D1429078

THE Knitting BOOK

THE
Knitting
BOOK

Vikki Haffenden • Frederica Patmore

LONDON, NEW YORK, MUNICH, MELBOURNE, DELHI

Project Editor Danielle Di Michiel
Senior Art Editor Jane Ewart
Editors Katie Hardwicke and Fiona Corbridge
Editorial Assistants Roxanne Benson-Mackey
and Kajal Mistry
Managing Editor Dawn Henderson
Managing Art Editor Christine Keilty
Senior Presentations Creative Caroline
de Souza
Senior Jacket Creative Nicola Powling
Senior Production Editor Jennifer Murray
Senior Production Controller Alice Sykes
Creative Technical Support Sonia Charbonnier

DK INDIA
Senior Editor Alicia Ingty
Photoshoot Coordinator and Designer
Devika Dwarkadas
Senior Art Editor Neha Ahuja
Assistant Designer Mansi Nagdev
Photographer Deepak Aggarwal
Managing Editor Glenda Fernandes
Managing Art Editor Navidita Thapa
DTP Manager Sunil Sharma
Production Manager Pankaj Sharma
DTP Designers Nand Kishor Acharya, Dheeraj
Arora, Arvind Kumar, and Anurag Trivedi

This edition first published in 2012.
First published in Great Britain in 2011 by
Dorling Kindersley Limited
80 Strand, London WC2R 0RL
Penguin Group (UK)

2 4 6 8 10 9 7 5 3 1
001-179420-Sept/12

A CIP catalogue record for this book
is available from the British Library.
ISBN 978-1-4093-8235-5

Printed and bound by Leo Paper Products, China

Discover more at www.dk.com

CONTENTS

INTRODUCTION

FREDERICA PATMORE

This book guides you through a huge variety of beginner, intermediate, and advanced techniques and tips. It is ideal for learning something new, experimenting, or fine-tuning your skills once you have some experience. The projects and swatches are a great opportunity to put what you have learned into practice, and make some lovely projects for you and your friends and family.

Happy Knitting!

VIKKI HAFFENDEN

This is a guide to a wealth of knitting skills. Each technique is explained with easy to follow, step-by-step instructions and clear colour photographs. Your knitting will look more professional when you work techniques correctly, and this section will also teach you the skills to incorporate individual design details into your knitting. From basic skills for beginners, to those for more experienced knitters, there really is something for every knitter here.

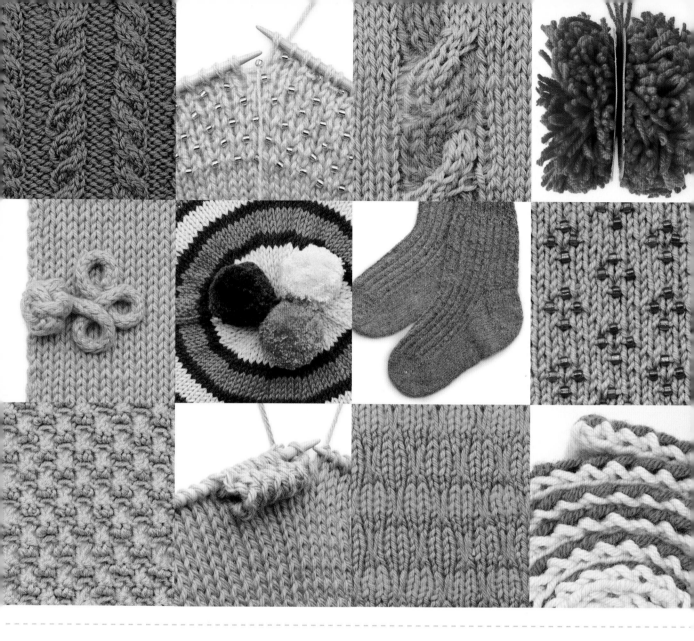

ABOUT THIS BOOK

This book is suitable for all knitters, whether you have never held a pair of knitting needles before or have been knitting for years. All the key areas are covered – tools and materials, stitch patterns, techniques, and projects – providing everything you need to get knitting. Start by familiarizing yourself with the Tools and Materials chapter – packed full of essential and specialist kit for a variety of disciplines. The Stitch Pattern Gallery shows all the beautiful fabrics you can

make using the techniques in this book – many of which only need simple stitches. The Techniques chapter makes up the majority of the book, taking you through more than 250 techniques, including beginner techniques and understanding a pattern, and then onto each specialist discipline, from cables to lace knitting and colourwork to embellishing. The Projects chapter contains forty fantastic ideas covering a range of skill levels – from basic to advanced – and a variety of techniques. Here you can bring your skills to fruition knitting scarves, gloves, baby accessories, and items for the home. With *The Knitting Book*, you'll find everything you need to knit with accuracy, confidence, and flair.

TOOLS
AND MATERIALS

YARNS

A yarn is the long, stranded, spun fibre that we knit with. There are many types of yarns, allowing knitters to enjoy a variety of sensory experiences as they express themselves through the medium. Yarns may be made of different fibres (see pp.12–19) and have a range of textures (see pp.20–23). Their possibilities are exciting: you can, in theory, knit with anything – from a skein of supple silk sock yarn to the plastic bag that you brought it home in. Choose from a colour palette that sweeps from subtle, muted tones to eye-popping brights.

FIBRES

Yarns, like fabrics, are made from fibres. A fibre may be the hair from an animal, man-made (synthetics), or derived from a plant. The fibres are processed and spun to make a yarn. A yarn may be made from a single fibre, such as wool, or mixed with other fibres to enhance its attributes (for example to affect its durability or softness). Different blends are also created for aesthetic reasons, such as mixing soft, luxurious cashmere with a rougher wool. As a result, all yarns have different properties, so it is important to choose an appropriate blend for your project.

NATURAL FIBRES

WOOL

The hair, or wool, of a variety of breeds of sheep, such as the Shetland Moorit or Bluefaced Leicester, is made into pure wool yarns, or blended with other fibres. It is very warm and hard-wearing, and great for winter wear such as jackets, cardigans, hats, and gloves. Some wool is rough, but it will soften with wear and washing. Wool sold as "organic" generally contains a high proportion of lanolin, offering a soft but strong yarn which retains some of its water-repellent properties.

MERINO WOOL

This is wool from the merino sheep, which is said to have one of the softest wools of any sheep breed. The bouncy, smooth-surfaced fibre is just as warm as a more wiry, coarse wool. Merino is a fantastic choice for wearing against the skin, and is often treated to make it suitable for machine-washing. Good for soft scarves, armwarmers, and children's garments.

MOHAIR

This fibre is the hair of the angora goat, and it produces a unique natural "halo" when knitted up. Working with it is quite challenging, as its frizzy appearance makes it difficult to see the structure of the knitting and any mistakes made. Mohair makes particularly interesting oversized jumpers or accessories. It is not advisable to use it for babywear as it may shed hair when newly made, which could be dangerous if inhaled.

ALPACA

This fibre has a luxurious feel and is one of the warmest natural fibres you can knit with. Even a fine, 4-ply garment provides sufficient insulation in bitterly cold weather. The alpaca is related to the llama. Alpaca yarn is perfect for ski hats, and thick, cosy jumpers and socks. You will also find baby alpaca yarn available, which is softer still.

TOOLS AND MATERIALS

CASHMERE

This fibre is the hair from a goat, which makes an ultra-luxurious, velvety-soft yarn. It is light but incredibly strong, and weighs very little by the metre; it often goes further than a pure wool or cotton. It is expensive to produce and is often blended with other fibres in a yarn to add softness. Cashmere should be enjoyed close to the skin in scarves, snoods, or jumpers. Treat it with great care; may be dry-clean only.

ANGORA

The lush coat of the angora rabbit produces a fibre that is softer and lighter than mohair, and produces the same furry "halo" effect. Each individual rabbit hair is very silky and long, and the resulting spun yarns, although soft, are inclined to shed slightly. Angora makes particularly pretty hats, but is very delicate and so is not recommended for bags or homewares.

SOYA OR MILK PROTEIN

Proteins derived from soya and milk can be used to make fibres, which are often seen in blended yarns. The stringy, sleek fibres add a soft, silky quality to rougher fibres such as linen or wool. Yarns containing soya or milk protein are less likely to be machine-washable, and do not retain heat particularly well. They are suitable for lightweight shrugs, flowing cardigans, and summer wear.

MATT COTTON
Cotton is the fluffy mass that grows around the seeds of the cotton plant. It is spun into a breathable, summery fibre. Most cotton yarns are easy to wash, and when cared for correctly, can be incredibly robust and last for decades. It is therefore a good fibre for homewares, knitted pouches, and shoulder bags. Pure, untreated cotton is ideal for hand-dyeing.

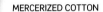

MERCERIZED COTTON
Cotton fibre can be mercerized, a treatment during which it undergoes mechanical and chemical processing to compress it and transform it into an ultra-strong yarn with a reflective sheen. It is a fine choice of fibre for a project that needs to be strong and hold its shape, such as a shiny evening bag, a long summer cardigan, or a throw.

TOOLS AND MATERIALS

BAMBOO
Modern technology has enabled us to derive flexible fibres from the inside of rigid, brittle bamboo canes. Bamboo fibre is a super-sleek imitation of silk fibre, and is made into a floppy and airy yarn that is ideal for lightweight shrugs and shawls.

SILK

The silkworm, a caterpillar that eats mulberry leaves, spins a cocoon in order to develop into a moth. It is from the fibres of the cocoon that silk is made. Silk is shiny and sleek, very delicate, and owing to its extraordinary source, very expensive. The luxurious texture of silk yarn makes it ideal for wedding and christening gifts, and indulgent fitted knitwear.

LINEN

This fibre is commonly derived from the flax plant. It is rather wiry, with an oily, waxy surface, but blossoms into a sleek, soft, breathable yarn that is ideal for knitting into lightweight cardigans and tops to wear in warm weather.

HEMP

The hemp plant is particularly versatile, and the use of its fibres for knitting yarn is one of its less common applications. Hemp has an earthy roughness that will soften with age and wear. It is usually produced in an environmentally friendly way, and the strong fibre is good for knitting openwork shopping bags and homewares such as placemats and coasters.

RAMIE

A plant from the nettle family yields the fibre called ramie. The bark of the plant is dried out into workable fibres, which are then spun into yarns. Like other plant fibres, this yarn does not insulate; it is desirable for its strength and airy quality. It is frequently blended with other fibres to produce a yarn that is breathable and wears well.

SYNTHETIC FIBRES

TOOLS AND MATERIALS

MICROFIBRE

With a quality of velvety softness, microfibre is increasingly common in multi-fibre yarns, as it is efficient at holding other fibres together as one yarn. Synthetic fibres such as this may not appeal to you, but they are often included in a yarn to reduce density, add texture, or to prevent excess spun fibre from migrating and pilling on the surface of a piece of knitting.

METALLICS

Although not a fibre, metallics are part of the library of yarns/fibres that is available to knitters. Lurex and other metallic yarns make highly effective trims and decorations. They may be uncomfortable to wear if used on their own, but if blended with other yarns, they create very interesting mixes and are fun to experiment with.

ACRYLIC

Acrylic fibres are produced from ethylene, which is derived from oil, and they are very cheap to manufacture. Acrylic yarn feels slightly rougher than other synthetics, and often comes in very bright and luminous shades which are hard to create with natural fibres. Robust and resistant to moths, acrylic yarn is ideal for toys, novelty knits, and budget projects. The yarn tends to accumulate static electricity.

NYLON

Polyamide, or nylon, is an incredibly strong and lightweight fibre. Its elasticity makes it perfect for use in knitted fabrics, and it is often used to reinforce yarn blends for items that may be subjected to heavy wear, such as sock and darning yarns. Like other man-made fibres, nylon improves the washability of the fibres it is blended with by preventing shrinkage and felting.

YARN BLENDS

WOOL AND COTTON MIXES

The strength and softness of cotton adds smoothness, breathability, and washability to wool's very warm (and sometimes scratchy) qualities. The blend is great for those with sensitive skin and babies. Cotton and wool absorb dye differently, which may lead to a stranded colour appearance in such blends. Wool sheds fewer hairs when mixed with a stabilizing plant fibre.

NATURAL AND SYNTHETIC MIXES

Man-made fibres are often blended with natural fibres to bring structure, strength, and washability; also to alter their appearance, such as to add a sheen. They help bind other yarns, such as mohair and wool together and prevent shedding; they also prevent animal fibres shrinking. The strength of such blends makes them perfect for socks or gloves.

SYNTHETIC-ONLY MIXES

Manufacturers can mix man-made, easily manipulated fibres to create a variety of textures such as furry eyelash yarns, soft and smooth babywear yarns, and rough aran substitutes. Although they do not hold much warmth in comparison to animal fibres, most synthetic-only blends can be washed at a high temperature and tumble-dried.

SPECIALITY YARNS AND TEXTURAL EFFECTS

For knitters who love something a bit different, speciality yarns make life very exciting. From velvety chenille to yarns with different textures, there is lots to experiment with. Each creates a different effect when knitted into a fabric, perhaps even looking like a fabric that has not been knitted at all! Read this section to bring out your inner textile artist, and let the yarns inspire you to create something fresh and edgy.

CHENILLE

This yarn is often composed of cotton and synthetics, and is made up of short fibres emerging from a strong core. A fabric knitted in it will have a luxurious, velvety feel. Chenille is ideal for a plain stocking stitch, but less so for intricate patterns and for work such as lace and cables, as it can hide the detail. It is a delicate yarn, which is likely to deteriorate with heavy wear and tear. It is therefore most suitable for plain-knitted garments for adults, and hats and scarves.

PLIED YARN

A plied yarn is made up from more than one strand of spun fibre. Originally, the number of "plies" held together in a yarn (i.e. 4-ply, 6-ply, or 8-ply) defined its thickness. Plied yarns often have a solid, bold appearance when knitted, with a good stitch definition, allowing you to see knitted textures and patterns clearly. They often contain several colours to give a mottled, tweedy effect. The yarn is widely available in a variety of fibre mixtures and is suitable for use in most knitting projects.

EYELASH YARN

When mixed in with other yarns, eyelash yarn is able to create a variety of effects, even resembling faux fur. This hairy yarn is an excellent choice for trims or edgings, looking like a machine-made fabric when knitted. It is a popular choice for scarves, and can be found in all sorts of forms, with combinations of metallic, ribbon, and silky "hairs" attached to a solid core.

SLUBBY YARN

This type of yarn is often spun by hand, and is characterized by a varying thickness along its length. This mixture of thick and thin areas creates a unique, uneven, and somewhat lumpy fabric when knitted. The texture produced by slubby yarn makes unusual accessories and outerwear such as jackets.

BRAIDED YARN

Two or more fibres are blended together to make a braided yarn. It often has a soft fibre, such as wool or cotton, for the core, which is then wrapped in a fibre such as nylon or a metallic blend. The mixture of fibres improves stitch definition: stitches are individually highlighted by the wrapping fibre around the core yarn.

TOOLS AND MATERIALS

LOOSE-SPUN YARN

This type of yarn is usually more aerated and less dense than a regular yarn, as it is more loosely spun. When knitted, it is light and bouncy, and very soft. Very thick yarns are often spun in this way to prevent knitted garments from feeling too heavy, or subsequently losing their shape when worn. These thick yarns are good for chunky, quick-to-knit accessories such as snoods and legwarmers.

TAPE YARN

The main characteristic of tape yarn is its flat shape. It may also be tubular, and is flattened when wound into a ball. A fabric knitted in it varies, depending on whether you twist the yarn when knitting, or lay it flat over the needle when working each individual stitch. Twisting it will produce a nubbly fabric; laying it flat will produce a smooth surface on the finished item.

RIBBON YARN

The shape of ribbon yarn is similar to that of tape yarn, but usually a bit wider. Both yarns are often comprised of synthetic or plant-fibre blends, to give them strength and sheen. Ribbon yarn lends itself especially well to making pretty accessories such as unique evening bags, scarves, and belts. It is also suitable for summer tops. Many ribbon and tape yarns are slippery, and special attention must be paid to tension and handling.

BOUCLÉ YARN

The curly appearance of bouclé yarn results from whirls of fibre attached to a solid core yarn. When knitted, these loops of fibre stand out and create a carpet-like looped fabric. (Bouclé is also the name of a type of fabric manufactured using a similarly spun yarn.) Bouclé yarns are completely unique and often specify a deceptively larger tension guideline as a result of their overall thickness. Bouclé is a lovely choice for very simply shaped garments, or for adding interest to plain stocking stitch knits by inserting an area using this alternative texture.

TWEED YARN

The term "tweed" describes a classic fibre mixture in both yarns and woven cloth. Tweed is most often composed of natural wool fibres spun with intermingled flecks of contrasting colours. The first tweeds were made of undyed cream wool and undyed wool from another breed of sheep with darker hair to create a cream yarn with brown or black flecks, most recognizable in traditional aran or fishermen's sweaters. Now tweed yarns come in a variety of colours with an assortment of contrasting flecks, from bright to subtle, for a knit with layers of artistic interest.

TOOLS AND MATERIALS

UNUSUAL YARNS

Subvert the traditional image of knitting with these radical departures from the historic heritage of wool and the convenience of modern synthetic yarns. Expand your horizons from everyday knitting and venture into the worlds of jewellery, sculpture, rugmaking, furnishings, and even homewares such as bowls and boxes. Many materials can be used as yarns: here are some ideas to experiment with.

PLASTIC BAGS

Recycle plastic bags by cutting them into strips and joining these together with tight knots to form yarn. Create interesting textures by mixing coloured and clear bags; the knots will add further texture. Knit on large needles, depending on the width of the strips you have cut – 10mm (UK000/US15) upwards is recommended; also choose the size according to whether you want a very tight or a floppy plastic fabric. Use this technique to make bags, mats, and waterproof items such as toiletry bags or garden seat covers.

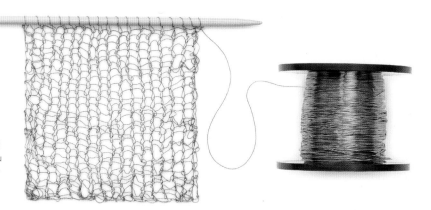

WIRE

This unusual medium is often used for knitting jewellery: buy beading wire, which is available in a range of colours, and knit it into chokers, necklaces, and bracelets. Try stranding beads on the wire before you work and place them in the knitting as you go along (see p.236). For a really unusual project, strand the wire with another yarn to knit a malleable fabric that holds its shape, and make three-dimensional sculptures.

FABRIC

Traditionally, fabric from old clothes and other textiles was often made into doormats and rugs by tying strips together. Think about using fabric strips to knit with, too. The needle size will depend on how thick the strips are. Some knitters have employed a pair of broom handles to knit very thick strips of raffia and furnishing fabric into hugely chunky and robust mats!

STRING

Ideal for knitting practical household items such as bowls and boxes, string is available in a range of colours and weights. Experiment on relatively small needles, such as 5mm (UK6/ US8), to create a very stiff fabric capable of holding its shape. Coat finished household items with diluted PVA glue to waterproof them and make future cleaning easy: just wipe with a damp cloth.

RUBBER YARN

Also known as "jelly yarn", rubber yarn is used to make decorative accessories such as belts, and three-dimensional sculptures. It is available in fluorescent, glittery, and glow-in-the-dark versions. The yarn may stick to knitting needles, so work with plastic or metal needles and use a lubricant such as baby oil. If the yarn has a hollow core, you can insert wire to make your work hold a shape.

BUYING YARN

Yarns are packaged for sale in specific quantities or "put-ups". The most common ones for knitting are balls, hanks, and skeins, which usually come in quantities of 25g, 50g, or 100g. You can also buy bigger put-ups, such as cones, designed for machine knitting.

◄ BALL
The stock in a yarn store will consist mostly of balls of yarn. These are ready to use: just pull the yarn from the centre to start knitting.

SKEIN ▶
The oblong-shaped skein of yarn is also ready to use without any special preparation. Keep the label in place as you work to ensure that the skein doesn't totally unravel.

◄ CONE
This is often too heavy to carry around in a knitting bag and the yarn is best wound into balls before you start knitting. Very fine yarns designed for machine knitting are sold in cones. If you plan to use this type of yarn, it is best to wind two or more strands together into a ball before you knit with it.

HANK ▶
A twisted ring of yarn, which needs to be wound into a ball before it can be used. You can do this by hand, or by using a swift and a ball-winder (see pp.40–41). This gives you the opportunity to check that there are no knots or faults in the yarn as you wind it. Some yarns avaliable as hanks consist of soft, delicate fibres, and these are unsuitable for certain industrial ball-winding machines.

YARN LABELS

Everything you need to know about a yarn is on its label. It will include symbols that tell you how to knit with it and how to clean it. Here is just a selection of the most common symbols. Always keep the labels: they are vital for identifying the yarn if you run short and need more. New yarn needs to have the same dye lot number as the original purchase in order to avoid a slight difference in colour in the finished item.

▲ **BALLBAND**

A yarn label is also known as a ballband. It features information on the yarn's weight and thickness, as well as washing guidelines. Yarns range from the very fine and light to the thick, dense, and heavy.

SYMBOLS

Yarn manufacturers may use a system of symbols to give details of a yarn. These include descriptions of suitable needles and the required tension.

YARN WEIGHT AND THICKNESS

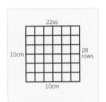

4.5mm (UK 7/US 7)

RECOMMENDED NEEDLE SIZE

TENSION OVER A 10cm (4in) TEST SQUARE

SHADE/ COLOUR

520

SHADE/COLOUR NUMBER

DYE LOT NUMBER

313

DYE LOT NUMBER

50g

NETT AT STANDARD CONDITION IN ACCORDANCE WITH BS984

WEIGHT AND LENGTH OF YARN IN BALL

100% WOOL

FIBRE CONTENT

MACHINE-WASH COLD

MACHINE-WASH COLD, GENTLE CYCLE

HAND-WASH COLD

HAND-WASH WARM

DO NOT BLEACH

DRY-CLEANABLE IN ANY SOLVENT

DRY-CLEANABLE IN CERTAIN SOLVENTS

DO NOT DRY-CLEAN

DO NOT TUMBLE-DRY

DO NOT IRON

IRON ON A LOW HEAT

IRON ON A MEDIUM HEAT

TOOLS AND MATERIALS

CHOOSING YARN COLOURS

When embarking on a new knitting project, the choice of colour is a very important decision. The colour wheel is a useful tool, which will introduce you to colour theory. Each segment shows the hue, shade, tone, and tint of a colour. A hue is the pure, bright colour; a shade is the colour mixed with black; a tone is the colour mixed with grey; and a tint is the colour mixed with white (pastels). The use of colour can affect the appearance of a project dramatically. When picking colours for Fair Isle, use a mixture of dark, mid-tone, and pale shades to optimize the contrasts in the pattern.

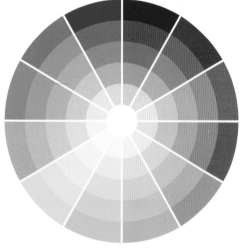

◀ USING A COLOUR WHEEL

Artists use this to see how colours work together. Blue, red, and yellow are primary colours; green, orange, and purple are secondary colours and the colours in between these are tertiary colours. Colours that lie side by side harmonize with each other. Colours that are directly opposite, such as purple and yellow, complement each other and provide a bold contrast in a design.

WARM SHADES ▶

The warm end of the colour spectrum consists mainly of red and yellow tones; browns, oranges, and purple are part of this group. Use these colours to bring richness and depth. A blend of warm shades can be a very flattering mixture to use, depending on your colouring: hold yarn against your face to see what suits you.

◀ COOL SHADES

Blue, green, and violet are at the cool end of the spectrum, and these can look very good used together. Cool colours are generally darker in tone than warm ones. If used with warm shades, their impact is lessened: if you need to balance a warm mixture in a project, you will need a higher proportion of cool than warm colours to do it.

PASTELS ▶

These very pale, often cool variations of deeper, darker colours are very popular for babies' and small children's garments; consequently, a variety of suitable synthetic yarns and blends are available. Pastels also feature strongly in spring/summer knitting patterns for adults: look for ice-cream colours in lightweight yarns, and enjoy using a delicate colour palette.

BLACK AND WHITE

Black and white are not included on the colour wheel as they are not classified as colours. Black is an absence of all colour and white is a combination of all colours in the spectrum. Bear in mind that when using black, not only is your work more difficult to see, but also that complex cables and texture work will not be seen to best effect in the final garment. White, however, guarantees that every stitch and detail will be clear; the drawback is that white knits show smudges of dirt more quickly and therefore need washing more frequently.

BRIGHTS ▶

Vivid and fluorescent shades are fun to use in a project, and often make particularly eye-catching accessories or intarsia motifs. A great way to liven up a colourwork project that consists of muted shades is to add a bright edging or set of buttons. This burst of colour can change the project's overall impact completely.

◀ SEASONAL MIXTURES

Nature can be a great source of inspiration, particularly when planning garments knitted in Fair Isle, intarsia, or stripes, where many colours will be used simultaneously. Think about sunsets, autumn leaves, frosted winter berries, or vibrant spring flowers. Keep a record in a sketchbook or in photographs, and notice the proportion of each colour in view. Most good yarn stockists change their range of colours according to season: in spring for example, more pastels and brights will be available.

TOOLS AND MATERIALS

YARN WEIGHTS

Yarns come in many different weights and thicknesses, which affect the appearance of a finished item and the number of stitches required to knit a sample tension square of 10cm (4in). Find the most suitable weight of yarn, according to project, below. The samples on p.31 show what the yarns look like when knitted in stocking stitch. The yarn weight names give the common UK term(s) first, followed by the US term(s).

YARN WEIGHT CHART

WHAT DO YOU WANT TO KNIT?	YARN WEIGHT	YARN SYMBOL	RECOMMENDED NEEDLE SIZES		
			METRIC	US	OLD UK
LACE	Lace, 2-ply, fingering	**0** Lace	2mm	0	14
			2.5mm	1	13
FINE-KNIT SOCKS, SHAWLS, BABYWEAR	Superfine, 3-ply, fingering, baby	**1** Superfine	2.75mm	2	12
			3mm	N/A	11
			3.25mm	3	10
LIGHT JUMPERS, BABYWEAR, SOCKS, ACCESSORIES	Fine, 4-ply, sport, baby	**2** Fine	3.5mm	4	N/A
			3.75mm	5	9
			4mm	6	8
JUMPERS, LIGHT-WEIGHT SCARVES, BLANKETS, TOYS	Double-knit (DK), light worsted, 5–6 ply	**3** Light	4.5mm	7	7
JUMPERS, CABLED MENSWEAR, BLANKETS, HATS, SCARVES, MITTENS	Aran, medium, worsted, Afghan, 12-ply	**4** Medium	5mm	8	6
			5.5mm	9	5
RUGS, JACKETS, BLANKETS, HATS, LEGWARMERS, WINTER ACCESSORIES	Bulky, chunky, craft, rug, 14-ply	**5** Bulky	6mm	10	4
			6.5mm	10½	3
			7mm	N/A	2
			8mm	11	0
HEAVY BLANKETS, RUGS, THICK SCARVES	Super bulky, super chunky, bulky, roving, 16-ply and upwards	**6** Super Bulky	9mm	13	00
			10mm	15	000

KNITTING WITH DIFFERENT WEIGHTS OF YARN

LACE/2-PLY

Extremely light and often sold in a plentiful quantity. If worked on needles of the recommended size, the yarn produces a very fine-knit, delicate result. It can be more pleasurable to use the yarn with slightly larger needles for a more open fabric and a slightly quicker knit.

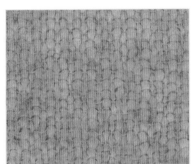

SUPERFINE/3-PLY

An ideal choice for lightweight lace work. It goes a long way per ball, and requires very slim needles. A gossamer yarn such as this one highlights stitch definition and very fine detail, and intricate lace work looks stunning in it.

FINE/4-PLY

Many knitters prefer Fine to Superfine, as it uses a more comfortable needle size yet still produces a very fine knit. This yarn is good for socks and baby clothes; the small stitches and neat appearance also suit items with designs that feature delicate texture or colourwork.

DOUBLE-KNIT (DK)/
LIGHT WORSTED/5–6 PLY

Double-knit yarn is used for anything from blankets and toys to jumpers and cardigans. It is commonly associated with 4mm (UK8/US6) needles, and this slightly thicker alternative to 4-ply yarn knits up more quickly and may therefore be preferable to work with.

ARAN/WORSTED/12-PLY

This thick, warm yarn commonly uses 5mm (UK6/US8) needles. It is good for men's garments with thick cabled detail, and the result is not too heavy. Good for functional items; many yarns in this thickness employ a large variety of fibres to make them machine-washable.

BULKY/CHUNKY/14-PLY

Although bulky, the yarn mainly consists of lightweight fibres to prevent garments from drooping out of shape over time. Commonly worked on 7mm (UK2/USn/a) needles to create a chunky fabric for outerwear, hats, and legwarmers. Quick to knit; perfect for gifts.

SUPER BULKY/
SUPER CHUNKY/16 PLY+

The yarn thickness varies, but it is commonly used with very large needles from 10mm (UK000/US15) upwards. A great choice for beginners, as stitches are so large that mistakes are easily visible. Knits up very quickly; good for rugged scarves.

KNITTING NEEDLES

Experienced knitters often settle on a preferred needle type according to their knitting style and tension. Needles come in assorted types and are made of different materials, and both have benefits when using particular techniques or working with certain fibres. Discover here how to choose the most suitable needles for the project you have in mind.

STRAIGHT NEEDLES

Straight needles give a great deal of support to the hand when knitting. If you are new to knitting, start with these. Short needles are recommended for small projects; long needles are more suitable for wider knits such as a pullover or a baby's blanket, and for knitters who like to work by holding the needles underneath their arms or elbows.

METAL NEEDLES ▶

When working with hairy fibres such as mohair or wool, which may stick, slippery metal needles are great. If you find that you tend to knit too tightly, the slippery surface can help as it will cause a knitter's tension to loosen. Needles of more than 8mm (UK0/US11) in diameter can be clunky to work with, so are rarely available.

EBONY/ROSEWOOD NEEDLES ▶

These wooden needles feel luxurious to work with, and can be quite expensive. They often have a waxy surface, which becomes smooth with wear, creating a soft and tactile surface. Like bamboo needles, they help to create an even tension; they hold their shape and remain straight when used, giving them a solid feel.

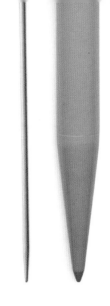

◀ SIZE

Knitting needles vary in diameter, from just 1.5mm ($\frac{1}{16}$in) thick to over 25mm (1in). There are three common needle-sizing systems: European metric, old British sizes, and American sizes. The chart opposite shows you how to convert between systems; notice that there are not always exact equivalents. Needles are also available in various lengths to suit different projects and different ways of holding needles.

◀ PLASTIC NEEDLES

For needles with a surface that is halfway between that of metal and that of bamboo, choose plastic. Plastic remains at a steady temperature during use, which may suit people who have arthritis. Avoid plastic needles of 4mm (UK8/US6) or smaller, as heavy projects may bend or break them.

◀ BAMBOO NEEDLES

Bamboo is a lightweight, flexible material, and makes excellent knitting needles. It helps to keep stitches regularly spaced, creating an even knitted fabric with a good tension. Great for slippery fibres such as silk, mercerized cotton, and bamboo yarn. Recommended for arthritis sufferers. Thin needles will gradually warp slightly with use, to fit the curvature of your hand.

◀ SQUARE NEEDLES

Most needles are cylindrical with a pointed tip; these unusual new needles have a faceted surface and a pointed tip. Made from metal, they lie over each other better, which is particularly useful when working with double-pointed needles, and cause less strain on the hands, making them especially suitable for arthritis sufferers.

CONVERSION CHART

This chart gives the closest equivalents between the three needle-sizing systems. If you have some old needles and are not sure of their size, buy a needle size gauge (see p.36) and push the needles through a selection of holes to establish their size.

EU METRIC	OLD UK	US
1.5mm	N/A	000
		00
2mm	14	0
2.25mm	13	1
2.5mm		
2.75mm	12	2
3mm	11	N/A
3.25mm	10	3
3.5mm	N/A	4
3.75mm	9	5
4mm	8	6
4.5mm	7	7
5mm	6	8
5.5mm	5	9
6mm	4	10
6.5mm	3	10½
7mm	2	N/A
7.5mm	1	N/A
8mm	0	11
9mm	00	13
10mm	000	15
12mm	N/A	17
15mm	N/A	19
20mm	N/A	35
25mm	N/A	50

TOOLS AND MATERIALS

DOUBLE-POINTED AND CIRCULAR NEEDLES

Some projects require you to knit in the round, to produce a tube of knitting without a seam. You can use both double-pointed needles and circular needles to do this, but the choice of needles is usually down to length. Most circular needles are too large to knit socks or gloves on, so double-pointed needles, which can knit a very narrow tube, are used instead. Your tension and style will change according to which you use.

BAMBOO DOUBLE-POINTED NEEDLES

METAL DOUBLE-POINTED NEEDLES

PLASTIC DOUBLE-POINTED NEEDLES

▲ DOUBLE-POINTED NEEDLES

The recommended option for socks and gloves, and narrow tubes. These needles are short and do not accommodate a large number of stitches. At first, some knitters may find that ladders form on each corner between the needles; however, this problem will disappear over time as you practise. Double-pointed needles are less slippery when made of bamboo or wood and most people agree that these types are more comfortable to work with.

CIRCULAR NEEDLES ▶

A flexible tube joins two needles to make a pair of circular needles. These come in a selection of different lengths and thicknesses. It is important to choose a length that is most appropriate for your project: it should match the anticipated diameter of the knitted tube. For instance, a hat would call for shorter circular needles than a jumper knitted in this way. Knitting patterns usually specify the size required. A piece of flat knitting can also be worked on circular needles: just turn your needles around after each row instead of working in the round.

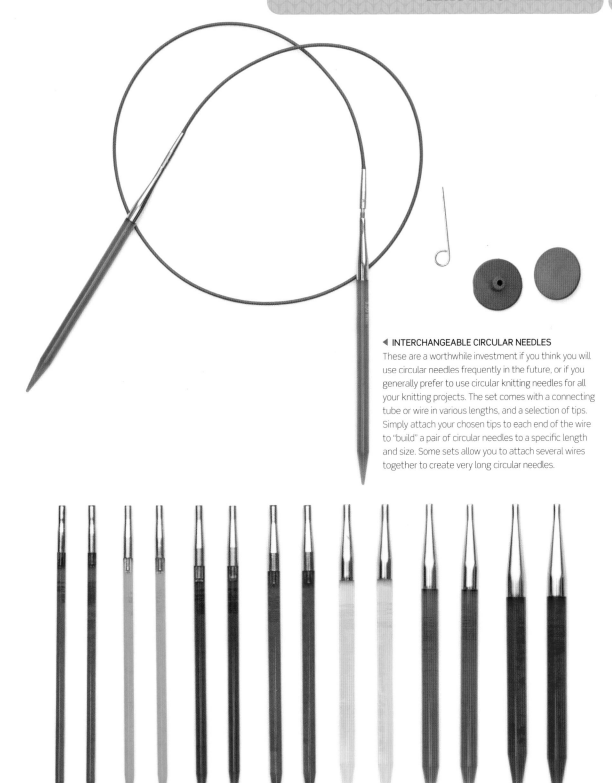

◀ INTERCHANGEABLE CIRCULAR NEEDLES

These are a worthwhile investment if you think you will use circular needles frequently in the future, or if you generally prefer to use circular knitting needles for all your knitting projects. The set comes with a connecting tube or wire in various lengths, and a selection of tips. Simply attach your chosen tips to each end of the wire to "build" a pair of circular needles to a specific length and size. Some sets allow you to attach several wires together to create very long circular needles.

TOOLS AND MATERIALS

OTHER EQUIPMENT

Hundreds of different gadgets are available to knitters. Some are merely for convenience, whereas others are absolutely vital and perform specific tasks. Here are the absolute essentials; the more advanced, specialized items are shown on pp.38–41.

THE ESSENTIALS

These basic items should always be to hand when you are working on a project. Most knitters have a portable knitting bag or case to keep them in, so that it is easy to take everything to wherever they want to sit and knit. The tools below are relatively inexpensive, and can be purchased from haberdashery stores and knitting suppliers.

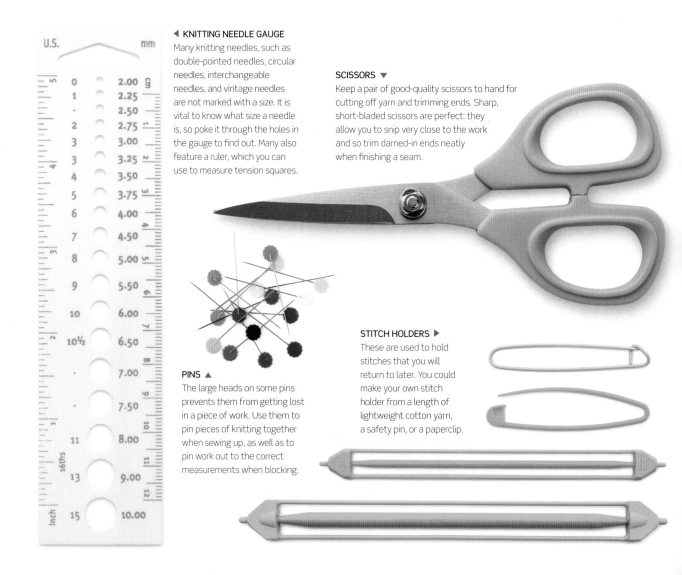

◀ KNITTING NEEDLE GAUGE

Many knitting needles, such as double-pointed needles, circular needles, interchangeable needles, and vintage needles are not marked with a size. It is vital to know what size a needle is, so poke it through the holes in the gauge to find out. Many also feature a ruler, which you can use to measure tension squares.

SCISSORS ▼

Keep a pair of good-quality scissors to hand for cutting off yarn and trimming ends. Sharp, short-bladed scissors are perfect: they allow you to snip very close to the work and so trim darned-in ends neatly when finishing a seam.

PINS ▲

The large heads on some pins prevents them from getting lost in a piece of work. Use them to pin pieces of knitting together when sewing up, as well as to pin work out to the correct measurements when blocking.

STITCH HOLDERS ▶

These are used to hold stitches that you will return to later. You could make your own stitch holder from a length of lightweight cotton yarn, a safety pin, or a paperclip.

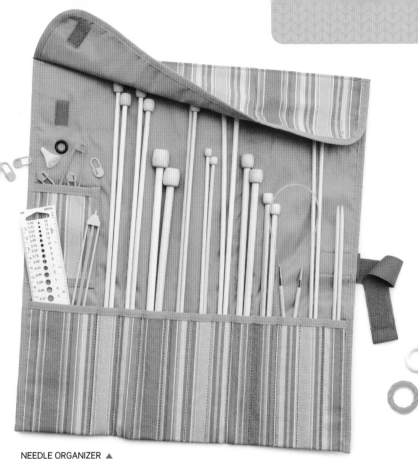

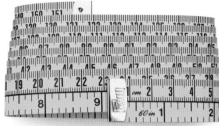

TAPE MEASURE ▲

Use this to measure the person you are knitting for, and for gauging sizing accurately. Also use it to check tension and measure knitting. Stick to using either metric or imperial measures, not a mixture of both.

◀ STITCH MARKERS

Use these to mark the beginning and end of a panel of stitches, and to identify the end of each row when working in the round. As you arrive at a marker, transfer it from the right-hand to the left-hand needle; continue working the row as normal.

NEEDLE ORGANIZER ▲

Use this to keep your knitting needles organized and protected against damage. Needle rolls and bags are available in a range of shapes and sizes. Thick needles are best suited to a needle bag (like a long pencil case); double-pointed needles can be stored in a short needle roll.

KNITTING BAG ▼

Bags for knitters often have many compartments, perfect for storing equipment and materials for your current project. To protect knitting from damp and moths, keep a cedar cube (see p.45) inside.

◀ ROW COUNTER

Available as a tube that sits at the end of a knitting needle: change the counter when you complete a row; also as a clicker, which you "click" each time you finish a row.

POINT PROTECTORS ▲

Pop these over fragile needle tips to guard against damage; use them to protect your knitting bag from punctures; and to stop stitches from sliding off needles and unravelling when not in use.

SPECIALIZED EQUIPMENT

As you begin to use more advanced techniques, you will find that you need specialized equipment. Each item is specific to a particular skill, such as colourwork, lace knitting, and patterning with cables. If you are a new knitter and just learning the basic stitches, do not worry about these items for now, but you will certainly need them in the future as you become more experienced and try more ambitious projects.

▲ TAPESTRY NEEDLES

These have a blunt tip in order to prevent damage to fibres, so are also suitable for use by knitters. Make sure that the eye is an appropriate size for the yarn: do not force yarn through an eye that is too small or it will spoil it.

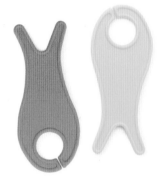

▼ YARN BOBBINS

In the intarsia method of colourwork, you create numerous lengths of yarn in different colours in order to work separate parts of each knitted row. These handy bobbins keep each colour tidily wound as you work.

▲ BLUNT-ENDED YARN NEEDLES

To sew up projects and darn in ends, you need a selection of blunt-ended yarn needles. These will not damage or split delicate fibres when penetrating knitting to sew a seam, instead nudging them out of the way. Some have a kinked tip, which will speed up the sewing-up process by resurfacing along your seam more quickly than a straight needle.

◀ CROCHET HOOK

Available in different materials such as metal, wood, and bamboo. A crochet hook makes it much easier to pick up previously dropped stitches. The slippery surface of the metal version probably makes this the most user-friendly type. You can also use a crochet hook for inserting tassels.

▲ SHARP-ENDED NEEDLES

Buy these with a large eye; use to secure darned-in ends after finishing with the blunt-ended needle. A sharp needle may also be required when inserting a zip or affixing trimmings to a piece of work.

▲ BLOCKING WIRE AND PINS

These are used to block very fine lace work. Thread the wire through the edge of the work, as though making a long running stitch. The wire stays in the knitting and supports it; it remains flexible after hand-washing the item, so the work can be reshaped and dried flat.

SOCK BLOCKER ▶

This is the best way to block finished socks to a neat shape. Hand-wash the sock and pull gently to shape on the blocker. As it dries, it will take on the shape of the blocker. Sock blockers are available in a selection of sizes. If you use a wooden version, the sock can be lightly steamed to shape instead.

▲ YARN CUTTER

A convenient alternative to scissors. Insert the yarn through the grooves in the yarn cutter in order to trim it off. You may prefer to attach it to a cord to wear around your neck while you work. When travelling by air, you can use this if you want to knit during the flight, because regulations prohibit scissors in hand luggage.

◀ CABLE NEEDLE

A kinked or U-shaped cable needle is used when working cables; this shape prevents cable stitches from sliding away. Choose a size that is closest to that of the needles used for the main body of the knitting.

TOOLS AND MATERIALS

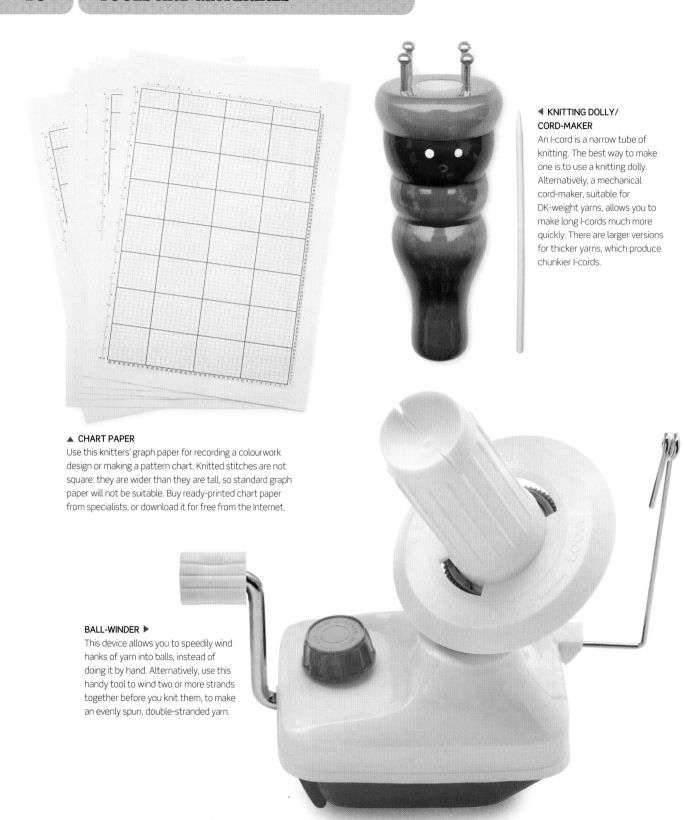

**◄ KNITTING DOLLY/
CORD-MAKER**
An I-cord is a narrow tube of
knitting. The best way to make
one is to use a knitting dolly.
Alternatively, a mechanical
cord-maker, suitable for
DK-weight yarns, allows you to
make long I-cords much more
quickly. There are larger versions
for thicker yarns, which produce
chunkier I-cords.

▲ CHART PAPER
Use this knitters' graph paper for recording a colourwork
design or making a pattern chart. Knitted stitches are not
square: they are wider than they are tall, so standard graph
paper will not be suitable. Buy ready-printed chart paper
from specialists, or download it for free from the Internet.

BALL-WINDER ▶
This device allows you to speedily wind
hanks of yarn into balls, instead of
doing it by hand. Alternatively, use this
handy tool to wind two or more strands
together before you knit them, to make
an evenly spun, double-stranded yarn.

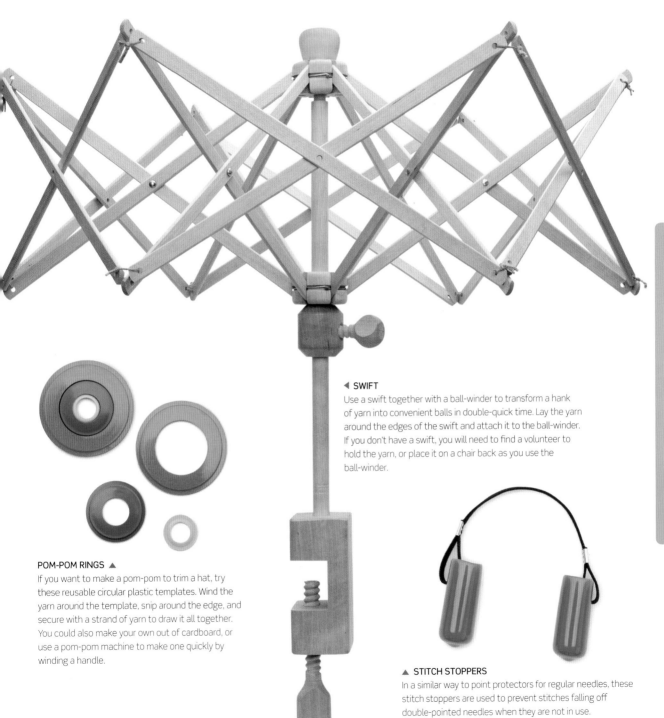

◀ SWIFT

Use a swift together with a ball-winder to transform a hank of yarn into convenient balls in double-quick time. Lay the yarn around the edges of the swift and attach it to the ball-winder. If you don't have a swift, you will need to find a volunteer to hold the yarn, or place it on a chair back as you use the ball-winder.

POM-POM RINGS ▲

If you want to make a pom-pom to trim a hat, try these reusable circular plastic templates. Wind the yarn around the template, snip around the edge, and secure with a strand of yarn to draw it all together. You could also make your own out of cardboard, or use a pom-pom machine to make one quickly by winding a handle.

▲ STITCH STOPPERS

In a similar way to point protectors for regular needles, these stitch stoppers are used to prevent stitches falling off double-pointed needles when they are not in use.

EMBELLISHMENTS

Add dazzle and give your knitting an edge by adding embellishments, from embroidery to beads, sequins, pretty trimmings, clever fastenings, and attractive notions such as handles. These can completely change the feel of a project, depending on the way that you use them. Embellishment gives you an opportunity to express your creativity: try some of the ideas here.

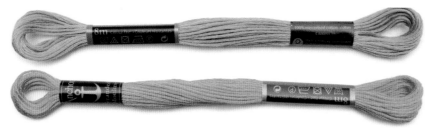

◀ EMBROIDERY THREAD

Silky, shiny embroidery threads come in a mixture of colours and styles. Metallic threads are particularly interesting and will jazz up a solid knitted background. Use a tapestry needle to embroider knitting, remembering that most embroidery threads stipulate that they must be hand-washed.

MACHINE EMBROIDERY THREAD ▶

This thread is very fine, and is sold on cones or small reels. It is intended for machine embroidery, but you could try double-stranding a metallic one (check its meterage) with a knitting yarn for a subtle hint of sparkle. Alternatively, use variegated threads, or several at the same time, with the yarn.

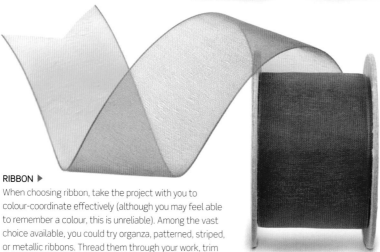

RIBBON ▶

When choosing ribbon, take the project with you to colour-coordinate effectively (although you may feel able to remember a colour, this is unreliable). Among the vast choice available, you could try organza, patterned, striped, or metallic ribbons. Thread them through your work, trim an edge, or form them into bows or rosettes.

KNITTING BEADS ▲

Most knitting beads are specially manufactured to be washable, and to not lose their colour over time, whereas other types may not withstand wear and washing. They come in sizes for a specific thickness of yarn, such as 4-ply, for example.

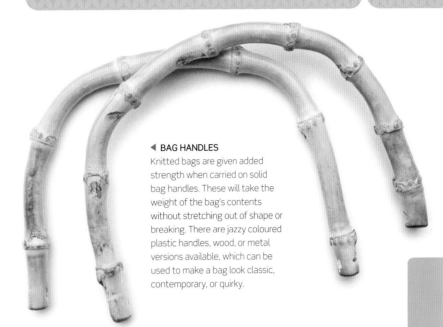

▲ TRIMMINGS

There is a whole world of trimmings for dressmaking: although these are less commonly used in knitting, they can impart a frilly, delicate feel to an otherwise blocky project. Trimmings come in all shapes and sizes, from the glittery to virginal broderie anglaise, fringing, and marabou feathers, to name but a few. Each can add an exciting dimension to your work.

◀ BAG HANDLES

Knitted bags are given added strength when carried on solid bag handles. These will take the weight of the bag's contents without stretching out of shape or breaking. There are jazzy coloured plastic handles, wood, or metal versions available, which can be used to make a bag look classic, contemporary, or quirky.

FASTENINGS ▶

Choose fastenings with care, according to the type of project and the yarn you are using, and make sure they are not so heavy that they will pull the knitting out of shape. Buttons usually double as a feature, but other fastenings are more discreet, such as a hook and eye or a press stud. Stitch these on with knitting yarn or sewing thread. Use push-on press studs for felted work.

SEQUINS ▲

Knit sequins into your work as you go, or embroider them on afterwards. If you're going to knit them in, look for pailettes, which have a larger hole than regular sequins, which are only suited to fine yarns. Choose flat sequins, which will sit flat against the work and each other, and are less inclined to get scratched and lose surface colour.

◀ BUTTONS

The choice of buttons for a garment is an important one. They are decorative as well as serving a practical purpose; make sure you select them to suit the way that the garment will be cleaned, or they may have to be removed beforehand. Coconut, shell, wooden, and metallic buttons are fairly neutral and work with many colours. Take your project to the store to assess the way that button shapes, colours, and sizes work with it.

GARMENT CARE

After all the hard work of knitting a garment, it is important to protect it from damage and to keep it looking new. Moths are one of the biggest threats: they love to lay their eggs in natural fibres and the larvae will chew tiny holes, which are unsightly and cause knitting to fall apart. The equipment below will help you to keep your hand-knits in good condition.

◀ LAVENDER SACHETS

Lavender is a traditional and natural deterrent to moths. Make your own sachets from dried garden lavender, crumbled into fabric or knitted bags (see our bow-tie version on p.336). Hang sachets in the wardrobe, or slip into drawers. Use also in sealed bags of yarn for storage.

BOBBLE REMOVER ▶

Knitted items may pill (form bobbles on the surface). If this is severe, shave them off with a bobble-removing comb or machine. Be gentle: do not pull at your work as it may damage it. Fabric softeners may aggravate the problem.

◀ MOTHBALLS

A chemical method of deterring moths and insects. Slip them into pockets or garment bags. They vary from strong-smelling to subtle; beware of the strong ones as the smell can be impossible to eradicate.

MOHAIR BRUSH ▶

Mohair can flatten and lose its aura-like furriness after a wash or prolonged storage. It is therefore essential to invest in a mohair brush to reinvigorate fuzzy knits with gentle brushstrokes. You can also prevent matting in areas subject to extra wear, such as the armpits of a jumper.

◀ GARMENT BAG

These are a must-have and are available in a variety of styles, ranging from simple zipped bags to lavender-scented plastic bags, and bags that allow vacuum packing in order to reduce bulk and save space. Make sure that bags are sealed properly to prevent damp and insects from getting in. Although a bag may appear secure when folded over, moths are able to wriggle in and out of small spaces and make themselves comfortable.

CEDAR RINGS OR CUBES ▶

An alternative moth deterrent. Cedarwood has a subtle aroma, which some people may prefer to that of lavender. Available as cubes, blocks, and rings to hang in the wardrobe, or to dot around a cupboard, or put inside bags or boxes of yarn. The aroma fades over time, but they can be sanded down to refresh the natural smell. Alternatively, apply a drop of grapefruit oil to each block, allow it to dry, and return the blocks to your yarn store for a moth deterrent with added antibacterial properties.

WOOL WASH ▶

This very gentle soap will gently cleanse fibres and remove dirt without damaging a yarn or pushing dye from it. It is now possible to buy a wool wash that does not need rinsing out, making the hand-washing of precious knitted items even more convenient.

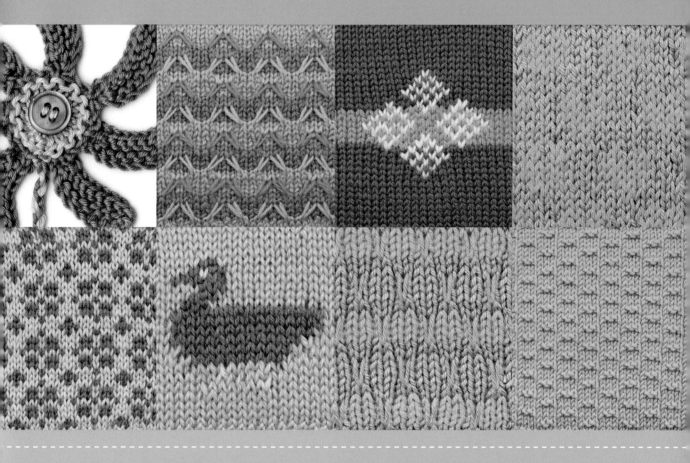

STITCH PATTERN GALLERY

STITCH PATTERN GALLERY

These swatches demonstrate how the techniques on pp.82–271 can be turned into interesting and original knitted fabrics. Even if you are new to knitting, you have probably already heard of some of the well-known stitches, such as Stocking and Moss, but what you might not know is that there are many, many alternatives, creating any number of attractive effects, from striking cables and colourwork to delicate lace patterns and beading. Take a look through this chapter to establish the kinds of effects that appeal to you. From there you can find the relevant techniques in the next chapter and the actual charts and patterns in the Stitch Patterns chapter at pp.354–389.

KNIT AND PURL STITCH PATTERNS

Here are a few of the vast array of stitch patterns created by combining knit and purl stitches. Each one produces a flat, reversible knitted fabric and is simple to work. Those that have no specific right side (RS) look exactly the same on both the front and the back, and the few with a marked right side have an attractive texture on the wrong side as well. Because the edges of these stitches do not curl, they are ideal for making simple scarves, baby blankets, and throws. See pp.114-117 for step-by-step guidance on knit and purl stitches.

MOSS STITCH (RICE STITCH) page 356

SINGLE RIB page 356

DOUBLE RIB page 356

BASKETWEAVE STITCH page 356

TEXTURED CHECK STITCH page 356

STRIPED CHECK STITCH page 356

STITCH PATTERN GALLERY

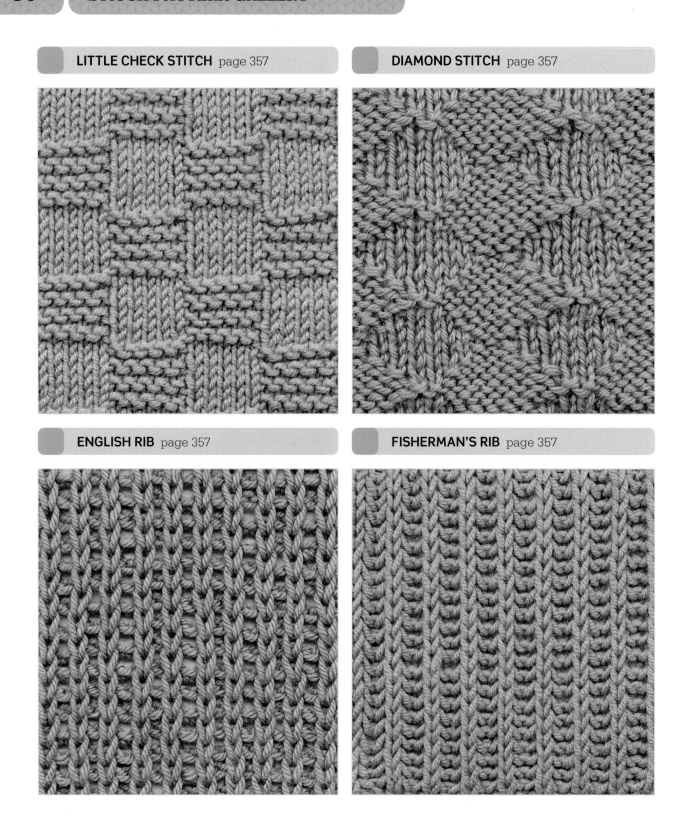

LITTLE CHECK STITCH page 357

DIAMOND STITCH page 357

ENGLISH RIB page 357

FISHERMAN'S RIB page 357

DOUBLE MOSS STITCH page 357

HALF MOSS STITCH page 357

TRAVELLING RIB page 358

BROKEN RIB page 358

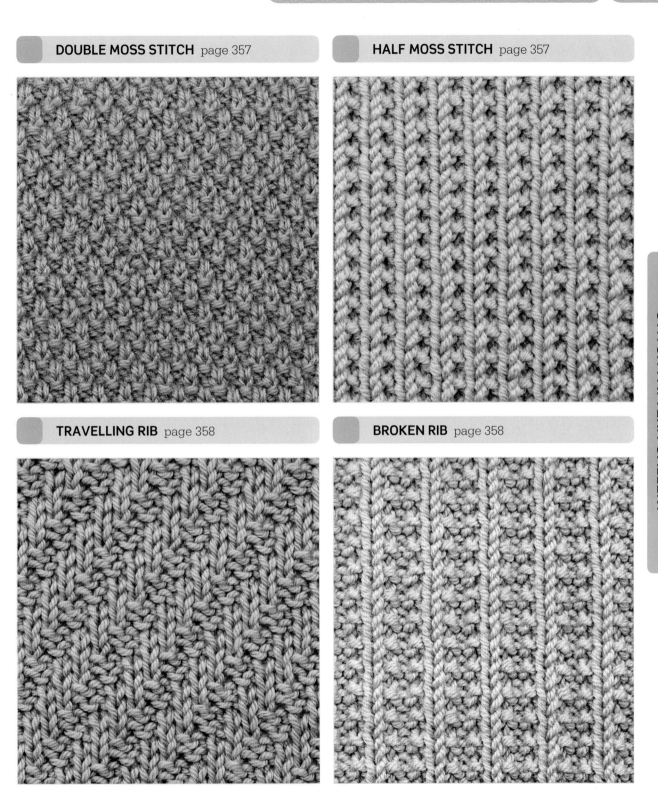

BROKEN MOSS STITCH page 358

GARTER RIB page 358

MOSS STITCH COLUMNS page 358

HONEYCOMB STITCH page 358

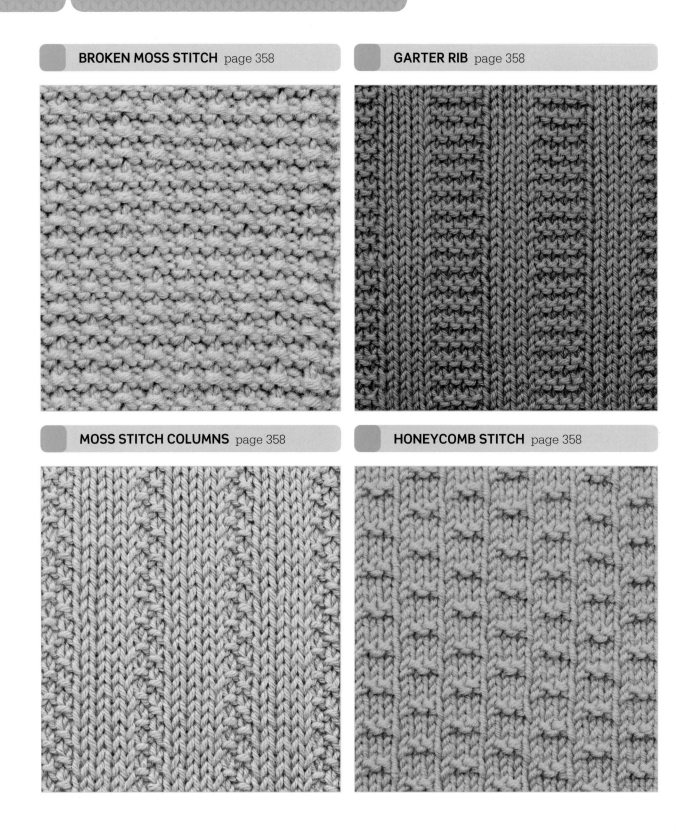

INCREASING AND DECREASING

Knitted increases and decreases add shape and texture to a knitted piece. A huge variety of shapes and patterns can be achieved by increasing or decreasing the number of stitches on the needle. As your knitted structure changes shape, the cast-on edge will not always remain straight, adding an attractive wavy edge in most cases. This selection of all-over patterns are worked by repeating a sequence, with each pattern repeat combining increases and decreases to cancel each other out so that the overall number of stitches remains the same. These stitches will produce particularly interesting scarves, shawls, and blankets. See pp.130–151 for step-by-step guidance on increases and decreases.

BASIC CHEVRON page 359

GARTER CHEVRON page 359

FEATHER AND FAN STITCH page 359

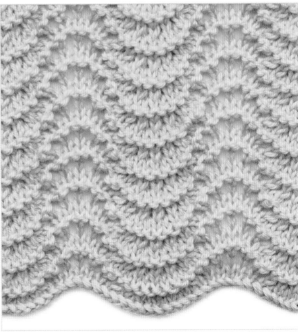

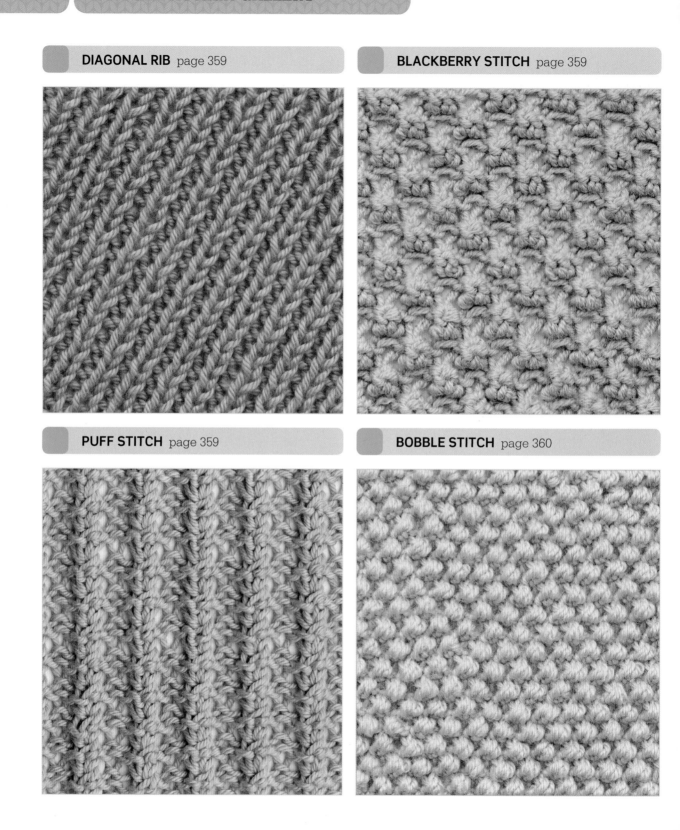

DIAGONAL RIB page 359

BLACKBERRY STITCH page 359

PUFF STITCH page 359

BOBBLE STITCH page 360

INCREASING AND DECREASING: FLOWER PATTERNS

These flowers have all been designed to be easy to make using simple increasing and decreasing techniques. Each flower is worked as one piece, with little or no sewing-up required. As a bonus, there is no need to darn in ends because you can use the yarn tails to plait a simple stem. The finished flowers are perfect for use as corsages, appliqué on blankets, cushion covers, bags, scarves, and sweaters, or to decorate greeting cards. See pp.130–151 for step-by-step guidance on increases and decreases.

TWELVE-PETAL FLOWER page 360

SPINNING-PETAL FLOWER page 360

FLOWER WITH SMALL CENTRE page 362

FLOWER WITH LARGE CENTRE page 362

ANEMONE page 361

LARGE LEAF page 361

PUFFBALL FLOWER page 361

CABLE AND TWIST STITCH PATTERNS

These patterns are all easy to work and are a good introduction to these textures for beginners. To knit these, try working the patterns from the written instructions for the first repeat; then follow the chart for the next repeat to see how much easier it is to use a chart for cables and twists. The twist patterns add a more subtle texture and, with no cable needle necessary, are quick to work, too. Cables and twists add texture and thickness to a project, and are therefore ideal for plain garments and accessories, such as a cushion cover. Cables will inevitably shrink your project widthways, so remember to cast on more stitches than you would normally need. See pp.152–153 for step-by-step guidance on cables and twists.

FOUR-STITCH CABLE PATTERN page 362

SIX-STITCH CABLE PATTERN page 363

CHAIN CABLE STITCH page 363

STITCH PATTERN GALLERY

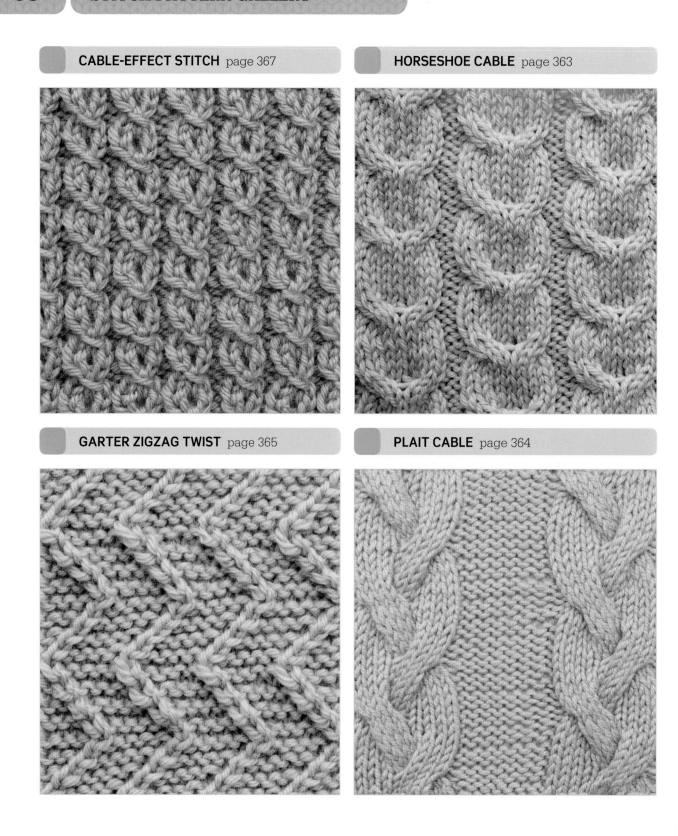

CABLE-EFFECT STITCH page 367

HORSESHOE CABLE page 363

GARTER ZIGZAG TWIST page 365

PLAIT CABLE page 364

DIAMOND CABLE page 364

GARTER STITCH CABLE page 365

BOBBLE CABLE page 366

SMOCKING page 364

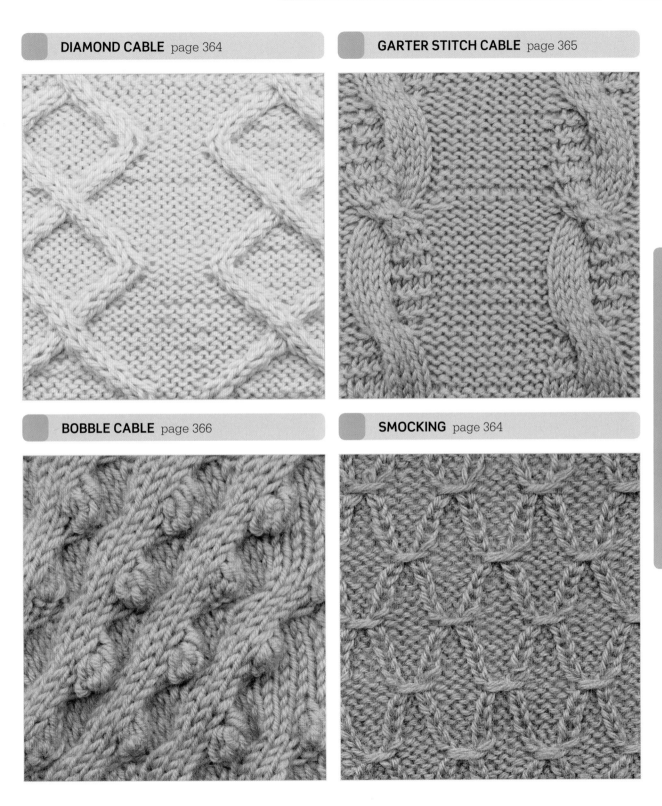

WOVEN CABLE page 366

WAVY CABLE page 367

FAN CABLE page 367

CABLE CHECK page 366

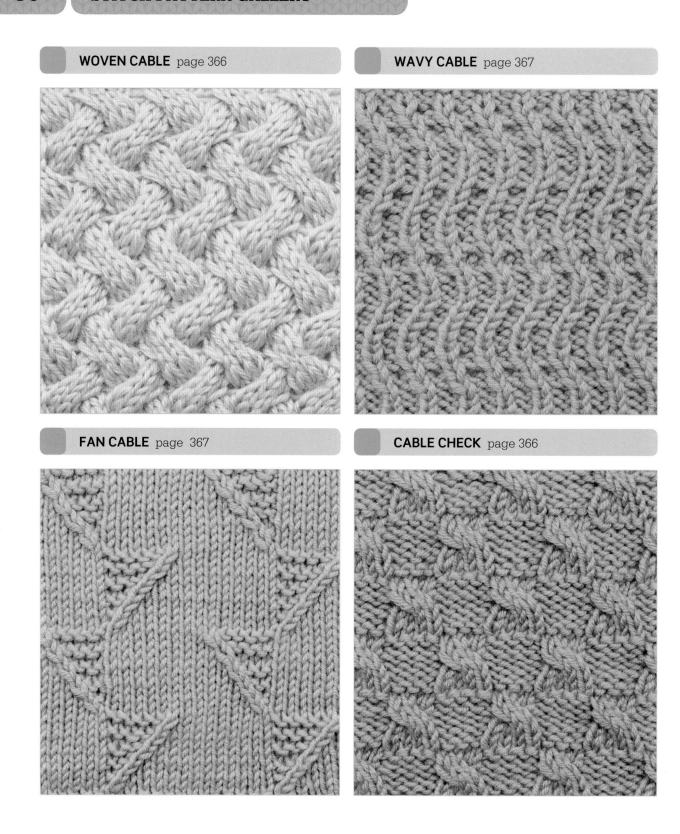

LACE STITCH PATTERNS

Lacework is an easy way to add a delicate and elegant look to shawls, scarves, garments, and blankets. If the ground of your chosen lace is stocking stitch, you will need to include a Garter or Moss stitch border around the piece. This can be achieved by either picking up stitches and working the border after the piece is complete; or working four rows of Garter stitch at the beginning and end of the knitted piece and four stitches of garter stitch at the sides of the knitting. Alternatively, sew a knitted or fabric trim edging all around the finished piece. See pp.158–159 for step-by-step guidance on lace techniques.

EYELET MESH STITCH page 368

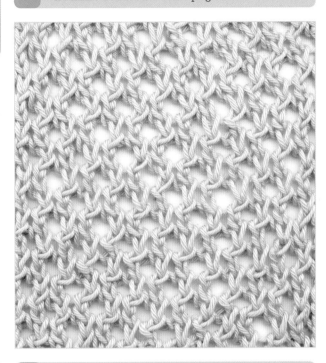

LEAF EYELET PATTERN page 368

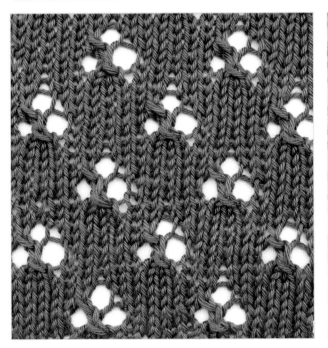

GRAND EYELET MESH STITCH page 368

VERTICAL MESH STITCH page 369

MINI-LEAF STITCH page 369

ARROWHEAD LACE page 369

ZIGZAG MESH STITCH page 370

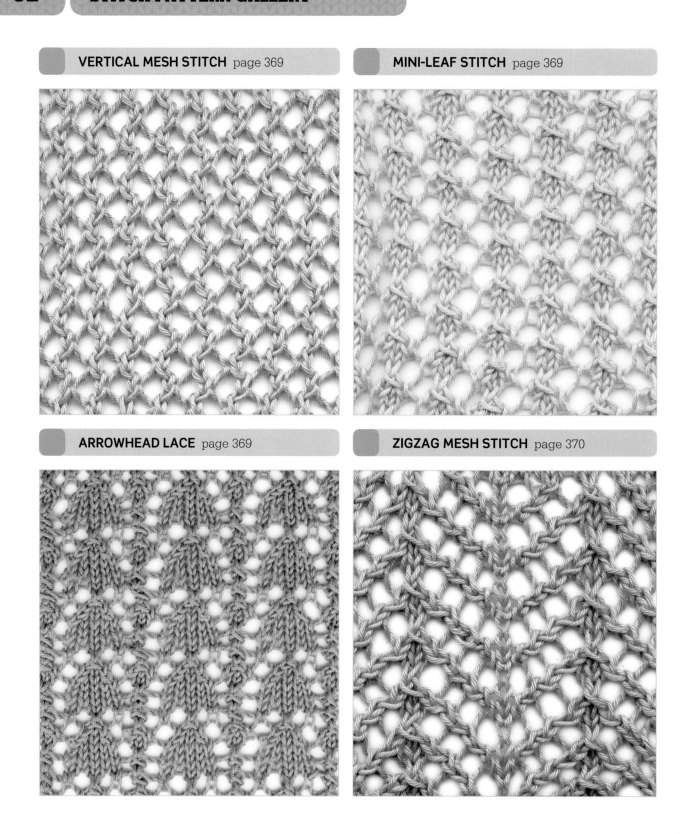

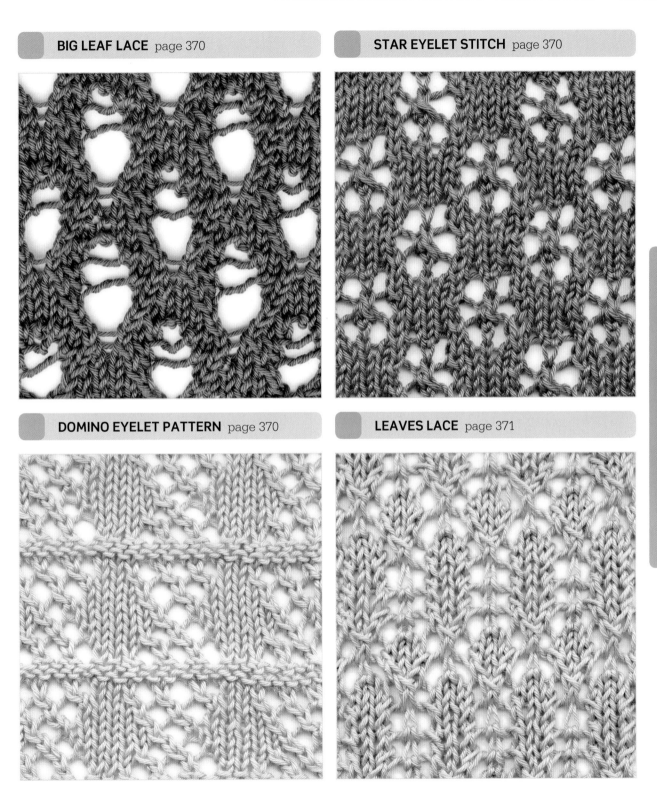

BIG LEAF LACE page 370

STAR EYELET STITCH page 370

DOMINO EYELET PATTERN page 370

LEAVES LACE page 371

DIAMOND LACE STITCH page 371

VICTORY LACE page 371

OPENWORK DIAMONDS page 371

FAGGOTING page 372

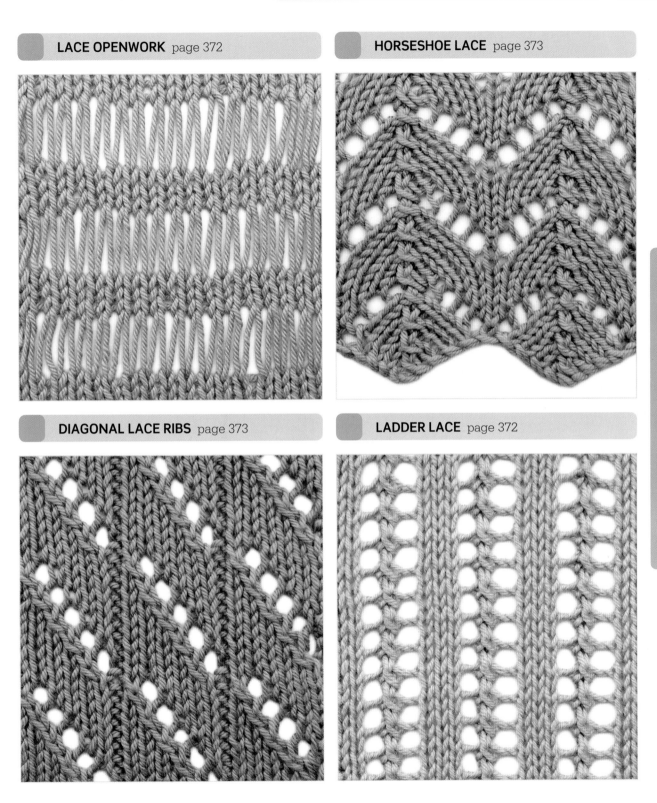

LACE OPENWORK page 372

HORSESHOE LACE page 373

DIAGONAL LACE RIBS page 373

LADDER LACE page 372

STITCH PATTERN GALLERY

EYELET LINES page 372

DROPPED STITCH PATTERN page 373

INTERWOVEN EYELETS page 373

NAUTICAL MOTIF page 372

COLOURWORK PATTERNS

Here are some easy-to-work Stocking stitch colourwork patterns. A few of the patterns are suitable for the Fair Isle technique, and the remainder for the intarsia technique or a combination of both. The borders can be worked individually for simple bands of colour, or repeated to make up an item in stripes. If you have never tried colourwork, start with the Fair Isle patterns as they only use two colours in every row. See pp.162–172 for step-by-step guidance on colourwork techniques.

SIMPLE BORDERS page 374

REPEATING CIRCLES page 374

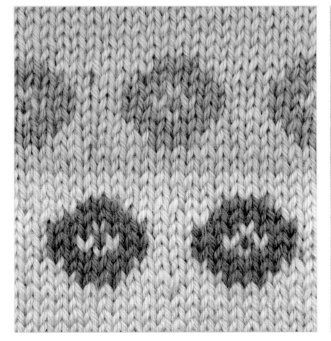

HEART MOTIF page 374

BIRD MOTIF page 375

FAIR ISLE BLOSSOMS page 375

INTARSIA FLOWERS page 376

FLOWER MOTIF page 376

TULIP MOTIF page 377

LITTLE LADY MOTIF page 377

PUSSY CAT MOTIF page 376

NUMBERS AND LETTERS page 376

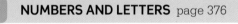

STITCH PATTERN GALLERY

DUCK MOTIF page 378

SKULL AND CROSSBONES MOTIF page 378

HEARTS page 377

ZIGZAGS page 375

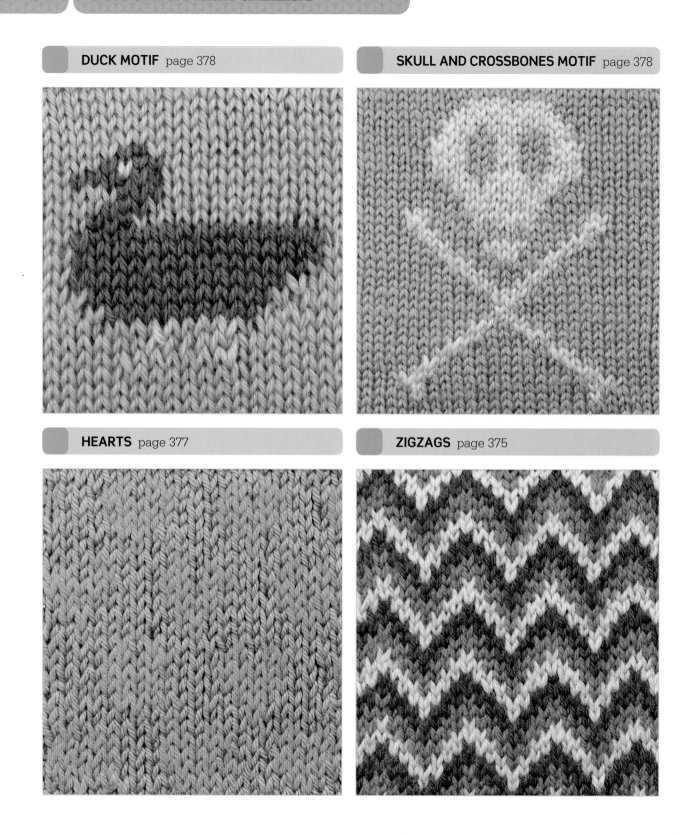

CLIMBING VINE page 379

ARGYLE page 378

SNOWFLAKE MOTIF page 379

STITCH PATTERN GALLERY

FAUX COLOURWORK PATTERNS

Faux Colourwork is a "cheat" technique where colour is mixed across your knitting without the need to work with two different yarns on the same row. You use stitches worked on previous rows to add a different colour to the rows above by pulling the stitches upwards, slipping them instead of knitting them (see p.124). All stitches are slipped purlwise unless otherwise stated. As these patterns feature a great deal of slipping stitches, the finished knitted fabric is stronger and makes excellent bags, cushion covers, and blankets.

PEEPING PURL STITCH page 379

GARTER SLIP STITCH page 380

BROKEN STRIPES page 379

ARROWHEAD STITCH page 380

WEAVER'S STITCH page 380

HONEYCOMB STITCH page 381

VERTICAL STRIPES page 380

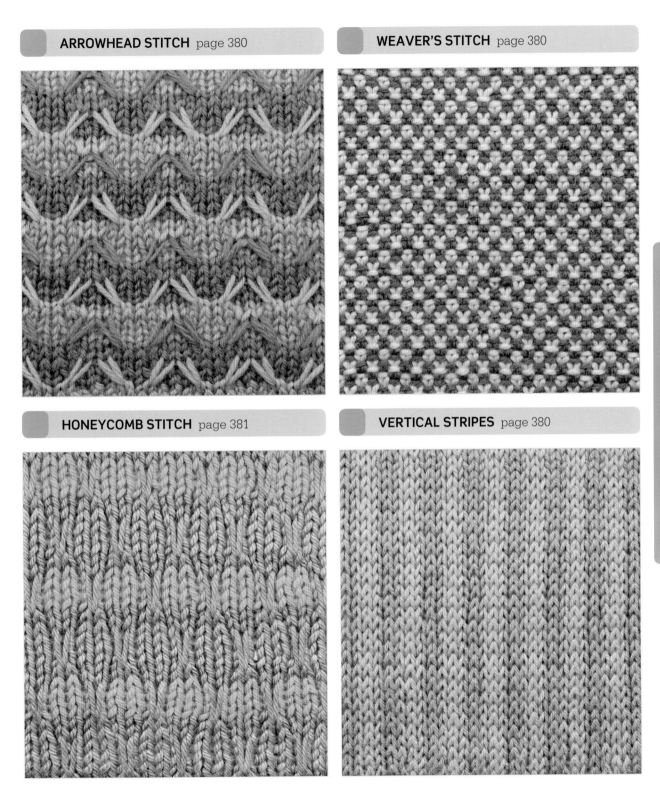

EDGING PATTERNS

Most of these easy edgings are worked lengthways. If adding the edging to a blanket, knit a little extra to gather at each corner. Do not cast off at the desired length; instead, slip the stitches onto a stitch holder and sew the edging on around the blanket. Before casting off, you can then work more rows if you need them. See pp.236–255 for step-by-step guidance on embellishing knitting.

PETAL EDGING   page 381

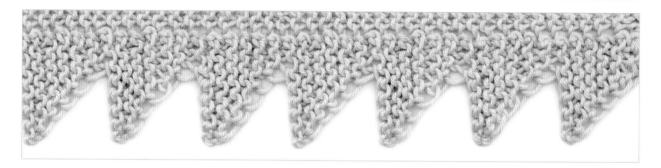

PEAKS EDGING   page 381

CHRISTENING EDGING   page 382

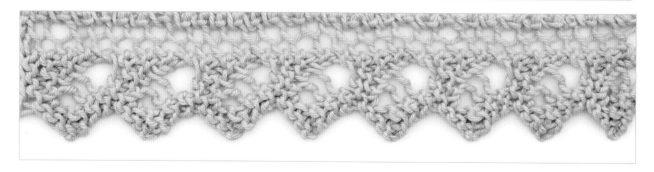

PICOT RUFFLE EDGING page 382

PICOT EDGING page 382

FRINGE EDGING page 383

GODMOTHER'S EDGING page 383

ARCHWAY EDGING page 383

BEADED EDGING page 384

OPEN WEAVE EDGING page 384

CABLED EDGING page 384

MEDALLIONS

These simple medallions can be stitched together to form larger pieces of fabric for throws, bags, and cushion covers. They can also be worked singly into pieces big enough for a cushion cover or table mat. Alternatively, the square and circle can form the base of a container worked in the round (see p.270). See pp.196–203 for step-by-step guidance on circular knitting.

SIMPLE CIRCLE page 385

SIMPLE SQUARE page 385

SQUARE WITH SWIRL INCREASES page 385

SQUARE WITH OPENWORK page 387

HEXAGON page 386

SIMPLE OCTAGON page 386

MITRED SQUARE page 386

BEADING STITCH PATTERNS

Beading adds a touch of sparkle to a project. The swatches shown here use the beading technique where you strand beads onto your yarn before you cast on for your project (see p.236). When estimating bead quantities, it is best to thread on more beads than you think is needed. This way, you will not need to stop knitting to thread on more beads. Bear in mind that adding beads will add weight to your project and it is therefore advisable to use fewer beads on big projects, such as jumpers and blankets. Always use washable knitting beads. It is not recommended to add beads to items intended for babies and small children. See pp.236–240 for step-by-step guidance on bead knitting.

SUBTLE SPARKLES page 387

DIAGONAL BEADING page 387

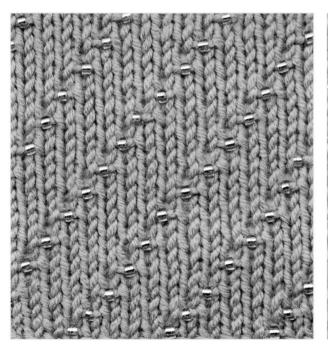

BEADED STOCKING STITCH page 387

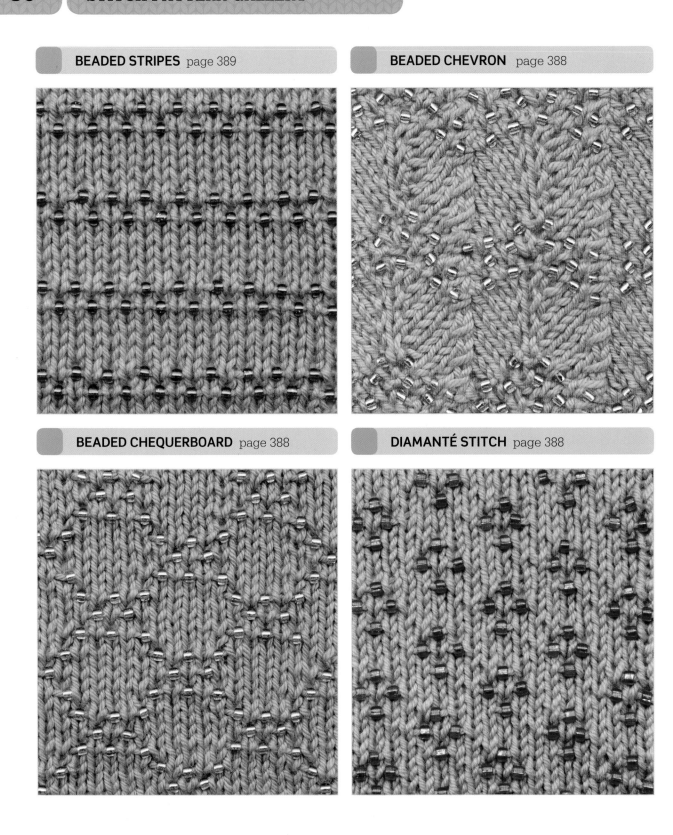

BEADED STRIPES page 389

BEADED CHEVRON page 388

BEADED CHEQUERBOARD page 388

DIAMANTÉ STITCH page 388

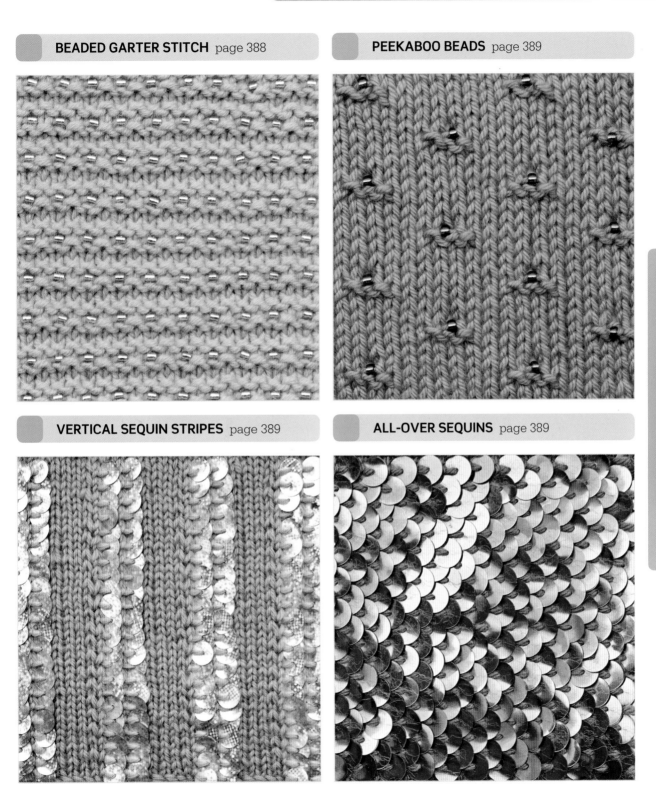

BEADED GARTER STITCH page 388

PEEKABOO BEADS page 389

VERTICAL SEQUIN STRIPES page 389

ALL-OVER SEQUINS page 389

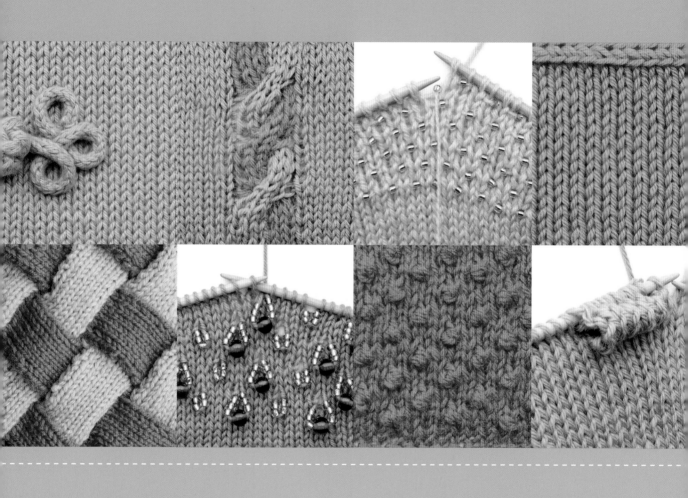

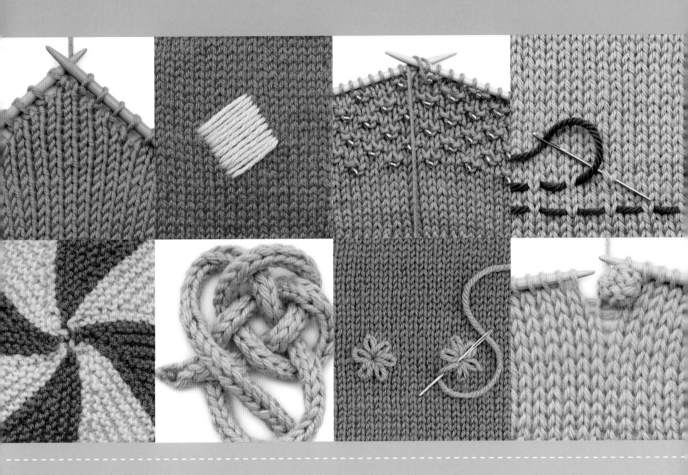

TECHNIQUES

KEY TECHNIQUES

Learning to knit is a very quick process. There are only a few key techniques to pick up before you are ready to make simple shapes like scarves, baby blankets, cushion covers, and throws. The basics include casting stitches onto the needle, the knit and purl stitches, and casting the stitches off the needles.

MAKING A SLIP KNOT

Before you start knitting, you must first learn how to place the first loop on the needle. This loop is called the slip knot and it is the first stitch formed when casting on stitches.

1 Begin by crossing the yarn coming from the ball over the yarn end (called the yarn tail) to form a circle.

Yarn coming from ball

Yarn tail

2 Insert the tip of a knitting needle through the circle of yarn, then wrap the needle tip around the ball end of the yarn and pull the yarn through the circle.

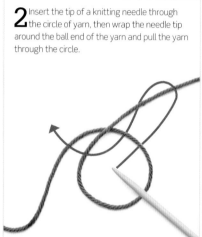

3 This forms a loop on the needle and a loose, open knot below the loop.

4 Pull both ends of the yarn firmly to tighten the knot and the loop on the needle.

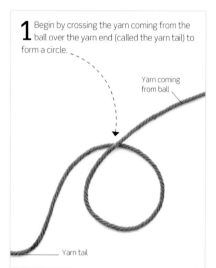

5 Make sure the completed slip knot is tight enough on the needle that it won't fall off but not so tight that you can't slide it along.

Make sure loop is secure but slides easily

Ball end of yarn

6 The yarn tail should be at least 10–15cm (4–6in) long so it can be darned in later. Your knitting pattern, however, may instruct you to leave an extra-long yarn tail (called a long loose end) to use for seams or other purposes.

Extra-long yarn tail

HOLDING YARN AND NEEDLES

Although all knitting is formed in exactly the same way, you can hold the yarn in either the right or left hand. These two yarn-holding techniques are called the "English" and "Continental" methods. Knitting is ambidextrous, so right-handed and left-handed knitters should try both knitting styles to see which one is easier.

KNITTING "ENGLISH" STYLE

1 The yarn is laced around the fingers of the right hand. Aim to control the yarn firmly but with a relaxed hand, releasing it to flow through the fingers as the stitches are formed.

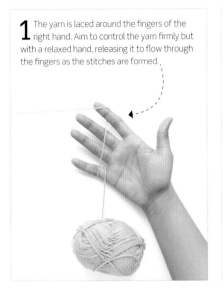

2 Try this alternative technique as well or make up your own. You need to tension the yarn just enough with your fingers to create even loops that are neither too loose nor too tight.

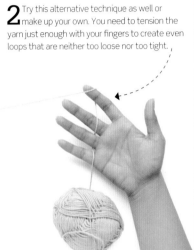

3 Hold the needles with the stitches about to be worked in the left hand and the other needle in the right hand. Use the right forefinger to wrap the yarn around the needle.

KNITTING "CONTINENTAL" STYLE

1 Lace the yarn through the fingers of the left hand in any way that feels comfortable. Try to both release and tension the yarn easily to create uniform loops.

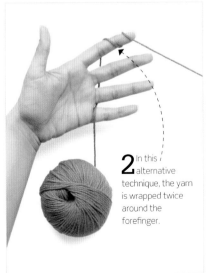

2 In this alternative technique, the yarn is wrapped twice around the forefinger.

3 Hold the needle with the unworked stitches in the left hand and the other needle in the right hand. Position the yarn with the left forefinger and pull it through the loops with the tip of the right needle.

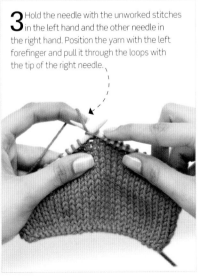

TECHNIQUES

ALTERNATIVE "CONTINENTAL" STYLE KNITTING

This alternative method makes knit stitches very easy, and is ideal for garter or circular stocking stitch. As you work near the tip, short tapered needles are best for this method. When knitting Continental style you may find your tension loosens, in which case use smaller needles.

For both the knit and the purl stitches, wrap the yarn around your left little finger, but keep it over all your fingers. This makes purling easier.

ALTERNATIVE "CONTINENTAL" KNIT STITCH

1 Hold your index finger up with the yarn over it and use the pad of your middle finger to hold the yarn against the left needle, slightly forwards of the stitch.

2 Insert the right tip into the stitch, pull and catch the yarn on your middle finger, draw it through the stitch on the left needle and off.

3 At the end of the row, keep the yarn around your left fingers. Swap the needles to start the next row.

ALTERNATIVE "CONTINENTAL" PURL STITCH

1 Hold the yarn as for knit stitch. Bring yarn to front. With your index finger raised and your middle finger touching the left needle near the tip, insert needle as for purl. Tilt the right tip towards you and then back in a small circular movement so that the yarn wraps over it.

2 At the same time, bring your left index finger with the yarn on it forwards, wrapping the yarn around the needle. Keep your index finger in constant contact with the left needle.

3 Immediately dip the right needle tip slightly away from you to hook the yarn and pull the old stitch open. Take the needle backwards through the old stitch and make a new purl loop. Slide the old stitch off the left needle.

ALTERNATIVE "CONTINENTAL" PURL STITCH – UNTWISTING AN INCORRECT STITCH

1 If the front "leg" of the stitch is further back along the needle than the rear "leg" the stitch is twisted.

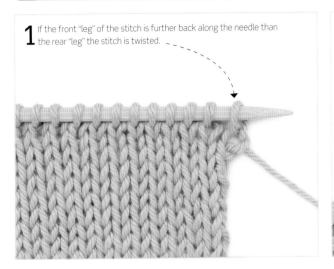

2 To untwist the stitches on the following row, knit into the back of the stitch. If you find it difficult to master the correct wrap, but still wish to purl in the Continental style, then work every knit row following a purl row by working into the back of the stitch.

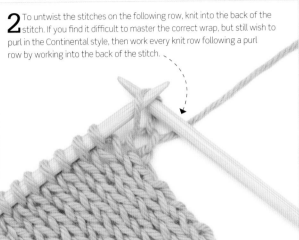

SINGLE STRAND CAST-ONS

These cast-ons are all related to the Single cast-on and use one strand. They tend to be soft, but can be made firmer by twisting. Alternating loop cast-on makes a decorative edge. Casting on knitwise and Cable cast-on are useful for casting on in the middle of a piece, for example if you need to add more than one stitch when increasing. When followed by Stocking stitch, Casting on knitwise can curl towards the knit side. For edges where this matters, choose a two strand Tubular cast-on (see p.100).

TECHNIQUES

SINGLE CAST-ON (also called *thumb cast-on*)

1 This is the easiest cast-on. Hold the needle with the slip knot in the right hand. Then wrap the yarn around the left thumb as shown and hold the yarn in place in the palm of the left hand. Insert the needle tip under and up through the loop on the thumb following the arrow.

Yarn going to ball — Yarn tail

2 Release the loop from the thumb and pull the yarn to tighten the new cast-on loop on the needle, sliding it up close to the slip knot.

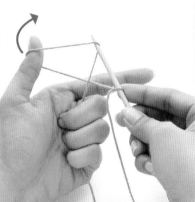

3 Loop the yarn around the thumb again and continue making loops in the same way until the required number of stitches is on the needle.

Yarn going to ball — Yarn tail

KNIT-ON CAST-ON (also called *knit-stitch cast-on*)

1 Holding the yarn in the left or right hand as explained on p.85, place the needle with the slip knot in the left hand. Then insert the tip of the right needle from left to right through the centre of the loop on the left needle.

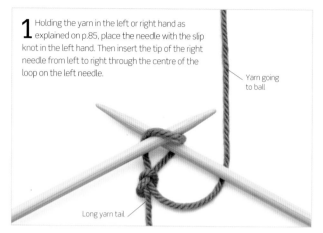

Yarn going to ball

Long yarn tail

2 With the yarn behind the needles, wrap it under and around the tip of the right needle. (While casting on, use the left forefinger or middle finger to hold the loops on the left needle in position.)

3 With the tip of the right needle, carefully draw the yarn through the loop on the left needle. (This is the same way a knit stitch is formed, hence the name of the cast-on.)

4 Transfer the loop on the right needle to the left needle by inserting the tip of the left needle from right to left through the front of the loop.

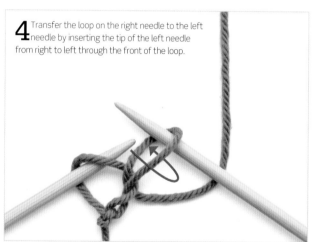

5 Pull both yarn ends to tighten the new cast-on loop on the needle, sliding it up close to the slip knot.

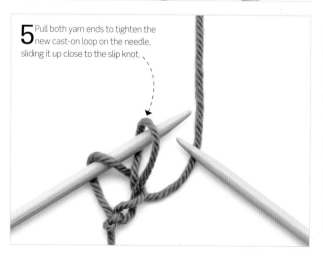

6 Continue casting on stitches in the same way until you have the required number of stitches. For a looser cast on, hold two needles together in your left hand whilst casting on.

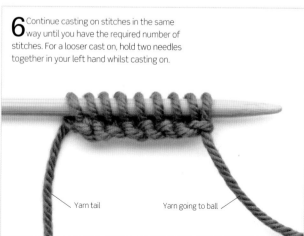

Yarn tail

Yarn going to ball

CABLE CAST-ON

1 Begin by working Steps 1–5 of the Knit-on cast-on (opposite). Then insert the tip of the right needle between the two loops on the left needle and wrap the yarn under and around the tip of the right needle.

Yarn going to ball

Long yarn tail

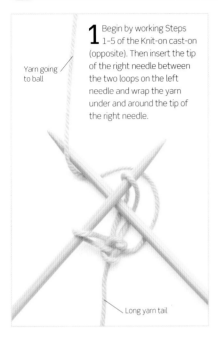

2 With the tip of the right needle, draw the yarn through to form a loop on the right needle.

3 Transfer the loop on the right needle to the left needle (see Step 4 opposite). Continue, inserting the needle between the first two loops on the left needle when beginning each new cast-on stitch.

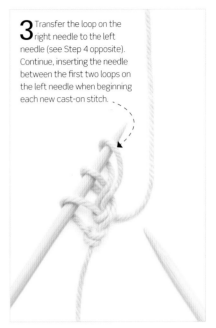

FINGER LOOP CAST-ON

1 This gives a soft cast-on. Hold the needle with the slip knot in the right hand. Lift the yarn from underneath with your left index finger pointing away from you. Bend and turn your finger to point towards you.

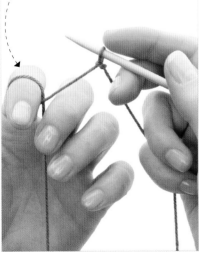

2 Insert the needle into the loop that lies on top of the finger from behind.

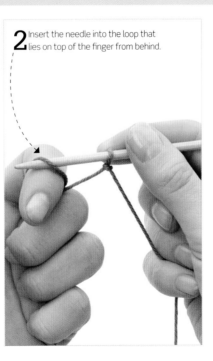

3 Release the index finger and tighten the stitch on the needle.

ALTERNATING LOOP CAST-ON

1 Work the first stitch as for Finger loop cast-on, as shown on p.89.

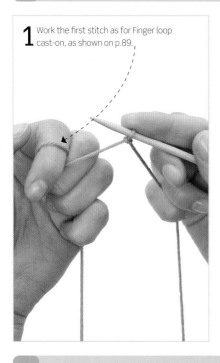

2 Work the second stitch as Single cast-on by lifting the yarn from behind with the left thumb, winding it round the thumb and inserting the needle into the front strand (see p.87),

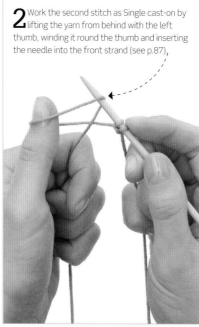

3 Repeat Steps 1 and 2 to cast on as many stitches as you need. On the first row, work into the front of the stitches, even if they look twisted.

DOUBLE TWIST LOOP CAST-ON

This is firmer than Single cast-on, and the first row is a little easier to knit.

1 Hold the needle with the slip knot in your right hand. Lift the yarn from behind with your left index finger.

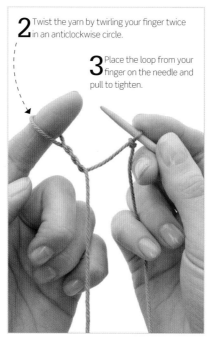

2 Twist the yarn by twirling your finger twice in an anticlockwise circle.

3 Place the loop from your finger on the needle and pull to tighten.

4 Repeat Steps 1–3 to cast on as many stitches as you need. The resulting decorative edge is open-textured.

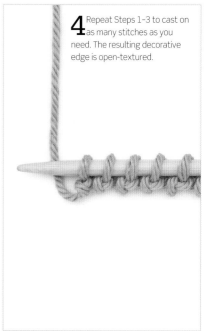

TWO STRAND CAST-ON

These cast-on techniques all use two strands, but generally only one needle, and are strong, elastic, and versatile. They are usually followed by a wrong side row, unless the reverse is the right side. As with Double cast-on, start all these with a slip knot made after a long tail at least three times as long as the planned knitting width.

DOUBLE CAST-ON (also called *long-tail cast-on*)

1 Make a slip knot on the needle, leaving a very long yarn tail – allow about 3.5cm (1⅜in) for each stitch being cast on. Hold the needle in your right hand. Then loop the yarn tail over the left thumb and the ball yarn end over the left forefinger as shown. Hold both strands in the palm of the left hand.

Long yarn tail

Yarn going to ball

2 Insert the tip of the needle under and up through the loop on the thumb.

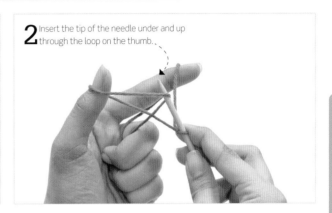

3 Wrap the tip of the needle around the loop on the forefinger from right to left and use it to pull the yarn through the loop on the thumb as shown by the arrow.

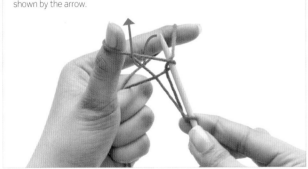

4 Release the loop from the thumb.

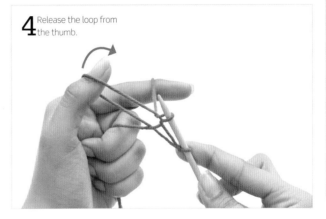

5 Pull both yarn ends to tighten the new cast-on loop on the needle, sliding it up close to the slip knot.

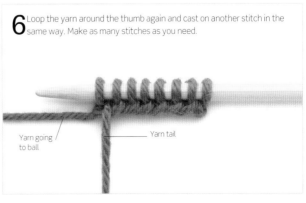

6 Loop the yarn around the thumb again and cast on another stitch in the same way. Make as many stitches as you need.

Yarn going to ball

Yarn tail

TECHNIQUES

CONTRAST EDGE CAST-ON

1 Cut a piece of contrast yarn three times the length of the cast-on, and tie one end onto the end of the ball of main coloured yarn.

2 Hold both strands of yarn in your left hand, with the contrast yarn towards you and the knot at the end.

3 Slide the needle along between the yarns so that the knot sits snugly on the right side of the needle. Hold it in place with your right index finger.

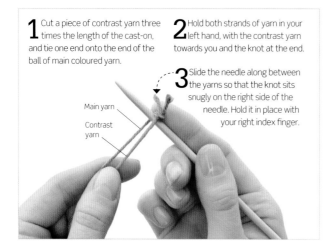

Main yarn

Contrast yarn

4 Loop the contrast yarn over your thumb by moving it in an anticlockwise circle, and loop the main colour over your index finger as shown.

5 Insert the needle from below under the front strand of the contrast yarn on the thumb.

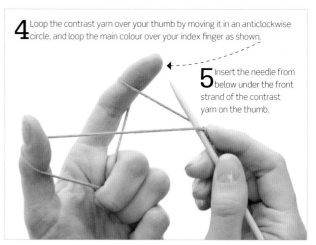

6 Move the needle towards your index finger and take the tip up and over the front index finger loop, pulling this back towards you, then pull this main colour loop through the contrast-coloured thumb loop.

7 Release the contrast yarn thumb loop. Pull both yarn ends to hold the needle snugly, and slide the cast-on stitch close to the slip knot. Repeat steps 4–7.

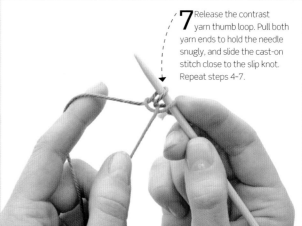

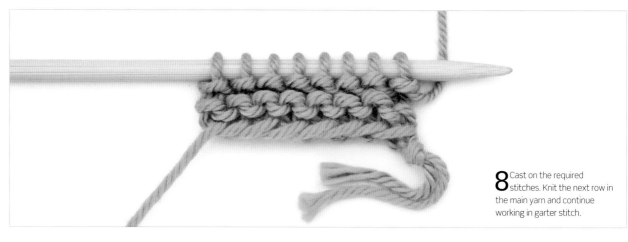

8 Cast on the required stitches. Knit the next row in the main yarn and continue working in garter stitch.

TWISTED DOUBLE CAST-ON

This cast-on is very stretchy, so is useful before a rib. It can be made even stretchier by working it over two needles held together.

1 Hold the yarn and needle as for Double cast-on (see p.91). Bring the needle towards you and then back under both thumb loops.

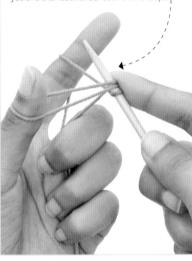

2 Bring the needle towards you over the top of the furthest thumb loop and down between both thumb strands. The thumb loop is now a figure of eight.

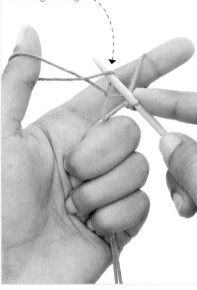

3 Take the needle over the first loop on your index finger.

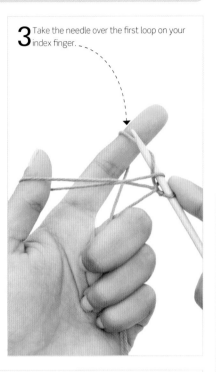

4 Bring the needle towards you. Drop the end of your thumb away from you and let the loop slide down towards the end to open the thumb loop. Bring the needle down through the open thumb loop.

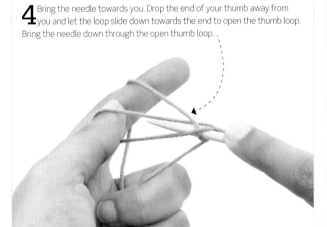

5 Release the thumb loop keeping the yarn around your index finger ready to start the next cast-on loop. Pull the short strand to tighten the stitch.

6 Loop yarn around thumb again and repeat Steps 1–4 to cast on another stitch in the same way. The stitches create a stretchy double twist effect.

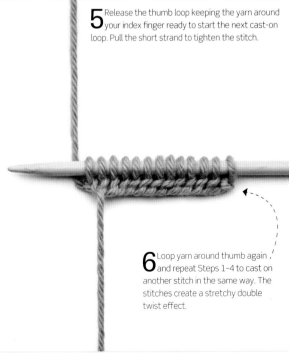

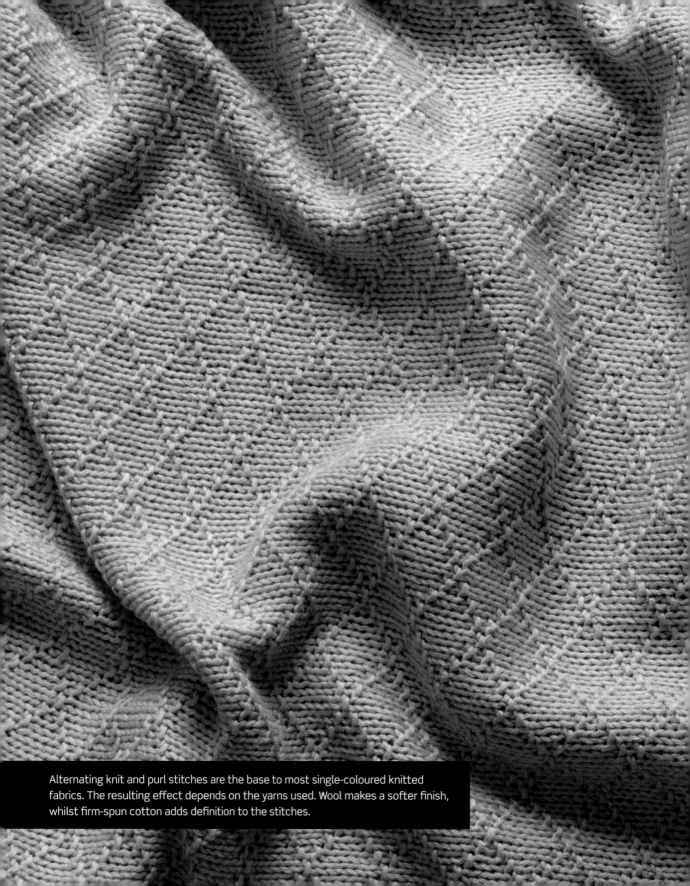

Alternating knit and purl stitches are the base to most single-coloured knitted fabrics. The resulting effect depends on the yarns used. Wool makes a softer finish, whilst firm-spun cotton adds definition to the stitches.

ITALIAN CAST-ON

1 Hold the needle with the slip knot and ball yarn end in the right hand, tail in the left.

2 Bring the left index finger and thumb forwards under the short yarn tail. Take the needle over and back under this strand, making a loop on the index finger.

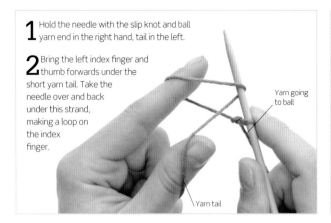

Yarn going to ball

Yarn tail

3 Holding this position, wrap the ball yarn around the needle from left to right.

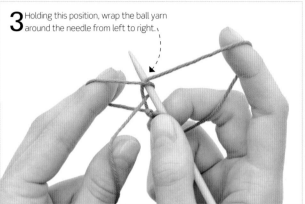

4 Slip the index finger loop over the tip of the needle. Pull the short yarn tail to tighten.

Slip loop over needle tip

5 Loop the yarn over the index finger and thumb again and continue making loops in the same way until the required number of sitches is on the needle.

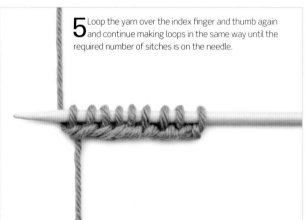

TWO-NEEDLE CAST-ON

1 Hold the needle with the slip knot in the left hand, with the short yarn tail at the back.

Yarn tail

Yarn going to ball

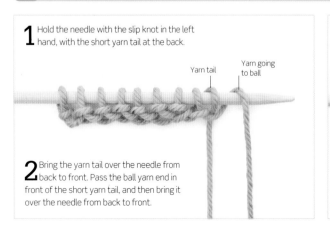

2 Bring the yarn tail over the needle from back to front. Pass the ball yarn end in front of the short yarn tail, and then bring it over the needle from back to front.

3 Using an empty needle in the right hand, pass the first loop over the second and remove the right needle.

Yarn going to ball

Yarn tail

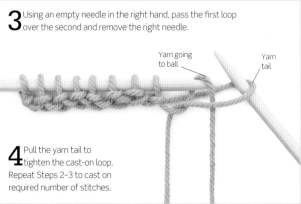

4 Pull the yarn tail to tighten the cast-on loop. Repeat Steps 2-3 to cast on required number of stitches.

COMBINED TWO-STRAND CAST-ON

1 Make the first stitch as for Double cast-on (see p.91). The second stitch is similar, except you turn your thumb in the opposite direction to catch the yarn. The end of the strand is now to the inside of your thumb.

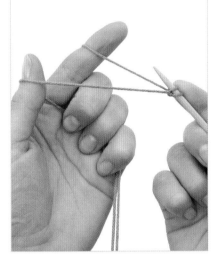

2 With the needle pointing away, take it over the first thumb loop and then under the loop on the inside of the thumb. Take the needle over the nearest loop on the index finger.

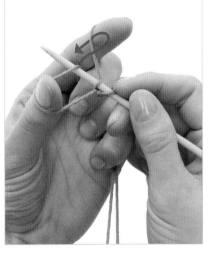

3 Draw the loop through the thumb loop.

4 Drop the thumb loop. Pull the yarn tail to tighten the new loop. Repeat to cast on the required stitches.

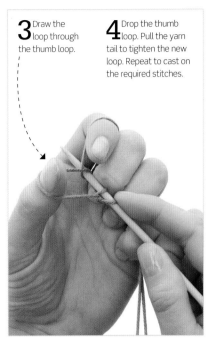

TECHNIQUES

TWO-STRAND DOUBLE CAST-ON

1 In preparation, measure the long tail length required for your cast-on. Fold the yarn so you have two strands of this length, and tie your slip knot at the free end of the yarn, catching both yarns.

2 Work as usual for Double cast-on (see p.91), or any other two-stranded cast-on, using the single ball end yarn to make the stitches and the doubled yarn for the foundation loop.

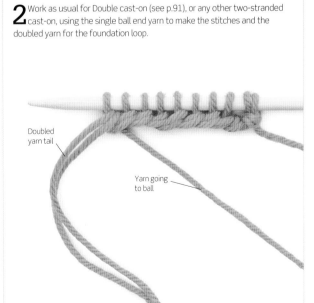

Doubled yarn tail

Yarn going to ball

Doubled yarn tail

Yarn going to ball

SPECIAL CAST-ONS

The following cast-ons are useful for specific purposes and may be specified in your pattern. However, many patterns simply say "cast on", in which case you should select one of these methods to add functionality or individuality to your project.

CHANNEL ISLANDS CAST-ON FOR SINGLE RIB

1 Fold the yarn tail, so that you have a doubled yarn four times the length of your cast-on edge, plus 10cm (4in).

2 Make a slip knot on the doubled strand, about 10cm (4in) down from the free end. Transfer to a needle. Hold the doubled strand in left hand, single strand and needle in the right.

3 Bring the left thumb under the doubled strand from the front, in a clockwise circle, winding the doubled yarn twice around the thumb. Insert the needle up through both loops.

4 Pass the single strand around the needle and slip thumb loops over to make a stitch as normal.

5 Release the loop from the thumb and pull the double strand first to tighten the loop on the needle.

6 To make the next stitch, take the single yarn over the needle to the back (yo).

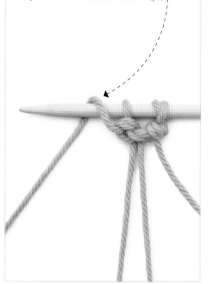

7 Repeat Steps 2–4 to the required cast-on length, finishing with a thumb wrapped stitch, making an even number of stitches.

8 To work the first row, knit the first stitch (thumb loop) and purl the next (yo). Finally, purl into the initial double strand slip knot.

PROVISIONAL CAST-ON

1 Take a length of contrast yarn over twice the required length of your cast-on, tie a slip knot at one end and transfer to a needle.

2 Make a slip knot in the main yarn. Transfer to the same needle.

3 Hold as for Double cast-on (see p.91), with contrast yarn around the thumb.

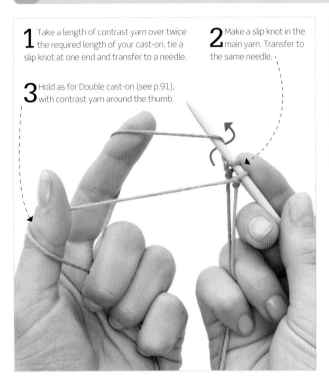

4 Flick your right wrist and take the needle down between the yarns and up under main yarn.

5 Turn the needle towards you and bring it over, and then back away from you under the contrast yarn.

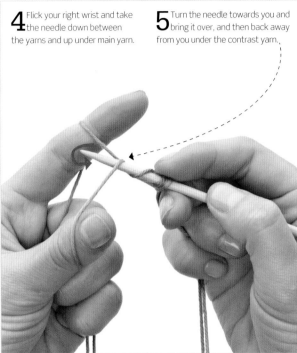

6 Catch the main yarn from above and behind, and bring it under the contrast yarn and around the needle. Let the contrast yarn slip to the back of the needle. Repeat steps 4–6 to cast on the required stitches.

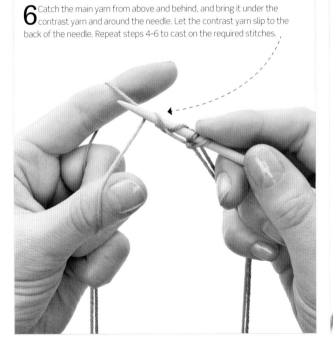

7 Drop the contrast slip knot at the end of the cast-on. Tie the contrast ends together until you want to pull the contrast yarn out and pick up the "live" open stitches. Knit into the front of the first row.

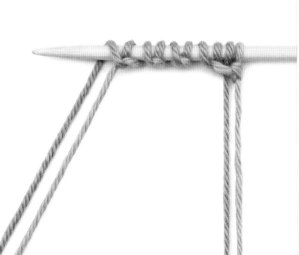

CROCHET PROVISIONAL CAST-ON

1 Make a slip knot on a crochet hook with contrast yarn. Hold yarn and needle in the left hand and hook in the right. Take the yarn behind the needle and over left index finger. Hold needle and hook crossed, with the hook in front. Lay yarn in the hook with left index finger.

2 Pull the yarn through the slip knot. The yarn will loop over the needle making a stitch. Take the yarn behind the needle and make another loop. Continue to cast on required stitches. Cut the yarn and pull it through the last chain on the hook. Mark this end so it is clear which end will unravel.

3 Work your knitting. When ready to work on the cast-on edge, pull the marked thread back out of the last chain after which the whole chain can be unravelled and the "live" open stitches picked up.

TUBULAR CAST-ON (also called *invisible cast-on*)

This is good for single rib, but can become wavy if over-stretched. Use needles at least two sizes smaller than those used for the main fabric.

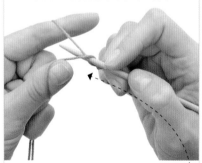

1 Hold yarn and needles as for Double cast-on (see p.91), but with the palm facing down, creating a "V" of yarn pointing to the right.

2 Bring the needle forwards, passing over and back under the thumb strand.

3 Catch the index-finger strand, going over and back towards you.

4 Turn your thumb away from you in a circular movement, flicking the thumb strand over the needle. Bring the left hand back to its original position, passing the yarn under the needle.

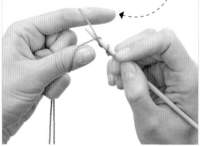

5 Make sure that the stitch goes all the way around the needle, and lies centrally under the needle.

6 Take the needle back over and under the index finger strand. With needle towards you, take it over and back under the thumb strand.

7 Move your index finger towards you in a circular movement, passing the yarn over the needle, and return your hand to its original position, making sure the stitch goes all the way around the needle. Repeat Steps 2–7 to cast on an even number of stitches.

The stitches must lie under the needle

8 At the end, tie the two strands together under the needle. Knit the first row by knitting into the back of the first stitch, bring the yarn to front and slip the next stitch purlwise. Repeat along the row. For the second row, repeat without knitting into back of stitch.

ALTERNATIVE ROLL EDGE TUBULAR CAST-ON

1 Using a smooth yarn, work a Crochet provisional cast-on (see opposite) of half the required stitches plus one. In main colour and on small sized needles, knit three rows of stocking stitch, starting with a knit row and ending with the wrong side facing.

2 Purl one stitch and take yarn to back. Insert the right needle tip from top to bottom through the purl bar of main colour bar at the colour join three rows down.

3 Insert the left needle from front to back into the picked up stitch. Knit into front of stitch. Bring yarn to front. Repeat Steps 2 and 3 until row is complete. Finish with a purl stitch, and no pick up.

4 Change to main needles. This cast-on makes an odd number of stitches. A single rib will have a knit stitch at each end and must be worked with rows starting as follows: knit one, purl one; then the next row purl one, knit one; and so on. Decrease one at the end of ribbing or when convenient. Remove Crochet provisional cast-on.

KNOTTED CAST-ON

This can be tight, so work loosely on thick needles. This makes a strong, decorative edge.

1 Make a slip knot on the needle and cast on one stitch as Double cast-on (see p.91).

2 Hold the second needle in the left hand, insert it into the slip knot and pass this over the last stitch made and off the right needle.

3 Repeat, casting on two stitches and passing first over second to required length of cast-on. Single cast-on may be substituted for Double cast-on if preferred. The first stitch of the first row should always be knitted.

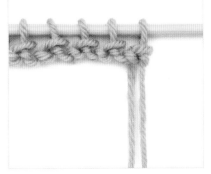

TWICE-KNITTED CAST-ON

Excellent for fringed edges and before Twice knitted work. Always knit first stitch of first row.

1 Working loosely, make a slip knot and cast on one stitch using the Knit-on method (see p.88).

2 Insert the right needle into both loops and knit together, but do not slip stitches off. Slip new loop from right needle to left. Knit new stitch together with the preceding stitch. Repeat Step 2 to cast on required stitches.

TECHNIQUES

FRILLY CAST-ON

1 Cast on an even number of stitches that is twice as many as required using Double cast-on method (see p.91). Other decorative cast-ons may be preferred.

2 Insert the right needle into the first two stitches from front to back and knit them together. Repeat across the row.

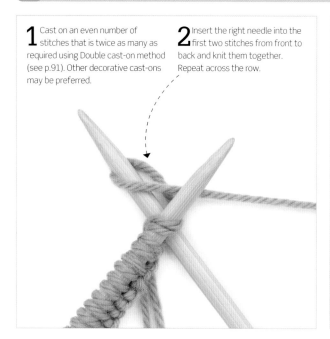

3 Work the next row as normal.

4 This creates a pretty, decorative edge. You may need extra yarn as the cast-on uses twice as many stitches.

EDGING CAST-ON

1 Knit a piece of a narrow edging to the required length of your cast-on. If you are unsure of the correct length, slip stitches onto a holder at end (see p.106) and alter as necessary.

2 Work along the right side. Hold the new yarn at the back. Insert the needle tip from front to back through the first edge stitch, wrap the yarn around the needle, and pull a loop through to the front.

New yarn tail

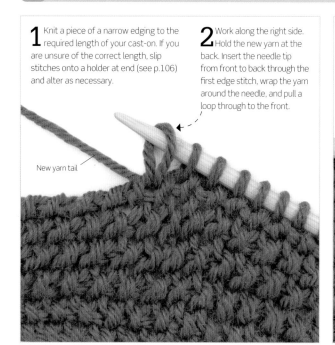

3 Continue along the full length of the edge, picking up the new yarn evenly to form stitches on the needle. If necessary, miss out some rows to prevent the cast-on distorting.

4 Knit the main fabric upwards from the edge trim as required. Start with a purl row if the main fabric is stocking stitch.

PINHOLE CAST-ON

This is ideal for starting circular medallions.

1 Wrap the yarn around your left index finger. Insert a crochet hook and draw a loop through as if making a slip knot.

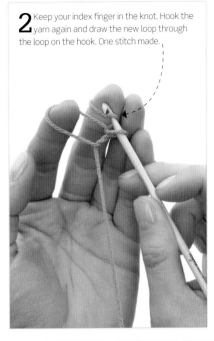

2 Keep your index finger in the knot. Hook the yarn again and draw the new loop through the loop on the hook. One stitch made.

3 Put the hook back into the knot loop on your finger and pull another loop through. Draw another loop through this one. There are now two stitches on the hook.

4 Repeat Step 3, adding a loop to the hook each time until you have enough loops for a quarter of the required stitches. Remove your finger after the first few stitches. Transfer these stitches to the first knitting needle, and repeat to cast on a circle to four needles.

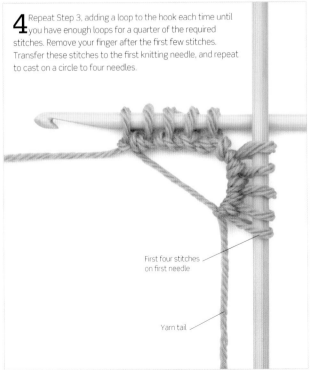

First four stitches on first needle

Yarn tail

5 When the project is complete, pull the yarn tail at the centre and the hole will close neatly.

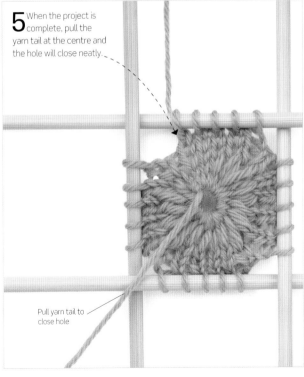

Pull yarn tail to close hole

Different stitch effects worked in one colour of yarn create fabrics where the subtleties of light and shade emphasize the surface texture. Careful choices of stitch patterns and yarn make many variations possible.

SIMPLE CAST-OFFS

When your piece of knitted fabric is complete you need to close off the loops so that they can't unravel. This is called casting off the stitches. Although casting-off is shown worked across knit stitches, the principle is the same for purl stitches. If instructed to retain stitches for future use, slip your stitches onto a spare needle or a stitch holder.

CASTING OFF KNITWISE

1 Begin by knitting the first two stitches. Then insert the tip of the left needle from left to right through the first stitch and lift this stitch up and over the second stitch and off the right needle.

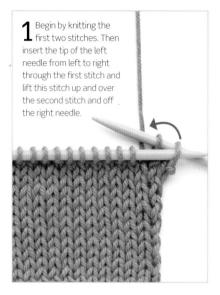

2 To cast off the next stitch, knit one more stitch and repeat Step 1. Continue until only one stitch remains on the right needle. (If your pattern says "cast off in pattern", work the stitches in the specified pattern as you cast off.)

3 To stop the last stitch from unravelling, cut the yarn, leaving a yarn tail 20cm (8in) long, which is long enough to darn into the knitting later. (Alternatively, leave a much longer yarn end to use for a future seam.) Pass the yarn end through the remaining loop and pull tight to close the loop. This is called fastening off.

SLIPPING STITCHES OFF NEEDLE

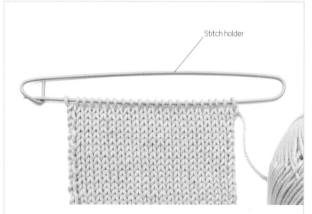

Stitch holder

Using a stitch holder: If you are setting stitches aside to work on later, your instructions will tell you whether to cut the yarn or keep it attached to the ball. Carefully slip your stitches onto a stitch holder large enough to hold all the stitches. If you are only slipping a few stitches, use a safety pin.

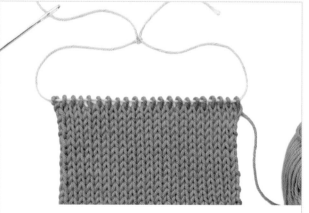

Using a length of yarn: If you don't have a stitch holder or don't have one large enough, you can use a length of cotton yarn instead. Using a blunt-ended yarn needle, pass the yarn through the stitches as you slip them off the knitting needle. Knot the ends of the cotton yarn together.

ALTERNATIVE CAST-OFFS

Try using one of these casting-off techniques to compliment your project. Consider using a contrast colour, either in the basic cast off or combined with a decorative style. Cast-offs are included that give more stretch to ribs or loosen an edge, and an adaptation of the Three-needle cast-off may even be used to join pockets and hems.

PURL CAST-OFF

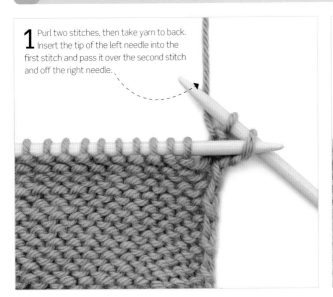

1 Purl two stitches, then take yarn to back. Insert the tip of the left needle into the first stitch and pass it over the second stitch and off the right needle.

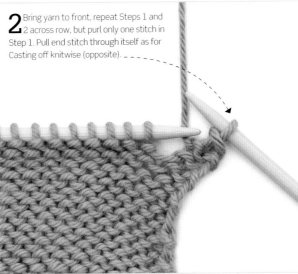

2 Bring yarn to front, repeat Steps 1 and 2 across row, but purl only one stitch in Step 1. Pull end stitch through itself as for Casting off knitwise (opposite).

CASTING OFF IN RIB EFFECT

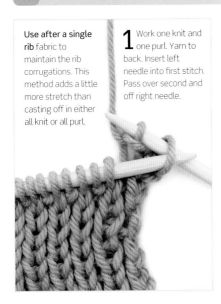

Use after a single rib fabric to maintain the rib corrugations. This method adds a little more stretch than casting off in either all knit or all purl.

1 Work one knit and one purl. Yarn to back. Insert left needle into first stitch. Pass over second and off right needle.

2 Knit the next stitch then pass the first stitch over the second and off the right needle as before.

3 Yarn to front and purl next stitch. Repeat Steps 2 and 3 across the row. Pull the final stitch through itself to fasten off.

TECHNIQUES

SUSPENDED CAST-OFF (also called *delayed cast-off*)

This is ideal after lace knitting.

1 Knit the first two stitches (this starts the row and is not repeated). Insert the left needle tip into the first stitch and pass it over the second and off the right tip. Do not drop it from the left tip.

2 Bring the right needle across the front of the "suspended" stitch, and knit the first stitch on the left needle.

3 Slip both loops off together as you complete the knit stitch. Continue passing and knitting stitches as in Steps 1 and 2 to the end of the cast off.

CROCHET CAST-OFF

1 Hold the yarn in your left hand and keep it at the back. Slip the first stitch purlwise onto the crochet hook.

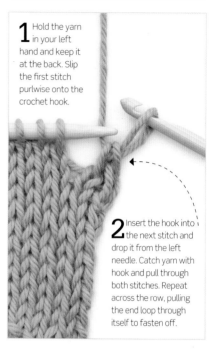

2 Insert the hook into the next stitch and drop it from the left needle. Catch yarn with hook and pull through both stitches. Repeat across the row, pulling the end loop through itself to fasten off.

THREE NEEDLE CAST-OFF

This seam can be worked on the right side of the knitting (as here) to form a decorative seam, or on the wrong side.

1 Hold the needles with the stitches to be joined together with the wrong sides facing each other. Insert a third needle through the centre of the first stitch on each needle and knit these two stitches together.

2 Continue to knit together one stitch from each needle as you cast off the stitches in the usual way. (A contrasting yarn is used here to show the seam clearly.)

3 When the pieces of knitting are opened out, you will see that this technique forms a raised chain along the seam.

PICOT POINT CAST-OFF

Where there is a seam, cast off the first stitch to leave a selvedge before starting the picot edge.

1 Knit two stitches, insert the left needle into the first stitch on the right needle and pass it over the second stitch and off the right needle (Casting off knitwise, see p.106).

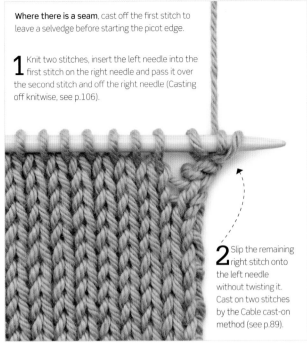

2 Slip the remaining right stitch onto the left needle without twisting it. Cast on two stitches by the Cable cast-on method (see p.89).

3 Cast off three stitches knitwise as described in Step 1. Cast off another two stitches. (These form the straight edge between the picots points).

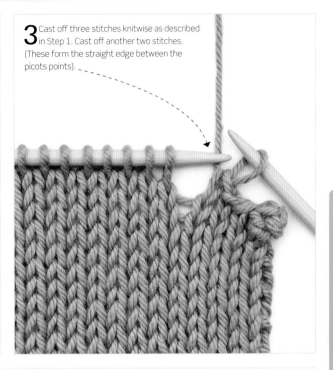

4 Repeat Steps 2–3 across the row.

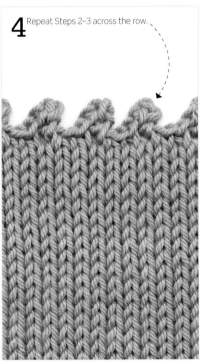

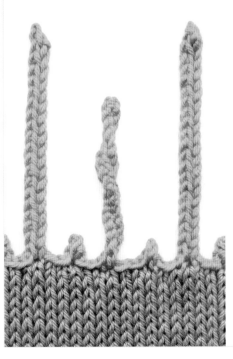

5 A lamb's tail edge can be made by casting on more stitches in Step 2 (the longer example shown has twenty stitches cast on). However many you choose, always cast off one more stitch in Step 3 than you cast on. To make the tails twist, as shown centre, cast off tighter than you cast on.

6 To use contrast colour for the picots, work the last row of the main fabric in contrast (purl row in stocking stitch). To prevent the edge rolling to the knit side, work the last two rows of the main fabric in Garter stitch (see p.116) or Moss stitch (see p.48). For a clean colour join introduce contrast yarn on the knit row before you start the garter or moss stitch. A picot cast-on can also be worked using this method of casting on and casting off the extra stitches between making each group of edge cast-on stitches (see p.92).

TECHNIQUES

TWO ROW CAST-OFF

1 Work on an even number of stitches. Knit the first stitch and purl the second. With the yarn at the back, insert the left needle in the first stitch and pass it over the second stitch and off the right needle.

2 Knit and purl the next two stitches on the left needle. Take yarn to back. Pass the second (knit) stitch over the third (purl) stitch on the right needle to cast off one stitch.

3 Repeat Step 2 across the row. This leaves you with half the number of original stitches on the needle. Cut the yarn leaving a tail. Do not turn the work.

4 Slip the last stitch on the right needle onto the left needle without twisting it, slip the next stitch in the same way. Pass the second stitch along on the left needle over the last stitch.

5 Repeat across the row, slipping only one stitch each time. Sew the last stitch in with a blunt-ended yarn needle and a separate piece of yarn.

DECREASE CAST-OFF

A decorative cast-off, this is better for single ribs than plain casting off knitwise.

1 Insert the tip of the right needle into the front of the first two stitches on the left needle and knit them together. Slip the new stitch on the right needle back onto the left without twisting it. Repeat across the row, pulling the thread through the last stitch to secure the end.

TUBULAR CAST-OFF

1 In preparation, and over an even number of stitches, work two rows as follows: knit the first stitch, bring yarn to front and slip the purl stitch that follows without twisting it (purlwise), take yarn to back. Repeat across row.

2 Stretch your ribbing out and cut the yarn end to about four times the length of the required cast-off edge. Thread onto a blunt-ended yarn needle. Hold the knitting with the tip to the right.

3 Insert the yarn needle into the first stitch knitwise. Pull the yarn through and drop the stitch.

4 Bring the yarn across the front and insert the needle purlwise into the third (knit) stitch. Pull it through but not too tightly. Take it to the right and insert purlwise into the second (purl) stitch, taking the yarn through to the back.

5 Take the yarn behind the third (knit) stitch, bring it to the front between the third and fourth stitch and insert it as shown into the fourth (purl) stitch. Then insert the needle through the centre of the preceding knit stitch, and out to the front around the left leg.

6 Repeat Steps 4–5. Tension the stitches evenly as you work.

VERY STRETCHY SINGLE RIB CAST-OFF

1 On a single rib fabric, make a yarn over before working the knit stitch at start of row.

2 Insert the left needle in the first stitch on the right needle. Lift it over the second stitch and off.

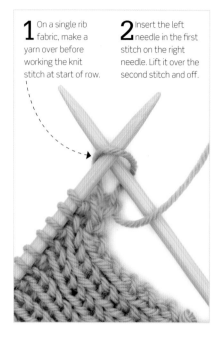

3 Bring yarn to front. Take yarn away from you over the top of the needle and back to the front. Purl the next stitch. There will be three stitches on the right needle.

4 Take yarn to back. Slip the first and second stitches on the right needle over the third and off.

5 Wrap the yarn round the needle and knit the next stitch. Slip the first and second stitches on the right needle over the third and off. Repeat Steps 3–5 along the row.

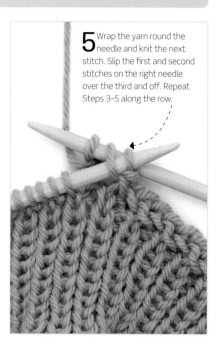

EDGING CAST-OFF

For a contrast edge, work the last row of the main fabric in a contrast colour.

1 Cast on three stitches for edging on an empty right needle. Hold the needle with the stitches to be cast off in your left hand. Slip the last stitch of the edging onto the left needle without twisting.

2 Knit the edging stitch and main colour stitch by putting the right needle into the back of both stitches from above.

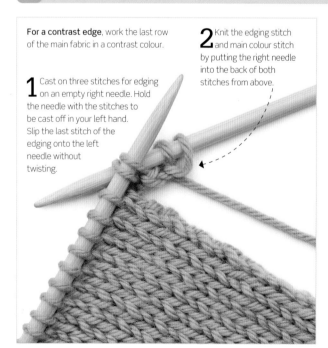

3 Turn the work, bring yarn to front. Slip the last stitch of the main fabric onto the left needle without twisting. Put the tip of the right needle into the back of both stitches from below, and purl together. Purl two remaining edging stitches.

4 Turn the work and knit all but one of the edging stitches, and then repeat Steps 2 to 4.

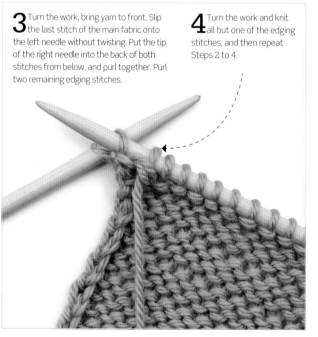

CROCHET CHAIN LOOP CAST-OFF

This decorative cast-off helps prevent edges from stretching, particularly on lacy knitting.

1 The stitches should be divisible by four. Hold the stitches with the RS facing you in your left hand. Slip the first stitch onto a crochet hook.

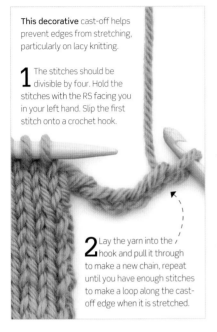

2 Lay the yarn into the hook and pull it through to make a new chain, repeat until you have enough stitches to make a loop along the cast-off edge when it is stretched.

3 Insert the hook into the first four stitches on the needle. Slip them onto the hook. Lay yarn into the hook and pull a loop through all four stitches.

4 Lay yarn into the hook and make another chain through both loops on the hook. Repeat Steps 2–4 across the edge, catching four stitches each time at Step 3.

SMOOTH DIAGONAL CAST-OFF

This example assumes you are working a pattern with a diagonal edge to cast off in groups of five (such as a shoulder seam).

1 Cast off four stitches using the Cast-off knitwise method (see p.106), leaving the last stitch of the cast-off on the right needle.

2 Knit to the end of the row on the left needle, turn the work and purl until there are only two stitches remaining on the left needle.

3 Purl these two stitches together. Turn the work. Repeat Steps 2–4 until the cast-off length is completed.

TECHNIQUES

KNIT STITCH
Abbreviation = *k*

All knitting is made up of only two basic stitches – knit and purl. Choose Single, Finger, or Knit-on cast-on and start with Garter stitch (see p.116), which uses only knit stitch. Try out some fun stripes and experiment with different yarns before you learn purl stitch. The odd dropped stitch doesn't matter so much, put a safety pin through it so it does not drop further and sew it in later. These steps will produce Stocking stitch.

1 Hold the needle with the unworked stitches in your left hand and the other needle in your right hand as explained on p.85. With the yarn at the back of the knitting, insert the tip of the right needle from left to right under the front loop and through the centre of the next stitch to be worked on the left needle.

Yarn at back of knitting

2 Wrap the yarn under and around the tip of the right needle, keeping an even tension as the yarn slips through your fingers.

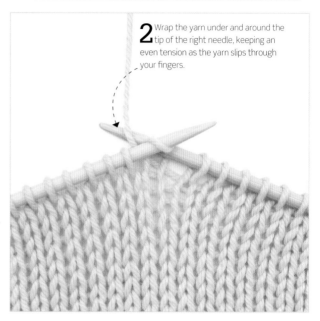

3 With the tip of the right needle, carefully draw the yarn through the stitch on the left needle. Hold the yarn firmly but not too tightly.

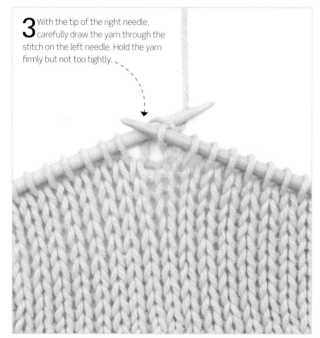

4 Let the old loop drop off the left needle to complete the knit stitch on the right needle. Work all the stitches on the left needle onto the right needle in the same way. To start a new row, turn the work and transfer the right needle to the left hand.

Completed new stitch

Old stitch

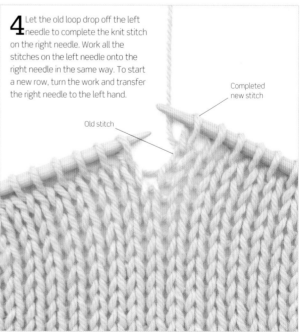

# PURL STITCH
Abbreviation = p

The purl stitch is a little more difficult than knit stitch, but like knit stitch it becomes effortless after a little practice. Once you are a seasoned knitter, you will feel as if your hands would know how to work these basic stitches in your sleep. Work your first purl row after you have cast on and knitted a few rows of garter stitch. You may find your tension alters on purl stitches, so try holding your yarn a little tighter or looser to compensate.

1 Hold the needle with the unworked stitches in your left hand and the other needle in your right hand as explained on p.85. With the yarn at the front of the knitting, insert the tip of the right needle from right to left through the centre of the next stitch to be worked on the left needle.

Yarn at front of knitting

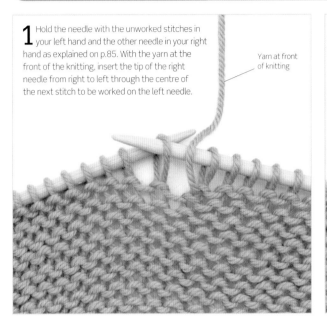

2 Wrap the yarn over and around the tip of the right needle. Keep an even tension on the yarn as you release it through your fingers.

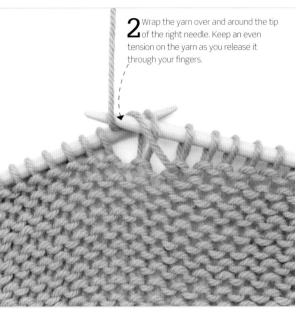

3 With the tip of the right needle, carefully draw the yarn through the stitch on the left needle. Keep your hands relaxed and allow the yarn to slip through your fingers in a gently controlled manner.

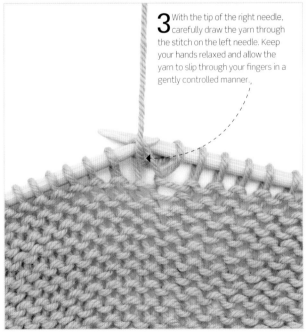

4 Let the old loop drop off the left needle to complete the purl stitch. Work all the stitches on the left needle onto the right needle in the same way. To start the next row, turn the work and transfer the knitting to the left hand.

Completed new stitch

Old stitch

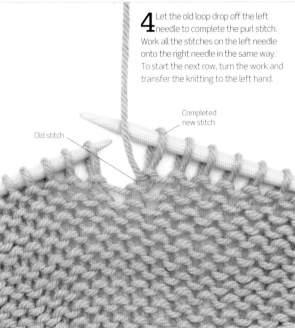

TECHNIQUES

BASIC KNIT AND PURL STITCHES

Once you know how to work knit and purl stitch with ease, you will be able to work the most frequently used stitch patterns – Garter stitch, Stocking stitch, Reverse stocking stitch, and Single ribbing. Stocking stitch and Reverse stocking stitch are commonly used for plain knitted garments, and Garter stitch and Single ribbing for garment edgings.

GARTER STITCH (Abbreviation = *g st*)

Knit right-side (RS) rows: Garter stitch is the easiest of all knitted fabrics as all rows are worked in knit stitches. When the right side of the fabric is facing you, knit all the stitches in the row.

Forms horizontal ridges

Edges of fabric lie flat and do not roll

Knit wrong-side (WS) rows: When the wrong side of the fabric is facing you, knit all the stitches in the row. The resulting fabric is soft, textured, and slightly stretchy.

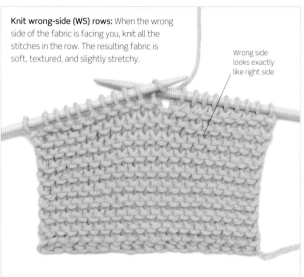

Wrong side looks exactly like right side

STOCKING STITCH (Abbreviation = *st st*)

Knit right-side (RS) rows: Stocking stitch is formed by working alternate rows of knit and purl stitches. When the right side is facing you, knit all the stitches in the row.

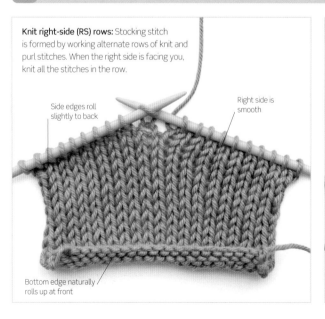

Side edges roll slightly to back

Right side is smooth

Bottom edge naturally rolls up at front

Purl wrong-side (WS) rows: When the wrong side is facing you, purl all the stitches in the row. The wrong side is often referred to as the "purl side" of the knitting.

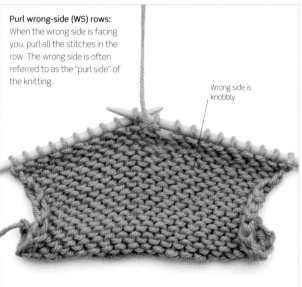

Wrong side is knobbly

REVERSE STOCKING STITCH (Abbreviation = *rev st st*)

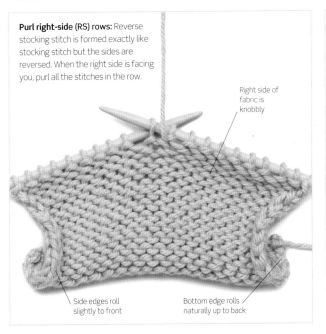

Purl right-side (RS) rows: Reverse stocking stitch is formed exactly like stocking stitch but the sides are reversed. When the right side is facing you, purl all the stitches in the row.

Right side of fabric is knobbly

Side edges roll slightly to front

Bottom edge rolls naturally up to back

Knit wrong-side (WS) rows: When the wrong side is facing you, knit all the stitches in the row.

Wrong side of fabric is smooth

SINGLE RIBBING (Abbreviation = *k1, p1 rib*)

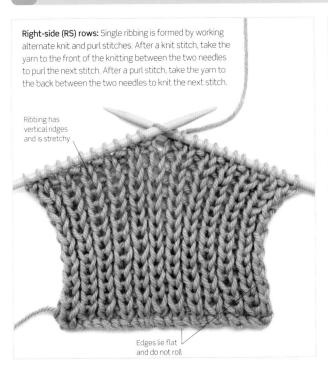

Right-side (RS) rows: Single ribbing is formed by working alternate knit and purl stitches. After a knit stitch, take the yarn to the front of the knitting between the two needles to purl the next stitch. After a purl stitch, take the yarn to the back between the two needles to knit the next stitch.

Ribbing has vertical ridges and is stretchy

Edges lie flat and do not roll

Wrong-side (WS) rows: On the wrong-side rows, knit all the knit stitches that are facing you and purl all the purl stitches. Work the following rows in the same way to form thin columns of alternating single knit and purl stitches.

Wrong side looks exactly like right side

TECHNIQUES

PREPARING AND REPAIRING

These useful tips will help both absolute beginners and more advanced knitters to prepare and complete their work with ease. Even experienced knitters can have problems joining on a new ball of yarn, and sewing in yarn ends correctly is the final touch for a professional finish.

WINDING AND JOINING YARNS

Knowing how to wind a hank into a ball is a useful skill, especially as many luxury yarns are sold as hanks. Joining a new ball of yarn when the first has run out, or a colour change is necessary, is a little daunting at first but easy to master.

WINDING A HANK INTO A BALL

1 Untwist the hank and carefully undo the knot joining the two ends of the yarn. Ask someone to hold the hank, or place it over a chair back. Pull out one of the yarn ends and wind it into a little yarn "butterfly" (see p.120). Then pinch the butterfly together at the centre and slip it off the left hand.

Yarn tail

2 Start wrapping the yarn around the butterfly and the thumb to create a hole in the centre of the ball. Keep winding until the whole hank is used up. Be sure to change the positioning of the wraps frequently to keep the ball round. Secure the yarn end under a few of the outer wraps. When you start knitting, pull the butterfly out of the centre and use this end. Pulling the yarn from inside stops the ball rolling around.

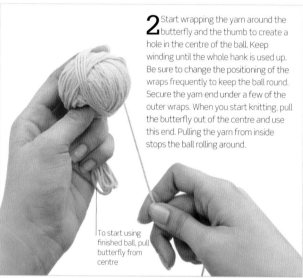

To start using finished ball, pull butterfly from centre

SQUARE KNOT

This is made like a Granny knot, but take left over right, then right over left. This is best made at the point where it is needed in the knitting so you can make sure it goes to the back.

WEAVER'S KNOT

Use when joining yarns of different thicknesses.

1 Make a loop of the thick yarn and pinch the neck together. Thread a longish end of the thin yarn through the loop from above, and wrap it over the neck of the loop from back to front, pinch this to the loop with your fingers.

2 Take the thin yarn end that is wrapped around the loop under the front thread of the thick yarn loop. Pass it over itself as you take it towards the back and then pass it under the rear thread of the thick yarn loop.

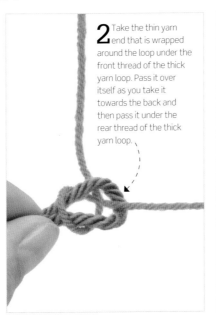

3 Holding both thick yarns in one hand and both thin in the other, gently pull the short ends apart with your fingers to close the knot.

JOINING ON A NEW YARN

To calculate if there is enough yarn to complete two rows, fold the remaining yarn in half and make a slip knot at the fold. Knit the first row. If the knot comes before the end of the row you don't have enough yarn and need to join on a fresh ball.

JOINING ON A NEW BALL

1 Always join on a new ball at the beginning of a row. Knot the new end of yarn onto the old yarn.

End of old ball

New ball

2 Slide the knot up very close to the knitting. The knot can be hidden in the seam later. If you are knitting a scarf or blanket, tie the knot loosely so you can undo it later and darn in the ends.

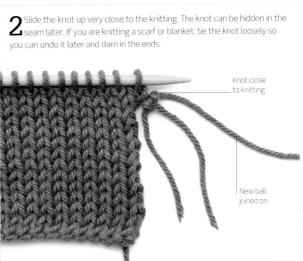

Knot close to knitting

New ball joined on

JOINING ON A NEW YARN – ALTERNATIVE METHOD

1 Lay the new yarn over the right needle with the old yarn tail. Knit the first stitch of the new row with both yarns. Drop the old yarn tail and continue with the new.

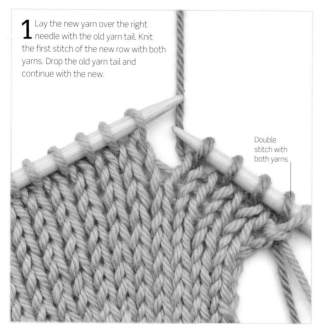

Double stitch with both yarns

2 When the knitting is complete, unpick the second thread from the old yarn before darning the ends in with a blunt-ended yarn needle.

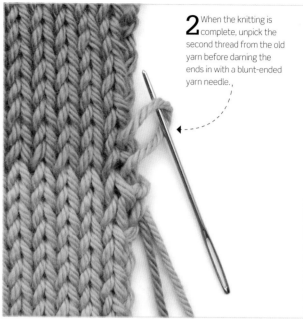

WINDING UP A LONG YARN TAIL

A long loose end on your slip knot can start to get tangled when it is packed away. To keep it tidy, wind it into a yarn "butterfly" close to your knitting.

1 Starting close to the knitting, wrap the yarn around your thumb and forefinger in a figure of eight.

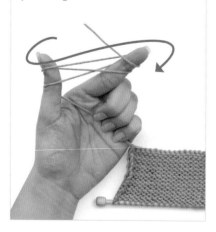

2 Remove the yarn "butterfly" from the thumb and forefinger and wrap the yarn end a few times around its centre. Tuck the end under the wrapping to secure it.

Yarn end tucked under wrapping to secure

DARNING IN AN END

Freshly completed knitting will have at least two yarn ends dangling from it – one at the cast-on and one at the cast-off edges. For every extra ball used, there will be two more ends. Thread each end separately onto a blunt-ended needle and weave it vertically or horizontally through stitches on the wrong side of work.

CORRECTING MISTAKES

The best thing to do if you make a mistake in your knitting is to unravel it back to the mistake by unpicking the stitches one by one. If you drop a stitch, be sure to pick it up quickly before it comes undone right back to the cast-on edge.

UNPICKING A KNIT ROW

Hold the needle with the stitches in your right hand. To unpick each stitch individually, insert the tip of the left needle from front to back through the stitch below the first knit stitch on the right needle, then drop the old knit stitch off the needle and pull out the loop.

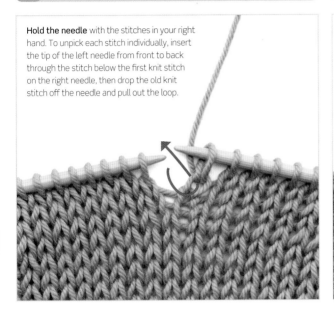

UNPICKING A PURL ROW

Hold the needle with the stitches in your right hand. Unpick each purl stitch individually with the tip of the left needle in the same way as for the knit stitch.

PICKING UP A DROPPED STITCH

If you drop a stitch on stocking stitch, you can easily reclaim it with a crochet hook. With the right side of the knitting facing you, insert the hook through the dropped loop. Grab the strand between the stitches and pull a loop through the loop on the hook. Continue up the rows in this way until you reach the top. Then slip the stitch back onto your needle.

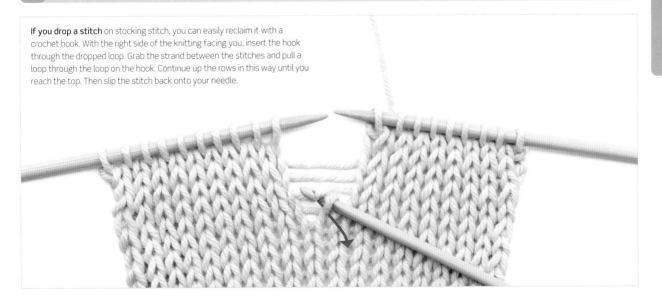

TECHNIQUES

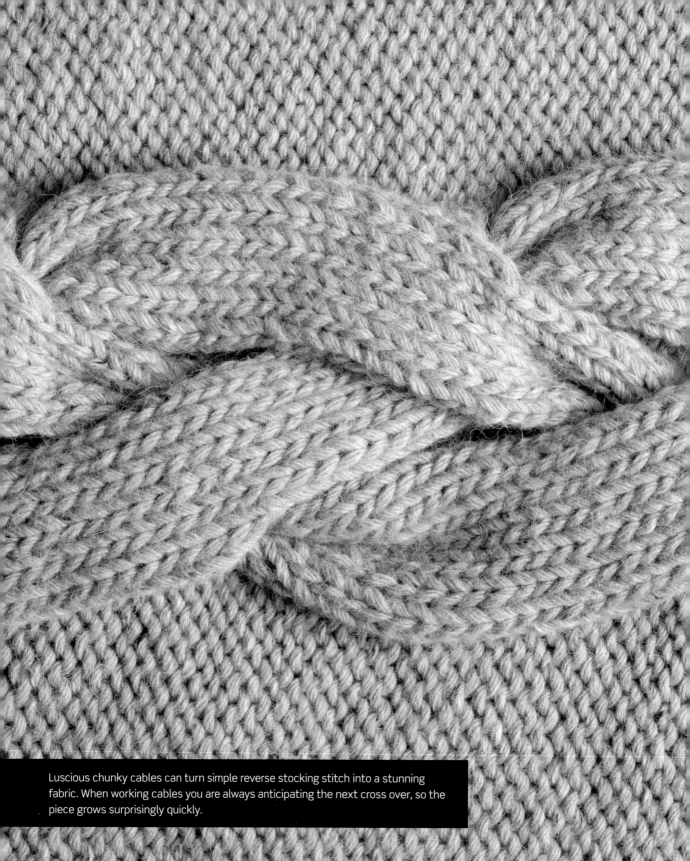

Luscious chunky cables can turn simple reverse stocking stitch into a stunning fabric. When working cables you are always anticipating the next cross over, so the piece grows surprisingly quickly.

FOLLOWING STITCH PATTERNS

Stitch pattern instructions are written or charted directions for making all sorts of textures – knit and purl combinations, lace, and cables. Knitting stitch pattern swatches is the best possible introduction to row instructions. Beginners should try some out before attempting to follow a proper knitting pattern (see pp.128–129).

UNDERSTANDING WRITTEN INSTRUCTIONS

Anyone who can cast on, knit and purl, and cast off will be able to work from simple knit-and-purl-combination stitch pattern instructions with little difficulty. It is just a question of following the instructions one step at a time and getting used to the abbreviations. A list of common knitting abbreviations is given on p.127, but for simple knit and purl textures all you need to grasp is that "k1" means "knit one stitch", "k2" means "knit two stitches", and so on. And the same applies for the purl stitches – "p1" means "purl one stitch", "p2" means "purl two stitches", and so on.

To begin a stitch pattern, cast on the number of stitches that it tells you to, using your chosen yarn and the yarn manufacturer's recommended needle size. Work the stitch row by row, then repeat the rows as instructed and the stitch pattern will grow beneath the needles. When your knitting is the desired size, cast off in pattern (see p.106).

The best tips for first-timers are to follow the rows slowly; mark the right side of the fabric by knotting a coloured thread onto it; use a row counter to keep track of where you are (see p.37); and pull out your stitches and start again if you get in a muddle. If you love the stitch pattern you are trying out, you can make a scarf, blanket, or cushion cover with it – no need to buy a knitting pattern.

The principles for following stitch patterns are the same for cables and lace (see pp.152–153 and 158–159), which you will be able to work once you learn cable techniques and how to increase and decrease.

Some stitch patterns will call for "slipping" stitches and knitting "through the back of the loop". These useful techniques are given next as a handy reference when you are consulting the abbreviations and terminology list.

SLIPPING STITCHES PURLWISE

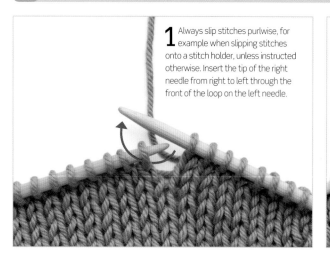

1 Always slip stitches purlwise, for example when slipping stitches onto a stitch holder, unless instructed otherwise. Insert the tip of the right needle from right to left through the front of the loop on the left needle.

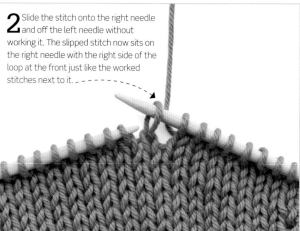

2 Slide the stitch onto the right needle and off the left needle without working it. The slipped stitch now sits on the right needle with the right side of the loop at the front just like the worked stitches next to it.

SLIPPING STITCHES KNITWISE

1 Slip stitches knitwise only if instructed to do so or if working decreases (see pp.139–141), as it twists the stitch. First insert the tip of the right needle from left to right through the front of the loop on the left needle.

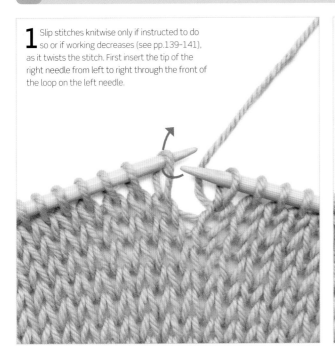

2 Slide the stitch onto the right needle and off the left needle without working it. The slipped stitch now sits on the right needle with the left side of the loop at the front of the needle unlike the worked stitches next to it.

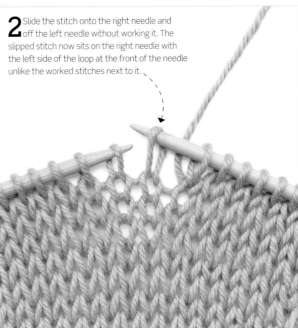

KNITTING THROUGH BACK OF LOOP (Abbreviation = *k1 tbl*)

1 When row instructions say "k1 tbl" (knit one through the back of the loop), insert the right needle from right to left through the side of the stitch behind the left needle (called the back of the loop).

2 Wrap the yarn around the tip of the right needle and complete the knit stitch in the usual way. This twists the stitch in the row below so that the legs of the stitch cross at the base. (The same principle applies for working p1 tbl, k2tog tbl, and p2tog tbl.)

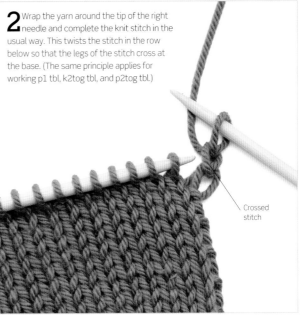

Crossed stitch

TECHNIQUES

USING BEADS AS STITCH AND ROW MARKERS

1 Use lightweight beads of various colours and shapes. Measure a length of slippery yarn twice the eventual length of your knitting, and either tie onto the long tail of the cast-on or leave loose.

2 Thread a bead onto the yarn for every two rows to be worked. Too many beads are better than too few, so add some spares. Tie an odd bead or button on the end to secure the beads.

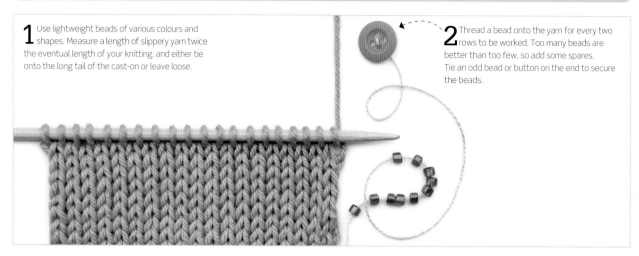

3 Hold the beaded thread at the back of your knitting. Choose a stitch position to be marked vertically upwards throughout the rows.

4 Work one row to marker position. Bring the beaded thread to the front between needles so it lies between two stitches and down the front of the work. Work remainder of row, taking care not to catch the beaded thread in the next stitch.

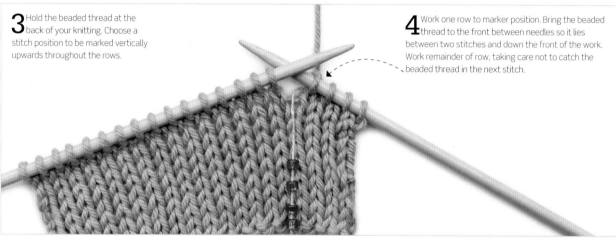

5 Work two or more rows, stopping at marker position on second row. Take the beaded thread to the back, leaving one bead at the front. Continue moving the beaded thread from back to front, placing markers as required. If you thread too many beads, leave any spares at the back. On completion, snip the beaded thread and pull it through the knitting to release the beads.

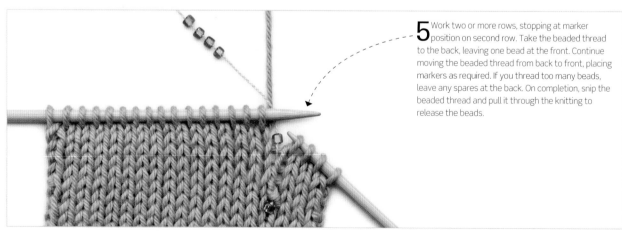

UNDERSTANDING STITCH SYMBOL CHARTS

Knitting instructions for stitch patterns can also be given in chart form. Some knitters prefer working stitch-symbol charts because they are easy to read, and they build up a visual image of the stitch repeat that is quick to memorize.

Even with charted instructions, there are usually written directions for how many stitches to cast on. If not, you can calculate the cast-on from the chart, where the number of stitches in the pattern "repeat" are clearly marked. Cast on a multiple of this number, plus any edge stitches outside the repeat.

Each square represents a stitch and each horizontal line of squares represents a row. After casting on, work from the bottom of the chart upwards. Read odd-numbered rows (usually RS rows) from right to left and even-numbered rows (usually WS rows) from left to right. Work the edge stitches, then work the stitches inside the repeat as many times as required. Some symbols may mean one thing on a RS row and another on a WS row (see below).

Once you have worked all the charted rows, start again at the bottom of the chart to begin the "row repeat" once more.

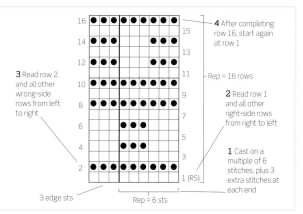

3 Read row 2 and all other wrong-side rows from left to right

4 After completing row 16, start again at row 1

Rep = 16 rows

2 Read row 1 and all other right-side rows from right to left

1 Cast on a multiple of 6 stitches, plus 3 extra stitches at each end

3 edge sts

Rep = 6 sts

KNITTING ABBREVIATIONS

These are the most frequently used knitting abbreviations. Any special abbreviations in knitting instructions are always explained within the pattern.

alt	alternate
beg	begin(ning)
cm	centimetre(s)
cont	continu(e)(ing)
dec	decreas(e)(ing)
foll	follow(s)(ing)
g	gram(s)
g st	garter stitch
in	inch(es)
inc	increase(s)(ing)
k	knit
k1 tbl	knit st through back of loop
k2tog (or dec 1)	knit next 2 sts together (see p.139)
kfb (or inc 1)	knit into front and back of next st (see p.148)
LH	left hand
m	metre(s)
M1 (or M1k)	make one stitch (see pp.131–133)
mm	millimetre(s)
oz	ounce(s)
p	purl
p2tog (or dec 1)	purl next 2sts together (see p.139)
patt	pattern, or work in pattern
Pfb (or inc 1)	purl into front and back of next st (see p.130)
psso	pass slipped stitch over
rem	remain(s)(ing)

rep	repeat(ing)
rev st st	reverse stocking stitch
RH	right hand
RS	right side (of work)
s1 k1 psso (skp)	slip one, knit one, pass slipped st over (see p.140)
s1 k2tog psso (or sk2p)	slip one st, knit 2sts together, pass slipped sts over (see p.140)
ssk	slip, slip, knit (see p.140)
s	slip stitch(es)
s2 k1 p2sso	slip 2, knit one, pass slipped stitches over (see p.141)
st(s)	stitch(es)
st st	stocking stitch
tbl	through back of loop(s)
tog	together
WS	wrong side (of work)
yd	yard(s)
yfwd	yarn forward (US yo; see p.137)
yfrn	yarn forward round needle (US yo; see p.137)
yon	yarn over needle (US yo; see p.137)
yrn	yarn round needle (US yo; see p.136)
[ ]*	Repeat instructions between brackets, or after or between asterisks, as

KNITTING TERMINOLOGY AND SYMBOLS

The following terms are commonly used in knitting patterns. Where terminology differs between the UK and US, the US equivalent is given in parentheses.

cast on Create a series of loops on a knitting needle to form the foundation for the piece of knitting.

cast off Close off stitches and drop from knitting needle (US: bind off).

cast off knitwise/purlwise Cast off while working stitches in knit/purl.

cast off in pattern Cast off while working stitches in the pattern used in the previous row.

cast off in ribbing Cast off while working stitches in the ribbing used in the previous row.

decrease Decrease the number of stitches in a row (see pp.139–141).

garter stitch Knit every row. In circular knitting (see p.196), knit one round and purl one round alternately.

tension The size of the stitches in a piece of knitting (US: gauge), measured by the number of stitches and rows to 10cm (4in), or to 2.5cm (1in) on fine knitting (see p.129).

increase Increase the number of stitches in a row (see pp.130–138).

knitwise Insert the right needle into the stitch on the left needle as if starting a knit stitch.

pick up and knit Draw loops through the edge of the knitting and place them on the needle (see p.208).

purlwise Insert the right needle into

the stitch on the left needle as if starting a purl stitch.

stocking stitch Knit all RS rows and purl all WS rows (US: stockinette stitch).

reverse stocking stitch Purl all RS rows and knit all WS rows (US: reverse stockinette stitch).

work straight Work in specified pattern without increasing or decreasing (US: work even).

yarn-over increase Wrap yarn around right needle to make a new stitch; abbreviated yfwd, yfrn, yon, or yrn (US yo; see pp.136–138).

STITCH SYMBOLS

These are some of the commonly used knitting symbols in this book. Any unusual symbols will be explained in the pattern. Symbols can vary, so follow the explanations in your pattern.

- ☐ = k on RS rows, p on WS rows
- ● = p on RS rows, k on WS rows
- ◎ = yarn over (see p.136)
- ☑ = k2tog (see p.139)
- ◨ = ssk (see p.140)
- ◭ = sk2p (see p.140)
- ◮ = sk2 k1 p2sso (see p.141)

FOLLOWING A PATTERN

Knitting patterns can look daunting to a beginner knitter, but if approached step by step they are easy to understand. This section provides an explanation of how to follow simple knitting patterns and gives tips for finishing details and seams.

SIMPLE ACCESSORY PATTERNS

The best advice for a beginner wanting to knit a first project from a knitting pattern is to start with a simple accessory. Cushion covers are especially good practice as the instructions are straightforward and usually the only finishing details are seams. This is an example of a pattern for a simple striped stocking stitch cushion cover.

At the beginning of most patterns you will find the skill level required for the knitting. Make sure you are confident that the skill level is right for you.

Check the size of the finished item. If it is a simple square like this cushion, you can easily adjust the size by adding or subtracting stitches and rows.

Try to use the yarn specified. But if you are unable to obtain this yarn, choose a substitute yarn as explained on p.30.

Make a tension swatch before starting to knit and change the needle size if necessary (see opposite page).

Instructions for working a piece of knitted fabric always start with how many stitches to cast on and what yarn or needle size to use. If there is only one needle size and one yarn, these may be absent here.

Consult the abbreviations list with your pattern (or in your book) for the meanings of abbreviations (see p.127).

The back of a cushion cover is sometimes exactly the same as the front or it has a fabric back. In this case, the stripes are reversed on the back for a more versatile cover.

After all the knitted pieces are complete, follow the Finishing (or Making Up) section of the pattern.

STRIPED CUSHION COVER

Skill level
Easy
Size of finished cushion
40.5 x 40.5cm (16 x 16in)
Materials
3 x 50g (1¾oz)/125m (137yd) balls in each of branded Pure Wool DK in Lavender 039 (**A**) and Avocado 019 (**B**) Pair of 4mm (US size 6) knitting needles
Cushion pad to fit finished cover
Tension
22 sts and 30 rows to 10cm (4in) over stocking stitch using 4mm (US size 6) needles or size necessary to achieve correct tension. To save time, take time to check tension.
Front
Using 4mm (US size 6) needles and A, cast on 88 sts. Beg with a K row, work in st st until work measures 14cm (5½in) from cast-on edge, ending with RS facing for next row.
Cut off A and change to B.
Cont in st st until work measures 26.5cm (10½in) from cast-on edge, ending with RS facing for next row.
Cut off B and change to A.
Cont in st st until work measures 40.5cm (16in) from cast-on edge, ending with RS facing for next row.
Cast off.
Back
Work as for Front, but use B for A, and A for B.
Finishing
Darn in loose ends.
Block and press lightly on wrong side, following instructions on yarn label.
With wrong sides facing, sew three sides of back and front together. Turn right-side out, insert cushion pad, and sew remaining seam.

Always purchase the same total amount in metres/yards of a substitute yarn; NOT the same amount in weight.

If desired, select different colours to suit your décor; the colours specified are just suggestions.

Alter the needle size if you cannot achieve the correct tension with the specified size (see left).

Extra items needed for your project will usually be listed under Materials or Extras.

Work in the specified stitch pattern, for the specified number of rows or cm/in.

Colours are usually changed on a right-side row, so end with the right-side facing for the changeover row.

If no stitch is specified for the cast-off, always cast off knitwise.

See p.120 for how to darn in loose ends.

Make sure you look at the yarn label instructions before attempting to press any piece of knitting. The label may say that the yarn cannot be pressed or to press it only with a cool iron. (See p.227 for blocking tips.)

See pp.227–229 for seaming options. Take time with seams on knitting. Practise on odd pieces of knitting before starting the main project.

GARMENT PATTERNS

Choosing the right size and knitting a tension swatch are the two most important things to get right if you want to create a successful garment. It is also possible to make simple alterations to patterns worked in plain garter or stocking stitch.

CHOOSING A GARMENT SIZE

Rather than looking at specific "sizes" when choosing which size to knit, select the one nearest to how you want the garment to fit. The best way to do this is to find a similar garment that fits you. Lay it flat and measure its width – choose the width on the pattern that is the closest match.

Photocopy your pattern and highlight the figures for your size throughout. Start with the number of balls of yarn, then the number of stitches to cast on, the length to knit to the armhole, and so on. The smallest size is given first and larger sizes follow in parentheses. Where only one figure is given, this applies to all sizes.

Choose your size by the width of a favourite, well-fitting sweater with the same shape and knitted fabric weight

Alter sweater length only where instructed

Check that circumference of sleeve suits your upper arm body measurement

Alter sleeve length only where specified in instructions

ALTERING PATTERNS

You can alter the length of garment patterns worked in plain garter or stocking stitch, but avoid altering armholes, necklines, or sleeve heads. As sleeves and some bodies have shaping, this must also be adjusted. Make notes at every step. In this example, length is being added to a sleeve:

1 Copy, photocopy, or draw out the pattern diagram. Write the new required length on the diagram (eg 48cm).
2 Find the number of rows to 10cm in the tension note. Divide that number by 10 to calculate how many rows there are in 1cm. For example, 30 rows per 10cm. $30 \div 10 = 3$ rows per 1cm.
3 Multiply the required new length by the number of rows in 1cm. The resulting figure is the total number in the new length. For example, $48 \times 3 = 144$ rows.

4 Any increasing, will also have to be re-calculated. From the pattern, note the number of stitches to cast on at the cuff and how many there will be on the needle just before the start of the underarm shaping (this figure should be shown at the end of the written instruction for the increases).
5 Subtract the smallest from the largest amount of stitches. The answer is the total number of stitches to be increased. Divide the answer by two (because a sleeve has two sides), to give the number of stitches to increase on each side. For example. $114 - 60 = 54$ sts. $54 \div 2 = 27$ sts.
6 To calculate the number of rows between each increase, divide the new number of rows found in Step 3 by the number of increases calculated in Step 5. If you have a fraction in this answer, round the number down. For example, $144 \div 27 = 4.22$. Increase one stitch each side every 4 rows. Knit the remainder rows straight before underarm cast-offs.

TECHNIQUES

MEASURING TENSION

Alway knit a swatch before starting your knitting in order to make sure that you can achieve the stitch size (tension) recommended in your pattern. Only if you achieve the correct tension will your finished knitted pieces have the correct measurements.

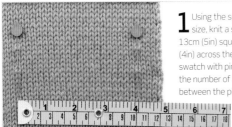

1 Using the specified needle size, knit a swatch about 13cm (5in) square. Mark 10cm (4in) across the centre of your swatch with pins and count the number of stitches between the pins.

2 Count the number of rows to 10cm (4in) in the same way. If you have fewer stitches and rows than you should, try again with a smaller needle size; if you have more, change to a larger needle size. Use the needle size for your knitting that best matches the correct tension. (Matching stitch width is more important than matching row height.)

INCREASES AND DECREASES

Increasing the number of stitches on the needle and decreasing the number of stitches is the way knitting is shaped, changing the edges from straight vertical sides to curves and slants. But increases and decreases are also used in combinations with plain knit and purl stitches to form interesting textures in the knitted fabric, from lace to sculptured relief.

SIMPLE INCREASES

The following techniques are simple increases used for shaping knitting. They create one extra stitch without creating a visible hole and are called invisible increases. Multiple increases, which add more than one extra stitch, are used less frequently and are always explained fully in the knitting pattern – one is given here as an example.

KNIT INTO FRONT AND BACK OF STITCH (Abbreviation = *kfb* or *inc 1*)

This popular invisible increase for a knit row is also called a bar increase because it creates a little bar between the stitches.

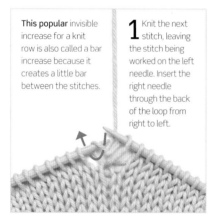

1 Knit the next stitch, leaving the stitch being worked on the left needle. Insert the right needle through the back of the loop from right to left.

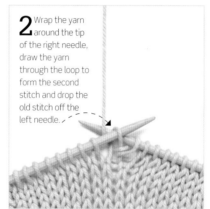

2 Wrap the yarn around the tip of the right needle, draw the yarn through the loop to form the second stitch and drop the old stitch off the left needle.

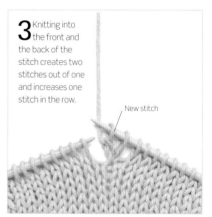

3 Knitting into the front and the back of the stitch creates two stitches out of one and increases one stitch in the row.

New stitch

PURL INTO FRONT AND BACK OF STITCH (Abbreviation = *pfb* or *inc 1*)

1 Purl the next stitch, leaving the stitch being worked on the left needle. Insert the right needle through the back of the loop from left to right.

2 Wrap the yarn around the tip of the right needle, draw the yarn through the loop to form the second stitch and drop the old stitch off the left needle.

3 Purling into the front and the back of the stitch like this creates two stitches out of one and increases one stitch in the row.

New stitch

LIFTED INCREASE ON KNIT ROW (Abbreviation = *inc 1*)

1 Insert the tip of the right needle from front to back through the stitch below the next stitch on the left needle. Knit this lifted loop.

2 Knit the next stitch (the stitch above the lifted stitch on the left needle) in the usual way.

3 This creates two stitches out of one and increases one stitch in the row. (The purl version of this stitch is worked using the same principle.)

New stitch

"MAKE-ONE" LEFT CROSS INCREASE ON A KNIT ROW (Abbreviation = *M1* or *M1k*)

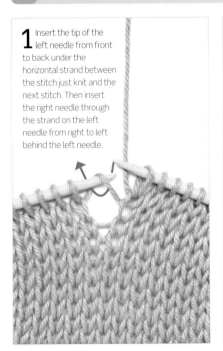

1 Insert the tip of the left needle from front to back under the horizontal strand between the stitch just knit and the next stitch. Then insert the right needle through the strand on the left needle from right to left behind the left needle.

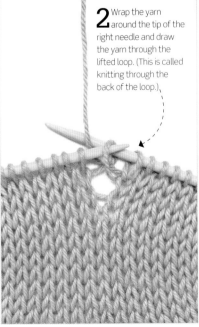

2 Wrap the yarn around the tip of the right needle and draw the yarn through the lifted loop. (This is called knitting through the back of the loop.)

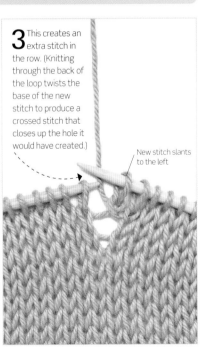

3 This creates an extra stitch in the row. (Knitting through the back of the loop twists the base of the new stitch to produce a crossed stitch that closes up the hole it would have created.)

New stitch slants to the left

"MAKE-ONE" RIGHT CROSS INCREASE ON A KNIT ROW (Abbreviation = *M1* or *M1k*)

Patterns do not always differentiate between left and right "make-one" increases. Choose the most suitable for your project.

1 Insert the tip of the left needle from back to front under the horizontal strand between the stitch just knit and the next stitch. Insert the right needle from left to right into the front of this new loop, twisting the stitch.

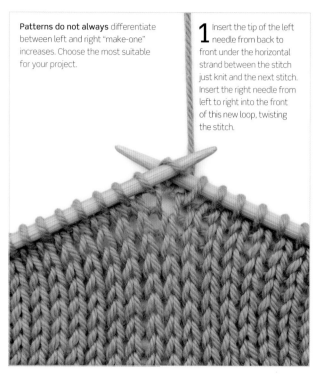

2 Wrap the yarn around the tip of the needle and draw the yarn through the lifted loop, knitting into the front of the stitch.

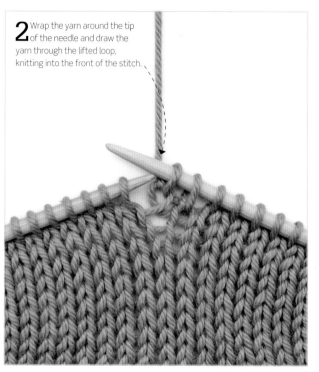

3 This action crosses the lifted stitch, and closes the hole made by picking up the loop. The resulting increase slants to the right and is normally worked at the end of a knit row.

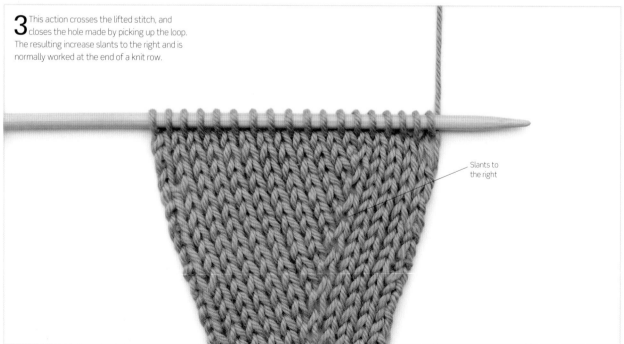

Slants to the right

"MAKE-ONE" INCREASE ON PURL ROW (Abbreviation = *M1* or *M1p*)

1 Insert the tip of the left needle from front to back under the horizontal strand between the stitch just knit and the next stitch. Then insert the right needle through the strand on the left needle from left to right behind the left needle.

2 Wrap the yarn around the tip of the right needle and draw the yarn through the lifted loop (known as purling through the back of the loop.)

3 This creates an extra stitch in the row. (Purling through the back of the loop twists the base of the new stitch to produce a crossed stitch that closes up the hole it would have created.)

New stitch

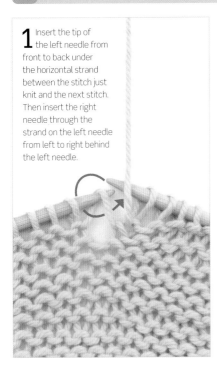
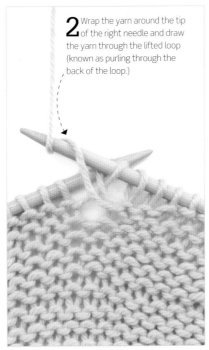
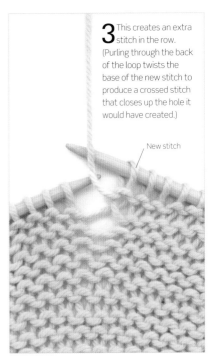

MULTIPLE INCREASES (Abbreviation = *[k1, p1, k1] into next st*)

This is a very easy increase if you need to add more than one stitch to an existing stitch, but it does create a small hole under the new stitches.

1 To begin the increase, knit the next stitch but leave the old stitch on the left needle.

2 Then purl and knit into the same loop on the left needle. This action is called knit one, purl one, knit one all into the next stitch. It creates two extra stitches in the row. You can keep alternating k and p stitches in the same loop to create more stitches if desired.

k1
p1
k1

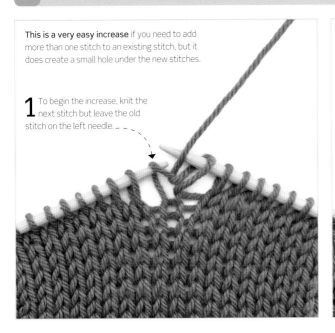
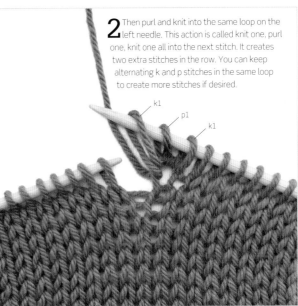

Colourwork checks are one of the easiest patterns to work as intarsia. Without strands of yarn across the back, the fabric is light and soft and many colours can be worked in one row.

YARNOVER INCREASES

Yarn-over increases add stitches to a row and create holes at the same time, so are often called visible increases. They are used to produce decorative laces (see pp. 158–159). A yarnover is made by looping the yarn around the right needle to form an extra stitch. It is important to wrap the loop around the needle in the correct way or it will become crossed when it is worked in the next row, which closes the hole.

YARNOVER BETWEEN KNIT STITCHES (Abbreviation = UK *yfwd*; US *yo*)

1 Bring the yarn forwards (yfwd) to the front of the knitting between the needles. Take the yarn over the top of the right needle to the back and work the next knit stitch in the usual way.

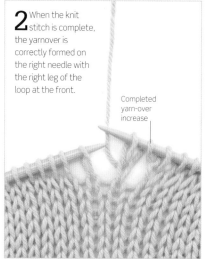

2 When the knit stitch is complete, the yarnover is correctly formed on the right needle with the right leg of the loop at the front.

Completed yarn-over increase

3 On the following row, when you reach the yarnover, purl it through the front of the loop in the usual way. This creates an open hole under the purl stitch.

Purl yarnover on next row

YARNOVER BETWEEN PURL STITCHES (Abbreviation = UK *yrn*; US *yo*)

1 Bring the yarn to the back of the work over the top of the right needle, then to the front between the needles. Work the next purl stitch in the usual way.

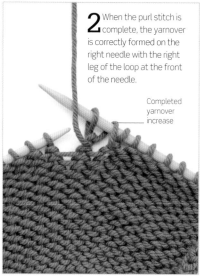

2 When the purl stitch is complete, the yarnover is correctly formed on the right needle with the right leg of the loop at the front of the needle.

Completed yarnover increase

3 On the following row, when you reach the yarnover, knit it through the front of the loop in the usual way. This creates an open hole under the knit stitch.

Knit yarnover on next row

YARNOVER BETWEEN KNIT AND PURL STITCHES (Abbreviation = UK *yfrn* and *yon*; US *yo*)

After a knit stitch and before a purl stitch (yfrn):
Bring the yarn to the front between the needles, then over the top of the right needle and to the front again. Purl the next stitch. On the following row, work the yarnover through the front of the loop in the usual way to create an open hole.

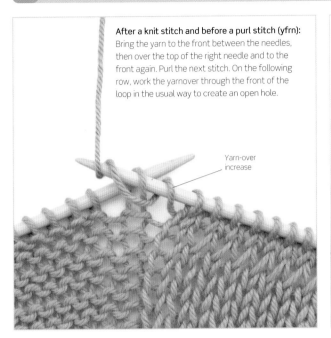

Yarn-over increase

After a purl stitch and before a knit stitch (yon):
Take the yarn over the top of the right needle and to the back of the work, then knit the next stitch. On the following row, work the yarnover through the front of the loop in the usual way to create an open hole.

Yarn-over increase

YARNOVER AT THE BEGINNING OF A ROW (Abbreviation = UK *yfwd* and *yrn*; US *yo*)

At the beginning of a row before a knit stitch (yfwd): Insert the tip of the right needle behind the yarn and into the first stitch knitwise. Then take the yarn over the top of the right needle to the back and complete the knit stitch. On the following row, work the yarnover through the front of the loop in the usual way to create an open scallop at the edge.

Yarnover increase

At the beginning of a row before a purl stitch (yrn):
Wrap the yarn from front to back over the top of the right needle and to the front again between the needles. Then purl the first stitch. On the following row, work the yarnover through the front of the loop in the usual way to create an open scallop at the edge.

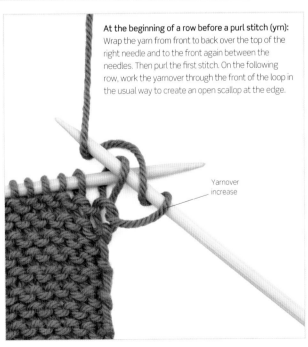

Yarnover increase

TECHNIQUES

DOUBLE YARNOVER (Abbreviation = UK *yfwd* twice; US *yo2*)

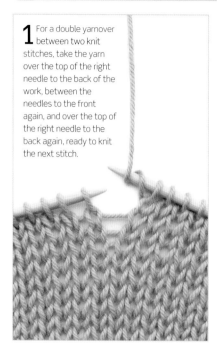

1 For a double yarnover between two knit stitches, take the yarn over the top of the right needle to the back of the work, between the needles to the front again, and over the top of the right needle to the back again, ready to knit the next stitch.

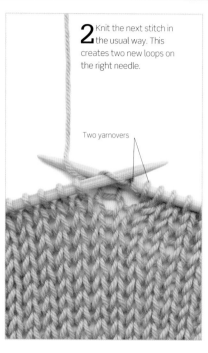

2 Knit the next stitch in the usual way. This creates two new loops on the right needle.

Two yarnovers

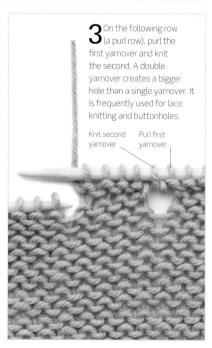

3 On the following row (a purl row), purl the first yarnover and knit the second. A double yarnover creates a bigger hole than a single yarnover. It is frequently used for lace knitting and buttonholes.

Knit second yarnover   Purl first yarnover

CLOSED YARNOVER ON GARTER STITCH

1 This is used as an "invisible" increase and is especially good for garter stitch. Take the yarn from back to front over the top of the right needle, then around the needle to the back of the work between the needles. Knit the next stitch in the usual way.

Yarnover increase

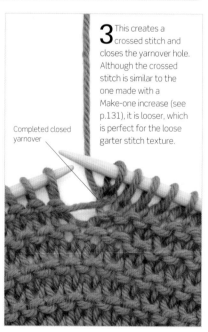

2 On the next row, knit the yarnover through the front loop (the strand at the front of the left needle).

Knit yarnover through front on next row

3 This creates a crossed stitch and closes the yarnover hole. Although the crossed stitch is similar to the one made with a Make-one increase (see p.131), it is looser, which is perfect for the loose garter stitch texture.

Completed closed yarnover

SIMPLE DECREASES

These simple decreases are often used for shaping knitting and, paired with increases, for textured and lace stitches. More complicated decreases are always explained in knitting instructions. Most of the decreases that follow are single decreases that subtract only one stitch from the knitting, but a few double decreases are included.

KNIT TWO TOGETHER (Abbreviation = *k2tog* or *dec 1*)

1 Insert the tip of the right needle from left to right through the second stitch then the first stitch on the left needle.

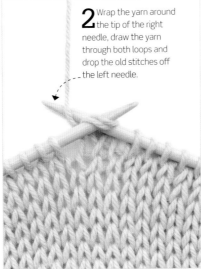

2 Wrap the yarn around the tip of the right needle, draw the yarn through both loops and drop the old stitches off the left needle.

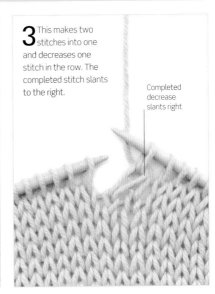

3 This makes two stitches into one and decreases one stitch in the row. The completed stitch slants to the right.

Completed decrease slants right

PURL TWO TOGETHER (Abbreviation = *p2tog* or *dec 1*)

1 Use the p2tog decrease where a pattern specifies "decrease 1" on a purl row. Insert the tip of the right needle from right to left through the first then the second stitch on the left needle.

2 Wrap the yarn around the tip of the right needle, draw the yarn through both loops and drop the old stitches off the left needle.

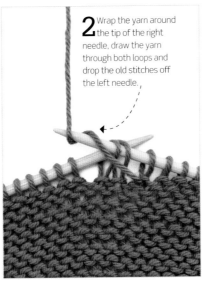

3 This makes two stitches into one and decreases one stitch in the row.

Completed decrease slants right on right side of work

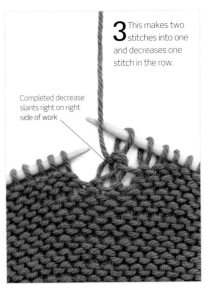
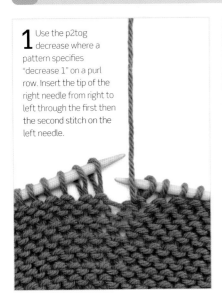

TECHNIQUES

SLIP ONE, KNIT ONE, PASS SLIPPED STITCH OVER (Abbreviation = *s1 k1 psso* or *skpo*)

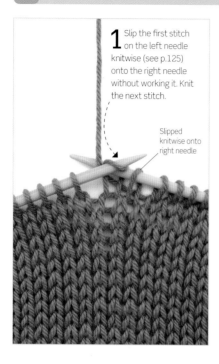

1 Slip the first stitch on the left needle knitwise (see p.125) onto the right needle without working it. Knit the next stitch.

Slipped knitwise onto right needle

2 Pick up the slipped stitch with the tip of the left needle and pass it over the knit stitch and off the right needle.

3 This makes two stitches into one and decreases one stitch in the row.

Completed decrease slants left

SLIP, SLIP, KNIT (Abbreviation = *ssk*)

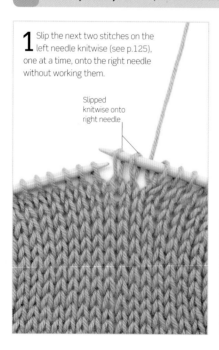

1 Slip the next two stitches on the left needle knitwise (see p.125), one at a time, onto the right needle without working them.

Slipped knitwise onto right needle

2 Insert the tip of the left needle from left to right through the fronts of the two slipped stitches (the right needle is now behind the left). Knit these two stitches together.

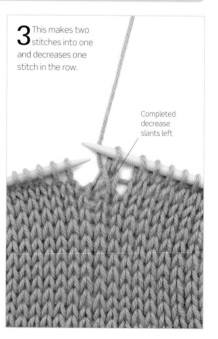

3 This makes two stitches into one and decreases one stitch in the row.

Completed decrease slants left

SLIP, SLIP, PURL (Abbreviation = *ssp*)

1 Keeping yarn at the front, slip two stitches, one at a time, knitwise (see p.125) onto the right needle without working them as for ssk decrease.

2 Holding the needles tip to tip, insert the left needle into both stitches and transfer back to the left needle without twisting them.

3 Holding the right needle at the back, bring the tip upwards from left to right through the back of the two stitches, bringing the right needle in front of the left as it comes through the stitches.

4 Lay the yarn between the needles as for purl. Take the right needle down and back through both loops, then slide them off the left needle together. This makes one stitch out of the two, and decreases one stitch.

DOUBLE DECREASES

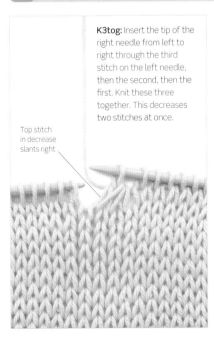

K3tog: Insert the tip of the right needle from left to right through the third stitch on the left needle, then the second, then the first. Knit these three together. This decreases two stitches at once.

Top stitch in decrease slants right

s1 k2tog psso: Slip one stitch knitwise onto the right needle, knit the next two stitches together, then pass the slipped stitch over the K2tog and off the right needle. This decreases two stitches at once.

Top stitch in decrease slants left

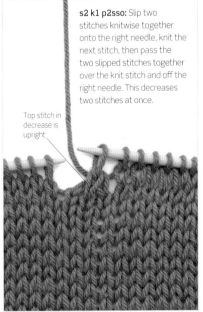

s2 k1 p2sso: Slip two stitches knitwise together onto the right needle, knit the next stitch, then pass the two slipped stitches together over the knit stitch and off the right needle. This decreases two stitches at once.

Top stitch in decrease is upright

TECHNIQUES

PAIRED INCREASES AND DECREASES

Increases or decreases at each end of a row can be worked to slant left or right so that the edges mirror each other. Paired shapings should be worked at consistent intervals, and are easier if worked on a knit row. When working a pattern, one or two edge stitches can be worked plain so that the shaping does not affect the pattern.

SUMMARY OF INCREASES AND DECREASES

PAIRED INCREASES

When made at end of a row	Abbreviation	When made at beginning of a row	Abbreviation
Slants left – increases the left edge of the knit side of stocking stitch		Slants right – shapes the right edge of the knit side of stocking stitch	
Left lifted increase	*inc1*	Right lifted increase	*inc1*
• virtually invisible • must have rows between or will pull • shows to right of increased stitch – slants the original stitch to the left and towards the selvedge when used for edge shaping		• virtually invisible • must have rows between or will pull • shows to left of increased stitch – slants the original stitch to the right and towards the selvedge when used for edge shaping	
Knit (or purl) in front and back of stitch	*kfb or inc1*	Knit (or purl) in front and back of stitch	*kfb or inc1*
Purl in front and back increases: • on a purl row seen from knit side, bar to the right of the stitch into which increase is made		Knit in front and back increases: • on a knit row seen from knit side, bar to the left of the stitch into which increase is made	
Make one knit (or purl) left cross	*M1k (M1p)*	Make one knit (or purl) right cross	*M1k (M1p)*
• virtually invisible • must have rows between or will pull • made between stitches, so shows where placed • slants the stitch worked after it to the left		• virtually invisible • must have rows between or will pull • made between stitches, so shows where placed • slants the stitch worked before it to the right	

PAIRED DECREASES

When made at end of a row	Abbreviation	When made at start of a row	Abbreviation
Right slant – decreases the left of the knit side of stocking stitch		Left slant – decreases the right of the knit side of stocking stitch	
Knit (or purl) two together	*k2tog (p2tog)*	Slip, slip, knit (or slip, slip, purl)	*ssk (ssp)*
Knit (or purl) two together	*k2tog (p2tog)*	Slip1, knit1, pass slipped stitch over	*skp, s1 K1 psso,* or *skpo*
Knit (or purl) two together	*k2tog (p2tog)*	Knit (or purl) two together through back of loops	*k2tog tbl (p2tog tbl)* or *k-b2tog (p-b2tog)*

PAIRED LIFTED EDGE INCREASE

This example increases each side of Stocking stitch using a Right lifted increase (see p.131) at the start, and its paired Left lifted increase at the end of every alternate knit row.

1 On an increase row, knit one stitch. Make a right lifted increase by inserting the tip of the right needle from front to back into the right side of the stitch below the next stitch on the left needle (be careful not to catch more than one strand of yarn). Knit this lifted loop.

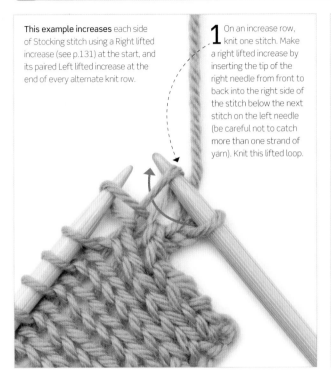

2 Knit to the last but one stitch of the row. Make a Left lifted increase by inserting the left needle tip from front to back into the left side of the stitch two rows below the new stitch on the right needle. Knit this loop, and knit the last stitch.

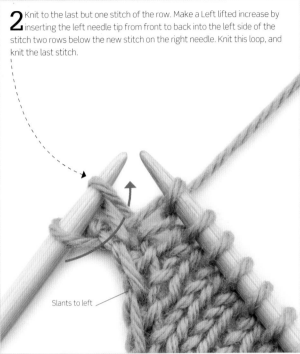

Slants to left

3 If you find the left lifted increase awkward, pick the loop up with the left needle from back to front, slip it onto the right needle, twisting it as it is returned to the left. Knit into the front of the loop.

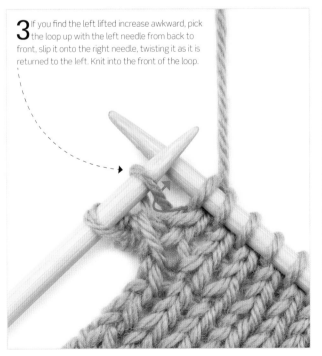

4 The paired increases look like this when completed over a number of rows.

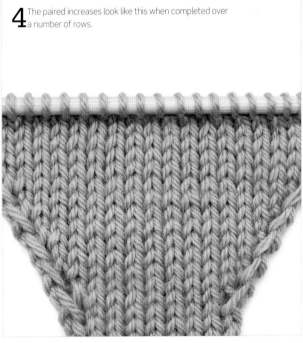

PAIRED EDGE DECREASES (Abbreviation = *skp* and *k2tog*)

This example has decreases on each side of Stocking stitch. It has a slip1, knit1, pass slipped stitch over (skp) at the beginning of the row, which is paired with knit two together (k2tog) at the end of the row. Slip, slip, knit (ssk) may be substituted for skp if preferred.

1 At the start of a knit row, work a slip1, knit1, psso as shown on p.140.

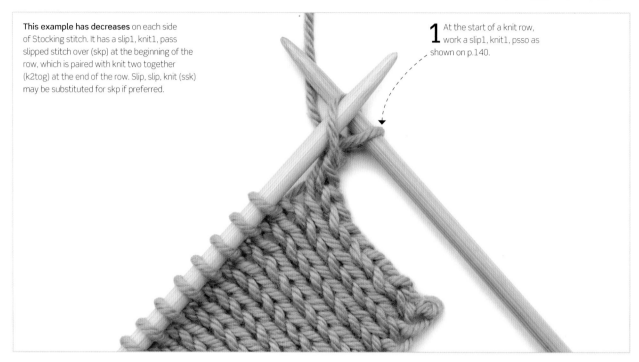

2 Knit to two stitches from the end of the row and knit two stitches together as shown on p.139.

"k2tog" slants to the right on left edge

"skp" slants to the left on right edge

FULLY FASHIONED SHAPING

This is a method of increasing or decreasing the width of stocking stitch whilst preserving a line of stitches that follow the outline of the piece. This looks attractive and makes sewing up easier. Use "paired" increases and decreases on a symmetrical piece: a left slope decrease must be mirrored by a right sloping one at the other side.

ON A KNIT ROW (Abbreviation = *ssk* and *k2tog*)

This example decreases one stitch at each end of a knit row but leaves two plain stitches at the selvedge.

1 Knit the first two stitches. Slip the next two stitches knitwise, one by one onto the right needle. Insert the left needle from left to right through the front of both stitches and knit together. This is a left-slanting ssk decrease (see p.140).

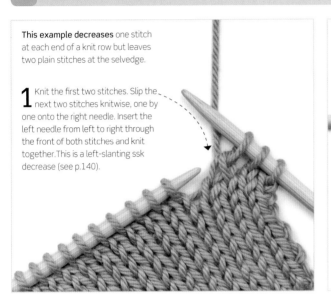

2 Knit to four stitches from the end of the row. Knit two stitches together (see p.139) and then knit the last two stitches. This slopes to the right.

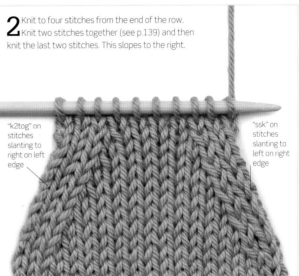

"k2tog" on stitches slanting to right on left edge

"ssk" on stitches slanting to left on right edge

ON A PURL ROW (Abbreviation = *ssp* and *p2tog*)

This example decreases one stitch at each end of a purl row but leaves two plain stitches at the selvedge.

1 Purl the first two stitches. Slip the next two stitches one at a time knitwise onto the right needle. Slip them back together without twisting. Insert the right needle into the front of both stitches from the right and purl them together (ssp). This slopes to the right.

2 Work to four stitches from the end, purl two stitches together (see p.139) and purl the last two stitches. This slopes to the left. Ssk and ssp work better than other decreases when paired with k2tog or p2tog.

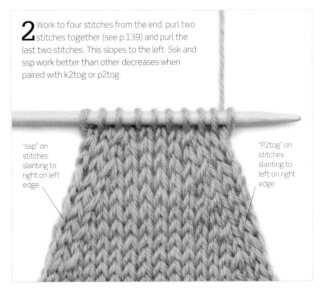

"ssp" on stitches slanting to right on left edge

"P2tog" on stitches slanting to left on right edge

TECHNIQUES

Stitch detail can be lost in dark yarns – pale-coloured yarns show cables to their best effect. Here, different-sized cables, worked together in a thick yarn, create a complex and beautiful tactile surface.

DECORATIVE CENTRAL INCREASES AND DECREASES

Although paired increases and decreases are most commonly used for edge shaping in knitting, they become highly decorative as well as functional when worked close together within the main fabric. For example, central decreases might be spaced around a flared peplum as part of the pattern whilst central increases could emphasize waist-to-bust darting. Decorative central decreases are sometimes combined with yarn over increases in more complex lace patterns.

KNIT INTO FRONT AND BACK AS A PAIRED CENTRAL INCREASE

1 This example works a central paired increase on the knit rows of Stocking stitch. It uses the Knit into front and back increase (see p.130). This forms a "bar" to the left of the stitch into which the increase is worked; therefore it must be offset when worked as a balanced, paired increase. Mark the centre stitch, moving this up as you work.

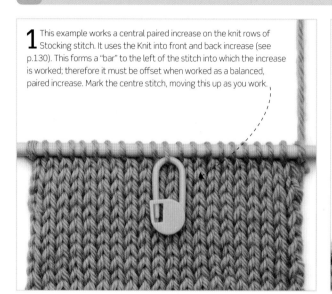

2 Knit to one stitch before the centre stitch. Knit into the front of next stitch and, leaving the stitch on the left needle, knit into the back of the stitch and drop the old stitch off left needle (this places bar to right of centre stitch). Work another of the same increase on the centre stitch (this places bar to left of centre stitch).

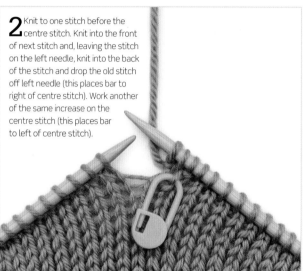

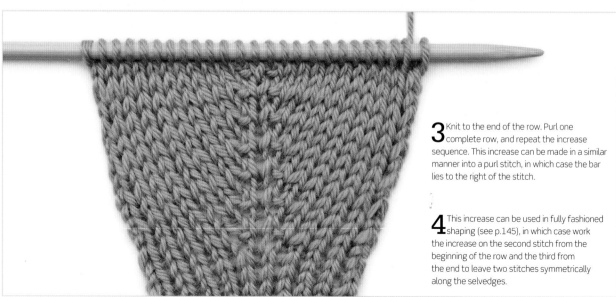

3 Knit to the end of the row. Purl one complete row, and repeat the increase sequence. This increase can be made in a similar manner into a purl stitch, in which case the bar lies to the right of the stitch.

4 This increase can be used in fully fashioned shaping (see p.145), in which case work the increase on the second stitch from the beginning of the row and the third from the end to leave two stitches symmetrically along the selvedges.

OPEN CENTRAL INCREASE

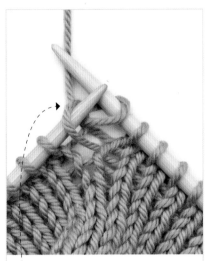

1 On the purl row before the increase, make a yarnover at the position of the increase. Knit to the increase position on the next row. Knit into the back of the yarnover, and drop the yarnover off the left needle.

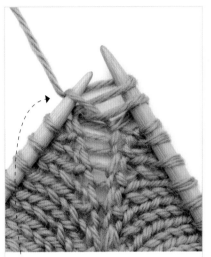

2 Insert the left needle back into the dropped loop from back left so it is twisted as shown, and knit into the front of the loop.

3 Repeat Steps 1 and 2 as you work up the piece. This increases two stitches every other row.

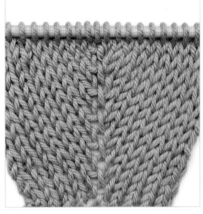

CLOSED CENTRAL INCREASE

1 Work the row, stopping before knitting the central stitch. Knit into the back and front of the central stitch and slide off the left needle. Gently pull the yarn to tension the last stitch.

2 Look for the vertical strand stretching downwards immediately to the right of this stitch. Insert the tip of the left needle from the left into this strand and knit into the back of the loop.

3 Knit to the end of the row. Purl the next row. Repeat Steps 1–3, remembering that there will be one more stitch to knit on each row before working the increase.

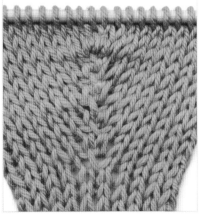

RAISED CENTRAL DECREASE

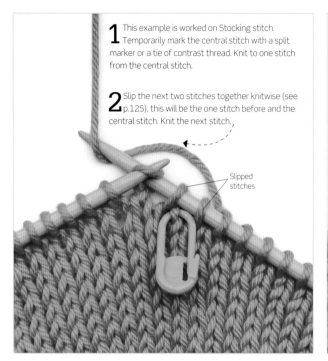

1 This example is worked on Stocking stitch. Temporarily mark the central stitch with a split marker or a tie of contrast thread. Knit to one stitch from the central stitch.

2 Slip the next two stitches together knitwise (see p.125), this will be the one stitch before and the central stitch. Knit the next stitch.

Slipped stitches

3 Insert the tip of the left needle into both slipped stitches and pass them together over the last stitch and off the right needle. This decreases two stitches. Purl the next row.

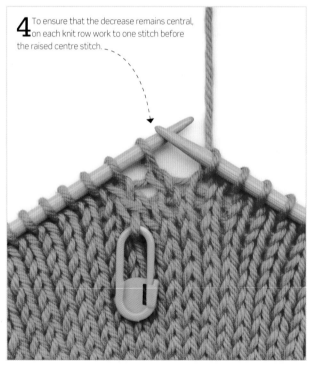

4 To ensure that the decrease remains central, on each knit row work to one stitch before the raised centre stitch.

5 Repeat Steps 2 and 3 as required.

FLAT CENTRAL DECREASE

1 This example is worked on stocking stitch. Working only on knit rows, knit to one stitch from the central stitch. Temporarily mark the central stitch with a split marker or a tie of contrast thread. Slip the next stitch knitwise (see p.125).

2 Insert the right needle knitwise through the next two stitches at once, and knit them together.

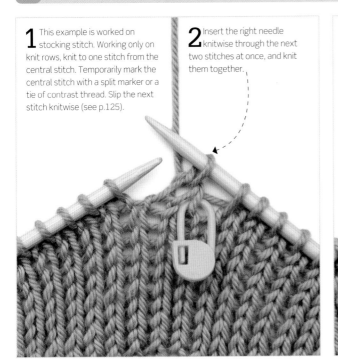

3 Insert the left needle into the second stitch on the right needle and pass it over the last stitch and off the needle. Knit to the end of the row.

4 To keep the decrease central, knit to one stitch before the central stitch of the decrease below before repeating Steps 1–3. This technique decreases one stitch either side of the central stitch.

TECHNIQUES

CABLES AND TWISTS

Many interesting textures can be created by combining knit and purl stitches in various sequences (see pp.48–52), but if you are looking for textures with higher relief and more sculptural qualities, cables and twists are the techniques to learn. Both are made by crossing stitches over each other in different ways to form an array of intricate patterns.

SIMPLE TWISTS

A simple twist is made over only two stitches, without a cable needle. Although twists do not create such high relief as cables, their ease and subtlety makes them very popular. The following twists are worked in Stocking stitch on a stocking stitch ground. They can also be worked with one knit and one purl stitch – the principle is the same.

RIGHT TWIST (Abbreviation = *T2R*)

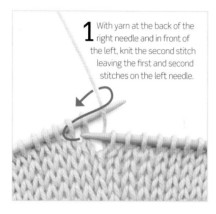

1 With yarn at the back of the right needle and in front of the left, knit the second stitch leaving the first and second stitches on the left needle.

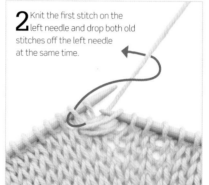

2 Knit the first stitch on the left needle and drop both old stitches off the left needle at the same time.

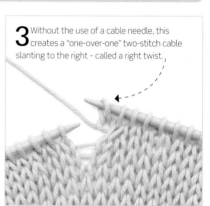

3 Without the use of a cable needle, this creates a "one-over-one" two-stitch cable slanting to the right – called a right twist.

LEFT TWIST (Abbreviation = *T2L*)

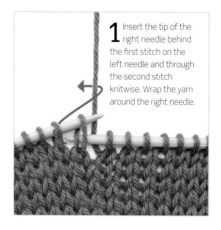

1 Insert the tip of the right needle behind the first stitch on the left needle and through the second stitch knitwise. Wrap the yarn around the right needle.

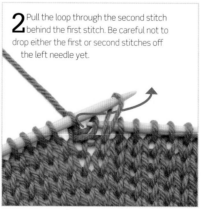

2 Pull the loop through the second stitch behind the first stitch. Be careful not to drop either the first or second stitches off the left needle yet.

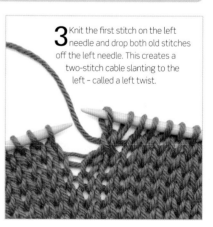

3 Knit the first stitch on the left needle and drop both old stitches off the left needle. This creates a two-stitch cable slanting to the left – called a left twist.

CABLES

Cables are usually worked in Stocking stitch on a Reverse stocking stitch (or garter stitch) ground. They are made by crossing two, three, four or more stitches over other stitches in the row. This technique is illustrated here with the cable 4 front and cable 4 back cables, which are crossed on every sixth row.

CABLE 4 FRONT (Abbreviation = *C4F*)

1 Work to the position of the four stocking stitches that form the cable and slip the first two stitches onto a cable needle. With the cable needle at the front, knit the next two stitches on the left needle.

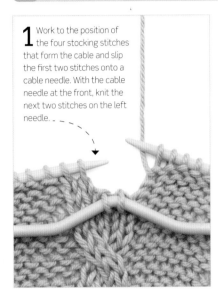

2 Next, knit the two stitches from the cable needle.

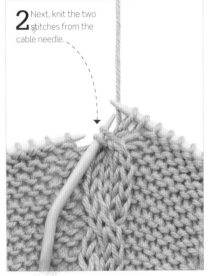

3 This creates a cable crossing that slants to the left. For this reason, a "front" cable is also called a "left" cable.

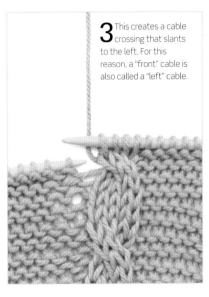

CABLE 4 BACK (Abbreviation = *C4B*)

1 Work as for Step 1 of Cable 4 front, but knit the first two stitches from the left needle with the cable needle at the back of the knitting.

2 Knit the two stitches from the cable needle.

3 This creates a cable crossing that slants to the right. For this reason, a "back" cable is also called a "right" cable.

TECHNIQUES

I-CORD

I-cord stands for "idiot" cord and is also known as slip cord. It is knitted on double-pointed needles and makes a neat edging or can be used for straps and ties, or for appliqué in a contrast colour. Use smaller needles for a tighter edge and it is best worked at a firm tension.

FREE FORM I-CORD

These cords can be applied to an item later, so it is possible to add extra detail as they are worked. Stripes, texture, structural effects, and even beads can be incorporated. With its simple method but multiple uses, I-cord is a very versatile technique.

SIMPLE I-CORD – FOR APPLIQUÉ, TIES, AND STRAPS

1 Cast on five stitches using the Single cast-on shown on p.87. Knit one row.

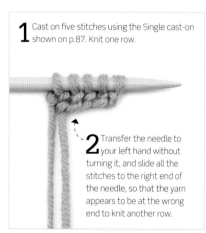

2 Transfer the needle to your left hand without turning it, and slide all the stitches to the right end of the needle, so that the yarn appears to be at the wrong end to knit another row.

3 Insert the right needle into the first stitch on the left needle, pull the yarn firmly from the left side of the knitting around the back to knit the first stitch. Tug the yarn again to pull the knitting round into a tube.

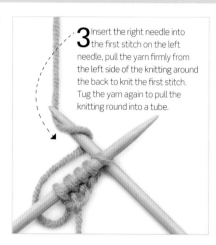

4 Repeat Steps 2 and 3 until the cord is the required length.

SPIRAL I-CORD

This version works up shorter than stocking stitch I-cord, but it is stretchier.

1 Cast on three stitches using the Single or Cable cast-on method (see pp.87 and 89). Knit one row. Continue as for Simple I-cord (see above), but purl the next row. Repeat, alternating knit and purl rows to the required length.

TWO COLOUR I-CORD

1 Cast on five stitches using Single cast-on (see p.87). Knit the first stitch in the main colour.

2 Insert the right needle into the second stitch and lay the contrast yarn between the needles. Knit the second stitch.

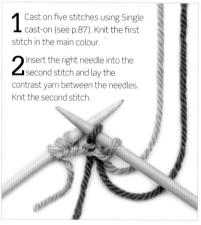

3 Drop the contrast, pick up the main colour, and knit the third stitch. Repeat, alternating colours, ending with main colour.

4 Slide stitches to other end of needle as in Simple I-cord (above). Keeping the colours in sequence, knit next row. Repeat Steps 2–4 to required length. See techniques for holding the yarns on p.167.

ATTACHED I-CORD

Attaching I-cords as you work saves time sewing up later on. I-cords can be added to a finished piece for edging, or form part of the main project as a cast-off. Their use as button loops and soft buttons add attractive and unique finishes to garments.

I-CORD EDGING

1 Cast on between two and five stitches. Knit one row. Transfer the needle to your left hand. Slide stitches as for Simple I-cord (see opposite).

2 Pull yarn around back of stitches and knit all but the last stitch of the next row. Slip the remaining stitch knitwise from left to right needle.

3 With empty left needle, pick up the extreme right loop of the lowest stitch on the main fabric edge from left to right. (This ensures the stitch is correctly positioned for the next step.)

4 Hold the needle with I-cord to the right of the edge of the main fabric. Knit the stitch on the left needle onto the right one. There will now be one extra stitch on the right needle. Insert the left needle into the second stitch on the right needle (slipped stitch) and pass it over the first stitch.

5 Repeat Steps 2-4. If the I-cord is joined, graft open stitches for a smooth join. When edging curves, use a larger needle in the right hand, reverting to the original size on straight sections.

I-CORD BUTTON LOOP

1 Leave a tail of yarn four times the selvedge length. Using a circular needle and the yarn, pick up the selvedge (RS facing). Return to the starting end of the needle, and cast on three stitches using Cable cast-on.

2 Knit two stitches. Work an ssk with last I-cord stitch and next picked up stitch.

3 Slip the three I-cord stitches to left needle without twisting (or use two double-pointed needles). Work a length of I-cord edging to the starting point of the button loop. Knit the three I-cord stitches, then slip them onto left needle. Continue with unattached I-cord until loop is correct size for button. Join I-cord to main fabric as in Step 2.

I-CORD CAST-OFF

1 If the I-cord is to be in contrast colour, work the last row of the main piece in the contrast yarn. Holding work to be cast off in the left hand, add three stitches to left needle using Cable cast-on (see p.89).

2 Knit two stitches. Slip the next two stitches (last of I-cord and first of edge stitches) onto the right needle one by one knitwise. Insert a double-pointed needle from left to right into the front of both stitches and knit together (ssk).

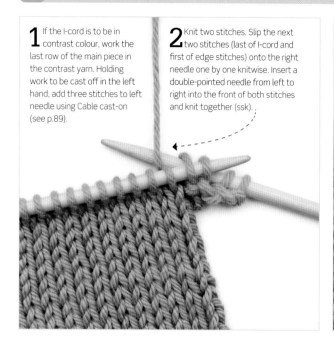

3 Slip the three stitches on the double-pointed needle to the opposite end. Repeat Steps 2 and 3 to end of cast-off. This technique is worked the same on the purl side of the work. Work loosely as I-cord can pucker the cast-off edge if worked tight.

I-CORD BOBBLE

1 At the bobble position, drop the straight right needle (use a point protector to hold stitches if necessary). With a double-pointed needle, knit into the front, back, front, and back again of the next stitch.

2 Slide stitches to the opposite end of the needle. Pull yarn across back and knit the four stitches again; repeat for the required number of rows.

Point protector

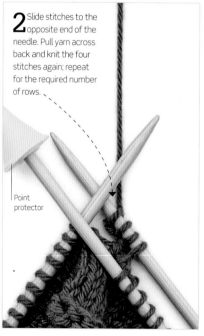

3 Starting with the second stitch, pass the stitches one by one over the first stitch. Slide the remaining stitch back onto the right needle and using the main needles, knit to the next bobble.

I-CORD BUTTON

For a bigger button, work a four or five stitch I-cord.

1 Knit 40cm (15¾in) of three stitch i-cord using a provisional cast-on and cast-off. Pin the left end to something secure with the I-cord stretching to the right. Make an anticlockwise loop that crosses back over itself to the right of the pin. This is Loop A and it points away from you.

Loop A

2 Make another anticlockwise loop that lies sideways on, facing to the right, and which crosses over Loop A except at the end, where it passes under the I-cord coming from the pin. This is Loop B.

Loop A

Loop B

3 Make another anticlockwise loop that faces towards you, this is Loop C. The end of this loop has to be woven over and under Loops A and B. It goes in over the first I-cord of Loop B, then under the first I-cord of Loop A, then over the second I-cord of Loop B and then out under the second I-cord of Loop A. Finally bring this end towards you over all the I-cords, and thread it down through Loop C.

Over B, under A, over B, under A, through C so ends lie together

Loop A

Loop B

Loop C

4 Gently pull both ends to shape the button into a ball. Either unravel the ends of the cord and sew the yarn ends in to complete the button, or cast off and appliqué the I-cord ends to the garment for a decorative "frogging" effect.

LACE KNITTING

The airy openwork texture of knitted lace is formed by combining yarnovers and decreases to create holes (also called eyelets) all over the fabric. Although lace knitting looks complicated, the techniques are relatively easy. If you choose a lace stitch with a short row repeat, you can work the openwork fabric quickly and still produce impressive delicate textures.

TIPS FOR LACE KNITTING

Eyelets arranged in various ways around each other are the basis of all lace stitches. Eyelets are made up of yarnovers (see pp.136–137), which produce the holes in the fabric, and decreases, which frame the eyelets and compensate for these increases in the row to keep the knitting the same width. The techniques for two simple eyelets are given here, but there are other ways of producing eyelets and these methods are always explained in full in the stitch instructions.

• **Cast on loosely** for lace patterns. This is best achieved not by trying to make loose loops but by spacing the cast-on stitches farther apart on the knitting needle, with at least 3mm (⅛in) between the loops. If you find this difficult to do evenly, then use a needle one or two sizes larger than the size you are using for the lace and switch to the correct needle size on the first row. Depending on your yarn, when knitting fine weight lace metal needles may be easier to work with than wooden ones.

• **Lace stitch patterns** sometimes have yarnovers and decreases in the very first row. These are not easy to work on cast-on loops, so you can start with a plain knit or purl row then begin the lace pattern on the following row.

• **Use a row counter** when working lace stitches to keep track of which pattern row you are on. This is especially important for intricate lace worked over a long row-repeat. If you do get lost in your pattern, stop and start over.

Use stitch markers to separate each pattern repeat until you are confident that you know it by heart.

• **Count your stitches** frequently when knitting lace to make sure you still have the right number of stitches. If you are missing a stitch you may have left out a yarnover. There is no need to undo stitches all the way back to the missing yarn. Simply work to the position of the missing yarnover on the following row, then insert the left needle from front to back under the strand between the stitch just worked and the next stitch on the left needle (see below). Work this stitch through the front of the loop in the usual way.

Picking up and working a missing yarn-over

CHAIN EYELET

1 For a chain eyelet on a stocking stitch ground, begin by creating a yarnover on the right needle (see p.136). Knit the next two stitches together (see p.139).

Yarn-over

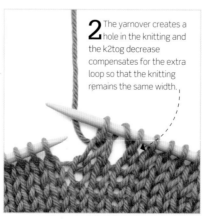

2 The yarnover creates a hole in the knitting and the k2tog decrease compensates for the extra loop so that the knitting remains the same width.

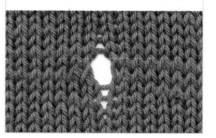

3 On the following row, purl the yarnover in the usual way. A single chain eyelet is shown here so that its structure is clear, but eyelets can be arranged separated by several rows and several stitches or sitting side by side.

OPEN EYELET

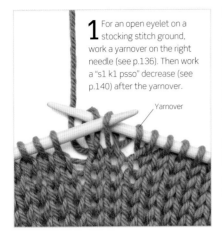

1 For an open eyelet on a stocking stitch ground, work a yarnover on the right needle (see p.136). Then work a "s1 k1 psso" decrease (see p.140) after the yarnover.

Yarnover

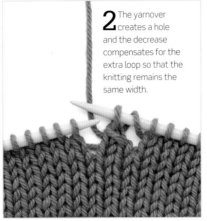

2 The yarnover creates a hole and the decrease compensates for the extra loop so that the knitting remains the same width.

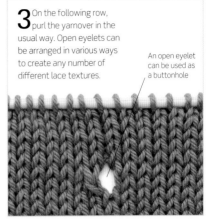

3 On the following row, purl the yarnover in the usual way. Open eyelets can be arranged in various ways to create any number of different lace textures.

An open eyelet can be used as a buttonhole

YARNS FOR LACE

Knitted lace was first designed to look similar to traditional needle lace, so it was worked on fine needles in white cotton thread. Fine yarn does enhance the delicacy, but openwork knitting can look interesting in other yarns as well. Here are a few examples.

PSEUDO LACE

The quickest way to produce a delicate effect is to knit Garter stitch using fine yarn and very large needles. You can make an attractive scarf this way in a flash, and any type of yarn, such as this metallic one, is suitable for the pseudo lace technique.

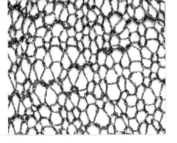

MULTICOLOURED OPENWORK

For added interest, use a double-knitting-weight yarn with variegated colours for openwork. This stitch pattern is Grand eyelet mesh stitch (see p.61), which looks the same on both sides and is extremely easy to work.

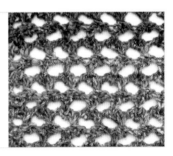

MOHAIR LACE

Fine mohair yarn highlights the delicacy of the lacy stitches. Try easy lace patterns like this Mini-leaf stitch (see p.62) when using mohair, as it is more difficult to knit with than smooth yarn, and complicated lace doesn't show up clearly in textured yarns.

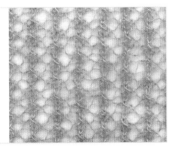

TRADITIONAL-STYLE KNITTED LACE

Fine cotton thread on very fine needles is used to work traditional-style knitted lace. You can see how much more delicate this Domino eyelet pattern looks when knitted with super-fine yarn instead of a lightweight cotton yarn as on p.63.

Fair Isle knitting is usually composed of small repeating patterns and is worked by carrying the non-working yarn along the back of the work until required again. This results in a richly coloured, thick fabric.

COLOURWORK

You have many technique choices if you like adding colours to your knitting. The easiest method is to knit plain stocking stitch using a multicoloured yarn or a variegated yarn, which changes colour along the strand. To add colours into the knitting yourself, you can work simple stripes, easy colourwork stitch patterns, or charted Fair Isle or intarsia motifs.

SIMPLE STRIPES

Horizontal stripes are perfect for knitters who want to have fun with colour without learning more advanced techniques. These examples show the variety of stripe widths, colours, and textures available. You can follow any plainly coloured pattern and introduce stripes without affecting the tension or shape of the knitting.

TWO-COLOUR GARTER STITCH STRIPE

This stripe pattern is worked in Garter stitch in two colours (A and B). To work the stripe, knit 2 rows in each colour alternately, dropping the colour not in use at the side of the work and picking it up when it is needed again.

TWO-COLOUR KNIT AND PURL PINSTRIPE

Knit this stripe in two colours (A and B). Work 6 rows in Stocking stitch in A. Drop A at the side and knit 2 rows in B – the second of these rows creates a purl ridge on the right side. Repeat this sequence for the pinstripe effect. To avoid loose strands of B at the edge, wrap A around B at the start of every RS row.

FIVE-COLOUR STOCKING STITCH STRIPE

To work multiple stripes and carry the colours up the side, use a circular needle. Work back and forth in rows. If a yarn you need to pick up is at the opposite end, push all the stitches back to the other end of the circular needle and work the next row with the same side of the knitting facing as the last row.

TEXTURED STOCKING STITCH STRIPE

This stripe is worked in a mohair yarn in two colours (A and B) and a smooth cotton yarn (C). The cotton yarn provides a good contrast in texture and sheen and highlights the fuzziness of the mohair.

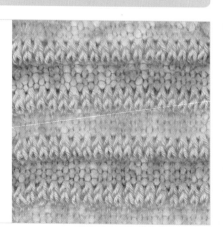

TIDYING THE EDGES

When working two coloured, even row stripes, twist the yarns around each other every 1-2cm (½–¾in) up the side of the piece. Alternating the direction of the twist after each colour change prevents the yarns becoming tangled. Be careful not to pull them tightly or the edge will pucker. This technique may make a bulky seam if used with more than two colours.

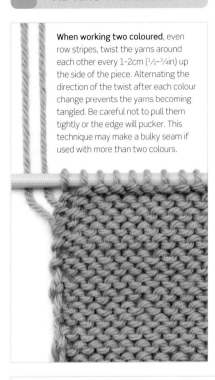

PLAIN-COLOUR DOMINO SQUARES

1 This technique works central decreases in garter stitch. Cast on 21 stitches with the Knit-on method (see p.88). First row is WS row. Slip first stitch knitwise, knit 8 stitches. Add a marker, knit 3 stitches, and add another marker. Knit next 8 stitches and purl the final one.

2 Knitting shown here with WS facing after completing first, non-decreasing row. Turn work. Slip first stitch knitwise, knit to first marker. S1, k2tog, psso (see p.141). Knit to end, purling the last stitch.

3 Slip first stitch knitwise, knit to last but one stitch, purl the last stitch. Right side rows, on which the s1 k2tog psso is worked on the centre three stitches, are indentified by the yarn tail being at the right.

4 Repeat Steps 2 and 3 until you have one stitch left. Cut the yarn and pull the end through as normal, but not tightly so that it can be re-threaded when another square is knitted on.

STRIPED DOMINO SQUARES

1 Working as Plain domino square, cast on 21 stitches. Knit the first row in the main colour.

2 Continue as Plain domino square, alternating two rows of contrast and main colour as you work. To join in the contrast yarn see p.119. Carry the yarns up the side as you work.

JOINING DOMINO SQUARES

1 With RS of original square facing and needle with remaining end stitch from last square in right hand, pick up and knit 10 stitches along the edge of the original square using yarn for new square (see p.121). Pick up through the centre of loops of edge stitches.

2 Cast on another 10 stitches on left needle using Knit-on method (see p.88). Knit this square as for Plain colour domino knitting (see p.163).

3 Continue to add squares, using different coloured yarns as required. When combined with the following technique, no sewing is required at all.

WEAVING IN ENDS DURING DOMINO KNITTING

1 On RS rows it is possible to weave in ends as you knit. Start with the lowest end, with the new colour held in the right hand, and the old colour over the left index finger.

2 Insert right needle into first left stitch, bring old colour (on left finger) around front of right needle from right to left.

3 Lay new colour between needles as normal and knit the stitch, as you pass the new colour loop off the needle, allow the old colour to slide to the right and over the tip of the right needle so that it does not catch in the new stitch. Knit one stitch without weaving the old colour.

4 Repeat Steps 2 and 3 until the tail of the old colour is woven in and then drop it for trimming later and complete the square. Trim it leaving about 1cm (½in) of yarn to prevent it unravelling on the right side.

COLOURWORK STITCH PATTERNS

Slip-stitch patterns are designed specially to use more than one colour in the overall pattern but only ever use one colour in a row. With this technique, geometric patterns are created by working some stitches in a row and slipping others. The pattern here is shown in two different colourways and is one of the easiest to work.

CHECK SLIP-STITCH PATTERN

Follow this pattern to work the stitch and use the steps below as a guide.

Use three colours for the pattern that contrast in tone: A (a medium-toned colour), B (a light-toned colour), and C (a dark-toned colour).

Note: Slip all slip stitches purlwise with the yarn on the WS of the work.

Using A, cast on a multiple of 4 stitches, plus 2 extra.

Row 1 (WS) Using A, P to end.

Row 2 (RS) Using B, K1, sl 1, *K2, sl 2; rep from * to last 3 sts, K2, sl 1, K1.

Row 3 Using B, P1, sl 1, *P2, sl 2; rep from * to last 3 sts, P2, sl 1, P1.

Row 4 Using A, K to end.

Row 5 Using C, P2, *sl 2, P2; rep from *.

Row 6 Using C, K2, *sl 2, K2; rep from *.

Rep rows 1–6 to form patt.

WORKING A CHECK SLIP-STITCH PATTERN

1 This shows the middle of a pattern row 2 (RS row) of the pattern above. Two stitches have been slipped. On RS rows, slip the stitches with yarn held at the back. Do not pull the yarn too tightly on the following stitches.

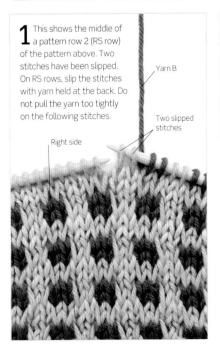

Yarn B

Two slipped stitches

Right side

2 Row 4 of the pattern is worked entirely with yarn A and no stitches are slipped. The slipped stitches on the previous row and on the following row pull the stitches in A up and down to produce the check effect.

Yarn A

Right side

3 On WS rows of the check pattern, slip the stitches with yarn held at the front. The principle of all the slip-stitch patterns is the same – only one colour is used in a row.

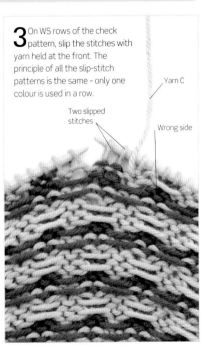

Yarn C

Two slipped stitches

Wrong side

CHARTED COLOURWORK

The techniques for charted stocking stitch colourwork – Fair Isle and intarsia – open up a world of richly coloured designs. In Fair Isle, a yarn colour is carried across the wrong side of the work until it is required. In intarsia, a separate length of yarn is used for each colour and the yarns are twisted together at the colour change junctures.

FOLLOWING A COLOURWORK CHART

The first step in understanding charted colourwork is to grasp how easy the charts are to follow. Rather than writing out how many stitches in which colours to work across a row, your knitting pattern provides a chart with the colours marked on it in symbols or in blocks of colour.

If a pattern covers the whole garment back, front, and sleeve and cannot be repeated, a large chart is provided for each of these elements with all the stitches on it for the entire piece. Where a pattern is a simple repeat, the repeat alone is charted. Each square on a stocking stitch colourwork chart represents a stitch and each horizontal row of squares represents a knitted

row. You follow the chart from the bottom to the top, just as your knitting forms on the needles.

The key provided with the chart tells you which colour to use for each stitch. All odd-numbered rows on a colourwork chart are usually right-side (knit) rows and are read from right to left. All even-numbered rows on a colourwork chart are usually wrong-side (purl) rows and are read from left to right. Always read your knitting pattern instructions carefully to make sure that the chart follows these general rules.

FAIR ISLE CHART

This example of a Fair Isle chart illustrates very clearly how easy it is to knit simple Fair Isle patterns. No more than two colours are used in a row, which makes it ideal for colourwork beginners. The colour not in use is stranded across the back of the knitting until it is needed again.

To identify if a colourwork chart should be worked in the Fair Isle technique, check that both colours in a row are used across the entire row. If each colour is used after every three or four stitches (as in this chart), use the stranding technique (opposite). If the colours are not used over a span of more stitches, use the weaving-in technique (see pp.170–171) so that the loose strands (called floats) don't become too long.

KEY
☐ = background colour
⬤ = motif colour

Read row 4 (a purl row) from left to right

Row 2 is a purl row

Read row 3 (a knit row) from right to left

Start here with a right-side row

INTARSIA CHART

This heart is an example of a simple intarsia colourwork chart. Each colour on the chart is represented by a different symbol. The blank square (the background) also represents a colour.

You can tell that a charted design should be worked in the intarsia technique if a colour appears only in a section of a row and is not needed across the entire row. Use a separate long length of yarn, or yarn on a bobbin, for each area of colour in intarsia knitting (including separated background areas). Twist the colours where they meet (see p.172).

KEY
☐ = background colour   ⦿ = motif colour 2
⬤ = motif colour 1   ⊠ = motif colour 3

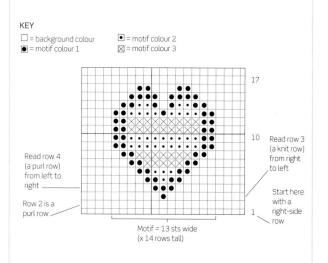

Read row 4 (a purl row) from left to right

Row 2 is a purl row

Read row 3 (a knit row) from right to left

Start here with a right-side row

Motif = 13 sts wide (x 14 rows tall)

FAIR ISLE METHOD

This is where two or more colours are used in a row of knitting – traditionally, the colours would make small repeating patterns in Stocking stitch. The non-working yarn is stranded along the wrong side, or may be woven into the back to prevent it catching.

FAIR ISLE STRANDING TECHNIQUE

1 On the knit rows, knit the stitches in the first colour, then drop it at the back and knit the stitches in the second colour. Strand the colour not in use loosely across the back of the work until required.

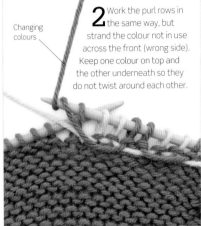

Changing colours

2 Work the purl rows in the same way, but strand the colour not in use across the front (wrong side). Keep one colour on top and the other underneath so they do not twist around each other.

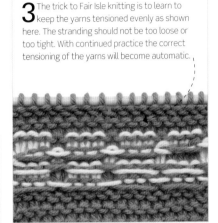

3 The trick to Fair Isle knitting is to learn to keep the yarns tensioned evenly as shown here. The stranding should not be too loose or too tight. With continued practice the correct tensioning of the yarns will become automatic.

HOLDING THE YARNS

These techniques for holding the yarns will speed up your work and produce more even results. To maintain consistent weight fabric, always carry both yarns to the edge even if no stitch is required there, and twist them before starting the next row.

HOLDING ONE YARN IN EACH HAND

1 This method works well when there are only two colours in a row. Hold the first yarn over your right index finger as normal and the second over your left index finger, as shown in Knitting "Continental" style (see p.85).

2 Knit the first colour stitches as usual. When you reach the second colour stitches keep the first colour over your right index finger. Insert the right needle into next stitch as if to knit. With your left index finger, lay the second colour forwards between the needles from left to right.

3 Pull the new knit loop through as usual, keeping both yarns over the correct index finger. On a purl row, follow the instructions for Alternative "Continental" purl stitch (see p.86) to work the colour over your left index finger.

BOTH YARNS IN RIGHT HAND

Place one colour over your right index finger, and one over your middle finger. Knit as normal, throwing the second colour with your middle finger. This method allows you the flexibility of potentially adding a third colour over your ring finger.

BOTH YARNS IN LEFT HAND

This is ideal for those who knit Continental style. Hold the first yarn over the index finger, and the second over the middle finger of your left hand. Throw the yarns with their respective finger for knit and purl as shown on p.86.

TECHNIQUES FOR WEAVING

When strands (or floats as they are also known) are longer than three or four stitches, they may catch on fingers or rings. To prevent this, weave the non-working yarn into the back of the knitting by taking the weaving yarn over and under the working yarn. This can be done on every other stitch, which makes a denser fabric, or whenever a float is longer than three stitches, in which case weave into occasional stitches.

WEAVING LEFT YARN, KNIT OR PURL

1 This method uses one yarn in each hand. Keep left yarn and finger below and to the left of needles when not weaving it in. Lift weaving yarn up, insert right needle through stitch to either knit or purl and underneath weaving yarn. Make stitch with main yarn, slipping weaving yarn over needle without catching in stitch.

2 Knit or purl the stitch, catching floating yarn in back of the fabric. Knit the next stitch without weaving in left yarn, by dropping left finger to back so the yarn lies below the needles before making the stitch. Weave in as necessary to prevent long floats.

Weaving yarn (left)

Working yarn (right)

WEAVING RIGHT YARN, KNIT STITCH

1 This method uses one yarn in each hand. Keep right yarn above and to the right of the needles when not weaving it in. To weave, insert right needle into stitch. Wind right yarn around needle as to knit, throw left yarn as usual to knit.

2 Return right yarn back along its route to original position and knit the stitch. Knit the next stitch without wrapping the right yarn. Weave in as necessary to prevent long floats.

Working yarn (left)

Weaving yarn (right)

WEAVING RIGHT YARN, PURL STITCH

1 This method uses one yarn in each hand. On a purl stitch, keeping the left index finger and yarn below the needles, wind the right yarn under the right needle. Throw left yarn as usual to purl, return right yarn back along its route to original position and purl the stitch. Work the next stitch without weaving the right yarn. Weave in as necessary to prevent long floats.

Working yarn (left)

Weaving yarn (right) – under needle

WEAVING INDEX FINGER YARN

1 Holding both yarns in right hand, insert right needle into stitch, wind both yarns around needle as if to knit.

2 Return index finger yarn to its original position. Knit the stitch with the remaining yarn. Keep weaving yarn above the needles when not weaving. Knit the next stitch without weaving the index finger yarn in. Weave in as necessary to prevent long floats.

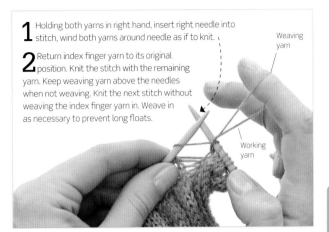

Weaving yarn

Working yarn

[RIGHT HAND] WEAVING MIDDLE FINGER YARN WHILST KNITTING OR PURLING A STITCH

1 Hold both yarns in right hand. Keep middle finger yarn above work when not weaving in. To knit or purl, insert right needle into stitch. Bring middle finger yarn above index finger yarn, across front of both needles to the left.

2 Holding yarn in place to the left of the needles, take it round to the right behind the needles.

Catch middle finger yarn with left thumb and/or index finger

Hold both yarns in right hand

3 Throw the index finger yarn as if to knit or purl, then return middle finger yarn back along its route to its original position at right back of work. Work next stitch without weaving, temporarily lowering middle finger so index finger yarn wraps around middle finger yarn. Weave in as necessary to prevent long floats.

Working yarn (index)

[LEFT HAND] WEAVING INDEX FINGER YARN WHILST KNITTING OR PURLING A STITCH

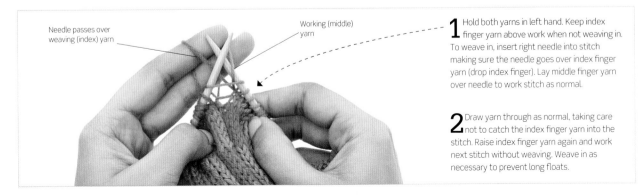

Needle passes over weaving (index) yarn

Working (middle) yarn

1 Hold both yarns in left hand. Keep index finger yarn above work when not weaving in. To weave in, insert right needle into stitch making sure the needle goes over index finger yarn (drop index finger). Lay middle finger yarn over needle to work stitch as normal.

2 Draw yarn through as normal, taking care not to catch the index finger yarn into the stitch. Raise index finger yarn again and work next stitch without weaving. Weave in as necessary to prevent long floats.

HOLDING BOTH YARNS IN LEFT HAND – WEAVING THE MIDDLE FINGER YARN

1 Here, the middle finger yarn is more awkward to weave than that on the index finger. Keep the middle finger below the work when not weaving. Insert the right needle into stitch, make sure it passes under both yarns.

2 Bring the tip back over the middle finger (weaving) yarn and catch the index finger yarn. Draw it under the middle finger yarn to make a new stitch. Work next stitch without weaving. Weave to prevent long "floats".

KNIT AND PURL FAIR ISLE

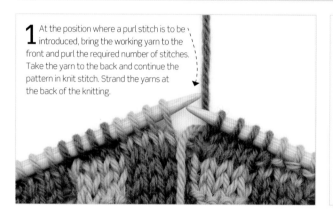

1 At the position where a purl stitch is to be introduced, bring the working yarn to the front and purl the required number of stitches. Take the yarn to the back and continue the pattern in knit stitch. Strand the yarns at the back of the knitting.

2 If you wish to maintain clear colour transitions, knit the first row of a new colour, purl the middle rows, and knit the row immediately before a colour change.

GARTER STITCH FAIR ISLE

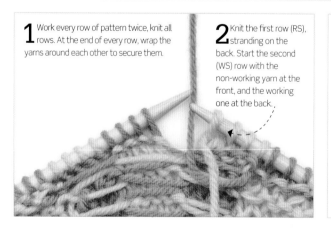

1 Work every row of pattern twice, knit all rows. At the end of every row, wrap the yarns around each other to secure them.

2 Knit the first row (RS), stranding on the back. Start the second (WS) row with the non-working yarn at the front, and the working one at the back.

3 When it is time to change colour, swap the yarn positions from front to back, and continue, stranding the non-working yarn at the front (WS) of the work.

4 For smooth transition when changing or finishing a colour, do so on the first of the two row pattern (RS) row.

TEA-COSY STITCH

1 Twist yarns at the start of each row. Pull stranding yarn gently throughout to slightly gather the knitting. Knit eight stitches in the first colour, stranding second yarn at back. Swap yarns, knit eight stitches in second colour stranding first yarn at back. Repeat along the row.

Wrong side of knitting

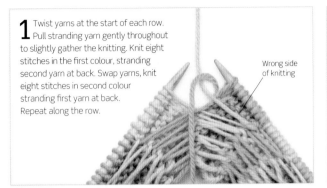

2 Next row. First colour to back, second yarn to front, knit first eight stitches. First colour to front, second to back, knit eight stitches in second colour. Repeat along row, swapping yarns from front to back so that both yarns strand on the front. Repeat Steps 1 and 2.

TWO STRAND LAYING-IN

1 Work Stocking stitch in main yarn, with all yarns at back. When decorative yarns are required on knit side, bring to front between needles. Work the number of stitches required in main yarn. Decorative yarns to back. Work in main yarn.

2 Do not twist main and decorative yarns when they are moved from front to back.

3 On a purl row, all yarns to front. When decorative yarns are required to lie on the knit side, take back between needles and work number of stitches required in main yarn. Decorative yarns to front between needles. Work in main yarn.

KNIT WEAVE

Shows on reverse of Stocking stitch. Always work one plain stitch between weaves. Twist the yarns at start of every row. Weaving yarn lies alternately over and under main yarn.

1 On a K row. Both yarns at back, insert needle to knit. Lay weaving yarn right to left between needles. Knit with main yarn, do not catch weaving yarn.

2 On a P row. Both yarns at front, weaving yarn below main yarn between weaves. Insert needle to purl, lay weaving yarn right to left between needles. Purl with main yarn.

INTARSIA

Here each yarn is worked separately and no strands are carried along the back. Each area of colour in a row must have its own small ball of yarn. Cut short lengths from the main balls and wind onto bobbins to prevent tangles.

INTARSIA TECHNIQUE

Right-slant colour change: To avoid holes, twist the colours around each other only on the knit rows.

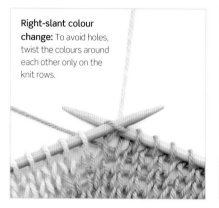

Left-slant colour change: To avoid holes, twist the colours around each other only on the purl rows.

Vertical colour change: To avoid holes, twist the colours around each other on both knit and purl rows.

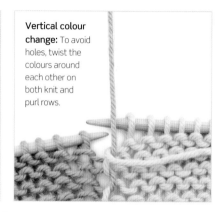

TWO-COLOUR CABLES

4 With C, and without twisting the yarn, knit the three C stitches off the cable needle and onto the right needle.

1 Wind sufficient small balls for intarsia. Work two vertical stripes of A with three-stitch vertical stripes in B and C in between (this is the six-stitch cable). Stop after the purl row before the first crossover.

2 Knit A to cable position. Slip the three C stitches off the left needle onto a cable needle and put to the back.

3 Bring B yarn under A yarn (this is the twist) and take behind stitches on cable needle. Knit the three B stitches off the left and onto the right needle.

5 Twist A under C and knit stitches between cables. On the next (purl) row, when twisting B and A the yarns will stretch diagonally at rear of crossover. Do not pull too tightly.

6 Work 7 rows of stripes to next crossover row. Work as Steps 2–5, reversing C and B.

TEXTURAL AND COLOUR EFFECTS

With a simple stocking and garter stitch base, prettily knotted, shaded, pulled, and gathered effects can be achieved. Loop stitch variations offer versatile decorative edging possibilities and careful yarn colour and type choices will also enhance these techniques.

WORKING INTO LOWER STITCHES

The following techniques add texture to the knitted surface. Combinations of textural and open lace-like knitting can be produced by dropping and unravelling stitches, while dip stitch adds colour. Pull up stitch creates three-dimensional effects.

TECHNIQUES

DOUBLE STITCH

1 Insert right tip from front to back into the centre of the stitch immediately below the next stitch to be taken off the left needle.

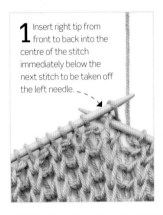

2 Wrap yarn around the tip of the needle at the back.

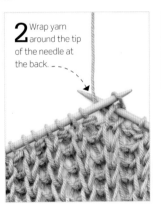

3 Pull new loop through to front and slide new loop and stitch above it off the tip.

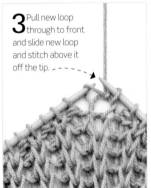

4 Knit the next stitch. Repeat Steps 1–3 for each double stitch. A plain stitch is always worked between each double.

DROPPING AND UNRAVELLING STITCHES AND ROWS

1 When you reach the desired position, drop the stitch that you wish to unravel and pull on it until it unravels to the desired position.

2 Making sure you put the needle beneath the unravelled strands, insert the right needle into the last stitch below that has not unravelled.

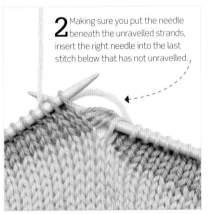

3 Knit the loose strands and the stitch together. Knit the next stitch before dropping another stitch.

PULL UP STITCH

1 Work Stocking stitch to position of pull up stitch, on a purl row. Reach right needle down purl side and insert tip into top loop of stitch to be pulled up.

2 Slip the stitch knitwise onto the left needle and purl together with the following stitch on the needle. Space as required along row.

3 When the piece is completed the pull up stitch creates a tucked, raised effect.

DIP STITCH

Dip stitch can be vertical or angled across the front or reverse of knitting, and worked in main colour for texture or contrast for a colour effect.

1 Knit to where the effect is to occur. Reach the right needle tip down a number of rows and insert tip through a stitch (or the space between two stitches).

2 Holding second yarn at back, catch "dip" yarn with needle and pull through to front. Pull enough through, and make the rear strands loose enough so that the main fabric is not distorted. On the next row, knit or purl the "dip" stitch together with the following stitch. Repeat Steps 1 and 2 whenever a dip stitch is required.

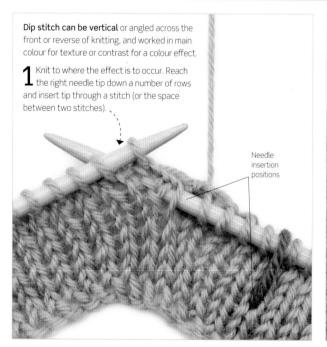

Needle insertion positions

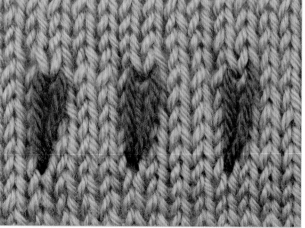

LOOP-PILE OR FUR KNITTING

Loops can be added to the front or the back, usually working a plain row between. Garter stitch or Stocking stitch make good base fabrics. You can adjust the density by altering the frequency of the loops. Try beading the loops, or varying their length for a surface effect.

LOOPS TO FRONT

1 At position of loop, with RS facing, knit the next stitch but do not drop from left needle. Bring yarn forwards between needles. Wind a loop around left thumb from back to front once.

2 Yarn back. Knit the original stitch again, dropping it off the left needle whilst withdrawing thumb from loop.

3 Insert left needle into last two stitches on right needle from front as in ssk (see p.140) and k2tog with main yarn.

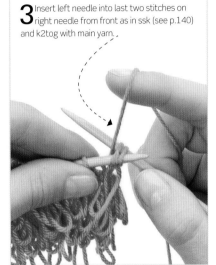

4 Repeat Steps 1–3 at regular intervals, keeping the length of the loop consistent. Gently tug the loops to tighten the stitches.

LOOPS TO BACK

1 At position of loop, with RS facing, wind the yarn around two left fingers as well as needle at back of work and knit the stitch. Do not drop stitch off left needle.

2 Slip new stitch loop onto left needle and k2tog through back of loops. Drop loop from finger. Gently tug loops at end of row to tighten stitches.

LONG LOOPS MADE WITH A RULER

1 Worked on a WS row. Hold a ruler at back to right of needles. Insert right needle into next stitch knitwise. Wind yarn clockwise around right needle, take it around ruler and bring yarn back under right needle.

2 Draw both loops on the right needle through the stitch on the left needle and drop this off left needle. Slide ruler out of loops at end of row. On next row, k2tog into the back of the two wraps made in last row.

Originating from Ireland, Aran-type knitting is a richly textured, traditionally cream-coloured fabric. Cables and travelling stitches, often in trellis and diamond patterns, are worked on reverse stocking stitch and moss stitch backgrounds.

DECORATIVE STITCHES

With a few uncomplicated moves, elaborate looking effects are possible. Elongated stitches lighten fabric and look particularly effective in slippery ribbon yarns. In their simplest form these can be worked in stripes, but may also form more elaborate effects, particularly in floral and lozenge patterns. Picot point chains can be worked into filet lace-like fabrics or make delicate trims.

THREE-INTO-THREE STITCH

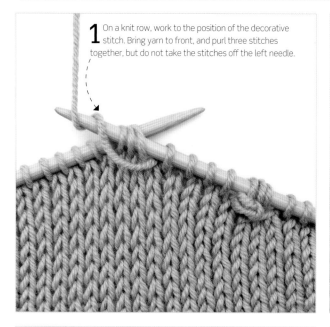

1 On a knit row, work to the position of the decorative stitch. Bring yarn to front, and purl three stitches together, but do not take the stitches off the left needle.

2 Yarn to back, knit into the three stitches that are still on the left needle, but do not take the stitches off the left needle.

3 Yarn to front, purl into the same three stitches again, then slide the three stitches off the left needle. Yarn to back and knit any intervening stitches in pattern.

4 The next row is usually a plain row, either knit or purl depending on your overall pattern.

5 The three-into-three stitch forms a raised bobble on the surface of the knitting, creating a pattern when worked regularly.

ELONGATED STITCHES

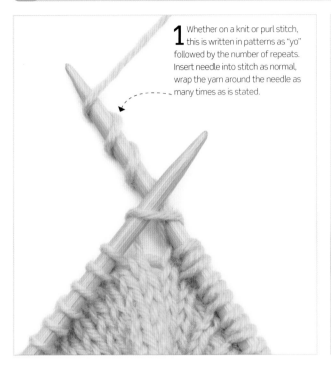

1 Whether on a knit or purl stitch, this is written in patterns as "yo" followed by the number of repeats. Insert needle into stitch as normal, wrap the yarn around the needle as many times as is stated.

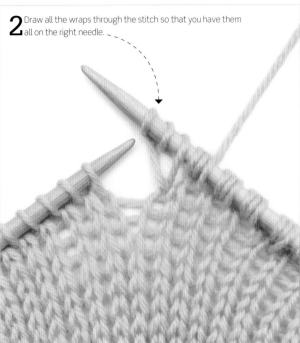

2 Draw all the wraps through the stitch so that you have them all on the right needle.

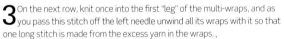
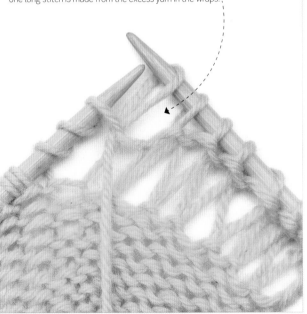

3 On the next row, knit once into the first "leg" of the multi-wraps, and as you pass this stitch off the left needle unwind all its wraps with it so that one long stitch is made from the excess yarn in the wraps.

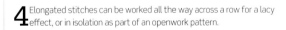
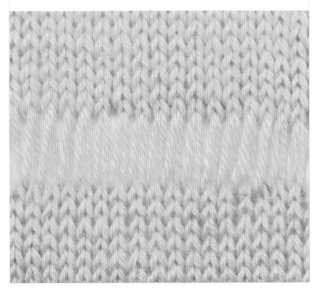

4 Elongated stitches can be worked all the way across a row for a lacy effect, or in isolation as part of an openwork pattern.

WRAPPED CLUSTERS

1 At the position of the cluster, slip the last five stitches on the right needle all together without twisting onto a cable needle.

2 Wrap the yarn in an anticlockwise direction around the stitches taking it underneath the cable needle. Wrap yarn six times, pulling it tight if you want the cluster to gather the stitches.

3 Slip the cable needle stitches straight back onto the right needle. Work row as normal to next cluster.

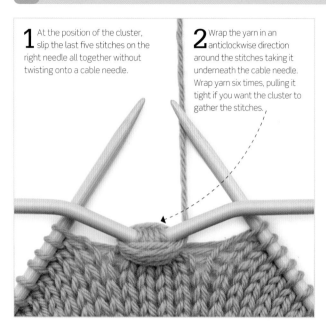

PICOT POINT CHAIN

1 Make a slip knot on the left needle.

2 Knit-on cast-on (see p.88) two more stitches. Knitwise cast off (see p.106) two stitches so there is one stitch remaining on right needle.

3 Slip the stitch onto the left needle without twisting. Repeat Step 2 to make a chain the required length.

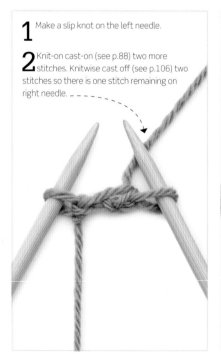

4 To make flower circles, work a five picot chain and then insert the needle into the base of the first picot, draw the loop through and cast off the last stitch.

KNITTED-IN SMOCKING

1 Cast on a multiple of eight stitches plus three, and work a purl three, knit one rib. This is a right side row. Knit an even number of rows in rib until the position of the first smocking is reached.

2 Work eight stitches of the rib. Slip last five stitches on right needle together onto a cable needle. Bring smocking yarn from back to front between right needle and cable needle leaving a 10cm (4in) tail at back. Wind this yarn twice clockwise around stitches on cable needle, leaving it at back of work.

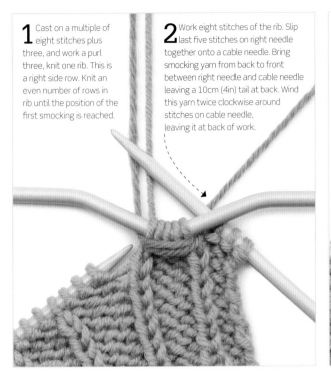

3 Slip stitches together off cable needle back onto right needle. Repeat Steps 2 and 3 across row, stranding smocking yarn across back of work and cutting with a 10cm (4in) tail at the end.

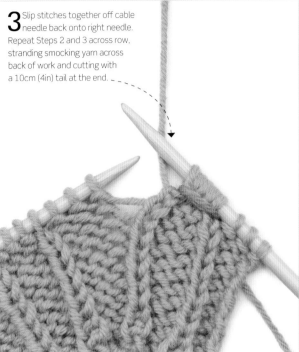

4 Work three rows of rib and then repeat Steps 2 and 3 but work the first twelve stitches before introducing smocking yarn.

5 Continue to work smocking alternating the start of eight or twelve stitches with three rows between. When complete, secure the ends of smocking yarn up one edge. Gently draw up each row of smocking, easing ribs together until finally securing the smocking yarn at the other edge.

SHADOW KNITTING

1 The design chart shows the finished effect.

2 This chart has to be "exploded", and drawn on a knitting chart that is four times as long as the original.

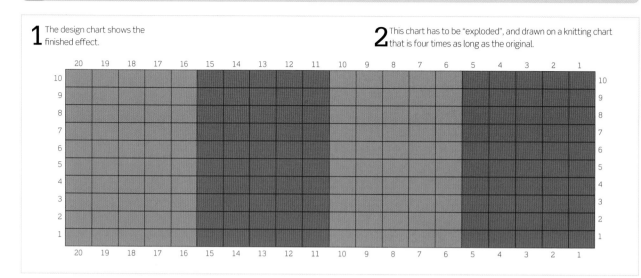

3 The first row of the exploded chart is always left blank. On the second row, draw the main (pink) stitches from row 1 of the original chart.

4 Leave three rows blank, then draw the main (pink) stitches from row 2 of the original chart; continue in this manner to the final row (row 10).

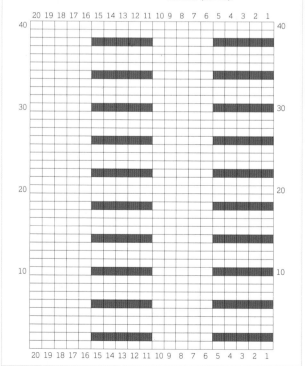

5 Go back to the beginning of the exploded chart, and on the middle row of the three blank rows, draw the contrast (grey) stitches from row 1 of the original chart. Continue up the exploded chart matching original chart stitches to the middle of the blank rows.

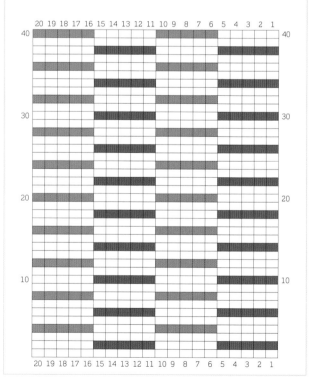

6 Annotate the chart in your own way to show purl and knit stitches. Colour every two rows in alternating colours, starting with two rows of main colour. This example shows purl stitches as white to help read the chart, but work them in whichever colour stripe they fall in.

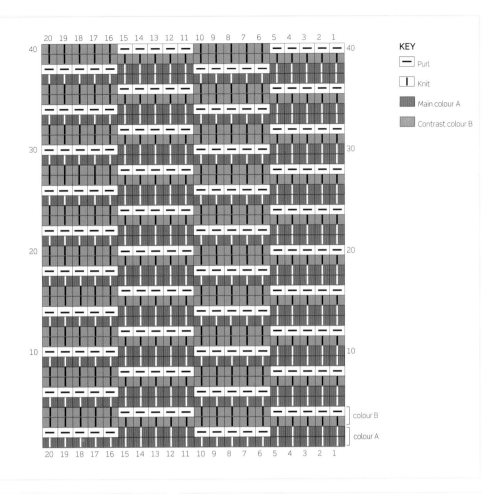

KEY

▭	Purl
Ⅱ	Knit
▨	Main colour A
▨	Contrast colour B

colour B
colour A

7 Cast on 20 stitches and, working from chart, knit the first row in colour A. Work second row in A, purling the white squares and knitting the coloured ones.

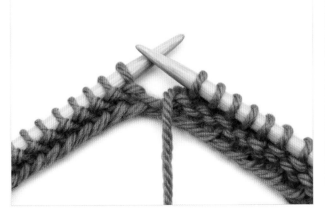

8 Change to colour B, knit one plain row and then work as row 4 of chart, purling the blank squares and knitting the coloured ones. Repeat the colour sequence of two rows of each colour as you follow the chart upwards.

STRUCTURAL EFFECTS

Structural knitting techniques are challenging and satisfying to work, and can be used in combination with varied colours and textural yarns. Entrelac squares offer scope for colour choices whilst Pleats, Gathering, and Doubling can add style details to garments. Tubular knitting is an interesting technique and alongside Bias knitting, may inspire new ideas.

ENTRELAC

Here, knitted squares create a diagonal basketweave effect. Squares can be worked in Stocking stitch, Garter stitch, cables, lace, or textural stitches. Each square has twice as many rows as stitches and alternating series of squares are worked in opposite directions. All the stitches for one series are on the needle at the same time, although the squares are worked individually. A line of short row triangles at the start, finish, and each side, create straight edges.

1 This example makes three eight-stitch squares. In colour A, loosely cast on 24 stitches using Knit-on method (see p.88). Knit 2 stitches and turn work. Purl one stitch, slip one purlwise, turn. This slip stitch makes picking up in Step 7 easier.

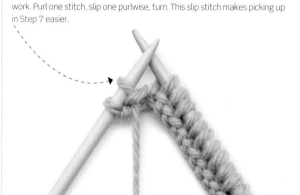

2 Repeat these two rows, knitting into one more cast-on stitch on left needle at end of each knit row, purling back and slipping the last stitch purlwise. Finish after knitting 8 stitches, do not turn (16 cast-on stitches remain).

Cast-on stitches

Completed first triangle

3 Work the next triangle as in Steps 1 and 2 over the following 8 stitches, and the third triangle over the final 8 stitches. There are now three triangles on the needle.

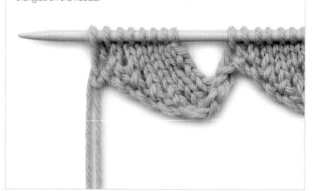

4 Left side triangle. WS facing, join in colour B and purl 2 stitches, turn, knit 2, turn. Purl into front and back of edge stitch (see p.130), this shapes the edge. Purl the last stitch in colour B together with the first stitch in colour A (p2tog, see p.139) on the right needle.

P2tog

5 Repeat Step 4, purling one more stitch for each repeat and knitting back to the edge each time. Stop after purling into front and back, purling 5 and purling colour B and colour A together. Do not turn work. Leave this completed edge triangle on the right needle.

6 To work squares. WS facing, yarn at front. Insert right needle from back to front into edge stitches and pick up and purl 8 stitches evenly along the free edge of first triangle.

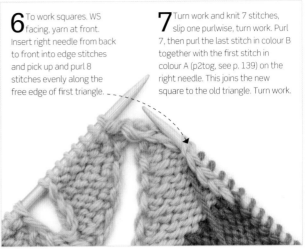

7 Turn work and knit 7 stitches, slip one purlwise, turn work. Purl 7, then purl the last stitch in colour B together with the first stitch in colour A (p2tog, see p. 139) on the right needle. This joins the new square to the old triangle. Turn work.

8 Repeat Step 7 seven more times, but do not turn work after last row, all stitches of first square are now on left needle. Work next square as Steps 6–8.

9 To work right edge triangle. WS facing, pick up edge as Step 6. Work every knit row, slipping the end stitch purlwise. P2tog at the end of all but the first purl row. One stitch remains.

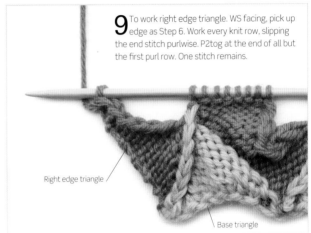

Right edge triangle

Base triangle

10 To work right edge square. Join in colour A. With RS facing, slip first stitch onto right needle. Pick up and knit 7 stitches along the edge of right-hand square (8 stitches on needle). Purl 7, slip 1 purlwise, turn.

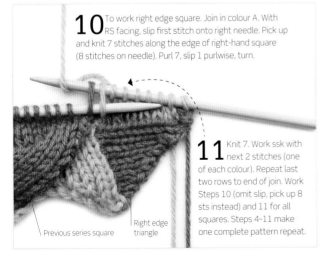

11 Knit 7. Work ssk with next 2 stitches (one of each colour). Repeat last two rows to end of join. Work Steps 10 (omit slip, pick up 8 sts instead) and 11 for all squares. Steps 4–11 make one complete pattern repeat.

Previous series square

Right edge triangle

12 Work finished triangles (these follow a series with edge triangles - see Steps 4-9). In appropriate colour, work as Step 10, purling 8 in final instruction. Turn. Knit 7, work an ssk as in Step 11. Turn, purl 6, p2tog at end to create flat top edge. Turn, knit 6 and ssk as before.

13 Continue working ssk and p2tog each time until triangle completed. Repeat for all triangles. Pull final stitch through itself to finish.

PLEATS

To make a pattern for pleats, fold a sheet of squared paper alternately away from and towards you along lines at 10 and 5 square intervals. Each square represents a stitch. Use the pattern to count the stitches required to make the visible face, underside, and turn-back of each pleat. Add one stitch at each fold – slipped on right side, purled on wrong side rows, or purled every row. Use the same method for all folds.

KNITTING PLEATS

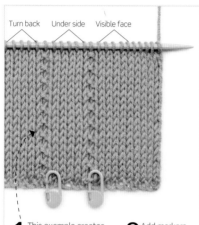

Turn back   Under side   Visible face

1 This example creates two left-facing 5-stitch pleats. Cast on 44 stitches (this includes an extra 4 stitches for fold lines).

2 Add markers as you work. First row: k10, p1, k5, p1, k10, p1, k5, p1, k10.

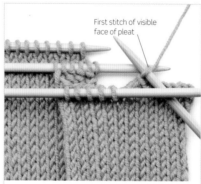

First stitch of visible face of pleat

3 Purl one complete row. Repeat to required length, finishing after a purl row.

4 When pleats completed, cast off 4 stitches knitwise (see p.106). Slip the next 5 stitches purlwise (including fold stitch) onto a double-pointed needle (dpn). Slip the next 6 stitches purlwise (including the fold stitch) onto another dpn. Turn the needles to fold the pleat.

5 Slip one stitch from rear dpn to right needle. Knit the first stitch on the left needle onto the right needle and pass both stitches on right needle over the first one and needle tip, one by one.

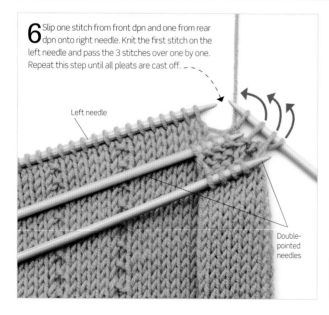

6 Slip one stitch from front dpn and one from rear dpn onto right needle. Knit the first stitch on the left needle and pass the 3 stitches over one by one. Repeat this step until all pleats are cast off.

Left needle

Double-pointed needles

7 Cast off remaining stitches as normal.

GATHERING AND DOUBLING

Gathering removes multiple stitches evenly along a row, and Doubling (also called Blousing) adds stitches in the same manner. Another form of gathering can be created by working multiple rows of rib on smaller needles preceded and followed by non-rib knitting. Doubling can be used after a cuff rib, giving fullness to a sleeve.

GATHERING

1 To calculate even gathering, decide how many stitches are to be removed, and divide the stitches on the needle by this number. For example if you cast on 30 stitches and wish to evenly remove 10 stitches, the sum is 30 ÷ 10 = 3. Therefore one stitch must be decreased in every three stitches. To do this, knit one stitch, then knit two stitches together (k2tog). Repeat along the row.

2 To make a fuller gather, try k2tog all across the row, or knit 3 stitches together or even work two consecutive k2tog, p2tog rows. To create a gathered edge, knit two or more stitches together as you cast off.

DOUBLING

1 To calculate doubling, do the same sum as for Gathering (above) but remember that doubling adds stitches. If the answer is three, then three stitches must be made out of every one stitch. To do this, knit into front, back, and front again of each stitch.

2 To use both doubling and gathering to work a horizontal ruffle, knit one row, knitting into front and back, and the next row purling into front and back of each stitch. Knit between 16 and 20 rows in stocking stitch. Knit one row k2tog across row, and then p2tog across next row. Continue in stocking stitch.

BIAS KNITTING

This method creates diagonal-shaped pieces, sloping left or right. Chevron knitting (see p.53) is created by working opposing bias panels in one piece. Increasing into lower rows or working increases tightly can force bias knitting to curve attractively.

BIAS KNITTING – STRAIGHT AND CURVED

1 Cast on 20 stitches. At the start of the first knit row, slip first and second stitch one by one onto right needle, insert left needle into front and knit them together (ssk, see p.140). Knit row to one before the end stitch, knit into front and back of edge stitch. Purl one row. Repeat knit row. This piece of knitting will slant to the left.

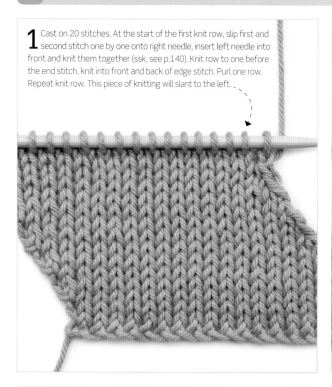

2 To slant to the right, knit into front and back of first stitch, knit to two from end and k2tog.

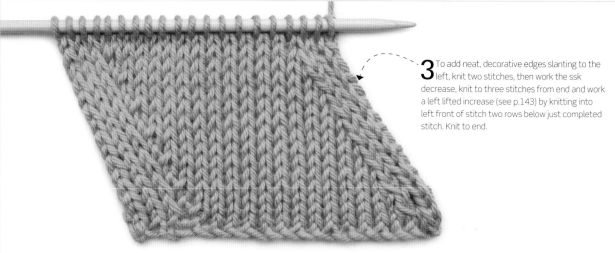

3 To add neat, decorative edges slanting to the left, knit two stitches, then work the ssk decrease, knit to three stitches from end and work a left lifted increase (see p.143) by knitting into left front of stitch two rows below just completed stitch. Knit to end.

TUBULAR KNITTING

Although commonly associated with circular knitting, tubular knitting, sometimes called double knitting, can be worked on straight needles by slipping every other stitch. To practise, work with two colours so that you can see which stitch belongs to which side of the knitting, as you work both sides at the same time. Tubular fabric knits up thick, firm, and flat. You may need to work with a smaller needle than normal.

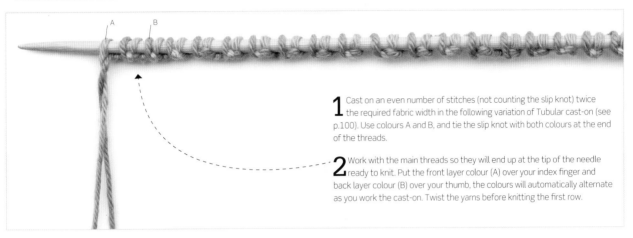

1 Cast on an even number of stitches (not counting the slip knot) twice the required fabric width in the following variation of Tubular cast-on (see p.100). Use colours A and B, and tie the slip knot with both colours at the end of the threads.

2 Work with the main threads so they will end up at the tip of the needle ready to knit. Put the front layer colour (A) over your index finger and back layer colour (B) over your thumb, the colours will automatically alternate as you work the cast-on. Twist the yarns before knitting the first row.

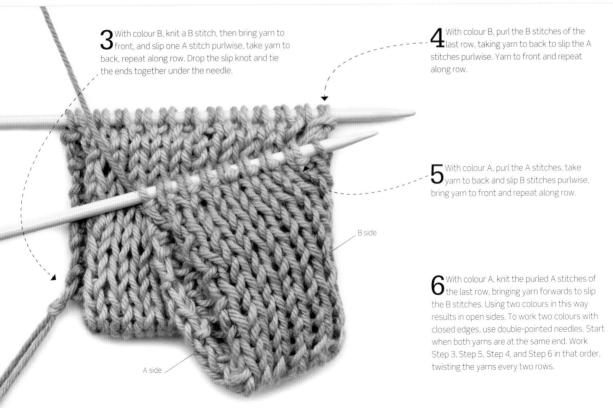

3 With colour B, knit a B stitch, then bring yarn to front, and slip one A stitch purlwise, take yarn to back, repeat along row. Drop the slip knot and tie the ends together under the needle.

4 With colour B, purl the B stitches of the last row, taking yarn to back to slip the A stitches purlwise. Yarn to front and repeat along row.

5 With colour A, purl the A stitches, take yarn to back and slip B stitches purlwise, bring yarn to front and repeat along row.

6 With colour A, knit the purled A stitches of the last row, bringing yarn forwards to slip the B stitches. Using two colours in this way results in open sides. To work two colours with closed edges, use double-pointed needles. Start when both yarns are at the same end. Work Step 3, Step 5, Step 4, and Step 6 in that order, twisting the yarns every two rows.

B side

A side

TECHNIQUES

SHORT ROWS

Rows of knitting do not necessarily have to be knitted end to end. Short rowing, or "partial knitting", involves knitting two rows across some of the stitches, thereby adding rows in only one part of the fabric. It is popular for creating smooth edges in shoulder shaping, curving hems, making darts, and turning sock heels. It is most commonly used on Stocking stitch.

PREVENTING HOLES

In most shaping applications a concealed turn is required and there are three ways to work this: the "wrap" or "tie" (easiest and neat); the "over" (loosest); and the "catch" (neatest). Garter stitch, as shown in the 3D ball, does not require wrapping.

WRAP OR TIE TO CLOSE HOLES

1 On a knit row: at turn position, slip next stitch purlwise onto right needle (see p.124), yarn to front. Return slip stitch to left needle, yarn back. Turn and purl short row. Repeat wrap at each mid-row turn.

2 On a purl row: at turn, slip next stitch purlwise, yarn to back. Slip stitch back, yarn to front. Turn and work knit short row. Repeat wrap at each mid-row turn.

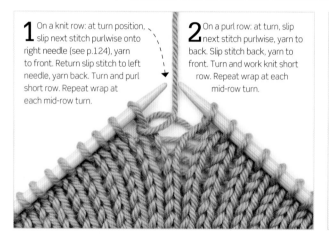

3 When working across all stitches on completion of short rowing: at wrap, insert right needle up through front (knit) or back (purl) of wrap. Work wrap together with next stitch.

OVER TO CLOSE HOLES

1 Knit or purl to turn position. Turn. Yarn to other side of work and bring yarn over needle (without moving yarn to back or front beforehand, so yarn does not go completely around needle). Work short row.

2 When knitting across all stitches on completion of short rowing, knit yarn over and next stitch together.

3 When purling across all stitches on completion of short rowing, drop yarn over and slip next stitch purlwise. Insert left needle downwards into dropped yarn, pick it up, and purl together with next stitch.

CATCH TO CLOSE HOLES

1 On either knit or purl rows, work a short row. Turn work, slip first stitch purlwise (see p.124), and work back along short row.

2 When knitting a completion row (knitting is temporarily reversed as this makes this step easier), insert right needle down through strand between first and second stitches on left needle as shown. Lift onto left needle.

Insert right needle one row below row just worked — Left needle

3 Turn work again and knit picked up loop together with next stitch on left needle.

4 If completion row is purl, insert left needle upwards through the strand between the first and second stitch two rows below right needle. Stretch this loop, then drop it. Slip next stitch from left to right needle. Pick up dropped loop again with the left needle. Return slipped stitch to left needle. Purl these two together.

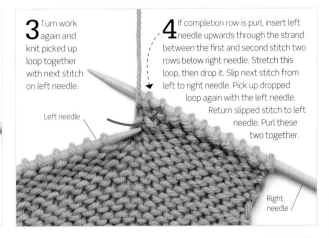

Left needle

Right needle

SHAPING: ADAPTING A CAST-OFF SHOULDER TO SHORT ROW SHAPING

1 This example adapts an existing left shoulder worked in stocking stitch. The left shoulder is 24 stitches wide and the original instruction is to cast off 8 stitches every alternate row. These cast offs can be substituted by working short rows with 8 less stitches every alternate row.

2 Cast on 24 stitches and work to the shoulder shaping. Ignore the cast-off instruction, and knit a row.

3 Turn the work. Purl to 8 stitches from the end and work a wrap (slip next stitch purlwise, yarn back, return slip stitch, yarn forwards, see opposite). Turn and knit to end.

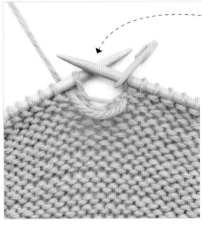

4 Purl to 16 stitches from the end, work wrap and turn. Knit to end (8 stitches on needle).

5 Purl across all the stitches, picking up wraps by slipping them onto left needle and purling together with next stitch (see opposite). Either cast off all stitches, or put them onto a stitch holder for grafting later.

TECHNIQUES

SHORT ROW CIRCULAR MEDALLION

This example is in Garter stitch, but medallions can be knitted in other stitches. There is no need to pick up the wraps in garter stitch.

1 Cast on 16 stitches in colour A with a Provisional cast-on (see p.99).

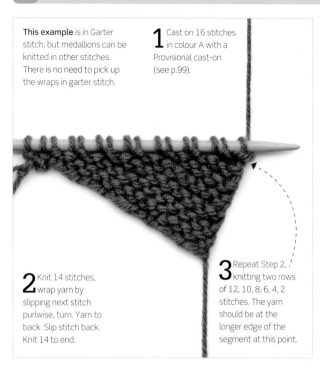

2 Knit 14 stitches, wrap yarn by slipping next stitch purlwise, turn. Yarn to back. Slip stitch back. Knit 14 to end.

3 Repeat Step 2, knitting two rows of 12, 10, 8, 6, 4, 2 stitches. The yarn should be at the longer edge of the segment at this point.

4 Turn work and knit 14 stitches. Yarn to front. Slip last two stitches on left needle purlwise onto right needle. Cut colour A yarn with a 10cm (4in) tail (yarn is part way along a row). One segment of the circle is completed.

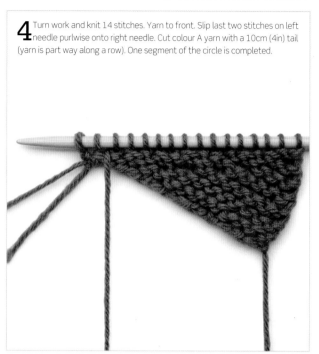

5 Hold the needle with stitches in the left hand, change to colour B, knit 16 stitches. Then repeat Steps 2-5 in B, swapping to colour A at Step 5.

6 Work 8 segments, alternating colours A and B. Finish by placing stitches on a holder (see p.106) after Step 5 on the final segment. Graft (see p.230).the seam and sew in the yarn ends to complete.

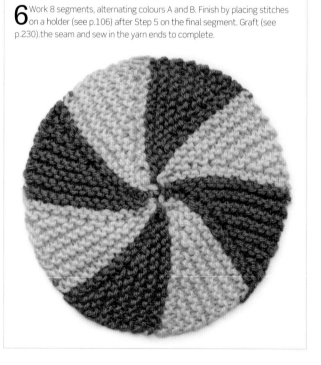

RUFFLES

By working a straight band vertically at the same time as working short rows, ruffles can be built up. The fullness of the ruffle is dictated by the number of times the short rows are worked compared to the rows of the vertical band. Varying the stitch, as shown in Edge ruffles, can add extra effect to the finished ruffle.

SHORT ROW EDGE RUFFLES

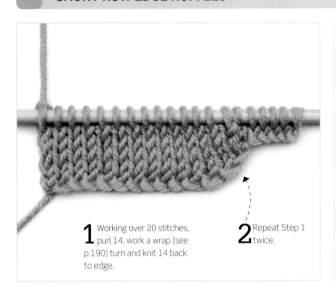

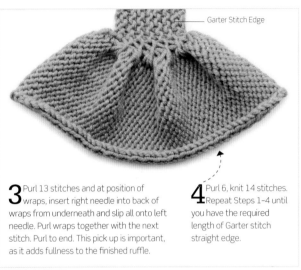

Garter Stitch Edge

1 Working over 20 stitches, purl 14, work a wrap (see p.190) turn and knit 14 back to edge.

2 Repeat Step 1 twice.

3 Purl 13 stitches and at position of wraps, insert right needle into back of wraps from underneath and slip all onto left needle. Purl wraps together with the next stitch. Purl to end. This pick up is important, as it adds fullness to the finished ruffle.

4 Purl 6, knit 14 stitches. Repeat Steps 1-4 until you have the required length of Garter stitch straight edge.

VERTICAL RUFFLES INSET INTO FABRIC

1 This example uses 24 stitches. The ruffle is worked over the middle 8 stitches. Knit 16, wrap (see p.190), and turn.

2 Purl 8 stitches, wrap, and turn.

3 Knit 8 stitches, wrap, and turn. Repeat Step 2.

4 Knit 16 stitches, picking up wraps (see p.190).

5 Purl 24 doing pick up on other side of ruffle, as in Step 4. This completes two rows of main fabric and four rows of the inset ruffle.

6 Repeat from knit instruction in Step 1 to end of Step 5 for required number of side panel rows. Group vertically for greater effect.

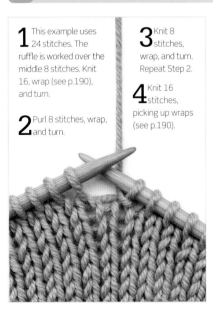

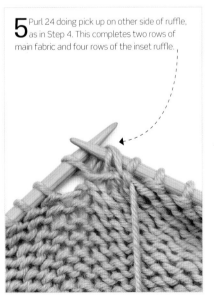

3D KNITTING

Planned use of short rows can make your knitting take 3D form. Peaks created in this way can be left open or sewn together at the base. Before joining, these can be padded to create a closed decorative "pocket". Un-graduated short rows flaps can also be sewn up, padded, and joined. Complete 3D shapes can also be worked.

SHORT ROW BALL

This example is in garter stitch and there is no wrapping included. If wrapping is required, follow the method shown in Short row circular medallion (see p.192).

1 Cast on 20 stitches in colour A.

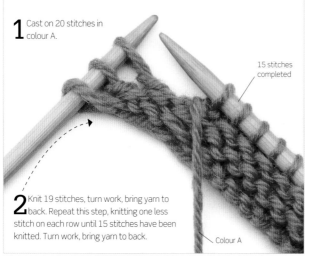

15 stitches completed

2 Knit 19 stitches, turn work, bring yarn to back. Repeat this step, knitting one less stitch on each row until 15 stitches have been knitted. Turn work, bring yarn to back.

Colour A

3 Knit 13 stitches, turn work, yarn to back. Repeat this step knitting 11 stitches.

4 Knit 7 stitches, turn work, yarn to back. Repeat this step knitting 5 stitches.

5 Knit 4 stitches, yarn to front. Slip all remaining stitches (9) on left needle purlwise onto right needle. Cut yarn with 10cm (4in) tail.

8 more stitches to slip

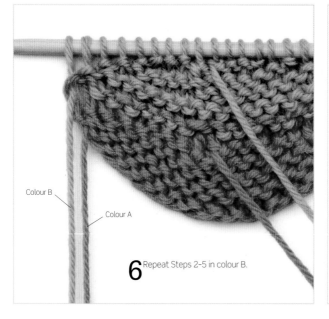

Colour B

Colour A

6 Repeat Steps 2–5 in colour B.

7 Work 8 segments in alternate colours to complete ball. Cast off or work a provisional cast-off. Sew in mid-row ends and gently pull top and bottom threads to neaten ends. Stuff with suitable material and either sew together with Mattress stitch (see p.227), or graft provisional open stitches to cast-on edge.

SHORT ROW PEAKS

1 Decide the width of the peak, for this example it is 9 stitches and there are 8 stitches on both sides of it (25 stitches on needle). At position of peak, knit 17 stitches, turn.

2 Purl 9 stitches, turn.

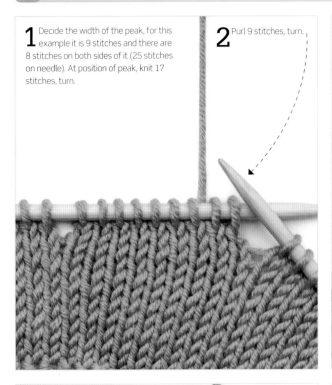

3 Knit 8 stitches, turn. Including a turn after each row, purl 7, knit 6, purl 5, knit 4, purl 3, knit 2, purl 1.

4 Knit 2, turn. Increasing in the reverse order to Step 3 and turning at end of each row, work until the last row completed is purl 9 stitches. Turn.

5 Knit 17 stitches, turn, and purl 25 stitches. There may be small "steps" visible along the edge of the peak, this is part of the short row effect.

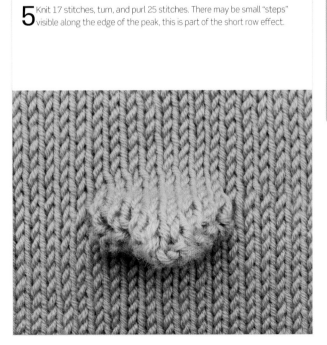

CIRCULAR KNITTING

Circular knitting, or knitting in the round, is worked on a circular needle or with a set of four or five double-pointed needles. With the right side always facing, the knitting is worked round and round to form a tube, or a flat shape (a medallion). A circular needle is easy to master, while working with double-pointed needles is best suited to knitters with intermediate skills.

KNITTING TUBES

For those who don't enjoy stitching seams, knitting seamless tubes is a real plus. Large tubes can be worked on long circular needles, for example for the body of a pullover or a bag. Short circular needles are used for seamless neckbands and armhole bands, and hats. Double-pointed needles are used for smaller items, like mittens and socks.

WORKING WITH A CIRCULAR KNITTING NEEDLE

1 Cast on the required number of stitches. Ensure that the stitches are untwisted and they all face inwards, then slip a stitch marker onto the end of the right needle to mark the beginning of the round.

Stitch marker

2 Hold the needle ends in your hands and bring the right needle up to the left needle to work the first stitch. Knit round and round on the stitches. When the stitch marker is reached, slip it from the left needle to the right needle.

Knit first stitch of first round tightly

3 If you are working a stocking stitch tube on a circular needle, the right side of the work will always be facing you and every round will be a knit round.

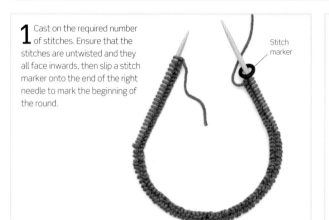

JOINING THE CIRCLE OF STITCHES

This is a neat way of closing the circle in circular knitting.

1 Cast on required number of stitches, plus one stitch.

2 Slip the first cast-on stitch onto the right needle next to last cast-on stitch. Place the join marker after this stitch.

3 Knit the round, and when you reach the end, knit the last two stitches before the marker together (this will be the first cast-on stitch and the extra stitch).

KNITTING A MOBUS LOOP

1 Using a Double cast-on (see p.91), cast on enough stitches to work a circle on a short circular needle. Knit the first round but stop before joining the circle.

2 Deliberately twist the stitches around the wire so that there is one clear twist visible, but the end stitches are facing each other with the loops facing inwards.

3 Join the circle, maintaining the twist, and knit the round. The first few rounds can be fiddly but once there are a few rows and the twist is established it becomes easier.

4 Continue until the loop is as deep as required. Cast off. A deep Mobus loop makes a great hair band.

5 If using the Magic loop technique (see p.198), moving the twist to the stitches on the right end of the needle for the first few rounds makes working them easier.

"MAGIC LOOP" KNITTING – WORKING A SMALL TUBE ON A CIRCULAR CABLE NEEDLE

1 Cast on a small amount of stitches onto a long circular cable needle using any method, but do not join the circle of stitches. Slide stitches down onto cable.

2 Find the middle point of the stitches and pull the cable through the gap between them.

3 Slide one group of stitches onto each point, and position the needle tips and yarn as normal. Make sure the stitches are not twisted; the cast-on loop should lie under the needle.

4 Hold both needle tips with your left hand and pull the right needle upwards through the stitches so that they slide onto the cable. The right needle tip needs to be sufficiently free to be able to work the left stitches, but the stitches must not join the end of the other group of stitches.

5 Loop the cable round and knit the first stitch tightly to join the circle, or use one of the methods shown in this chapter. Continue to knit the first half of stitches off the left needle.

6 The left needle is now empty. Pull the cable backwards through the stitches on the cable so that they slide onto the left needle tip. Repeat Steps 4–6.

KNITTING TWO TUBULAR ITEMS AT ONCE ON TWO CIRCULAR NEEDLES

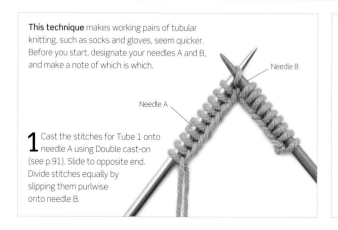

This technique makes working pairs of tubular knitting, such as socks and gloves, seem quicker. Before you start, designate your needles A and B, and make a note of which is which.

Needle B

Needle A

1 Cast the stitches for Tube 1 onto needle A using Double cast-on (see p.91). Slide to opposite end. Divide stitches equally by slipping them purlwise onto needle B.

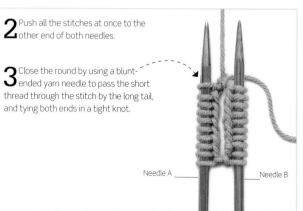

2 Push all the stitches at once to the other end of both needles.

3 Close the round by using a blunt-ended yarn needle to pass the short thread through the stitch by the long tail, and tying both ends in a tight knot.

Needle A   Needle B

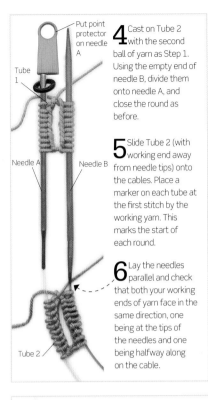

4 Cast on Tube 2 with the second ball of yarn as Step 1. Using the empty end of needle B, divide them onto needle A, and close the round as before.

5 Slide Tube 2 (with working end away from needle tips) onto the cables. Place a marker on each tube at the first stitch by the working yarn. This marks the start of each round.

6 Lay the needles parallel and check that both your working ends of yarn face in the same direction, one being at the tips of the needles and one being halfway along on the cable.

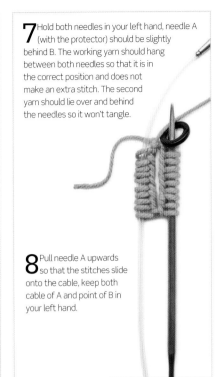

7 Hold both needles in your left hand, needle A (with the protector) should be slightly behind B. The working yarn should hang between both needles so that it is in the correct position and does not make an extra stitch. The second yarn should lie over and behind the needles so it won't tangle.

8 Pull needle A upwards so that the stitches slide onto the cable, keep both cable of A and point of B in your left hand.

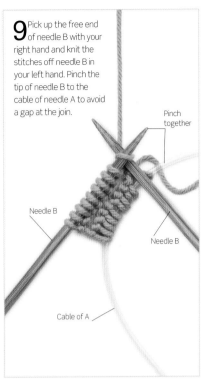

9 Pick up the free end of needle B with your right hand and knit the stitches off needle B in your left hand. Pinch the tip of needle B to the cable of needle A to avoid a gap at the join.

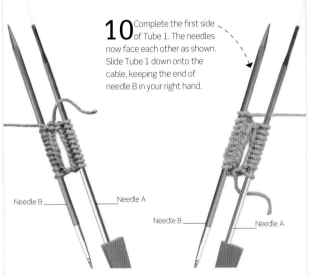

10 Complete the first side of Tube 1. The needles now face each other as shown. Slide Tube 1 down onto the cable, keeping the end of needle B in your right hand.

11 Slide Tube 2 up to the tips of the other end of needle B, and holding this end in your left hand knit the first side of Tube 2 with needle B.

12 Turn your work so that the working end of yarn is on the tip in your left hand, and slide a tube to each end. You will now see that you are halfway around both tubes.

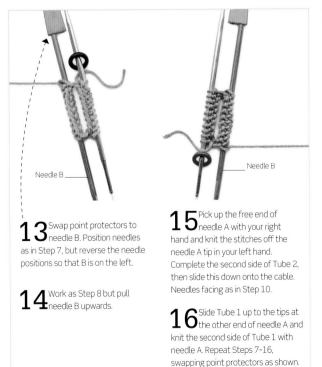

13 Swap point protectors to needle B. Position needles as in Step 7, but reverse the needle positions so that B is on the left.

14 Work as Step 8 but pull needle B upwards.

15 Pick up the free end of needle A with your right hand and knit the stitches off the needle A tip in your left hand. Complete the second side of Tube 2, then slide this down onto the cable. Needles facing as in Step 10.

16 Slide Tube 1 up to the tips at the other end of needle A and knit the second side of Tube 1 with needle A. Repeat Steps 7–16, swapping point protectors as shown.

TECHNIQUES

HELIX KNITTING

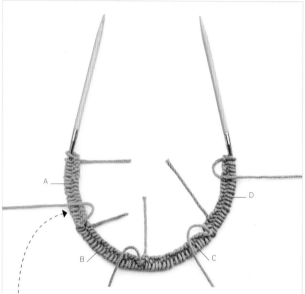

1 Cast on a quarter of the total number of stitches required in each colour, (for example if 80 stitches are required, cast on 20 in A, 20 in B, 20 in C, and 20 in D). Leave yarns attached.

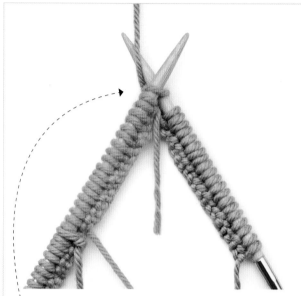

2 Without turning the needle, start to knit the colour A stitches off the left needle using the working thread of D. At colour joins, do not pull the new thread tight but keep the stitches even, otherwise the stripes will become distorted. Knit until all A stitches are worked.

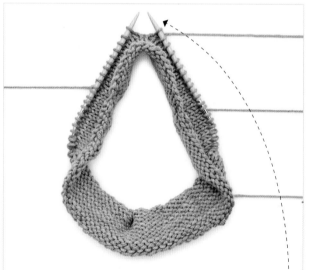

3 Pick up the working thread of A and knit the next colour. Continue to the end of each colour, picking up yarn above next colour.

4 After one round, there will be no yarn waiting at the end of the last colour, so work to the point at which the next yarn is attached, pick it up and continue as Step 3.

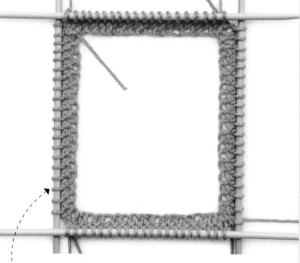

5 To work on double-pointed needles, using A, cast on, knit one round and join circle. Next round, knit a quarter of the stitches in A, followed by a quarter in the other three colours, one after the other on the next round. Continue as Steps 2–4.

WORKING WITH A SET OF FOUR DOUBLE-POINTED NEEDLES

1 Your knitting instructions will specify how many double-pointed needles to use for the project you are making – either a set of four or a set of five. When working with a set of four double-pointed needles, first cast on all the stitches required onto a single needle.

2 Slip some of the stitches off onto two other needles – your knitting pattern will tell you precisely how many to place on each needle. Ensure that the bottoms of the cast-on loops are all facing inwards.

Make sure stitches are not twisted

3 Place a stitch marker between the first and second stitches on the first needle to mark the beginning of the round. Then pull the first and third needles close together and start to knit with the fourth needle. Knit round and round in this way as for knitting with a circular needle.

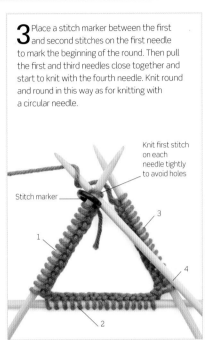

Knit first stitch on each needle tightly to avoid holes

Stitch marker

1

3

4

2

WORKING WITH A SET OF FIVE DOUBLE-POINTED NEEDLES

1 Cast on, distribute the stitches and position a stitch marker as for working with four needles, but distribute the stitches over four needles.

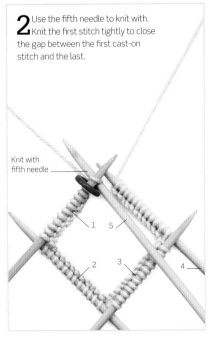

Stitch marker

Make sure stitches are not twisted

1

4

2

3

2 Use the fifth needle to knit with. Knit the first stitch tightly to close the gap between the first cast-on stitch and the last.

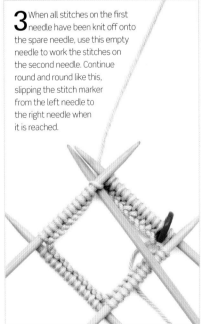

Knit with fifth needle

1

5

2

3

4

3 When all stitches on the first needle have been knit off onto the spare needle, use this empty needle to work the stitches on the second needle. Continue round and round like this, slipping the stitch marker from the left needle to the right needle when it is reached.

TECHNIQUES

SPIRAL KNITTING

1 Cast on 24 stitches and divide equally between three double-pointed needles (8 on each, see p.201).

2 Join the circle and add marker as you work first round as follows: knit 4 stitches, purl 4 stitches, repeat for complete round. Work another 3 rounds.

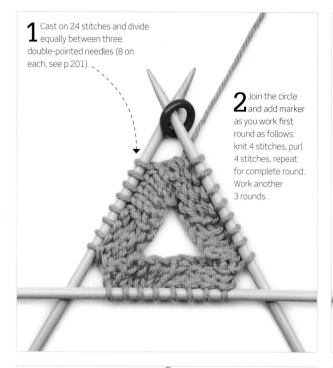

3 On the next row, purl the first stitch, then knit 4, purl 4 around complete round, finishing with purl 3 to meet the first purl stitch.

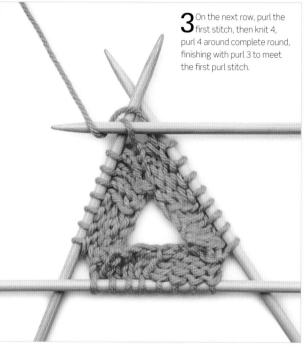

4 This has moved the whole rib one stitch over. Continue moving the rib one stitch in the same direction every four rows as you work the required length.

5 This technique is particularly successful as jewellery when it incorporates fancy and sparkly yarns or beading.

KNITTING MEDALLIONS

Knitted medallions are flat shapes knitted from the centre outwards. They are worked on a set of four or five double-pointed needles. Although the steps below show a square being worked, the technique is the same for knitting circles, hexagons, octagons, and so on.

WORKING A SIMPLE SQUARE

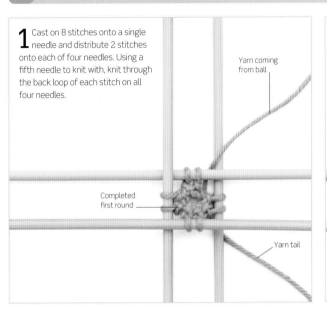

1 Cast on 8 stitches onto a single needle and distribute 2 stitches onto each of four needles. Using a fifth needle to knit with, knit through the back loop of each stitch on all four needles.

Yarn coming from ball

Completed first round

Yarn tail

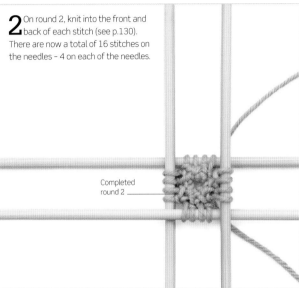

2 On round 2, knit into the front and back of each stitch (see p.130). There are now a total of 16 stitches on the needles – 4 on each of the needles.

Completed round 2

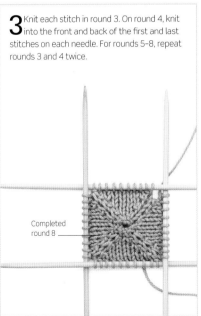

3 Knit each stitch in round 3. On round 4, knit into the front and back of the first and last stitches on each needle. For rounds 5–8, repeat rounds 3 and 4 twice.

Completed round 8

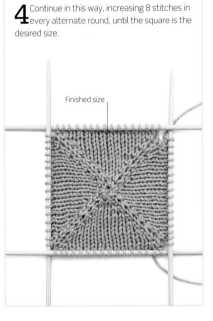

4 Continue in this way, increasing 8 stitches in every alternate round, until the square is the desired size.

Finished size

5 Cast off in the usual way, leaving a long yarn tail. Using a blunt-ended yarn needle, pass the yarn tail under the top of the first cast-off stitch and back though the centre of the fastened-off stitch. Darn in the yarn ends on the wrong side of the work, using the yarn end at the centre to pull the hole together if necessary.

Bobbles add texture to a surface. Whether large or small, they are created by making extra stitches and then decreasing them, which is why they stand proud of the main knitting.

REVERSE, TWICE KNIT, AND TUNISIAN

Reverse knitting is simply a quicker way of working. The techniques produce a quite different, firmer, and less stretchy result than traditional knitting. In some cases the results can look more like crochet than knitting and can be used for a similar effect.

REVERSE KNITTING

Reverse, or backwards, knitting is useful for narrow areas when frequent turning is otherwise required. When working Reverse knit stitches on Stocking stitch, every row is worked from the right side. Reverse knitting purl stitches is more unusual.

REVERSE KNIT STITCH

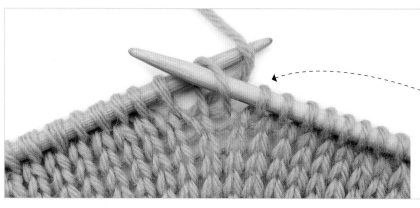

1 At the end of a knit row, do not turn the work.

2 Insert the left needle into the back of the first stitch on the right needle. Bring yarn forwards between the needles from left to right.

3 Slide the right needle along the left needle and slip the loop over the left tip, then slide the right needle down out of the old stitch.

REVERSE PURL STITCH

1 At the end of a purl row, do not turn the work. Keep yarn at front.

2 Insert the left needle from back to front through the left leg of the first stitch on the right needle and in front of the right needle. Take the yarn in an anticlockwise circle and between the needles from right to left.

3 Slide the left needle through the stitch backwards under the right needle to catch the loop. Slide the left needle to the right to slip the old stitch over the right tip.

TWICE KNIT KNITTING

Twice knit is not stretchy, which makes it very dense, and should be worked on larger needles than normal for the yarn. The stitches will work out wider than the rows unless larger needles are used, and work will be very slow to grow.

1 Cast on with Twice knitted cast-on (see p.101).

2 Knit two stitches together. Drop only the first stitch, leaving the second on the left needle.

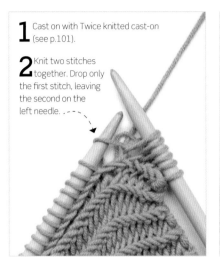

3 Insert the right needle into both the remaining stitch and the following one on the left needle and knit them together. Repeat this step to end of row.

4 Every row is knitted the same way. The resulting fabric is firm, slow to unravel or snag, and can be cut much like a woven fabric.

TUNISIAN KNITTING

Tunisian knitting results in flat, dense, and thick fabric that looks a little like crochet. It can be worked on standard needles, although it is usually worked loosely or on slightly larger needles than normal for the yarn. The first row is always a wrong side row.

1 Slip one stitch knitwise, then make a yarnover from front to back, taking yarn right round needle and to the front. Slip the next stitch knitwise, yarn over. Repeat this slip and yarnover along the row.

Slip stitch

2 The last yarnover will be loose, so hold it at the front with your left thumb. Turn the work, keeping thumb and yarnover in place (it will now be at the back of the work).

3 Work the next row by knitting each yarnover and stitch together through back of loop (k2 tbl). To start the row, insert the right needle into the back of the first stitch and yarn-over on left needle, bring yarn-over thread round the right needle (see p.137) and knit yarnover and first stitch together. Repeat steps 1–3.

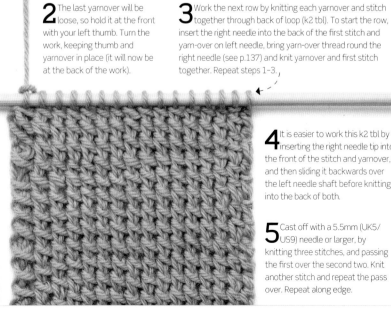

4 It is easier to work this k2 tbl by inserting the right needle tip into the front of the stitch and yarnover, and then sliding it backwards over the left needle shaft before knitting into the back of both.

5 Cast off with a 5.5mm (UK5/ US9) needle or larger, by knitting three stitches, and passing the first over the second two. Knit another stitch and repeat the pass over. Repeat along edge.

TECHNIQUES

FINISHING DETAILS

Finishing, as its name suggests, is the final stage of a project. Details that will make your knitting easier to assemble and look more professional, such as adding borders, hems, pockets and fastenings, can, with a little planning, be incorporated into the actual knitting itself.

PICKING UP STITCHES

Picking up edges is a technique that even experienced knitters can find challenging. Careful preparation and lots of practise will help. Try it out on small pieces of knitting to perfect the technique before moving on to more important projects.

CAST-ON/OFF EDGE

With RS facing, insert the needle in the first stitch. Leaving a long, loose end, wrap the yarn around the tip and pull it through, as if knitting a stitch. Continue, picking up and knitting one stitch through every cast-on or cast-off stitch.

ALONG ROW-ENDS

1 On lightweight or medium-weight yarn, pick up about three stitches for every four row-ends. To begin, mark out the row-ends on the right side of the knitting, placing a pin on the first of every four row-ends as shown here.

2 Pick up and knit the stitches as for picking up stitches along a cast-on edge, inserting the tip through the centre of the edge stitches. Skip every fourth row-end.

Remove pin before picking up stitch

Skipped row-ends

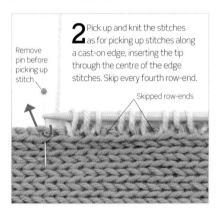

WITH A CROCHET HOOK

1 Use a hook that fits through the stitches. With RS facing, insert the hook through the first stitch, wrap the hook behind and around the yarn from left to right and pull through.

Yarn going to ball

Yarn tail

2 Transfer the loop on the hook onto a needle. Pull yarn to tighten. Repeat, transferring the loops to the needle.

TIPS FOR PICKING UP STITCHES

• **A yarn in a contrasting colour** is used in the step-by-step instructions for picking up stitches to clearly illustrate the process. You can hide picking-up imperfections, however, if you use a matching yarn. For a contrasting border, switch to the new colour on the first row of the border.

• **Always pick up** and knit stitches with the right side of the knitting facing you, as picking up stitches creates a ridge on the wrong side.

• **Your knitting pattern** will specify which needle size to use for picking up stitches – usually one size smaller than the size used for the main knitting.

• **After you have picked up** the required number of stitches, work the border following the directions in your pattern, whether it is ribbing, moss stitch, garter stitch, or a fold-over hem.

• **It is difficult** to pick up stitches "evenly" along an edge. To help, try casting it off again, either looser or tighter. If this doesn't work, pull out the border and try again, adjusting the number of stitches or spreading them out in a different way. Alternatively, try a smaller needle size if the border looks too stretched, or a larger needle size if it looks too tight.

ALONG A CURVED EDGE

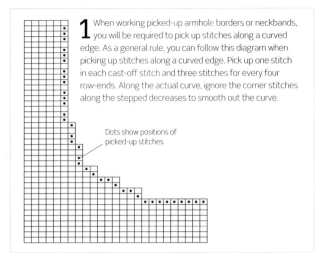

1 When working picked-up armhole borders or neckbands, you will be required to pick up stitches along a curved edge. As a general rule, you can follow this diagram when picking up stitches along a curved edge. Pick up one stitch in each cast-off stitch and three stitches for every four row-ends. Along the actual curve, ignore the corner stitches along the stepped decreases to smooth out the curve.

Dots show positions of picked-up stitches

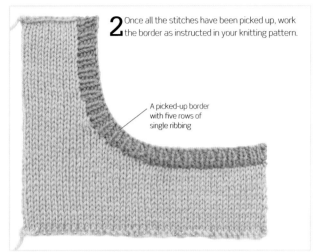

2 Once all the stitches have been picked up, work the border as instructed in your knitting pattern.

A picked-up border with five rows of single ribbing

SELVEDGES

The selvedge can make all the difference to a free edge and there are many methods that are decorative as well as functional. Loose edges can be tightened with Chain or Slipped garter and rolling edges controlled with a Garter selvedge. Both selvedges do not have to be worked the same.

GARTER SELVEDGE

1 This is best for edges that will not be sewn together as it can make a bumpy seam. It encourages the edge of Stocking stitch to lie flat. Each "bump" equals two rows.

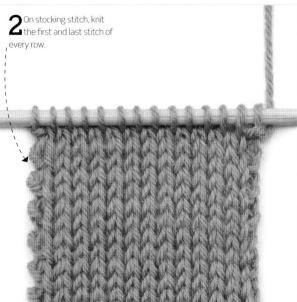

2 On stocking stitch, knit the first and last stitch of every row.

SLIPPED GARTER SELVEDGE

Firmer than Garter selvedge.

1 Slip first stitch knitwise and knit last stitch on all rows.

2 The resulting edge is firmer than Garter selvedge, and smoother. The slipped stitches can aid picking up on some projects.

DOUBLE SLIPPED GARTER SELVEDGE

Good for slightly decorative free edges.

1 Work all rows the same. Insert the right needle into back of first stitch from right to left and slip the stitch.

2 Knit the second stitch. Work as pattern to two from end of row and knit the last two stitches.

CHAIN SELVEDGE

Best for picking up stitches into (see pp.208–209), Crochet edgings, and Backstitch (but not Mattress stitch) seams (see p.227).

1 On Stocking stitch, all right side rows slip first stitch knitwise, and knit last stitch. On all wrong side rows, slip first stitch purlwise, and purl last stitch.

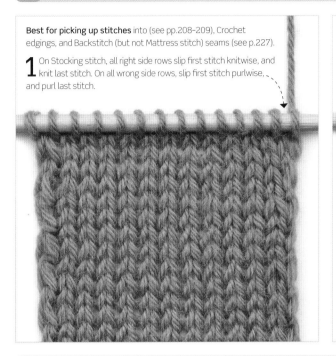

2 On Garter stitch, with yarn in front slip first stitch purlwise, yarn back and knit to end.

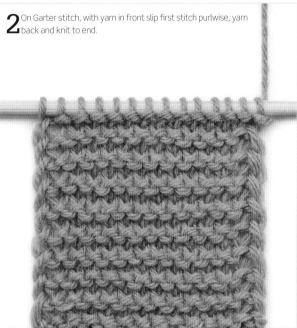

PICOT LOOP SELVEDGE

1 Right side rows, insert right needle knitwise into first two stitches, bring yarn around front of right needle from left to right and work a yarnover (see p.137) whilst knitting first two stitches together. Knit to last two stitches, slip them knitwise one by one and insert left needle into front to make an ssk decrease (see p.140).

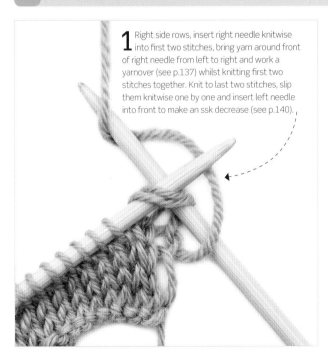

2 Wrong side rows, loosely work a purl yarnover (see p.137, hold it open with your thumb if necessary), and purl rest of row. On garter stitch, purl first and last two stitches.

PICOT POINT SELVEDGE

1 On stocking stitch on a knit row, knit-on cast-on two stitches, then cast off knitwise the same two stitches.

2 Slip the remaining stitch on the left needle without twisting onto the right needle. Knit to end of row.

3 On the purl row, cast on two stitches as Step 1, yarn to front and cast off both stitches purlwise (see p.107).

4 Yarn to front, slip remaining stitch on left needle, without twisting, onto right needle. Purl to end of row.

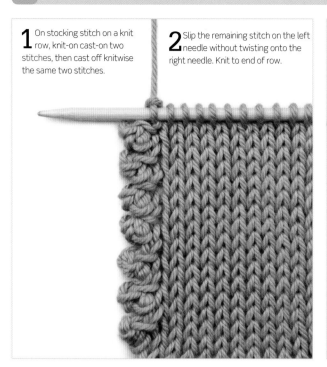
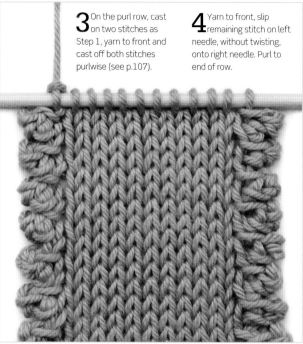

FRINGED SELVEDGE

1 For a four stitch fringed selvedge, using Single cast-on (see p.87), cast on knit width plus an extra eight stitches. Work as many rows as required in stocking stitch or a variation of knit and purl stitches. On the last row drop four stitches at each end of the row. Cast off the remaining stitches.

2 Unravel the edge stitches all the way down the fabric. To make the fringe straight, thread a long needle through all loops and block them whilst stretched flat (see p.227).

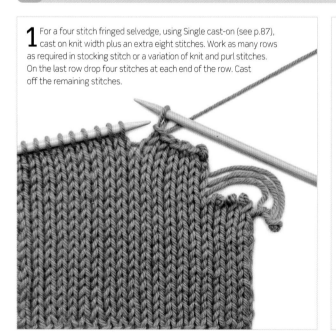
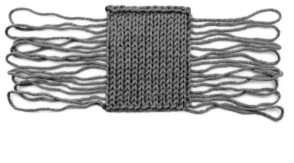

BUTTONHOLES

The simplest form of buttonhole is an eyelet, but there are techniques for larger, stronger ones that will take different sized buttons. Although horizontal buttonholes are the most common, vertical and diagonal variations are also included in this section.

POSITIONING BUTTONS AND BUTTONHOLES

Decide on the number of buttons before knitting buttonholes. Work holes to match button size. Top and bottom buttons are usually positioned between 1cm (½in) and 3cm (1¼in) from neck and hem edge. Start buttonholes at least 3 stitches from the edge. Count rows and stitches, as measuring may be inaccurate. For vertically worked bands, knit and attach the buttonband first. Mark the top and bottom button position with thread.

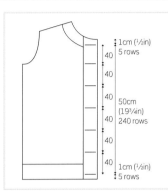

1cm (½in) 5 rows
40
40
40
50cm (19¾in) 240 rows
40
40
40
1cm (½in) 5 rows

1 Knit the buttonhole band, working the calculated number of rows between buttonholes, allowing two rows for a two-row buttonhole. Work vertical buttonhole rows so that they centre on the marker.

2 For a horizontally worked picked up buttonband, count stitches rather than rows to calculate the spacing as described in Step 1.

MAKING BUTTON LOOPS

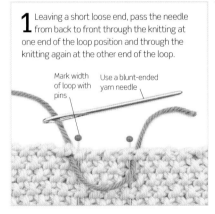

1 Leaving a short loose end, pass the needle from back to front through the knitting at one end of the loop position and through the knitting again at the other end of the loop.

Mark width of loop with pins
Use a blunt-ended yarn needle

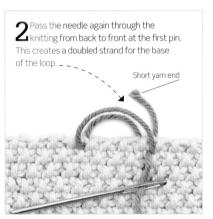

2 Pass the needle again through the knitting from back to front at the first pin. This creates a doubled strand for the base of the loop.

Short yarn end

3 Work buttonhole stitches tightly over the doubled strand and the short yarn end. Secure the yarn to the knitting. Pass the yarn through a few buttonhole stitches and trim.

KNITTED BUTTON LOOP

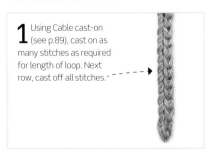

1 Using Cable cast-on (see p.89), cast on as many stitches as required for length of loop. Next row, cast off all stitches.

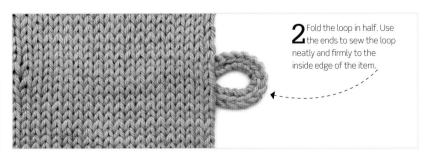

2 Fold the loop in half. Use the ends to sew the loop neatly and firmly to the inside edge of the item.

REINFORCED EYELET BUTTONHOLE

1 On a knit row, work to position of buttonhole. Make a yarnover (see p.136). Work to end of row.

2 On next row, slip the yarnover purlwise and make another front to back yarnover. Work to end of row.

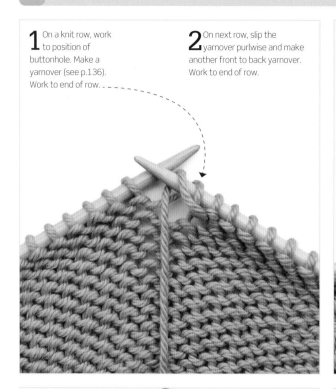

3 On next row, slip the stitch before the yarnovers knitwise. Knit both yarnovers together but do not drop from left needle.

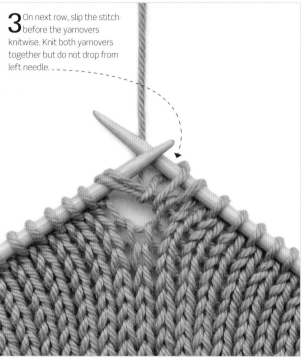

4 Pass slipped stitch over the newly made stitch. Knit three stitches together (the yarnovers and the following stitch). Work to end of row.

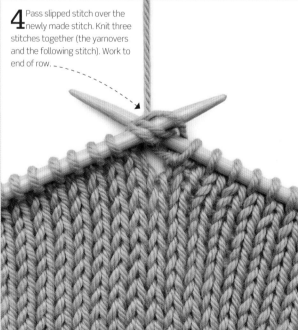

5 This buttonhole is stronger and neater than a simple eyelet buttonhole (see p.159).

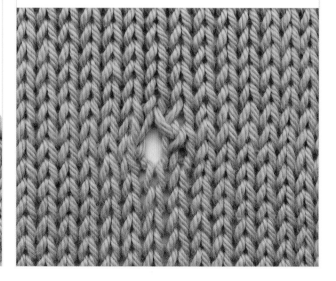

ONE ROW HORIZONTAL BUTTONHOLE

A strong buttonhole which is worked on Stocking stitch in this example, but looks particularly neat on a Garter stitch or Reverse stocking stitch project.

1 Work to buttonhole position (this should be a knit row on reverse stocking stitch). Yarn to front. Slip one stitch purlwise. Yarn back.

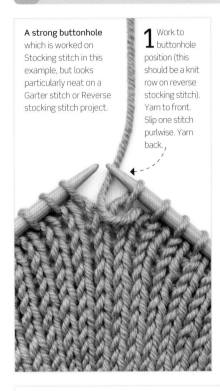

2 Slip one stitch purlwise and pass previous stitch over. Repeat this step across the number of buttonhole stitches required.

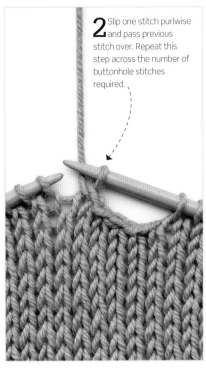

3 Slip last stitch on right needle back to the left. Turn work. Yarn back.

4 Cast on the number of stitches for the buttonhole using Cable cast-on (see p.89). Cast on one more stitch, bring yarn forwards after making stitch but before placing it on left needle. Turn work.

5 Slip one stitch knitwise and pass the last cast-on stitch over it. Work rest of row.

6 This buttonhole is worked the same on Reverse stocking stitch.

TECHNIQUES

Lace can be one of the most delicate knits. Even a simple lace pattern such as Eyelet mesh stitch (see p.61), which only requires you to learn to yarn over and knit two together, can be highly effective.

CAST-OFF HORIZONTAL BUTTONHOLE

1 On a knit row, work to buttonhole position. Work two more stitches before passing one over the other in a knitwise cast-off (see p.106) for the number of buttonhole stitches. When the last cast-off loop is on right needle, slip the first stitch on left needle onto right needle and pass last cast-off loop over this stitch. Pull yarn tight. Work next row to buttonhole.

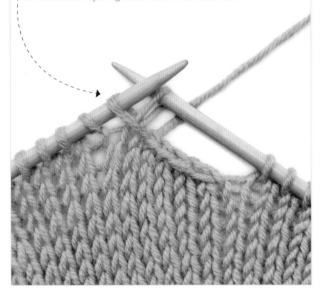

2 For advanced completion using buttonhole cast-on, miss this step and work Steps 3–5. For simple completion, turn work and use Cable cast-on (see p.89). When last cast-on loop is still on right needle bring yarn to front between needles and transfer the stitch to the left needle. Yarn to back, turn, and knit rest of row. Buttonhole is now completed.

3 Drop left needle (use point protector to retain stitches if necessary) and work only with right. Hold yarn and needle in right hand. With left thumb pointing downwards, pick up yarn from behind, and wind thumb to right in an anticlockwise circle so yarn crosses near needle. Insert right needle into front thumb loop.

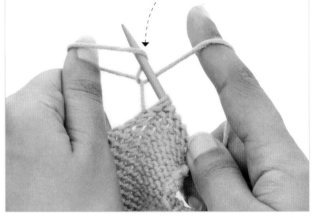

4 Bring left index finger from beneath, catching the yarn. Take yarn left behind needle and then wind to right, over needle.

5 Slip thumb loop over point of right needle. Hold new loop in place with right index finger and tighten yarn with left hand, making sure the loop goes all round the needle. Repeat for each cast-on stitch. Knit to end of row.

INCREASED HORIZONTAL BUTTONHOLE

1 Work to buttonhole position. Work two more stitches before passing one over the other in a knitwise cast-off (see p.106) for number of buttonhole stitches (five in this example).

2 When last cast-off loop is on right needle, slip it onto left needle and pass second stitch over cast-off loop. Pull yarn tight

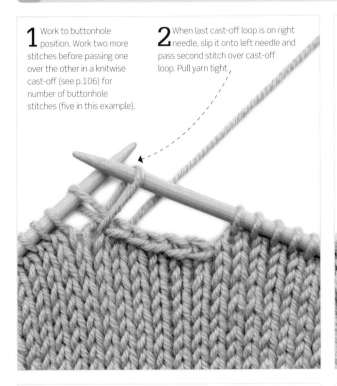

3 Yarn over twice (once for a two to three stitch buttonhole – dependant on tension and yarn). Knit to end of row.

4 Next row, work to the yarnovers. Drop the yarnovers and pull up the end stitch on the left needle so that it draws the yarn from the overs and is elongated.

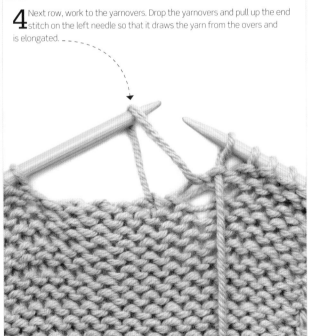

5 Purl into front and back (see p.130) repeatedly for the same number of times as stitches cast off plus one. Work to end of row.

VERTICAL BUTTONHOLE

1 This example is in Stocking stitch. Work to position of buttonhole. Slip the stitches that will be to the left of the buttonhole onto a stitch holder. Turn work.

2 Work right side of buttonhole starting with a purl row, making a chain selvedge (see p.211) by slipping first edge stitch purlwise on all wrong side rows, and knitting last edge stitch on all right side rows.

3 Once right side is long enough, finish on a purl side row, cut yarn with a long tail and slip right side stitches onto another holder. Slip held stitches back onto left needle with knit side facing. Join in new end of yarn (leaving a long tail) and make a right lifted increase (see p.132) between the first and second stitches.

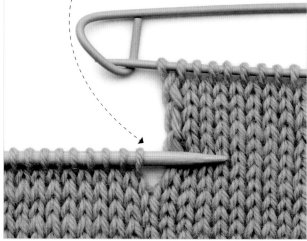

4 Slip the last stitch knitwise on the next and all wrong side rows and knit it into the back of the first stitch on all right side rows. This creates a variation of a chain selvedge on the left side of the buttonhole.

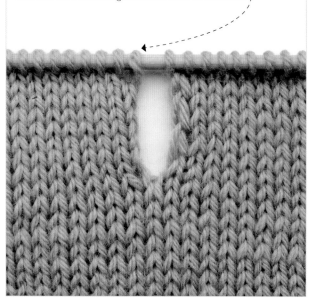

5 When both sides have equal rows, making sure you finish on a purl row, cut the yarn with a long tail and restore all stitches to the needles in the correct order. Join yarn in and work a complete row, working the two selvedge stitches of the buttonhole together. Sew in ends neatly.

DIAGONAL BUTTONHOLE

1 Working in stocking stitch. Knit to position of buttonhole. Slip the stitches that will be to the left of the buttonhole onto a stitch holder. Turn work. Slip first stitch purlwise. Make a yarnover. Purl to end.

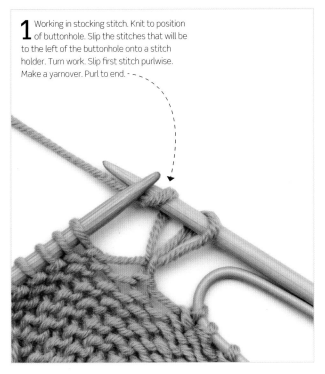

2 Knit next row to yarnover, and knit into back of yarn-over, twisting it to close the hole. Knit last stitch. Repeat for required length of buttonhole, ending with a purl row. Repeat knit instruction in Step 1.

3 Cut yarn with a long tail and slip right side stitches onto another holder. Slip held stitches back onto the left needle with knit side facing. Join in new end of yarn and make a right lifted increase (see p.132) between the first and second stitches.

4 Knit into the back of the first stitch and knit to end. Purl next row to three stitches from end. Purl next two stitches together and slip last stitch knitwise. Repeat this step for required length of buttonhole, ending with a purl row.

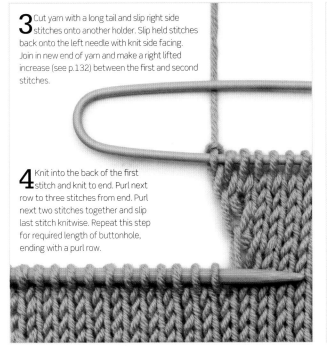

5 Cut yarn with a long tail and restore all stitches to needles in the correct order. Join yarn in and work a complete row, working the two selvedge stitches of the buttonhole together. Sew in ends neatly. To slant the buttonhole the other way, reverse the increase and decrease.

POCKETS

Patch pockets can be knitted separately and sewn on or picked up from the main knitting. Inset versions are particularly neat on garments and can be edged with textural and colour stitch details, and even knitted in lighter yarns to avoid bulk.

PICKED-UP PATCH POCKET

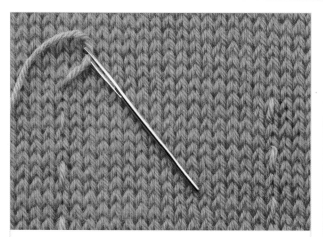

1 Work garment piece first. Tack the side and bottom position of the pocket on the garment with thin contrast colour yarn. To ensure a straight pocket bottom, either pick up into the row after welt or tack through left side of stitches along the base row.

2 Thread pocket yarn on a large-eyed needle, take the end to the wrong side and secure it, leaving a long tail. Have a knitting needle ready to receive stitches as they are made. Starting at the lower right-hand corner of the marked stitches, insert a crochet hook through the middle of the "V" of the first stitch, under the top loop and back out to the front. Lay the yarn from right to left into the hook, and draw a loop of yarn through.

3 Slip loop onto right needle. Repeat Steps 2 and 3 to left along the row for each pocket base stitch.

4 Beginning with a wrong side row, work as many rows as necessary for the pocket depth, adding a ribbed or patterned welt as desired. Cast off.

5 Sew sides in place with Mattress stitch (see p.227) using the yarn ends if possible. Remove tacking stitches.

HORIZONTAL INSET POCKET

1 Knit the pocket lining before you knit the garment piece, this will be two stitches wider than the cast off for the pocket. Leave on needle after working last knit row or put on stitch holder.

2 With right side facing, work to pocket position. Cast-off knitwise (see p.106) the stitches for the pocket opening and knit to end of row.

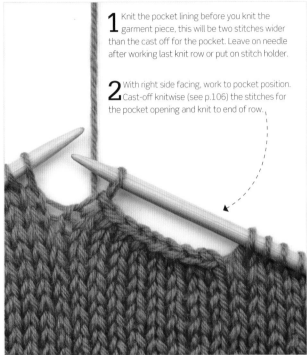

3 Turn and purl back to one stitch from pocket position. Take needle with lining stitches on it in left hand, and purl last main stitch and first lining stitch together.

4 Purl across lining stitches. Purl last stitch together with first one on left needle. Continue. Complete garment piece.

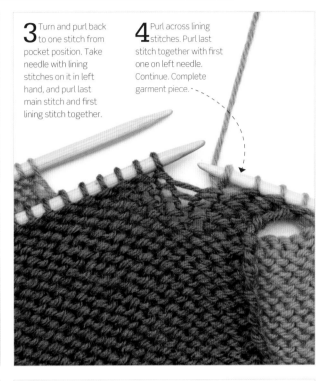

5 An alternative to Step 2 is to place the opening stitches without casting off onto a stitch holder. This allows you to knit an edging to the pocket later on.

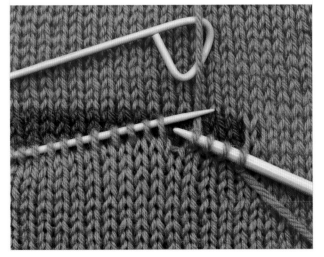

6 When sewing garment together, whipstitch the lining to the garment without pulling the stitches too tight. This example has a contrast lining, but the lining would normally be made in the main yarn.

TECHNIQUES

VERTICAL INSET POCKET

1 The opening is at the left of the actual pocket in this example, and the lining is worked at the same time as the pocket front. On a right side row, work to pocket position, slip remaining stitches on left needle onto a stitch holder.

2 Work front of pocket: Turn work and work Garter stitch edge border by knitting first two stitches, purling the rest of the row. On next row, work to two from end and then knit both edge stitches. Continue to work rows, with border stitches included, for depth of pocket. Finish pocket front by working a purl row and slip stitches onto a stitch holder. Cut yarn with a long end.

3 The right side and lining is worked in one: with right side facing, slip stitches off first stitch holder onto a needle, unless you use a double-pointed needle, you may need to transfer them from this needle to one that has its tip facing to the right. Join in yarn.

4 Cable cast-on (see p.89) the number of stitches required for width of pocket lining. Turn and work the same number of rows for the lining and left side as were worked for the pocket front. End with a purl row.

5 Join top of pocket: With right side facing, slip stitches off second stitch holder onto a needle pointing right (stitch holder should be pointing left). Knit next row. At pocket position, place lining needle behind left needle and knit them together. Complete row.

6 Complete piece and sew lining to garment front.

HEMS

A traditional ribbed hem is often knitted at the start of a garment, whereas others may be sewn on afterwards. Colour detail and stitch structures such as Garter stitch, Moss stitch, or Cables can be incorporated to add flair to hems. Hems make great cuffs and can be added vertically along front openings. They also make good accessory trims.

PICKED UP HEM

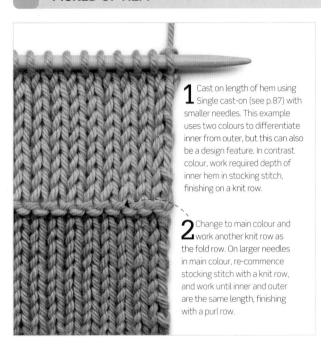

1 Cast on length of hem using Single cast-on (see p.87) with smaller needles. This example uses two colours to differentiate inner from outer, but this can also be a design feature. In contrast colour, work required depth of inner hem in stocking stitch, finishing on a knit row.

2 Change to main colour and work another knit row as the fold row. On larger needles in main colour, re-commence stocking stitch with a knit row, and work until inner and outer are the same length, finishing with a purl row.

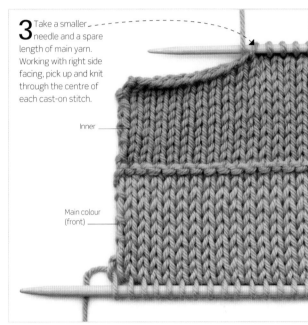

3 Take a smaller needle and a spare length of main yarn. Working with right side facing, pick up and knit through the centre of each cast-on stitch.

Inner

Main colour (front)

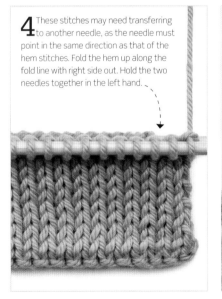

4 These stitches may need transferring to another needle, as the needle must point in the same direction as that of the hem stitches. Fold the hem up along the fold line with right side out. Hold the two needles together in the left hand.

5 Taking a larger needle and re-joining main yarn if necessary, knit the corresponding stitches of both needles together onto the right needle.

6 Block hem with garment to achieve the final effect.

TECHNIQUES

PICOT HEM

1 Using smaller needles, cast on an even number of stitches to the length of the hem using Single cast-on (see p.87).

2 Work required depth of hem in Stocking stitch, ending with a purl row.

3 Next row, knit first two stitches together (see p.139), make a yarnover by bringing yarn forwards and back over the needle (see p.137). Repeat to end of row.

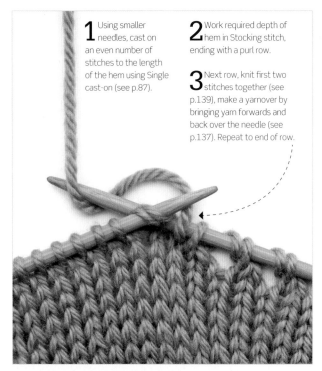

Yarnover lace holes

4 Change to larger needles. Knit stitches and yarnovers on first row, work equal depth of hem in stocking stitch, ending on a purl row.

5 When piece is completed, fold the hem up at lace holes with wrong sides together. Pin so that the stitches are in line. Working from the wrong side, oversew in place along a row using hem yarn and blunt-ended needle as follows: insert needle into a reverse stitch loop and then its vertically matching cast-on loop, pull yarn through and repeat. Do not allow the sewing to pucker the knitting.

6 Block hem with garment to achieve final effect.

BLOCKING

Always refer to your yarn label before blocking. Textured stitch patterns, such as Garter stitch, ribbing, and cables, are best wet blocked or steamed extremely gently so that their texture is not altered – they should not be pressed or stretched.

WET BLOCKING

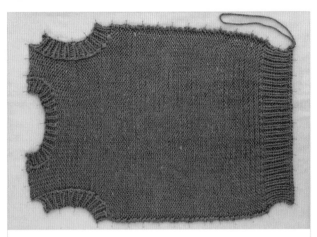

If your yarn allows, wet blocking is the best way to even out your knitting. Using lukewarm water, either wash the piece or simply wet it. Squeeze and lay it flat on a towel, then roll the towel to squeeze out more moisture. Pin the piece into shape on layers of dry towels covered with a sheet. Leave to dry.

STEAM BLOCKING

Only steam block if your yarn allows. Pin the piece to the correct shape, then place a clean damp cloth on top. Use a warm iron to create steam, barely touching the cloth. Do not rest the iron on the knitting, and avoid any garter stitch or ribbed areas. Before removing the pins, let the piece dry completely.

SEAMS

The most popular seam techniques for knitting are Mattress stitch, Edge-to-edge stitch, Backstitch, and Overcast stitch. Cast-off and Grafted seams are sometimes called for and learning to graft open stitches together for a seamless join is very useful.

TIPS

- **Block knitted pieces** before sewing together. After seams are completed, open them out and steam very lightly if the yarn allows.
- **Always use** a blunt-ended yarn needle for all seams on knitting. A pointed needle will puncture the yarn strands and you won't be able to pull the yarn through the knitting successfully.
- **Although the seams** are shown here worked in a contrasting yarn for clarity, use a matching yarn for all seams.
- **If knitting** is in a fancy yarn, find a smooth strong yarn of a similar colour to sew in. It is generally better, particularly with mattress stitch, to work with shorter lengths as long strands become weakened and may break.
- **Before starting a seam**, pin the knitting together at wide intervals. At the start of the seam, secure the yarn to the edge of one piece of knitting with two or three overcast stitches.
- **Make seams firm** but not too tight. They should have a little elasticity, to match the elasticity of the knitted fabric.

MATTRESS STITCH

1 Mattress stitch is practically invisible and is the best seam technique for ribbing and stocking stitch. Start by aligning the edges of the pieces to be seamed with both the right sides facing you.

2 Insert the needle from the front through centre of first knit stitch on one piece of knitting and up through centre of stitch two rows above. Repeat on the other piece, working up the seam and pulling edges together.

FIGURE OF EIGHT START FOR SEAMS

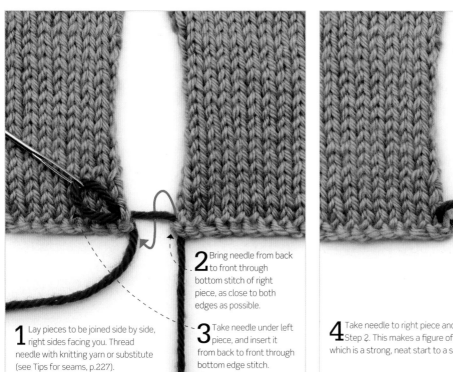

2 Bring needle from back to front through bottom stitch of right piece, as close to both edges as possible.

1 Lay pieces to be joined side by side, right sides facing you. Thread needle with knitting yarn or substitute (see Tips for seams, p.227).

3 Take needle under left piece, and insert it from back to front through bottom edge stitch.

4 Take needle to right piece and repeat Step 2. This makes a figure of eight which is a strong, neat start to a seam.

5 To use before Mattress stitch, after Step 4, take needle back under the left piece and bring it through the same place as before. This positions the first stitch in the correct place.

EDGE-TO-EDGE SEAM

This seam is suitable for most stitch patterns. To start, align the pieces of knitting with the wrong sides facing you. Work each stitch of the seam through the little pips formed along the edges of knitting as shown.

Wrong sides

BACKSTITCH SEAM

Backstitch can be used for almost any seam on knitting, but is not suitable for super-bulky yarns.

1 Align the pieces of knitting with the right sides together. Make one stitch forwards, and one stitch back into the starting point of the previous stitch as shown. Work the stitches as close to the edge of the knitting as possible.

Right sides of knitting together

OVERCAST SEAM

This seam is also called an Oversewn seam or a Whipped stitch seam.

1 With the right sides together, insert the needle from back to front through both layers, working through the centres of the edge stitches (not through the pips). Make each stitch in the same way.

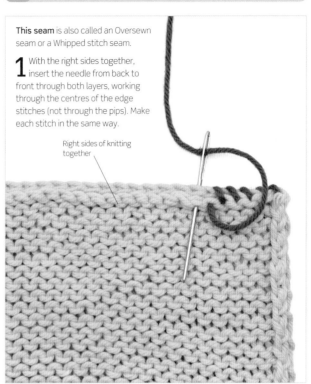

Right sides of knitting together

GRAFTED SEAM

This seam can be worked along two pieces of knitting that have not been cast off or along two cast-off edges as shown here; the principle for both is the same.

1 With the right sides facing you, follow the path of a row of knitting along the seam as shown.

2 When worked in a matching yarn as here, the seam blends in completely and makes it look like a continuous piece of knitting.

GRAFTING OPEN STITCHES TOGETHER

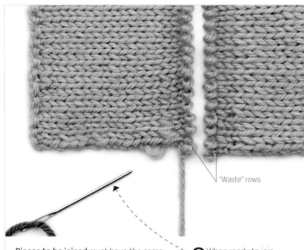

"Waste" rows

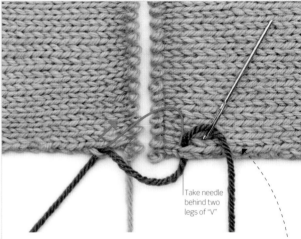

Take needle behind two legs of "V"

Pieces to be joined must have the same number of stitches. Knit row stitches can be recognized as "Vs".

1 At the end of main knitting, do not cast off, but knit four rows of stocking stitch "waste" rows in a thinner, contrast coloured yarn. Leave on needles or holder.

2 When ready to join pieces, remove needle or holder. Lay pieces right side up, open edges facing as shown. Thread a blunt-ended needle, ideally with a long end from one of the rows to be grafted.

3 Insert needle from the back through the first main colour stitch on the left piece (so it comes out through the "V" of the stitch).

4 Insert needle from front through main colour edge loop on the right, across behind two "legs" (behind "V"), and out to the front between two stitches (between "V"s).

5 Continue, taking the needle back into the "V" of the left-hand stitch that it emerges from, behind the two "legs" and out of the next "V". Gently pull yarn until sewn stitch is same size as knit stitches. As you pull, fold the waste fabric under to close the gap.

6 Repeat, taking needle to right side.

7 Repeat Steps 5 and 6 along the row. Secure the ends and unravel the waste yarns. With more experience it becomes possible to graft the pieces together straight off the needles without knitting waste rows.

SEWING ON AN EDGING

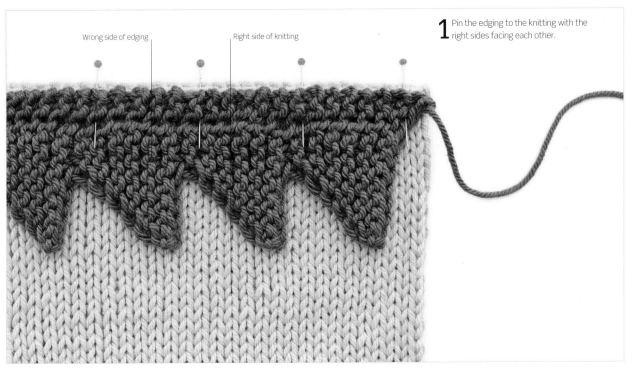

1 Pin the edging to the knitting with the right sides facing each other.

Wrong side of edging

Right side of knitting

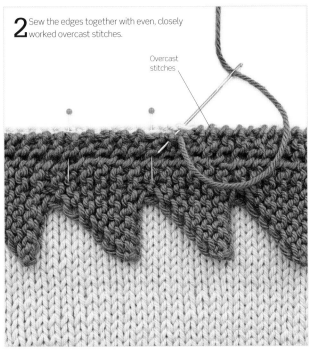

2 Sew the edges together with even, closely worked overcast stitches.

Overcast stitches

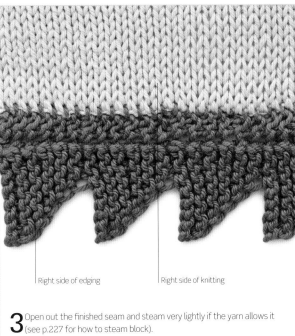

Right side of edging

Right side of knitting

3 Open out the finished seam and steam very lightly if the yarn allows it (see p.227 for how to steam block).

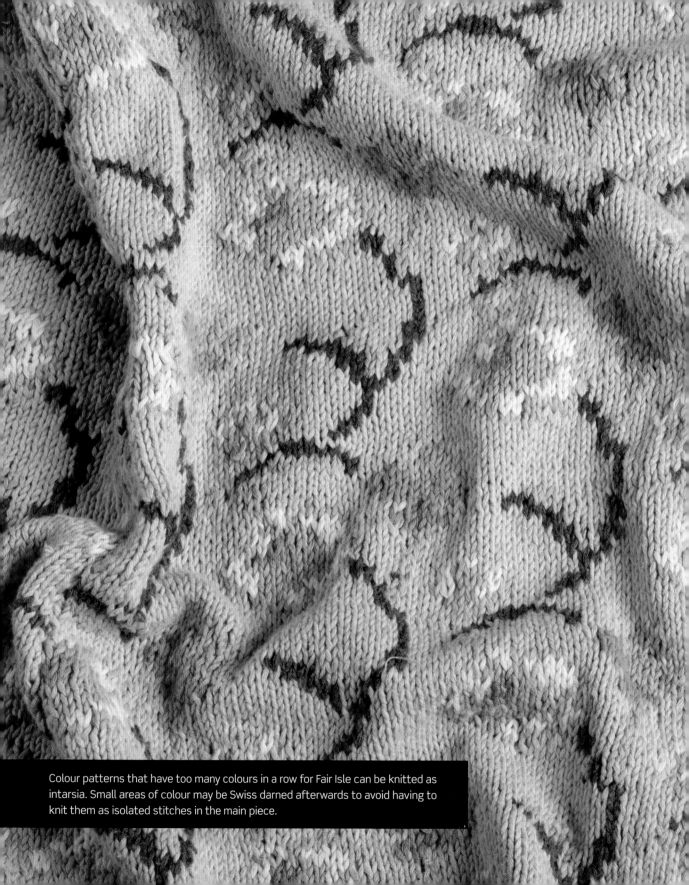

Colour patterns that have too many colours in a row for Fair Isle can be knitted as intarsia. Small areas of colour may be Swiss darned afterwards to avoid having to knit them as isolated stitches in the main piece.

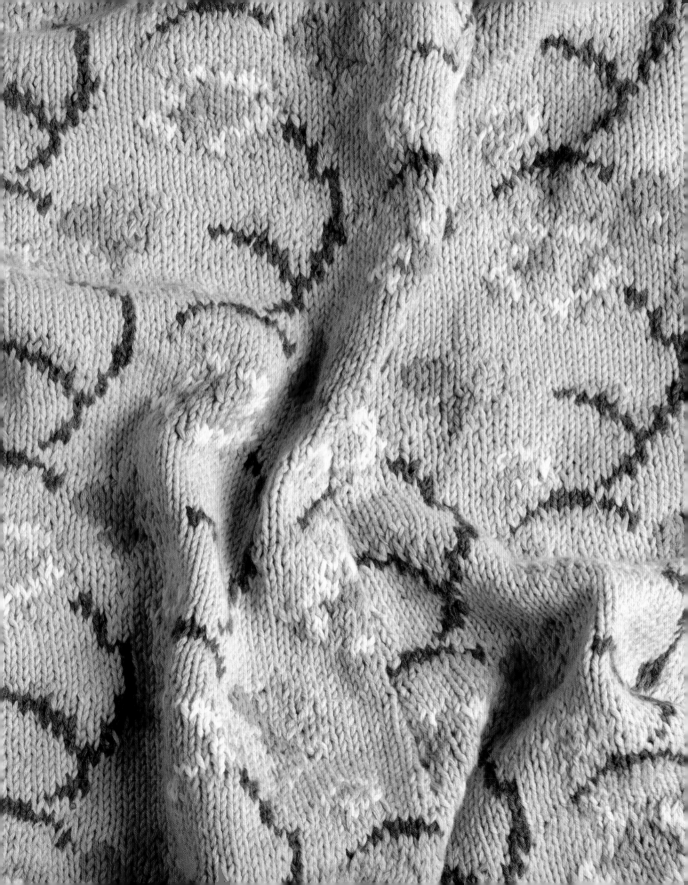

CUTTING INTO YOUR KNITTING

Cutting can be a time-saving way of completing projects, particularly for circular knitted garments. Hairy wool that clings to itself and felts slightly when washed is ideal. "Steek" or "bridge" are common terms for the extra stitches knitted where openings will later be cut. You can machine sew edges prior to picking up.

STEEKS OR BRIDGES

1 To work a steek as, for example, a cardigan opening, cast on an extra nine stitches for the steek at the centre front. Work these stitches in one stitch vertical stripes if knitting Fair Isle and in stocking stitch when working with one colour. Use markers to identify the steek.

2 Work complete front. Block the piece and cut straight up the centre stitch of the steek. If the knitting unravels easily, run a line of small machine stitches along inside the open edge to prevent them unravelling further.

3 Pick up and knit (see p.208) between the last steek stitch and the first main fabric stitch all along the edge. Work required edging. Cast off.

4 Turn work inside out, trim any unravelled ends with sharp scissors and oversew the cut edge down to the back of the main fabric using main colour yarn. Sew back, crossing the first stitches.

5 The cut edge is neatly folded under and invisible on the right side of the completed cardigan opening.

FASTENINGS

Choose an appropriate size and material for your project. Although nylon and plastic fastenings are lighter and less obtrusive, metallic or contrast coloured ones can make a statement. Riveted press studs can be used; insert the shank between stitches and when connecting top to bottom, make sure there are no sharp edges to cut stitches.

ATTACHING PRESS STUDS

The male side of the stud goes on the inside of the outer of a garment. Decide position of studs. Measuring can be inaccurate; count exact stitches and rows on each piece and mark positions with contrast thread.

1 Make a knot and sew in end of thread at marker, catching only half of each strand of yarn so that stitches don't go through to right side. Place stud in position centrally over marker and insert needle inwards through surface of yarn near a stud hole just below the stud edge, then bring it up through the stud hole.

2 Repeat this three or four times through each hole, never taking the needle through to the right side. Move needle to next hole and repeat. To secure thread, sew two small backstitches, then sew a loop, thread the needle back through and pull tightly to secure thread.

SEWING IN A ZIP

1 Match colour and weight of zip to yarn, and knit length of garment to match zip lengths available. Work a Garter stitch selvedge (see p.209) at the zip edge.

2 Close the zip. With RS facing, pin the top and bottom of knitting to the zip first, making sure the teeth are covered by the knitted edge. Pin the centre, then the centres of the remaining sections, easing the rows so they are evenly distributed. Pin horizontally rather than vertically. Do one side at a time and use plenty of pins.

3 Tack the zip in place with contrast sewing thread, sewing between the same vertical lines of stitches.

4 With a sharp large-eyed needle and knitting yarn (or matching sewing thread), backstitch neatly upwards from hem, sewing between the same vertical lines of stitches.

5 Turn garment inside out. With knitting yarn, or matching sewing thread, slip stitch outer edges of zip to knitting, sewing into the back of the same vertical lines of stitches.

TECHNIQUES

EMBELLISHMENTS

Plain knitting sometimes calls out for a little embellishment. Embroidery, a few well placed beads, or a decorative edging are good candidates for the perfect finishing touch. Pockets, collars, hems, and cuffs are ideal positions for these.

BEAD KNITTING

Choose beads carefully, glass beads are attractive, but can weigh knitting down. Make sure that the bead hole is large enough for the yarn, or consider using a second thread or enclosing large beads. Beaded cast-on or cast-off make effective edgings.

THREADING BEADS ONTO YARN

Make sure you have the right beads before starting to thread them onto the yarn. Consider their size and weight. If your knitting is to be entirely covered with scattered beads, large heavy beads will be unsuitable as they would weigh the knitting down too much. Adding a little weight to the knitting can, however, produce the extra drape needed for a graceful shawl, scarf, or evening knit.

Thread the beads onto the yarn before you begin knitting. The last bead to be used is threaded on first and the first bead to be used is threaded on last. Fold a short length of sewing thread in half, thread both cut ends together through the eye of an ordinary sewing needle, and pass the end of the yarn through the sewing-thread loop. Thread the beads onto the sewing needle, over the thread and onto the yarn.

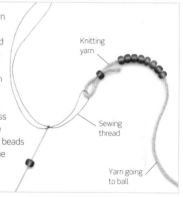

Knitting yarn

Sewing thread

Yarn going to ball

SLIP STITCH BEADING

1 There is usually a chart provided for positioning the beads on Slip stitch beading, unless only a few beads are to be added, in which case the bead placements will be within the written instructions. The sample chart here illustrates how slip-stitch beads are staggered. This is because the slipped stitches at the bead positions pull in the knitting and alternating the bead placements evens out the fabric.

□ = k on RS rows, p on WS rows
● = place bead and slip stitch

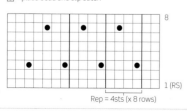

8

1 (RS)

Rep = 4sts (x 8 rows)

2 The beads are placed on knit (right-side) rows. Knit to the position of the bead, then bring the yarn to the front (right side) of the work between the two needles. Slide the bead up close to the knitting and slip the next stitch purlwise from the left needle to right needle.

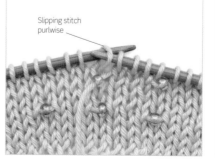

Slipping stitch purlwise

3 Take the yarn to the wrong side between the two needles, leaving the bead sitting on the right side in front of the stitch just slipped. Knit the next stitch firmly to tighten the strand holding the bead at the front.

Slipped stitch

SIMPLE GARTER STITCH BEADING

1 This method can be used to create bands of beads along borders or at intervals for beaded stripes. Start with a right-side row and work at least three rows of plain Garter stitch before adding any beads. On the next row (a wrong-side row), knit two edge stitches before adding a bead. Then push a bead up close to the knitting before working each stitch. At the end of the row, add the last bead when two stitches remain on the left needle, then knit the last two stitches.

Wrong side of knitting

2 Knit the next row with no beads. Alternate a bead row and a plain row to form a band of beads of the desired depth. This technique could be used to create a piece entirely covered with beads for a small bag, but would create a fabric too heavy for a large garment.

Right side of knitting

REVERSE STITCH BEADING

1 Thread beads onto knitting yarn. Working in Stocking stitch, knit to one stitch before bead position. Yarn to front.

2 Purl one. The bead must sit tight against the right needle, so slide it along the yarn to this position and hold it there. Purl the next stitch. Yarn to back and work to next bead position.

Hold bead in position

INSET BEAD WITH A HOOK

1 Bead shows from both sides and is inset into the knitting. Knit to bead position.

2 Place bead on a fine crochet hook. Pick the next stitch off the left needle with a hook. Slide bead onto stitch and return it to left needle. Knit or purl the stitch as required. Needle and thread can be used instead of a crochet hook. In which case, make a loop of thread through stitch and slide bead down the thread.

CLOSE BEADING

1 Work at a tight tension so beads stay at front. Thread beads on yarn. Slide bead along close to needle.

2 On a knit row: knit into back of stitch, draw loop and bead through stitch, with bead behind right needle. Tighten stitch with bead at front.

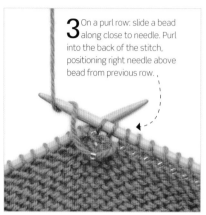

3 On a purl row: slide a bead along close to needle. Purl into the back of the stitch, positioning right needle above bead from previous row.

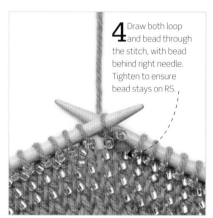

4 Draw both loop and bead through the stitch, with bead behind right needle. Tighten to ensure bead stays on RS.

USING A SECOND YARN

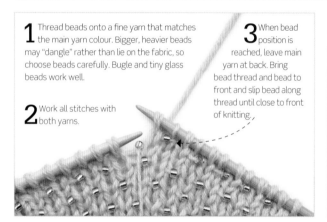

1 Thread beads onto a fine yarn that matches the main yarn colour. Bigger, heavier beads may "dangle" rather than lie on the fabric, so choose beads carefully. Bugle and tiny glass beads work well.

2 Work all stitches with both yarns.

3 When bead position is reached, leave main yarn at back. Bring bead thread and bead to front and slip bead along thread until close to front of knitting.

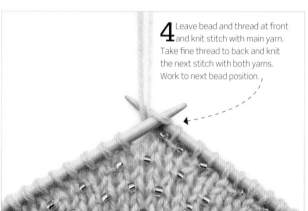

4 Leave bead and thread at front and knit stitch with main yarn. Take fine thread to back and knit the next stitch with both yarns. Work to next bead position.

BEADED LOOPS AND CLUSTERS

1 Thread beads onto knitting yarn in desired colour/shape sequence (here 4 small beads per cluster, 3 small, 1 larger, and 3 small per loop).

2 Cluster: work stocking stitch to position of cluster. Yarn to front, slide 4 small beads along yarn. Yarn to back, tighten yarn and knit into back of next stitch and knit to next cluster position.

3 Loop: work in Stocking stitch to position of loop. Yarn to front, slide 3 small round beads, 1 larger one, and 3 more small ones along yarn to needles. Yarn to back. Knit into back of next stitch and knit to next loop. If the beads are heavy and a hole forms, try the following variation after taking yarn back: knit next stitch, but do not remove from left needle, knit into stitch again, sliding it off left needle afterwards. Slip both loops of the stitch to the right needle, insert left needle into front of both loops and knit together (ssk).

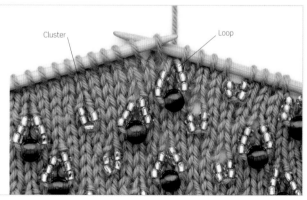

Cluster

Loop

TUBULAR POCKETS FOR LARGE BEADS

1 Knit to position of bead. Insert needle and knit front and back of the stitch (see p.130), repeat on next stitch (or work across more stitches depending on bead size). Knit to next bead.

2 On next row, purl to bead position. Purl the first increased stitch wrapping yarn twice round needle, slip the second purlwise, knit the third wrapping yarn twice round needle, slip fourth purlwise. Purl to next bead.

3 On next row, at bead position: knit the first stitch wrapping yarn twice round needle, yarn to front and slip the second purlwise releasing the wrapped loops, yarn to back, knit the third stitch wrapping yarn twice round needle, yarn to front, slip the fourth stitch purlwise releasing the wrapped loops as shown. Yarn to back and knit to next bead.

4 Repeat Steps 2 and 3 once or twice more (depending on bead size).

5 Purl to bead position. Slip the first stitch onto the right needle, the second onto a cable needle, third onto the right needle and fourth onto the cable needle. This opens the tubular pocket. Insert bead. Return the four stitches to the left needle in correct order without twisting. Purl two together twice to close pocket. Purl to next bead.

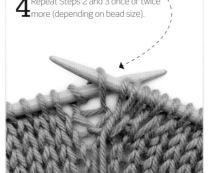

6 The completed pocket holds the bead in position. Large flat objects can be inserted in this way as well.

BEADED CAST-ON

1 Thread beads onto knitting yarn. Make a slip knot at the end of the yarn leaving a 10cm (4in) tail, and place on needle. Hold needle in right hand, yarn in left. Push a bead along the yarn between left hand and needle. Hold yarn and wrap it around thumb as shown, then insert right needle to work a Single cast-on (see p.87). Make sure the bead remains under the needle.

2 Repeat for each cast-on stitch, or space the beads as required along the edge, this example has three stitches between each bead.

BEADED CAST-OFF

1 Cut a piece of main colour yarn five times the width of the knitting. Thread one bead for each stitch to be beaded, less one, onto the yarn. Tie the last bead (which will not be worked) to the end of the yarn to prevent beads sliding off.

2 With beaded yarn, knit first two stitches of cast-off. Pass second over first as normal. This leaves a selvedge stitch for seaming.

3 Push a bead close to back of fabric. For a firm edge (as shown here), knit stitch drawing both bead and yarn through stitch. To alter lie of bead, change which side of the bead the stitch is passed over in Step 4. For a dangling bead, knit the next stitch leaving bead at back as new loop is formed.

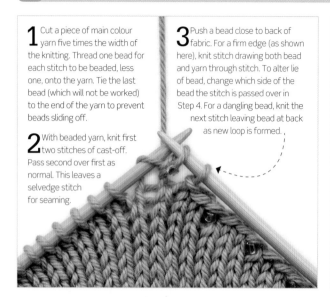

4 For either method, pass second stitch on right needle over first and off tip of needle.

5 Repeat Steps 3 and 4 along the cast-off, either working one bead per stitch or some plain cast-offs in between, depending on size of bead and effect required.

6 The last stitch should not be beaded if it will be seamed, so remove and discard end bead, work last stitch plain and pull end through as normal.

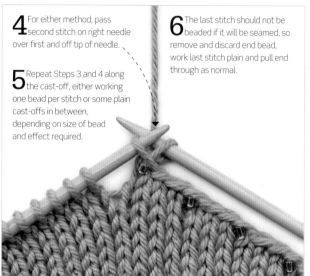

BOBBLES AND EMBOSSING

Popcorns and bobbles look similar but are worked differently. Bells are larger variations of tulip clusters but become partially detached from the knitting. Flaps are worked separately and integrated as the work progresses, whilst curls combine short rows with tubular knitting. Try using Reverse knitting (see p.206) to avoid turning the work.

POPCORNS

1 This example is worked on a knit row on stocking stitch fabric. Knit to popcorn position.

2 Insert right needle as if to knit into next stitch, then knit into front, back, front, then back of the stitch. Slip stitch off needle. Four stitches are made from one. Knit to next popcorn position.

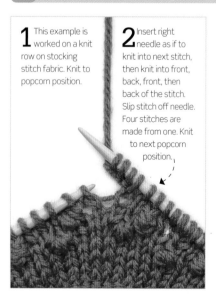

3 On next row, purl to popcorn position. Insert tip of left needle into second stitch on right needle and pass it over the first stitch and over the tip. Repeat with the third and fourth stitches.

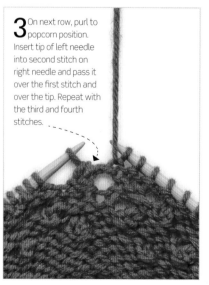

4 Purl to next popcorn position. On next row, knit to next popcorn position and repeat Steps 2–4 as required.

DETACHED BOBBLES

1 This example is worked on a knit row on stocking stitch fabric, making a reverse stocking stitch bobble. Knit to bobble position. Insert right needle knitwise into next stitch. Knit it without removing from left needle. Bring yarn to front between needles and purl into same stitch, yarn to back and knit it again, yarn to front, purl it again, yarn to back, knit it again. ,

2 Slide stitch off left needle. Five stitches are made from one.

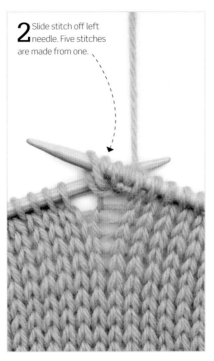

3 Turn the work. Knit across the five stitches and loops just made.

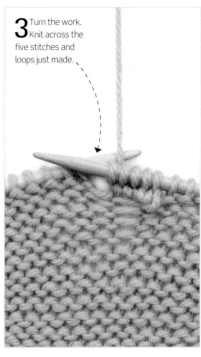

4 Turn and purl across the five stitches just worked. Yarn to back.

5 Insert tip of left needle into second stitch on right needle and pass it over the first stitch and over the tip of needle. Repeat with the third and fourth stitches. One bobble stitch left. Knit to next bobble position. ,

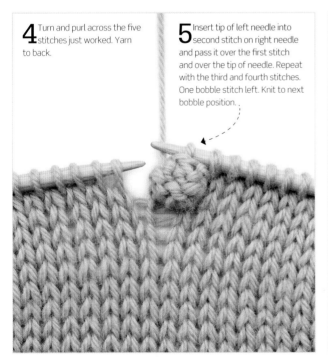

6 Repeat Steps 1-5 to make next bobble. Bobbles can be purely decorative, or used as a functional fastener on garments or accessories.

TULIP CLUSTER BOBBLE

1 Makes a stocking stitch cluster on a reverse stocking stitch fabric. On a right side row, purl to bobble position. Make five stitches out of one as described in Step 1 of Bobbles (see p.241). Purl to next bobble, or end of row.

2 Work three rows, working the background as stocking stitch and the bobble as reverse stocking stitch. (When background is knit, purl bobbles and vice versa).

Wrong side

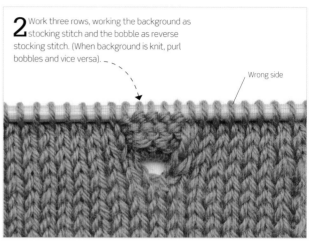

3 Next row, with right side facing, purl to bobble position. Slip first bobble stitch to right needle, knit one and pass the slipped stitch over it. Knit one, k2tog, three stitches remain of bobble.

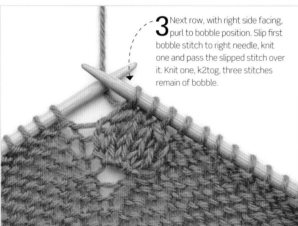

4 On next row, knit to bobble position and purl the three bobble stitches.

5 On next row, purl to bobble position, slip first stitch, k2tog and pass the first stitch over and off the right needle. Purl to next bobble.

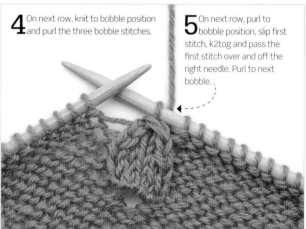

6 Bobbles can be made larger by working more rows. For a more prominent version try working Bells (opposite).

BELLS

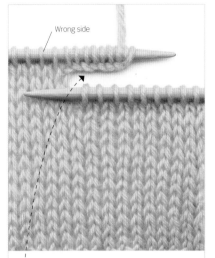

Wrong side

1 This example works a stocking stitch bell on a reverse stocking stitch background. With right side facing, purl to position of bell. Turn work and Cable cast-on (see p.89) 8 stitches onto what is temporarily the left needle. Turn work and work to next bell or end of row.

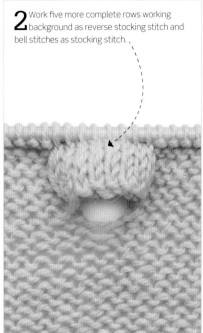

2 Work five more complete rows working background as reverse stocking stitch and bell stitches as stocking stitch.

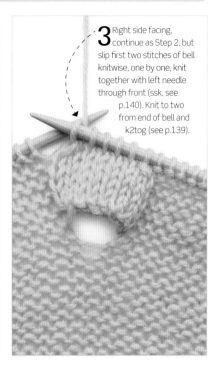

3 Right side facing, continue as Step 2, but slip first two stitches of bell knitwise, one by one, knit together with left needle through front (ssk, see p.140). Knit to two from end of bell and k2tog (see p.139).

4 Repeat Step 3 on every right side row, until only two stitches are left of bell. Knit these together on next knit row, and then knit last remaining stitch of bell together with the following one to complete the bell.

FLAPS

1 Working on separate needles, knit a garter stitch triangle by casting on one stitch. Knit into front, back, and front of this stitch. Kfb each end stitch on alternate rows until nine stitches wide. Place stitches on a spare needle. Work to flap. Place needle with flap stitches in front of main needle. Insert right needle into first stitch of both left-hand needles. Knit together.

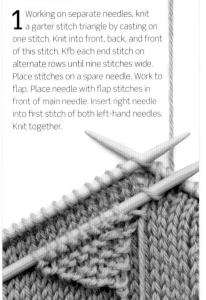

2 For the purl version, see Step 3 of Horizontal inset pocket (see p.223). Flaps can be made from any shape knitted in a stitch that lies flat, try moss stitch rectangles or diamonds.

TECHNIQUES

CURLS

1 Work in Stocking stitch. With wrong side facing, purl to position of curl in colour A.

2 Work a purl right lifted increase using colour B by picking up and purling into right side of stitch below next stitch (this is picked up the same as a right lifted increase on a knit row, see p.131).

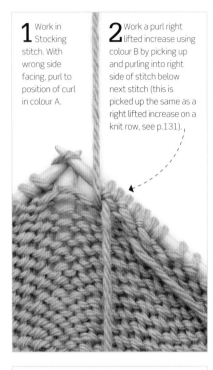

3 Purl one stitch in colour A. Repeat this increase, purl one sequence across the width of the curl (six for this example, so the curl will be twelve stitches wide). Purl to end of row.

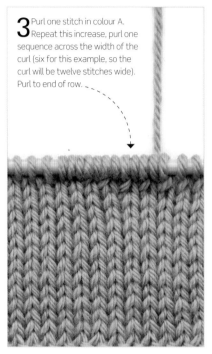

4 Knit to curl in colour A. Colour A and B at back. Knit all the colour B stitches in colour B, taking yarn forwards and back to slip each colour A stitch purlwise in between. Turn at end of curl.

5 Keep colour A at front. In colour B, purl all colour B stitches, taking yarn back and forwards to slip each colour A stitch in between. Turn at end of curl.

6 Repeat Steps 4 and 5 two or more times, working only over curl stitches.

7 Colour A and B to back. With colour A work to end of row and then work a complete row, knitting each colour B stitch together with the following colour A stitch. Trim ends of colour B and sew in on reverse.

EMBROIDERY ON KNITTING

Swiss darning, Bullion stitch, Lazy daisies, and Chain stitch are most commonly used on knitting, although Running and Satin stitch can be very attractive. Use a smooth yarn that is the same weight as that used for the knitting, or slightly thicker, together with a blunt-ended needle to avoid splitting the knitting yarn.

SWISS DARNING CHART

As Swiss darning embroidery imitates and covers the knit stitches on the right side of the Stocking stitch, you can work any charted colourwork motif using the technique. (Cross stitch books are also good sources of motifs for Swiss darning.) The completed embroidered motif will look as if it has been knitted into the fabric.

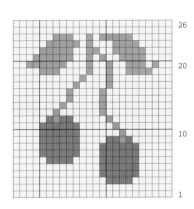
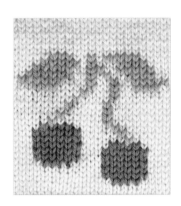

SWISS DARNING WORKED HORIZONTALLY

1 Secure the embroidery yarn to the wrong side of the stocking stitch, then pass the needle from back to front through the centre of a knit stitch, and pull the yarn through. Next, insert the needle from right to left behind the knit stitch above as shown and pull the yarn through gently so it "mirrors" the knit stitch size.

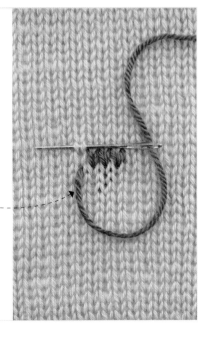

2 Insert the needle from right to left into the knit stitch below and out at the centre of the next knit stitch to the left to complete the stitch as shown. Continue in this way, tracing the path of the knitting horizontally.

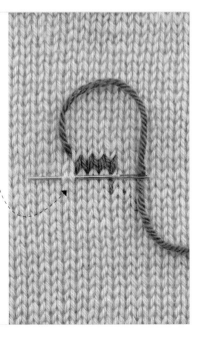

SWISS DARNING WORKED VERTICALLY

1 Secure the embroidery yarn on the wrong side of the stocking stitch, then pass the needle from back to front through the centre of a knit stitch and pull the yarn through. Next, insert the needle from right to left behind the knit stitch above as shown and pull the yarn through.

2 Insert the needle from front to back and to front again under the top of the stitch below so it comes out in the centre of the stitch just covered, as shown. Continue in this way, tracing the path of the knitting vertically.

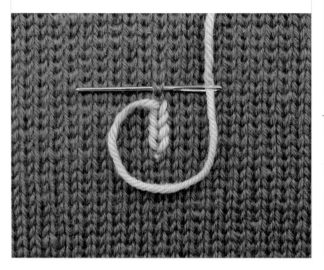

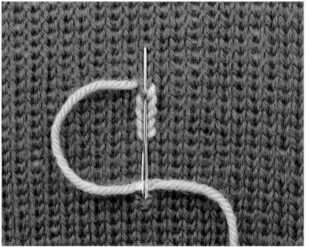

SATIN STITCH

1 Secure yarn on the wrong side. Bring needle through to front between two stitches, at one side of the shape to be worked.

2 Take needle to back between two stitches at the opposite side of the shape.

3 Bring the needle to the front again at the original side, but spacing it a yarn-width away by angling the needle very slightly whilst at back of work. The stitches should lie flat and parallel to each other.

4 Continue to work the shape in long smooth stitches that do not pucker the fabric.

RUNNING STITCH

1 Secure yarn on wrong side of work. Bring needle through to front between two stitches, at the end of the line to be worked.

2 Take needle to back between two stitches a measured number of stitches or rows to the right (or left).

3 Repeat, spacing the stitches in an even pattern as required being careful not to pucker the fabric.

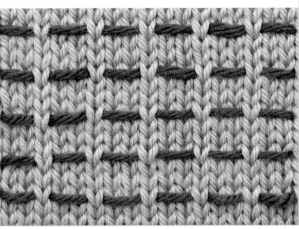

BULLION STITCH

To begin the stitch, secure the yarn on the wrong side and bring the needle through to the right side at one end of the position for the stitch. Then insert the needle through to the back a short distance from the starting point and out to the front again at the starting point. Wrap the yarn at least six times around the needle close to the knitting and holding the wraps with your fingers, pull the needle carefully through the wraps. To complete the stitch, reinsert the needle through the knitting at the same place (as shown by the arrow). Arrange the bullion stitches in spirals to form rose shapes, or as here to form simple star or flower-petal shapes.

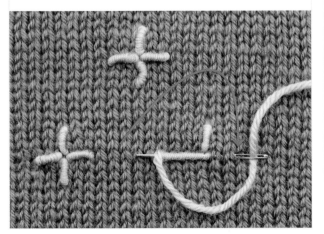

LAZY DAISY STITCH

Lazy daisy stitches are individual chain stitches held down at the loop end by a short stitch. They are traditionally used to form flower shapes. To begin the stitch, secure the yarn on the wrong side and bring the needle through at the centre of the flower. Reinsert the needle through to the back at the starting point and bring it out to the front a short distance away as shown. Secure the loop with a short stitch. Work all the "petals" in the same way, starting each one at the flower centre.

CHAIN STITCH ON STRIPES

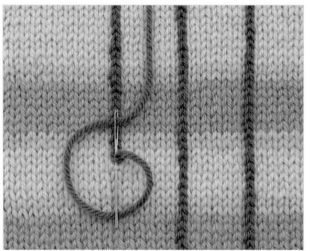

Knitted stripes can be turned into a plaid or check pattern with simple vertical lines of chain stitch. Bring a blunt-ended yarn needle out in position for the first stitch. Re-insert the needle where it emerged and bring the tip out a short distance below with the yarn looped under it. Pull the yarn through. To continue, insert the needle back into the hole from which it has just emerged and bring it out a short distance below.

3 Working to left, re-insert needle to the back after the third rib knit stitch. Re-thread yarn in same direction once more, making sure not to catch the yarn with the needle and ending with the needle at the back. Gently pull the yarn to gather the two ribs together. Continue along the row, working into each pair of rib stitches as shown. Gather each wound stitch as it is completed. Fasten and cut yarn at the other end.

EMBROIDERED SMOCKING

Smocking draws the knitting in, so knit the fabric one and half times the required width.

1 Cast on a multiple of 8 plus three extra stitches (35 in this example). Work a wide rib fabric starting with 3 purl stitches and 1 knit stitch that repeats across the row, ending with 3 purl stitches. This is the right side. Work 30 rows and cast off.

2 Mark second rib stitch from right four rows up work from cast on. Thread a needle with contrast yarn, secure yarn to right side back of work and bring needle from back to front just between last purl stitch and the knit stitch of the marked rib stitch.

4 Move four rows up and work next gathers. Re-fasten yarn to right edge, bring needle from back to front just before first rib knit stitch, re-insert just after second rib knit stitch, thread yarn around and gather as in Step 3. Repeat along row, starting by bringing the yarn to front after the next 3 purl stitches as described in Step 3. Continue alternating the stitches as Step 3 and 4, spacing each repeat four rows apart up the fabric.

3D EMBELLISHMENTS

Surface embellishments and edge decorations can be attached to knitting once it is completed. These are easy and fun to make and extremely effective, but remember to buy extra yarn. Simple tools are required to make Pom-poms and Tassels whilst a specially worked cast-on, cast-off, or selvedge will make adding a fringe easier.

TWIZZELS

1 Cast on 8 stitches using Single cast-on (see p.87) or another soft cast-on method.

2 Turn work. Knit 2 together along row. Cast on eight stitches using same method as before.

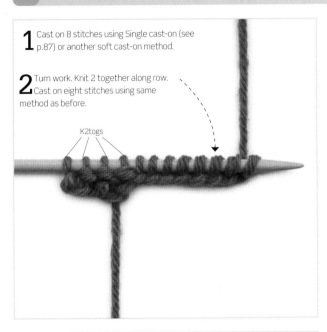

K2togs

3 Turn work. Knit 8, then knit 2 stitches together twice.

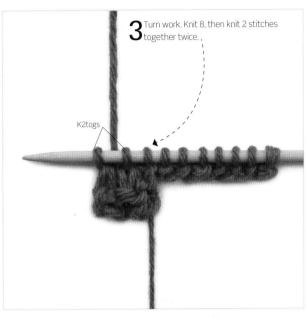

K2togs

4 Turn work. Knit 2 stitches together 5 times. Cast on 8 stitches.

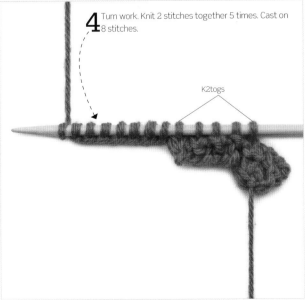

K2togs

5 Turn work. Knit 8, then knit 2 stitches together and last 3 stitches together. Repeat Steps 4–5 until required length is reached.

6 To finish, turn work and knit 2 stitches together 5 times. Turn, knit 2 together, and knit 3 together. Turn, knit 2 together, and pull thread through.

TECHNIQUES

Combining stitches, such as twisted stitches and brioche stitch, can create quite interesting effects in one fabric. Decreasing on rib fabric makes an attractive feature, especially when worked in a pale colour.

POM-POMS

1 Draw two 8cm (3¼in) diameter circles on firm card. Draw another 2.5cm (1in) diameter circle in the centre. The diameter of the outer circle minus that of the inner will be the approximate size of the pom-pom. A smaller centre circle makes a denser pom-pom. Cut out circles and centres so they look like doughnuts.

2 Cut a few 1m (1yd) lengths of yarn and wind together into a small ball. Put the circles together. Hold yarn ends at the edge of the circle, and insert ball into centre, winding yarn through the circles. Continue winding.

3 When the first ball runs out make another. If the centre becomes too tight, thread as many strands of yarn as possible onto a large-eyed needle, and use this to complete the winding. Insert the point of scissors into the outside of the circle and cut through the wraps.

4 Slide a long doubled strand of yarn between the circles, wrap and knot it tightly around the core.

5 Thread the yarn onto a needle and make a few stitches through the knot. Gently remove the circles. Shake and trim the pom-pom, but do not cut the tie strands. Suspending a wool pom-pom in steam will make it even fuller (hang it at the end of a long needle for safety).

TASSELS

1 Select a template approximately the length of the finished tassel, this can be cut card, but a book is often ideal. Holding the end with your thumb, wrap the yarn repeatedly around the template using single or varied colours. Fifty wraps is average, more wraps make a thicker tassel. With a threaded needle, pull a long doubled strand of yarn between yarn and template, and slide it up to end. Tie tightly around strands, leaving long ends.

2 Insert scissors at the base of the wraps and cut across all strands. Remove the template.

3 Wrap another strand of yarn tightly around the top a short distance below the head, then tie securely and sew the ends through the wraps and into the tassel head a few times.

4 Trim the ends of the tassel and sew to project with remaining long strand at head. Light pressing or steaming at the end of Step 2 makes the tassel sleeker.

FRINGE

1 Cut a card template a little wider than the fringe length. Wind yarn repeatedly around the card. Cut along one side of the card, making lengths of yarn double the width of the card.

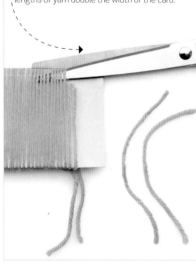

2 Take several lengths (more make a thicker fringe), fold in half and hold the folded loop in front of fabric edge. Insert a crochet hook through back of fabric close to edge or through purpose-made selvedge holes. Catch the folded loop and pull it through to back.

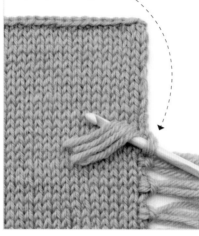

3 Catch strands in hook again and pull through the first loop. Repeat along edge, spacing as required. Trim ends evenly. Fringes can be beaded, knotted, or worked in silky or contrast coloured yarns.

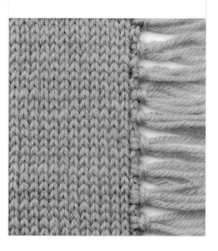

DRAWTHREAD BOBBLE

1 Using smaller needles than normal for yarn, cast on five stitches using Single cast-on (see p.87). Work a number of rows in garter or stocking stitch as desired. Finish with wrong side facing, and slip all the stitches, one by one, over the first one.

2 Cut yarn leaving a 20cm (8in) tail and pull through the remaining stitch. Sew a running stitch with yarn tail around the edge, and pull tightly. (Contrast yarn has been used here for clarity.)

3 Sew together to secure and use the same thread to attach to the project.

COVERED BUTTONS

1 This example uses Moss stitch. On smaller needles than normal for yarn, knit a square that is at least one and a half times as big as the button front. If using a kit, go to Step 4.

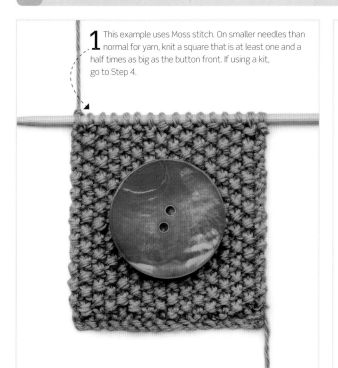

2 Cut the yarn with a 20cm (8in) tail, thread a large-eyed needle with the tail and thread back through stitches as they are removed from the needle. Sew small running stitches around the three edges of the knitting, leave the thread end loose. (A contrast thread has been used here for clarity.)

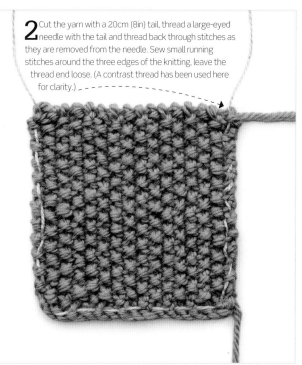

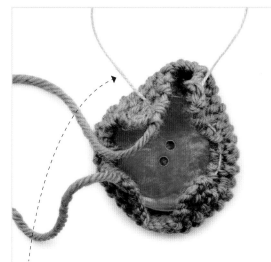

3 Gently draw the knitting up into a shallow bag. Insert the button into the bag and draw the threads tight. Sew closed with yarn end. Sew to garment with knitting yarn or matching thread. To secure big buttons, try sewing through a small plastic button at the back of the knitting at the same time.

4 If using a kit, cast off the square, and follow the manufacturer's instructions to complete the button in either method. A layer of fine woven fabric can be inserted under the knitting to prevent the button showing through the stretched stitches.

KNITTED TOYS

If you have never knitted a toy before, try this very easy striped monkey. These step-by-step instructions for making a toy include lots of tips for knitting toy pieces, for stuffing, for assembling parts, and for stitching facial features. (Toy directions are given on p.390.)

MAKING THE TOY

Knit on a pair of needles instead of in the round, the monkey is easy, even for a beginner. The toy pattern has been specially devised to be easy to understand as well. Follow the steps to learn practical general toy-making tips.

CHOOSING MATERIALS

Start your toy project by choosing the yarns, needles, and extras. For the monkey, you need six colours of yarn. One ball of each yarn is often enough for a whole toy, but your toy pattern will specify a yarn amount. For striped toys, small amounts of leftover yarns are ideal, as long as they are all the same weight.

As for most toys, the extras needed for the monkey include embroidery thread for facial features, buttons for eyes, and toy filling. If you are making the toy for a small child, you should either embroider the eyes or select safety eyes that meet safety regulations. Safety eyes have a shank that is pushed through the fabric and held by a metal back that clamps onto the shank.

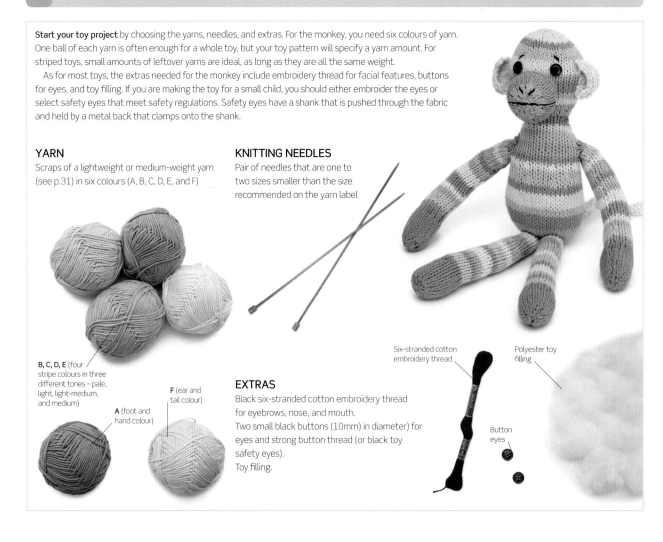

YARN
Scraps of a lightweight or medium-weight yarn (see p.31) in six colours (A, B, C, D, E, and F)

KNITTING NEEDLES
Pair of needles that are one to two sizes smaller than the size recommended on the yarn label

B, C, D, E (four stripe colours in three different tones – pale, light, light-medium, and medium)

F (ear and tail colour)

A (foot and hand colour)

EXTRAS
Black six-stranded cotton embroidery thread for eyebrows, nose, and mouth.
Two small black buttons (10mm) in diameter) for eyes and strong button thread (or black toy safety eyes).
Toy filling.

Six-stranded cotton embroidery thread

Polyester toy filling

Button eyes

KNITTING THE BODY AND HEAD

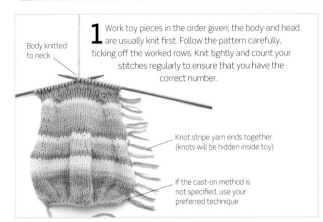

1 Work toy pieces in the order given; the body and head are usually knit first. Follow the pattern carefully, ticking off the worked rows. Knit tightly and count your stitches regularly to ensure that you have the correct number.

Body knitted to neck

Knot stripe yarn ends together (knots will be hidden inside toy)

If the cast-on method is not specified, use your preferred technique

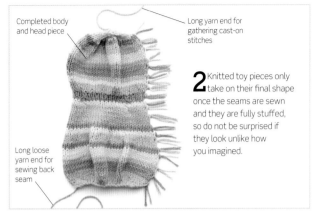

2 Knitted toy pieces only take on their final shape once the seams are sewn and they are fully stuffed, so do not be surprised if they look unlike how you imagined.

Completed body and head piece

Long yarn end for gathering cast-on stitches

Long loose yarn end for sewing back seam

KNITTING THE LEGS AND ARMS

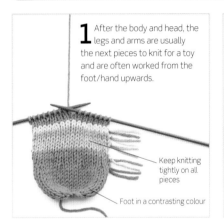

1 After the body and head, the legs and arms are usually the next pieces to knit for a toy and are often worked from the foot/hand upwards.

Keep knitting tightly on all pieces

Foot in a contrasting colour

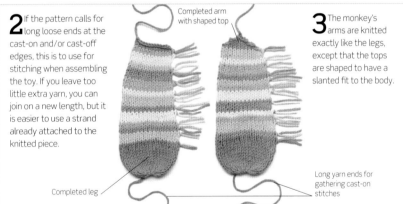

2 If the pattern calls for long loose ends at the cast-on and/or cast-off edges, this is to use for stitching when assembling the toy. If you leave too little extra yarn, you can join on a new length, but it is easier to use a strand already attached to the knitted piece.

Completed arm with shaped top

Completed leg

3 The monkey's arms are knitted exactly like the legs, except that the tops are shaped to have a slanted fit to the body.

Long yarn ends for gathering cast-on stitches

KNITTING OTHER BODY PARTS

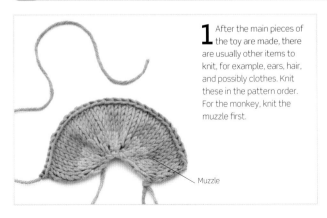

1 After the main pieces of the toy are made, there are usually other items to knit, for example, ears, hair, and possibly clothes. Knit these in the pattern order. For the monkey, knit the muzzle first.

Muzzle

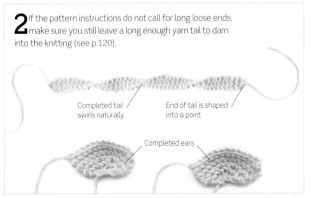

2 If the pattern instructions do not call for long loose ends, make sure you still leave a long enough yarn tail to darn into the knitting (see p.120).

Completed tail swirls naturally

End of tail is shaped into a point

Completed ears

TECHNIQUES

FINISHING THE TOY

Finishing the toy successfully is the most difficult part of the toy-knitting process. Take your time and stitch slowly. Do not be afraid to unpick and redo any sewing that you are unhappy with. The following finishing tips are useful for all knitted toys.

STUFFING AND ASSEMBLING THE MAIN TOY PIECES

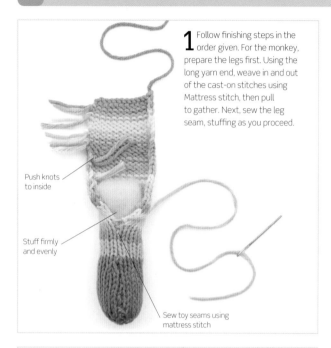

1 Follow finishing steps in the order given. For the monkey, prepare the legs first. Using the long yarn end, weave in and out of the cast-on stitches using Mattress stitch, then pull to gather. Next, sew the leg seam, stuffing as you proceed.

Push knots to inside

Stuff firmly and evenly

Sew toy seams using mattress stitch

2 Pinch the end of each leg together, with the seam at the centre of the back of the leg, and sew the end closed with overcast stitches. Prepare the other leg in same way.

Use a blunt-ended yarn needle for all toy seams

Finished leg seam is invisible at back of leg

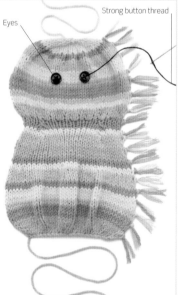

3 Before starting seams on the body, sew the button eyes onto your toy (or snap on safety eyes). Position the monkey's eyes about three or four stitches apart at the centre of the head. Use strong button thread and an ordinary sewing needle.

Eyes

Strong button thread

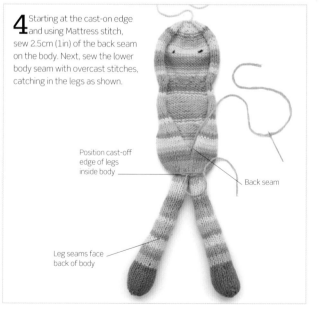

4 Starting at the cast-on edge and using Mattress stitch, sew 2.5cm (1in) of the back seam on the body. Next, sew the lower body seam with overcast stitches, catching in the legs as shown.

Position cast-off edge of legs inside body

Back seam

Leg seams face back of body

5 Continue the back body seam, stuffing firmly with toy filling.

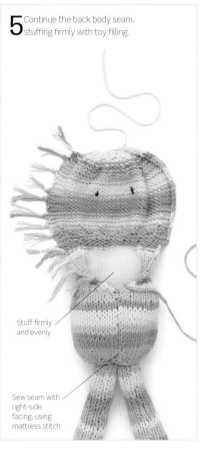

Stuff firmly and evenly

Sew seam with right-side facing, using mattress stitch

6 Continue the seam up the back of the head. Make sure the head is firmly packed with toy filling before completing the seam. Secure the yarn with two or three small stitches.

Stuff very firmly all the way to top of head

Back of head

7 Prepare the arms in the same way as the legs, but do not sew the tops of the arms closed.

Leave end open

Finished arm seam is invisible

8 Look at the photograph of the toy in your pattern to see how to position the arms. On the monkey, keep the arm ends open so that they meet the body in a circle and slant downwards.

Safety note: Only use pins on toys when absolutely necessary and ensure that none have been lost inside the toy.

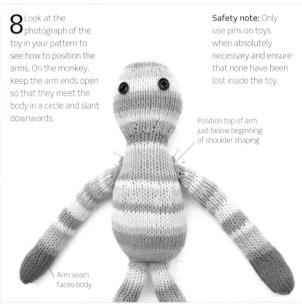

Position top of arm just below beginning of shoulder shaping

Arm seam faces body

9 Sew the arms in place, turning the edge of the arm inside the arm as you stitch. Remove the pins carefully as you stitch.

ADDING SMALL BODY PIECES AND FACIAL FEATURES

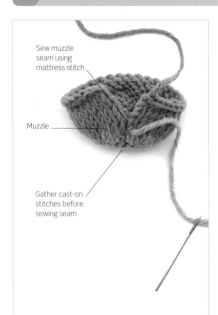

Sew muzzle
seam using
mattress stitch

Muzzle

Gather cast-on
stitches before
sewing seam

1 Using the yarn end, stitch in and out of the cast-on stitches and pull to gather. Sew the muzzle seam, starting at the cast-on end.

2 Trim the seam yarn to 5cm (2in) long and place inside the muzzle. Fill the muzzle with toy filling.

Fill firmly and evenly
with toy filling

3 Pin the muzzle to the head just below the eyes, forming an oval shape covering about ten stitches across the face and about twelve rows. Sew the muzzle in place with short overcast stitches.

Seam at centre of
bottom of muzzle

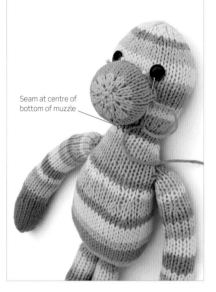

Darn in
yarn end

Ear

Gather
straight edge

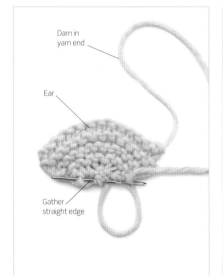

4 Make widely spaced overcast stitches along the straight edge of each ear. Gather these stitches to form the ear into a cup shape.

5 Using the gathering yarn, sew the ears to the sides of the head. Position toy ears following the photograph with your pattern.

Pull stitches tight
so they disappear

Use long yarn
ends to sew on
small pieces

6 Sew the tail at the base of the monkey's back. Darn in the other yarn end at the cast-off edge of the tail.

7 Use a blunt-ended yarn needle and all six strands of the embroidery thread for the facial features. Embroider the mouth in Backstitch along the centre of the muzzle. Work toy features carefully, redoing them if necessary.

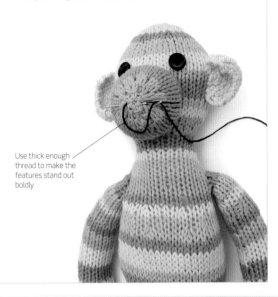

Use thick enough thread to make the features stand out boldly

8 For each nostril, work two stitches in the same place, the second on top of the first.

9 For each eyebrow, work two stitches in the same place, the second on top of the first. The slant of the eyebrows will give your toy its expression. To personalize your toy, alter the position and size of the eyes, and the shape of the mouth and eyebrows.

Slanting eyebrows upwards towards centre gives an innocent, relaxed expression

Even changing the ear positions can give your toy its unique look

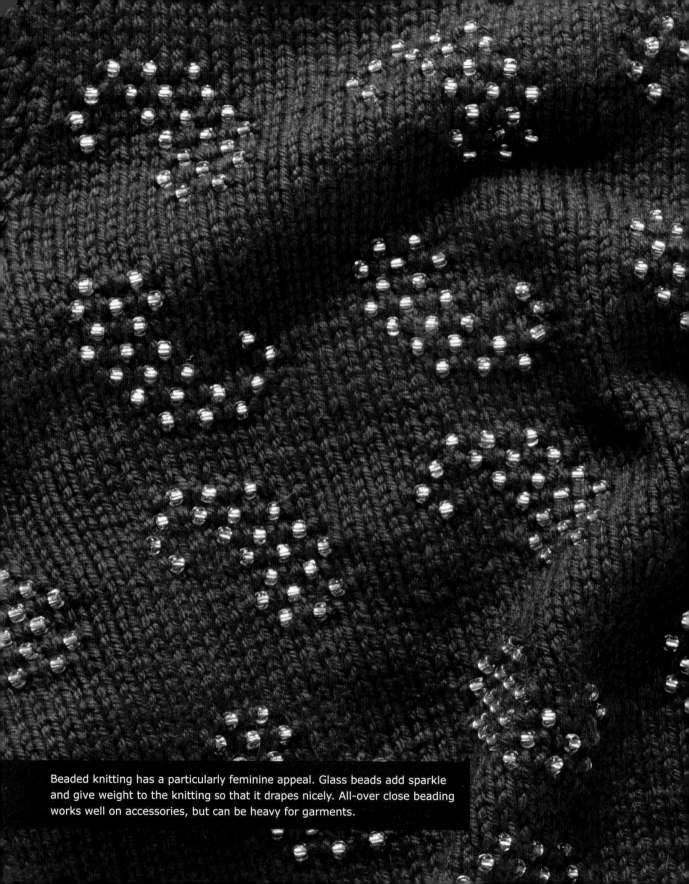

Beaded knitting has a particularly feminine appeal. Glass beads add sparkle and give weight to the knitting so that it drapes nicely. All-over close beading works well on accessories, but can be heavy for garments.

FELTED KNITTING

When felted, knitting shrinks, and it is not possible to control the exact amount of shrinkage. There are many things you can make from felted knitting that do not require precise sizes, from cushion covers to simple bags. Motifs cut from felt also make great embellishments.

FELTED BASICS

If you are a beginner, avoid attempting a felted garment pattern until you have gained some experience with felting smaller items. Before taking the plunge into a specific project, read all about the felting basics below and discover some helpful tips.

CHOOSING THE YARN

Super-fine and lightweight 100 per cent wool tweed yarn will create a knitted felt of average thickness.

Medium-weight wool-blend yarn containing mohair will felt very readily because of the mohair content.

Medium-weight and bulky-weight 100 per cent wool tweed yarn will create a thick knitted felt.

The best yarns for felted knitting are 100 per cent wool yarns, and other animal fibre yarns, that have not been too tightly spun. As a rule, the longer the fibres of a yarn, the more easily they felt. Avoid wool yarns marked "machine washable".

PREPARING FOR TEST-FELTING

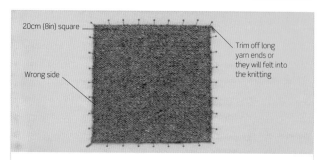

20cm (8in) square

Wrong side

Trim off long yarn ends or they will felt into the knitting

By test-felting a swatch of your yarn you can determine how much it will shrink. However, felting is not an exact science. Washing machine agitation, water temperature, detergent type, and yarn fibre content, spin, and colour all vary.

Knit a swatch of stocking stitch at least 20cm (8in) square; accurate shrinkage measurements cannot be obtained with smaller swatches. Block the swatch carefully. If unblocked, the side edges will felt too thickly due to the curling.

HAND FELTING

First, hand test the yarn to see if it will felt. Roll a 90cm (36in) long strand into a ball. Add a drop of detergent and rub it together for 2 minutes under hot running water. If the yarn clumps and is difficult to pull apart, it is a good candidate for test-felting. Next, knit and block a 10cm (4in) swatch. Submerge it in soapy hand-hot water. Squeeze and knead it gently, keep agitating and adding more hot water for up to 30 minutes. Rinse and squeeze out the water (do not wring) and roll in a towel. Pat the felt, right-side up, into a rectangle and leave to dry overnight. If the yarn has felted successfully, test a bigger swatch in a washing machine.

MACHINE FELTING

Put a swatch in the washing machine along with a large towel (this increases the agitation; use for all felting). Add half the amount of detergent used for a full load. Wash at 40°C (104°F) for yarn that contains mohair, and 60°C (140°F) for 100 per cent wool yarns, using the full washing and spin cycle. Tug the washed swatch gently in both directions, lay it right-side up and pat into a rectangle. Leave to dry completely. If necessary, do more tests with new swatches, altering the temperature or the length of the wash cycle. Keep detailed records of tension, needle size, sizes of pre-felted and felted swatches, wash settings, and type and amount of detergent.

TIPS FOR FELTING

• **If you are trying** felting for the first time, make several test swatches in different weights of yarn and felt them together in the same load. This way you can get a feel for the different thicknesses of knitted felt.
• **When using highly contrasting colours**, put a colour catcher in the machine to absorb loose dye and prevent colours from running.
• **Wool will fade slightly** when felted, due to the high temperatures and the detergent, but this adds an attractive quality to the felt.
• **Clean your washing machine** after a felting load by wiping it out with a damp cloth to remove any stray fibres.

BEFORE AND AFTER FELTING

Knitting changes character when it is felted, becoming dense and usually shrinking more lengthways than widthways. Integrated decorative effects can be achieved with knitted stripes or embroidery worked onto the knitting prior to felting.

100 per cent wool yarn: The wool yarn used for these samples is a lightweight, loosely spun tweed. A 60°C (140°F) wash was used to felt the knitting.

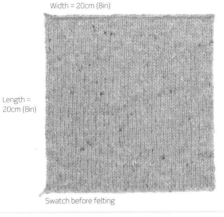

Width = 20cm (8in)

Length = 20cm (8in)

Swatch before felting

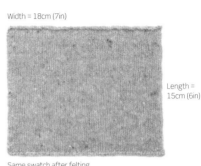

Width = 18cm (7in)

Length = 15cm (6in)

Same swatch after felting

Mohair-mix yarn in stripes: The yarn used here is a medium-weight mohair mix. A 40°C (104°F) wash was used to felt the knitting. Felted stripes merge together gently in the felting process. When making striped knitting for felting, cut off the old colour each time a new colour is started and knot the yarn ends together at the edge of the knitting. Clip off the yarn ends close to the knot so that they do not become felted into the knitting.

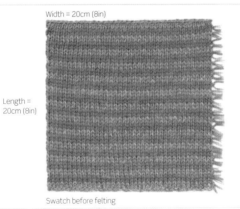

Width = 20cm (8in)

Length = 20cm (8in)

Swatch before felting

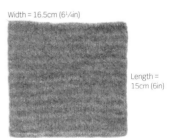

Width = 16.5cm (6¼in)

Length = 15cm (6in)

Same swatch after felting

Felted knitting with embroidered lines: The yarn used here is the same medium-weight mohair mix used above; and the same felting wash was used. Prior to felting, contrasting horizontal lines were embroidered in backstitch using the same yarn as the base. This embroidery merges attractively into the felt. (Notice how the backstitch shrinks and narrows the swatch more than usual.) This technique can be used to integrate a variety of embroidered motifs into felt.

Width = 20cm (8in)

Length = 20cm (8in)

Swatch before felting

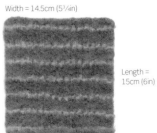

Width = 14.5cm (5¾in)

Length = 15cm (6in)

Same swatch after felting twice

TECHNIQUES

FELTED DECORATIONS

Felted knitting is a great base for embroidery because it is firm and stable. For a first project, felt a plain cushion cover then embroider with cotton stitches or, alternatively, appliqué with motifs cut from contrasting knitted felt. Cut-out motifs also make ideal decorations for knitted hats, or they can be made into stand-alone brooches.

EMBROIDERED FELTED KNITTING

Simple star stitches stand out beautifully on knitted felt. Try this, or other embroidery stitches, on a 20cm (8in) stocking-stitch square worked in lightweight 100 per cent wool yarn and felted as explained on p.264.

1 To work star stitches, mark the positions for the stars with pins. Thread a sharp-pointed crewel (embroidery) needle with a contrasting doubled six-strand cotton embroidery thread.

2 Work the two arms of the base crosses on each star 2cm (¾in) long and the arms of the small crosses on top 1.5cm (⅝in) long.

3 Your finished sample provides a good starting point for designing your own cushion cover.

MAKING FELTED CUT-OUT DECORATIONS

For a simple flower, knit two 20cm (8in) stocking stitch squares – one striped and one plain – and felt as explained on p.264. Use a medium-weight wool yarn with some mohair content.

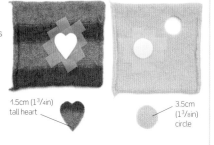

1.5cm (1¾in) tall heart

3.5cm (1³⁄₈in) circle

1 Make a paper template for the petal shape and the circle centre. Tape the templates to the wrong side of the felted pieces.

2 Using very sharp small scissors, cut out the shapes, cutting through the tape. Cut a total of five petals and two circles.

4 With the wrong side of the petals still facing upwards, place the second felt circle right-side up on top of the petals and aligned with the circle underneath. Sew the circle in place with neat overcast stitches.

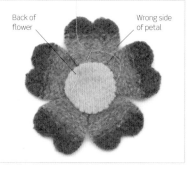

Back of flower

Wrong side of petal

3 Lay one of the circles wrong-side up, then pin the petals wrong-side up on top. Using a thread that matches the circle and a sharp sewing needle, sew the petals to the circle with running stitches, catching the circle with each stitch but not sewing all the way through it.

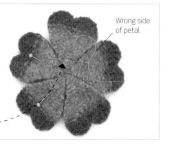

Wrong side of petal

5 Turn the flower over so it is right-side up and decorate it with beads as here or with contrasting embroidery.

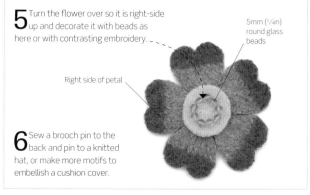

5mm (¼in) round glass beads

Right side of petal

6 Sew a brooch pin to the back and pin to a knitted hat, or make more motifs to embellish a cushion cover.

USING UNUSUAL YARNS

Knitting is even more fun if you know you are helping the environment. Undoing old sweaters and reusing the yarn is the most obvious type of recycling for knitters. But you can also choose more "unusual" yarns – rag strips, plastic strips, and string – for your eco knitting.

RECYCLING YARN

Old sweaters are perfect candidates for recycling, whether they are hand-knit or machine-made. The thickness of the yarn is irrelevant, as you can use thin strands doubled or tripled to create yarns thick enough to hand knit with.

PREPARING RECYCLED YARN

1 Carefully undo all the seams. This is very easy on some manufactured sweaters because the seams pull out in a chain. Cut other seams stitch by stitch with sharp scissors.

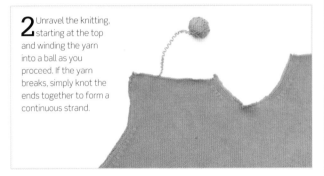

2 Unravel the knitting, starting at the top and winding the yarn into a ball as you proceed. If the yarn breaks, simply knot the ends together to form a continuous strand.

KNITTING WITH VARIEGATED RECYCLED YARN

1 To enliven your rescued yarns, cut them in 30–61cm (12–24in) lengths and knot together to form a unique yarn with variegated colours. Use yarns of similar thicknesses, doubling thin yarns if necessary.

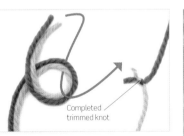

Completed trimmed knot

2 Roll the newly formed yarn into a ball as you knot the ends together.

3 Use the yarn for your chosen project. A garter stitch scarf is perfect for showing off your unique variegated yarn. The knots are a decorative feature, so make sure some fall on each side of the scarf.

TECHNIQUES

RAG KNITTING

Old shirts, cotton blouses, and patchwork remnants provide the best fabrics to recycle for rag knitting. Knitting thicker fabric strips is strenuous on the hands, and very thin fabrics are more liable to tear during the knitting process.

PREPARING RAG STRIPS

1 To make your rag "yarn", start by trimming the fabric pieces into even straight-edged shapes. Press remnants and cut off ragged edges. On clothing, trim off all seams, then press the fabric.

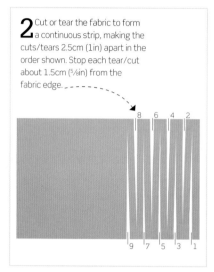

2 Cut or tear the fabric to form a continuous strip, making the cuts/tears 2.5cm (1in) apart in the order shown. Stop each tear/cut about 1.5cm (⅝in) from the fabric edge.

3 As you cut the strip, wind it into a ball. At the end of a strip, knot on the next strip of the same colour. Keep the fabric colours separate so that you can create patterns in your knitting.

KNITTING WITH RAG STRIPS

1 Garter stitch is the easiest stitch to work with rag strips. For 2.5cm (1in) wide patchwork-fabric-weight cotton strips, use 10mm (UK000/US15) needles.

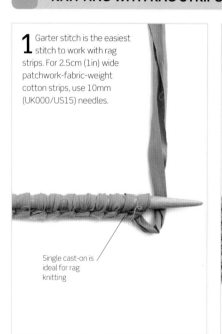

Single cast-on is ideal for rag knitting

2 Add interest by working in stripes. To change colours, knot on the new colour (see p.267). Position the knot as close as possible to the edge of the knitting.

Trim ends to 3cm (1¼in) from knot

3 When you finish your rag knitting, cast off the stitches knitwise (see p.106).

4 You can use your rag knitting to make a rag rug or a simple bag. For a bag, make one long rectangle, fold it in half (with the knots inside) and sew the seams using sewing thread. Add a plaited bag handle.

PLARN KNITTING

Most of us have a collection of plastic shopping bags. Cutting them into strips for knitting is a great way to put these bags to use. Because plastic strips (called plarn) are so flexible, they are even easier to knit with than rag strips.

PREPARING PLARN STRIPS

1 Select lightweight plastic bags, as these are easier to knit with than thicker ones and produce a springier fabric. To cut strips, smooth the bag out flat, then fold it in half lengthways.

Fold line

2 Smooth the bag flat again and fold at the second, third, and fourth fold lines as shown, smoothing the bag flat after each fold.

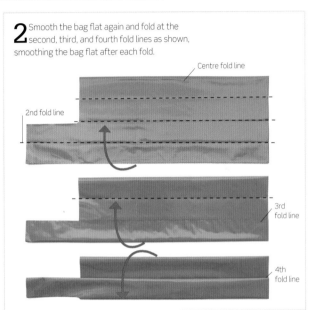

Centre fold line

2nd fold line

3rd fold line

4th fold line

3 Trim the handles and the bottom seam of the folded bag. Cut segments 3cm (1¼in) wide; each of these form a ring of plastic. Keep these rings folded until required.

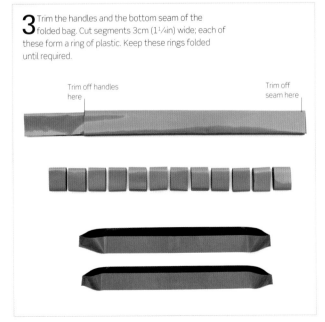

Trim off handles here

Trim off seam here

4 To link the rings together, lay one ring out horizontally on the table. Lay a second ring out vertically next to it. Then pass the first ring through the top of the second ring and pass the tail of the second ring through the centre of the first ring. Pull the tail of the second ring to knot it tightly to one end of the first.

Knots linking rings

5 Continue looping the rings together, rolling the continuous strip into a ball. When the ball gets too big to handle, start a new one.

TECHNIQUES

KNITTING WITH PLARN STRIPS

1 Plarn is very easy to knit into a tube that can be used to make a bag. Prepare the plarn (see previous page) and cast your stitches onto a 9mm (UK00/US13) circular knitting needle. Knit every round to form Stocking stitch (see p.116).

2 At the top work several rounds in knit and purl alternately to form a garter stitch border. (For handles, cast off and cast on stitches in the first two rounds to form a slot on each side.) Sew the bottom seam with overcast stitches and a blunt-ended yarn needle threaded with plarn.

KNITTING WITH STRING

If you have balls of old string languishing on a shelf or in a drawer, why not put them to use by knitting them into a useful household item? Because of its relative stiffness, string is perfect for making attractive knitted boxes.

DESIGNING A STRING BOX

Choose a twine of medium thickness. Brightly coloured strings are useful for adding contrasting seams or a border. Using a needle size that will produce a very stiff fabric, knit a tension swatch and calculate how many stitches to cast on for the sides of your box.

KNITTING A STRING BOX

1 So that the top edge of the box won't curl, begin each of the four sides of the box with two rows of Garter stitch. Complete each side in Stocking stitch and cast off knitwise on the right side.

2 Once the four sides are complete, work the base in stocking stitch only, making sure the sides fit it exactly.

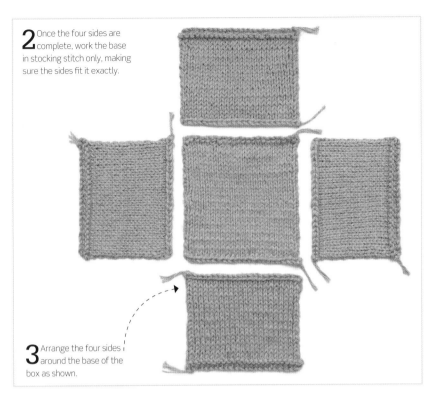

3 Arrange the four sides around the base of the box as shown.

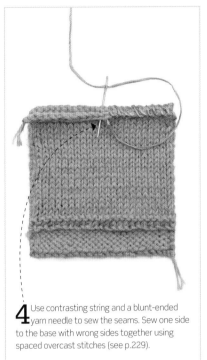

4 Use contrasting string and a blunt-ended yarn needle to sew the seams. Sew one side to the base with wrong sides together using spaced overcast stitches (see p.229).

5 Sew the three remaining sides to the base in the same way.

6 Sew the seams joining the sides together in the same way.

TECHNIQUES

PROJECTS

STRIPED SCARF

This vibrant scarf is an enjoyable, simple way to build up your knitting rhythm and skills. In a simple knit 1, purl 1 rib (also known as a 1 x 1 rib), it involves frequent colour changes that make it seem as though the knitting is growing quickly. The rib is double-sided and will not curl, producing a neatly knitted scarf. To trim, add a fringe in your choice of remaining yarn.

DIFFICULTY LEVEL
Easy

SIZE
180cm (71in) or desired length

YARN
Rowan Pure Wool DK 50g

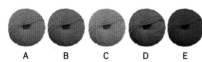

A: 028 Raspberry x 2 **B:** 026 Hyacinth x 3
C: 047 Geranium x 1 **D:** 042 Dahlia x 2
E: 030 Damson x 1

NEEDLES
A: 1 pair of 4mm (UK8/US6) needles
B: 1 pair of 3.25mm (UK10/US3) needles

A

B

TENSION
22sts and 30 rows to 10cm (4in) over st st on 4mm (UK8/US6) needles.

PATTERN
Using 3.25mm (UK10/US3) needles and yarn A, cast on 50sts. Change to 4mm (UK8/US6) needles and cont as follows:
Row 1 (RS): S1p, p1, [k1, p1] to end.
Row 2: S1p, p1, [k1, p1] to end.
These 2 rows form a 1 x 1 rib with a slipped stitch at the beginning of each row.
Repeat these 2 rows six times more (14 rows worked in total), ending with a WS row.
Join in yarn B using a slipknot.

Work in 14-row stripes of rib in the following colour sequence: C, B, A, D, E, D, A, B. Repeat four times. To finish stripe sequence, work 14-row stripes in colour C, B, then A. Cast off in rib.
Cut yarn B (or your choice of yarn) into lengths approximately 22cm (9in) long. Affix these as a fringe along each end of the scarf using the method shown on p.254.

FRINGE

LEAVE SHORT GAPS to prevent the knots from warping the edge of the scarf and pulling it out of shape. The gaps should be made slightly larger according to the number of strands in the fringe.

PROJECTS

SCARF EDGE

SLIPPED STITCHES at the beginning of each row, referred to as a Chain selvedge (see p.211), create a neat and professional-looking edge to the scarf.

COLOUR CHANGES

DARN ENDS up the side of the scarf to prevent unsightly ridges forming (see p.120). The stripes will remain cleanly divided, without uneven lines or puckering.

STRIPED HAT

This quick and simple beanie can be made to match the Striped scarf on p.274, and is a recommended project to follow on from a basic strip or square. You use a smaller knitting needle for the ribbed edge, and use the knit two together (k2tog) decreasing technique to shape the top of the hat. The hat is knitted flat and then sewn up with a hidden mattress stitch seam (see p.227): try to keep the stripes aligned for an especially neat finish.

DIFFICULTY LEVEL
Easy

SIZE
To fit an adult female

YARN
Rowan Pure Wool DK 50g

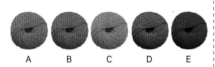

A   B   C   D   E

A: 028 Raspberry x 1 B: 026 Hyacinth x 1
C: 047 Geranium x 1 D: 042 Dahlia x 1
E: 030 Damson x 1

NEEDLES
A: 1 pair of 3.25mm (UK10/US3) needles
B: 1 pair of 4mm (UK8/US6) needles

——————————————————— A

——————————————————— B

TENSION
22sts and 30 rows to 10cm (4in) over st st on
4mm (UK8/US6) needles

PATTERN
Using 3.25mm (UK10/US3) needles and yarn A,
cast on 122 stitches.
Row 1: K2 [p2 k2] to end.
Row 2: P2 [k2 p2] to end
Repeat these 2 rows four times more, decreasing
one stitch at end of last row. (121sts)
Change to 4mm (UK8/US6) needles and
yarn B.
Work in st st for 8 rows, ending with a WS row.
Working all colour changes using the alternative
method on page 120, work 8-row stripes in the
following sequence: C, B, A.
Change to yarn D and work 4 rows st st.

SHAPE CROWN
Row 1: [K10, k2tog] to last st, k1. (111sts)
Row 2 and all foll alt rows: P.
Row 3: K.
Row 5: Change to yarn E. [K9, k2tog] to last st, k1.
(101sts)
Row 7: [K8, k2tog] to last st, k1. (91sts)
Row 9: [K7, k2tog] to last st, k1. (81sts)
Row 11: [K6, k2tog] to last st, k1. (71sts)
Row 13: Change to yarn D. [K5, k2tog] to last st,
k1. (61sts)
Row 15: [K4, k2tog] to last st, k1. (51sts)
Row 17: [K3, k2tog] to last st, k1. (41sts)
Row 19: [K2, k2tog] to last st, k1. (31sts)
Row 21: Change to yarn A. [K1, k2tog] to last st,
k1. (21sts)
Row 23: [K2tog] to last st, k1. (11sts)
Draw yarn through rem stitches and join side seam
using mattress stitch (see p.227).

ELASTICATED EDGE

AREAS THAT MUST FIT WELL, such as hat
bands and sleeve cuffs, use stretchy rib stitch
(see p.117) knitted in a smaller needle size for
a tight knit and elasticity.

FINISHING THE CROWN

FOR A SECURE JOIN, leave a long yarn tail at the end of the last row, draw it through the remaining stitches twice, then use it to sew the seam.

INVISIBLE SEAM

USING MATTRESS STITCH (see p.227) to sew the seam, worked with the right side of the work showing, allows you to keep the stripes aligned.

CABLED SCARF

This scarf is knitted from an attractive tweedy wool made from reclaimed clothing. The chunky helix cable moves every 4 rows, and is very enjoyable to work. The long length of the scarf means that it will wrap around your neck at least once and hang to a reasonable length.

LEVEL OF DIFFICULTY
Moderate

SIZE
19cm x 2m (7½in x 6½ft)

YARN
Rowan Purelife Renew 50g

682 Digger x 6

NEEDLES
A: 1 pair of 6mm (UK4/US10) needles
B: Cable needle

A

B

TENSION
20sts and 19 rows to 10cm (4in) over cable patt using 6mm (UK4/US10) needles

SPECIAL ABBREVIATIONS
C10F Place 5sts on cable needle and leave at front of work, k5, then k5 from cable needle.
CR7R Place 2sts on cable needle and leave at back of work, k5, then p2 from cable needle.
CR7L Place 5sts on cable needle and leave at front of work, p2, then k5 from cable needle.

PATTERN
Using 6mm (UK4/US10) needles, cast on 31sts.
Work 4 rows g st.
Row 5 (RS): K3, p to last 11sts, k5, p3, k3.
Row 6: K6, p5, k to end.
Row 7: As row 5.
Row 8 (increase row): K6, (M1, p1) five times, k to end. (36 sts)
Row 9: K3, p17, k10, p3, k3.
Row 10: K6, p10, k to end.

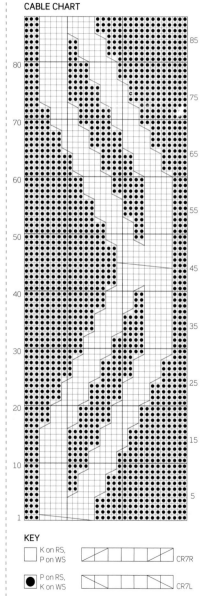

CABLE CHART

SET CABLE PANEL
When working the chart, read as all RS (odd) rows from R to L and all WS (even) rows from L to R.
Next row (RS): K3, work next 30sts as row 1 of cable chart, k3.
Next row: K3, work next 30sts as row 2 of cable chart, k3.
These 2 rows set sts.
Continue repeating the 88-row pattern repeat from chart, until work measures 198cm (78in), or desired length, ending after chart row 1.
Decrease row (WS): K6, (p2tog) five times, k to end. (31 sts)
Row 1: K3, p17, k5, p3, k3.
Row 2: K6, p5, k to end.
Row 3: As row 1.
Work 5 rows g st.
Cast off on WS.
Darn in all ends and block lightly under a damp cloth, being careful not to squash the cables.

KEY

☐ K on RS, P on WS	▱ CR7R
⬤ P on RS, K on WS	▱ CR7L
	▱ C10F

TEXTURED EDGE

LONG STRIPS OF KNITTING in single-sided stitches can lead to curled edges, but a border in garter or moss stitch and careful blocking (both sides) will prevent the work from losing its shape.

CABLE TWISTS AND TURNS

THE TRAVELLING NATURE of this cable pattern makes it easy to identify where the next cable will move. After a few pattern repeats, you may not need to be constantly consulting the chart.

CABLED HAT

This hat is designed to match the Cabled scarf on p.278. The cables climb upwards in a unique spiralling effect to merge at the top of the hat. The design is achieved by knitting the entire hat in circular rounds; there is no wrong-side row to deal with. This is a challenging knit, but the unusual spiral is a fun way to practise your circular knitting skills.

DIFFICULTY LEVEL
Difficult

SIZE
To fit an adult male

YARN
Rowan Purelife Renew 50g

682 Digger x 2

NEEDLES
A: 1 x 5.5mm (UK5/US9) circular needle, 60cm (24in) long,
B: 1 x 6mm (UK4/US10) circular needle, 60cm (24in) long
C: 4 x 6mm (UK4/US10) double-pointed needles
D: Cable needle

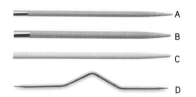

TENSION
30sts and 36 rows to 10cm (4in) over patt, when slightly stretched.

SPECIAL ABBREVIATIONS
CR4L Place 2 stitches on cable needle and leave at front of work, p2, then k2 from cable needle.
CR5L Place 2 stitches on cable needle and leave at front of work, p3, then k2 from cable needle.
rib Work in rib, knitting all presented knit stitches and purling all presented purl stitches.
rib2tog Working in rib, either k2tog, or p2tog as appropriate.

PATTERN
HAT PATTERN
Using 5.5mm (UK5/US9) needles and cable cast-on method (see p.89), cast on 96sts.
Join into a round being careful not to twist cast on sts. Place marker at start of round.
Round 1: K1, *p2, k2 to last 3 sts, p2, k1.
Cont to rep last round until work measures 3.5cm (1⅜in).
Next round: Rib 2, *rib2tog, rib 5, rep from * to end, ending rib 3. (83sts)

WORK RIDGES
Rounds 1 and 2: P.
Rounds 3 and 4: K.
Round 5: P.
Round 6: P3, *M1p, p6, rep from * to last 2sts, p2. (96sts)

SET CABLE PATT
Change to 6mm (UK4/US10) needles and work in cable patt as follows:
Patt round 1: *P2, k2, p2, rep from * to end.
Patt round 2: *CR4L, p2, rep from * to end.
Patt round 3: *K2, p4, rep from * to end, to last 2sts. Disregard end of round; start next round immediately.
Patt round 4: [CR4L, p2] sixteen times.
Patt round 5: *P4, k2, rep from * to end.
Patt round 6: *P2, CR4L, rep from * to end.
Previous 6 rows set pattern. Working in patt as set, continue rep these 6 rows until work measures 17cm (6¾in) from cast-on edge, ending with pattern row 6.

SHAPE TOP
Round 1: *P2tog, k2, p2, rep from * to end of round. (80sts)
Round 2: *P1, CR5L, slip next 2sts on to cable needle and leave at back of work, p2tog then k2 from cable needle, rep from * to end. (72sts)
Round 3: [P2, k2, p2, p2tog, p1] eight times. (64sts)

Round 4: [P2tog, CR5L, p1] eight times. (56sts)
Round 5: [P1, p2tog, k2, p2] eight times. (48sts)
Round 6: [P1, slip next 2sts on to cable needle and leave at front of work, p3, then k2tog tbl from cable needle] eight times. (40sts)
Round 7: [p3, k2tog tbl] eight times. (32sts)
Rounds from this point onwards will not finish at actual start point of rounds, but will overlap to form the crown spirals.
Round 8: [p1, slip next st on to cable needle, p2tog then k1 tbl] eight times. (24sts)
Round 9: [k2tog tbl, p1] eight times. (16sts)
Draw yarn through rem sts and fasten off.
Darn in ends.

TOP OF CROWN

THIS EYE-CATCHING SWIRL creates a tidy end for the circling cables. As you decrease, you need to transfer the stitches from circular needles to double-pointed needles – the work will get smaller and smaller.

PROJECTS

TEXTURE

THERE IS NO NEED TO TURN THE WORK and no wrong-side row. You knit in the direction of the cables, constantly going anticlockwise, to produce the texture.

JELLYFISH SCARF

This cosy scarf is designed to look like a string of jellyfish. It's not too difficult to create the unique texture, but you need to have mastered skills such as increasing and decreasing (see pp.130–151), and knitting into the stitch below (see pp.173–174). This deep-sea creature eats a lot of yarn, but it's worth knitting it up for the warmth it brings.

DIFFICULTY LEVEL
Moderate

SIZE
2m (6½ft) long (approx)

YARN
Rowan Alpaca Cotton 50g

409 Intense Slate x 7

NEEDLES
A: 1 pair of 5mm (UK6/US8) needles
B: 1 pair of 6mm (UK4/US10) needles

A

B

TENSION
16sts and 23 rows to 10cm (4in) over st st using 5mm (UK6/US8) needles.

SPECIAL ABBREVIATIONS
k1b Knit into the loop below the next presenting stitch on the left-hand needle.
s1 wyif Slip 1 with yarn in front.
s1 wyib Slip 1 with yarn in back.

PATTERN
Using 5mm (UK6/US8) needles, cast on 28sts. Work 7 rows garter st.
Row 8 (WS): **[K1, p1, k1] into every stitch to end. (84sts)
Change to 6mm (UK4/US10) needles and work in fisherman's rib as follows:
Row 9: *K1, p1, rep from * to end.
Row 10: S1 *p1, k1, rep from * to last st, p1.
Row 11: S1 wyib, *p1, k1b, rep from * to last st, s1 wyib.

Row 12: S1 wyif, *p1, k1b, rep from * to last st, s1 wyif.
Rows 13, 15, and 17: As row 11.
Row 14: As row 12.
Row 16: K1 tightly, *p1, k1b, rep from * to last st, p1 tightly.
Rows 11–17 set fisherman's rib, with long slipped stitches holding the shape of the puffball along the side of the scarf. Rep rows 11–16 five times more, and rows 11–13 once more.
Decrease for puffball (WS): [K3tog] to end. (28sts)
Change to 5mm (UK6/US8) needles, and work 7 rows in garter stitch (knit every row)**.
Rep from ** to ** a further eight times.
Cast off. Darn in all ends. Do not block.

GARTER STITCH BANDS

THE THICK, STURDY nature of garter stitch (see p.116) is used to create "ribs" in the scarf, which help to keep the puffs supported and raised.

FISHERMAN'S RIB

TO WORK FISHERMAN'S RIB (see p.50), revisit existing stitches and fill them with more yarn. This results in a thick fabric that is a good insulator.

PUFFY SHAPE

THE PUFFY SHAPE is achieved with a combination of needle sizes and by increasing and decreasing the number of stitches worked at one time.

JELLYFISH HAT

This exceptionally warm hat goes with the Jellyfish scarf on p.282. Its slouchy, contemporary design includes some fully-fashioned shaping techniques (see p.145). These prevent nasty tucks and clumps forming and blend in without being too noticeable. The needles used for the rib are larger than those recommended by the manufacturer, to add bounciness to the knitted fabric.

DIFFICULTY LEVEL
Moderate

SIZE
To fit an adult female

YARN
Rowan Alpaca Cotton 50g

409 Intense Slate x 3

NEEDLES
A: 1 pair of 5mm (UK6/US8) needles
B: 1 pair of 6.5mm (UK3/US10½) needles

A

B

TENSION
12sts and 11 rows to 10cm (4in) over patt on 6.5mm (UK3/US10½) needles, when slightly stretched.

SPECIAL ABBREVIATIONS
k1b Knit into the loop below the next presenting stitch on the left-hand needle.
p5tog Purl 5 stitches together.

PATTERN
Using 5mm (UK6/US8) needles, cast on 92sts.
Starting with a k row, work 5 rows g st.
Inc row (WS): (K1, p1, k1) into next st, *(k1, p1) into next st, rep from * to end. (185sts)
Change to 6.5mm (UK3/US10½) needles.
Row 1 (RS): K1, *p1, k1, rep from * to end.
Row 2: S1p, *k1b, p1, rep from * to end.
Row 3: S1k, *p1, k1b, rep from * to end.
Rows 2 and 3 set patt. Cont in patt until work measures 17cm (6¾in), ending with a RS row.
Next row (WS): S1p, k1b, *p3tog, k1b, p1, k1b to last 3 sts, p1, k1b, p1. (155sts)
Work 3 rows in patt without shaping.
Next row: *P5tog, k1b, p1, k1b, rep from * to last 3sts, k1b, p1, k1b. (79sts)
Next row: S1k, *k3tog, p1, rep from * to last 2sts, k2tog. (40sts)
Cut off yarn leaving a long tail and draw through rem sts twice. Use this end to sew side seam, with RS facing, using mattress stitch (see p.227).
Do not block.

DECREASES

THESE DECREASES use k3tog (see p.141) and p5tog (see Special abbreviations, left) to blend in with the ribbing at the top of the hat, leading to a "puffball" finish.

FISHERMAN'S RIB

FISHERMAN'S RIB (see p.50) has extra lines of yarn running through the work, creating a "meshy" effect and a three-dimensional texture.

BAND

THE GARTER STITCH BAND (see p.116) uses a smaller needle than the body of the hat to give enough elasticity to keep the hat on your head.

HARLEQUIN SCARF

This scarf is a fantastic opportunity to experiment with blending effects. The colour gradation is achieved by holding two strands of fuzzy mohair together as you knit, gently blending these two yarns to create a third "in between" colour. Basic increases and decreases cause the stripes to slant. This 1 x 1 rib is double-sided and so produces a thicker knitted fabric, making the scarf lovely and warm.

DIFFICULTY LEVEL
Moderate

SIZE
2m (6½ft) long (approx.)

YARN
Rowan Kidsilk Haze 25g

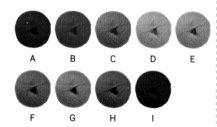

A: 595 Liqueur x 1 **B:** 627 Blood x 1
C: 596 Marmalade x 1 **D:** 644 Ember x 1
E: 597 Jelly x 1 **F:** 629 Fern x 1 **G:** 582 Trance x 1
H: 632 Hurricane x 1 **I:** 641 Blackcurrant x 1

NEEDLES
1 pair of 4mm (UK8/US6) needles

TENSION
22sts and 30 rows to 10cm (4in) over st st with yarn held double

PATTERN
Note: The whole scarf is made by holding two strands of yarn together. For example, the first stripe uses two strands of yarn A, therefore referred to as AA. Yarn AB is one strand of A and one of B, and so on.
Using yarn AA, cast on 50sts.
Row 1 (WS): [K1, p1] to end.
Row 2: S1, p1, psso, [k1, p1] to last 2sts, k1, [p1, k1] into next st. (50sts)
Row 3: [P1, k1] to last 2sts, p2.

Row 4: S1 k1 psso, [p1, k1] to last 2sts, p1 [k1, p1] into next st. (50sts)
Last 4 rows set diagonal pattern. Work a further 24 rows as set.
Working in diagonal pattern as set, break off one strand of yarn and join in one of yarn B. Commence stripe patt as set, working 28 rows in each colour pattern.
AB, BB, BC, CC, CD, DD, DE, EE, EF, FF, FG, GG, GH, HH, HJ, JJ.
17 stripes worked in total.
Cast off. Darn in all ends.

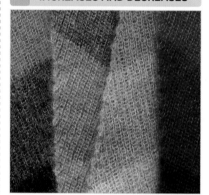

THE BASIC INCREASES and decreases are used to form the slanted stripes in the pattern. They add a geometric element to the scarf.

STITCH CHOICE

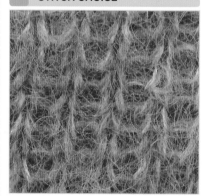

AVOID COMPLEX KNITTED TEXTURES, such as cables, when working with mohair. The fuzzy fibres will conceal any fine detail or texture.

DARNING IN ENDS

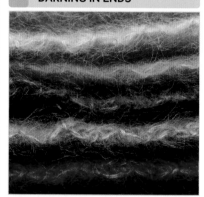

FINE MOHAIR really lends itself to the darning-in process (see p.120). The ends are well hidden beneath the furry surface fibres.

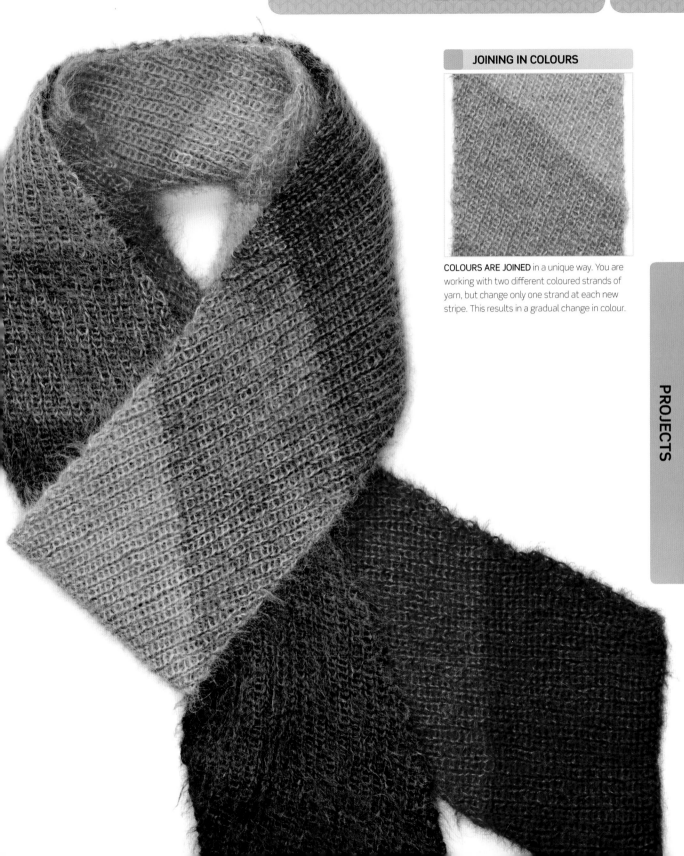

COLOURS ARE JOINED in a unique way. You are working with two different coloured strands of yarn, but change only one strand at each new stripe. This results in a gradual change in colour.

PROJECTS

LACE SHAWL

Knitting a luxurious, lace-weight shawl can be a little tricky, but the result is truly rewarding. The gossamer shawl will add an elegant touch to any outfit, and the mohair blend feels soft and warm against the skin. Knits and purls add further texture to the umbrella-style lace pattern.

DIFFICULTY LEVEL
Difficult

SIZE
50cm x 130cm (20in x 51in)

YARN
Rowan Kidsilk Haze 25g

606 Candy Girl x 4

NEEDLES
A: 1 pair of 3.75mm (UK9/US5) needles
B: 1 pair of 4.5mm (UK7/US7) needles
C: 1 pair of 6mm (UK4/US10) needles

TENSION
19sts and 28 rows to 10cm (4in) over patt

PATTERN
Using a knit-on cast-on (see p.88) and 6mm (UK4/US10) needles, cast on 190sts. Change to 4.5mm (UK7/US7) needles and cont as follows:

WORK EDGING
Row 1 (WS): K.
Row 2: [Knit but wrap yarn twice around needle, bringing both loops through] to end.
Row 3: [Purl into one of two loops in next stitch, knock off other loop] to end.
Change to 3.75mm (UK9/US5) needles.
Row 4: [K2tog] to end. (95sts)

COMMENCE PATTERN
Row 1: K3 *[p2, k1] twice, yo, k2tog, yo, k1, yo, s1 k1 psso, yo, [k1, p2] twice, k1; repeat from * to last 2sts, k2.

Row 2: K2, [p1, k2] twice, p9, *k2, [p1, k2] three times, p9; repeat from * to last 8sts, k2, [p1, k2] twice.
Row 3: K3, *[p2, k1] twice, yo, k2tog, yo, k3, yo, s1 k1 psso, yo [k1, p2] twice, k1; rep from * to last 2sts, k2.
Row 4: K2, [p1, k2] twice, p11, *k2, [p1, k2] three times, p11; repeat from * to last 8sts, k2, [p1, k2] twice.
Row 5: K3, *[p2tog, k1] twice, yo, k2tog, yo, s1 k1 psso, k1, k2tog, yo, s1 k1 psso, yo, [k1, p2tog] twice, k1; repeat from * to last 2sts, k2.
Row 6: K2, [p1, k1] twice, p11, *k1, [p1, k1] three times, p11; repeat from * to last 6sts, [k1, p1] twice, k2.
Row 7: K3, *[p1, k1] twice, yo, k2tog, yo, k1 tbl, yo, s1 k2tog psso, yo, k1 tbl, yo, s1 k1 psso, yo, [k1, p1] twice, k1; repeat from * to last 2sts, k2.
Row 8: K2, [p1, k1] twice, p13, *k1, [p1, k1] three times, p13; repeat from * to last 6sts, [k1, p1] twice, k2.
Row 9: K3, *[k2tog] twice, yo, k2tog, yo, k3, yo, k1, yo, k3, yo, s1 k1 psso, yo [s1, k1, psso] twice, k1; repeat from * to last 2sts, k2.
Row 10: K2, p to last 2sts, k2.
Row 11: K3, *[k2tog, yo] twice, s1 k1 psso, k1, k2tog, yo, k1, yo, s1 k1 psso, k1, k2tog, [yo, s1, k1, psso] twice, k1; repeat from * to last 2sts, k2.
Row 12: As row 10.
Row 13: K2, [k2tog, yo] twice, k1 tbl, yo, s1 k2tog psso, yo, k3, yo, s1 k2tog psso, yo, k1 tbl, yo, s1 k1 psso, *yo, s1 k2tog psso, yo, k2tog, yo, k1 tbl, yo, s1 k2tog psso, yo, k3, yo, s1 k2tog psso, yo, k1 tbl, yo, s1, k1, psso; repeat from * to last 4sts, yo, s1 k1 psso, k2.
Row 14: As row 10.
Row 15: K3, *yo, s1 k1 psso, yo, [k1, p2] four times, k1, yo, k2tog, yo, k1; repeat from * to last 2sts, k2.
Row 16: K2, p5, [k2, p1] three times, k2, *p9, [k2, p1] three times, k2; repeat from * to last 7sts, p5, k2.
Row 17: K4, yo, s1 k1 psso, yo, [k1, p2] four times, k1, yo, k2tog, *yo, k3, yo, s1 k1 psso, yo, [k1, p2] four times, k1, yo, k2tog; repeat from * to last 4sts, yo, k4.

Row 18: K2, p6, [k2, p1] three times, k2, *p11, [k2, p1] three times, k2; repeat from * to last 8sts, p6, k2.
Row 19: K3, *k2tog, yo, s1 k1 psso, yo, [k1, p2tog] four times, k1, yo, k2tog, yo, s1 k1 psso, k1; rep from * to last 2sts, k2.
Row 20: K2, p6, [k1, p1] three times, k1, *p11, [k1, p1] three times, k1; rep from * to last 8sts, p6, k2.
Row 21: K2, k2tog, yo, k1 tbl, yo, s1 k1 psso, yo, [k1, p1] four times, k1, yo, k2tog, yo, k1 tbl, *yo, s1 k2tog psso, yo, k1 tbl, yo, s1 k1 psso, yo, [k1, p1] four times, k1, yo, k2tog, yo, k1 tbl, repeat from * to last 4sts, yo, s1 k1 psso, k2.
Row 22: K2, p7, [k1, p1] three times, k1, *p13, [k1, p1] three times, k1; repeat from * to last 9sts, p7, k2.
Row 23: K3, *yo, k3, yo, s1 k1 psso, yo, [s1, k1, psso] twice, k1, [k2tog] twice, yo, k2tog, yo, k3, yo, k1; repeat from * to last 2sts, k2.
Row 24: As row 10.
Row 25: K3, * yo, s1 k1 psso, k1, k2tog, [yo, s1, k1, psso] twice, k1, [k2tog, yo] twice, s1 k1 psso, k1, k2tog, yo, k1; repeat from * to last 2sts, k2.
Row 26: As row 10.
Row 27: K4, yo, s1 k2tog psso, yo, k1 tbl, yo, s1 k1 psso, yo, s1 k2tog psso, yo, k2tog, yo, k1 tbl, yo, s1 k2tog psso, *yo, k3, yo, s1 k2tog psso, yo, k1 tbl, yo, s1 k1 psso, yo, s1 k2tog psso, yo, k2tog, yo, k1 tbl, yo, s1 k2tog psso; repeat from * to last 4sts, yo, k4.
Row 28: As row 10.
These 28 rows set lace patt. Repeat rows 1–28 twelve times more, ending with a WS row.

WORK TOP EDGING
Row 1 (RS): [(K1, p1) into next stitch] to end. (190sts)
Change to 4.5mm (UK7/US7) needles and work as follows:
Row 2: [Purl but wrap yarn twice around needle, bringing both loops through] to end.
Row 3: [Knit into one of two loops in next stitch, knock off other loop] to end.
Cast off using a 6mm (UK4/US10) needle.
Handwash and wet block (see p.277), making sure to stretch lace pattern out until visible and keep edges of scarf straight.

LACE DIAMONDS

THE FILIGREE DIAMONDS create a delicate geometric pattern by using yarn overs and increases and decreases.

FRILLED EDGE

LARGER NEEDLES create the pronounced frill and bring double wraps of yarn through each stitch, producing a wavy edge.

PEEKABOO LACE SCARF

A combination of techniques is used to create this fuzzy, lightweight scarf. In the "knit one below" technique, you push the right-hand needle into a stitch worked 3 rows earlier to tug the gathered loops of yarn into place. To create intricate webs and gathers, make yarnovers and drop them on the next row. If you wish, you can continue knitting to a length of 150cm (60in) with the same two balls of yarn required for a regular-length scarf.

DIFFICULTY LEVEL
Difficult

SIZE
28 x 100cm (11 x 40in)

YARN
Rowan Kidsilk Haze 25g

596 Marmalade x 2

NEEDLES
1 pair of 4.5mm (UK7/US7) needles

TENSION
15sts and 16 rows to 10cm (4in) over patt

SPECIAL ABBREVIATIONS
k1b3 As k1b (knit one below), but instead of knitting one below, knit 3 rows below the next stitch, allowing above stitches to come undone.

PATTERN
Note: When dropping yos/yrns from needle, please be aware that this refers to the yo/yrn worked on the previous row, and it will therefore present on the left-hand needle. Yarn may have to be teased into shape after rows 5 and 9.
Cast on 42sts using knit-on cast-on method (see p.88).
Row 1 (RS): K.
Row 2 (WS): K1, yrn, p1, yrn, *p1, k1, p1, yrn, p1, yrn, rep from * to last 5sts, p1, k1, p1, yrn, p1, yfwd, k1. (65sts)
Row 3: K1, *drop next yrn off LH needle, yfwd, k1, drop next yrn off LH needle, yfwd, k3, rep from * to last 4sts, drop next yrn off LH needle, yfwd, k1, drop next yrn off LH needle, yfwd, k1. (65sts)

Row 4: K1, drop next yo off LH needle, yrn, p1, drop next yo off LH needle, yrn, *p3, drop next yo off LH needle, p1, drop next yo off LH needle, yrn, rep from * to last 5sts, p3, drop next yo off LH needle, p1, drop next yo off LH needle, yfwd, k1. (65sts)
Row 5: Dropping all yrns from previous row, k1, *yfwd, k1b3, yrn, p3tog tbl, rep from * to last 2sts, yfwd, k1b3, yfwd, k1. (46sts)
Row 6: K1, p1, k1, p1, *yrn, p1, yrn, p1, k1, p1, rep from * to last st, k1. (65sts)
Row 7: K1, *k3, drop next yrn off LH needle, yfwd, k1, drop next yrn off LH needle, yfwd, rep from * to last 4sts, k4. (65sts)
Row 8: Dropping all yrns from previous row, k1, *p3, drop next yo off LH needle, yrn, p1, drop next yo off LH needle, yrn, p3, rep from * to last st, k1. (65sts)
Row 9: K1, *p3tog tbl, yfwd, k1b3, yfwd, rep from * to last 4sts, p3tog tbl, k1. (43sts)
Rows 2 to 9 set patt. Cont working until work measures 100cm (40in), or desired length, ending with a WS row.
Next row: K.
Cast off. Darn in ends.

(see p.88)

LACE CAST-ON

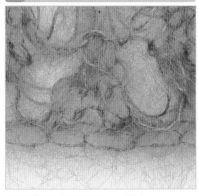

THE KNIT-ON CAST-ON (see p.88) forms a flexible mesh, which blends nicely with the lightweight nature of this pattern.

USING PREVIOUS ROWS

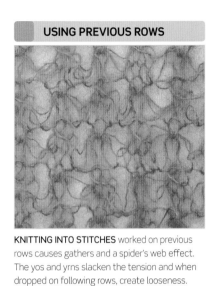

KNITTING INTO STITCHES worked on previous rows causes gathers and a spider's web effect. The yos and yrns slacken the tension and when dropped on following rows, create looseness.

LIGHTWEIGHT YARNS

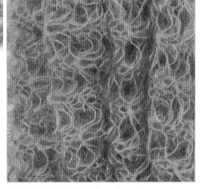

LACE-WEIGHT SCARVES are luxuriously soft and great at retaining warmth if knitted in suitable fibres. You can use larger needles to spread the stitches further and make the scarf even lighter.

DOUBLE-SIDED SCARF

This challenging project enlists the use of circular needles, but is also workable on double-pointed needles. The double-sided effect is achieved by working backwards and forwards across two separate pieces of knitted fabric in different colours, on the same needle, joined together using the intarsia technique (see p.172) as you go along.

DIFFICULTY LEVEL
Difficult

SIZE
15 x 150cm (6 x 60in)

YARN
Rowan Wool Cotton 50g

A   B

A: 969 Bilberry x 3 **B:** 974 Freesia x 3

NEEDLES
1 x 40cm (15¾in) long, 3.75mm (UK9/US5) circular needle

TENSION
23sts and 31 rows to 10cm (4in) over st st using 3.75mm (UK9/US5) circular needle

PATTERN
Using yarn A and tubular cast-on method (see p.100), cast on 70sts. Do not join.

Row 1: Using yarn A, * k1, s1 wyif, rep from * to end. Without turning your work, push sts up to tip of circular needle in your left hand, to be reworked. This will be where you worked the beginning of the last row.

Row 2: Using yarn B, * s1 wyib, p1, rep from * to end of row. Turn work over, to now go in the opposite direction. Twist yarns together once to prevent holes from forming.

Row 3: Using yarn B, work as given for row 1.

Row 4: Using yarn A, work as given for Row 2. Turn work over, to now go in the opposite direction. Twist yarns together once.

These last 4 rows form the pattern.

Cont repeating last 4 rows until work measures 150cm (60in), ending with patt row 4.

Cast off, using tubular cast-off (see p.111), in yarn B. Fasten off.

Darn in ends. Block lightly with a warm iron under a damp cloth.

DOUBLE-SIDED KNITTING is framed perfectly by this cast-on and cast-off (see pp.100, 111). It looks like the knitted fabric has been folded or grafted to create a seamless edge all the way round.

THIS REVERSIBLE FABRIC is most effective when each side is worked in a contrasting colour. Try making a striped hat to match (see pp.276–277).

INTARSIA EDGES

BY TWISTING YARNS over each other once when the two coloured yarns meet, you are essentially weaving the two separately knitted coloured fabrics together, row by row.

EASY ARMWARMERS

These armwarmers are simply knitted as a flat piece and sewn up afterwards. Using knit and purl, the stripes are easily and neatly worked by carrying yarns up the side of the work. We have used an elasticated yarn to help the armwarmers fit more snugly. Always be careful to check your tension, and change needle sizes where necessary.

DIFFICULTY LEVEL
Easy

SIZE
To fit an adult female

YARN
Rowan Calmer 50g

A   **B**

A: 500 Tree x 1 **B**: 498 Aqua Marine x 1

NEEDLES
A: 1 pair of 3.75mm (UK9/US5) needles
B: 1 pair of 4.5mm (UK7/US7) needles

——————————————————— A
——————————————————— B

TENSION
23sts and 33 rows to 10cm (4in) over st st on 4.5mm (UK7/US7) needles

PATTERN
LEFT ARMWARMER
Using yarn A and 3.75mm (UK9/US5) needles and single cast-on method (see p.87), cast on 46sts. Starting with a k row, work 10 rows in st st ending with a WS row.

Change to 4.5mm (UK7/US7) needles and work a further 6 rows in st st, ending with a WS row. Join in yarn B.

Next row (RS): Using yarn B, k1, s1 k1 psso, k to last 3sts, k2tog, k1. (44sts)
Work 9 rows without shaping.
Work 10 rows in yarn A without shaping.
Last 20 rows set stripe patt; 10 rows yarn B, 10 rows yarn A. Cont working stripe patt throughout, at same time dec as set on next and foll 20th row. (40sts)

Work 9 rows without shaping, ending with a WS row.**

Thumb Gusset
Row 1: (Working in yarn A) [k4, M1] three times, k to end. (43sts)
Row 2 and all foll alt rows: P.
Row 3: K5, M1, k to end. (44sts)
Row 5: K5, M1, k4, M1, k6, M1, k to end. (47sts)
Row 7: K9, M1, k8, M1, k to end. (49sts)
Row 9: K9, M1, k10, M1, k to end. (51sts)
Row 11: Using yarn B, k21 and turn, leaving rem sts unworked. Leaving yarn B hanging, join in yarn A, cast on 2sts and p12. You may leave the unworked stitches on stitch holders if desired. (14 live sts remain)

Thumb
Working on these 14sts only, and starting with a k row, work 8 rows st st.
Change to 3.75mm (UK9/US5) needles and using yarn A, work a further 7 rows st st. Cast off loosely using 4.5mm (UK7/US7) needles on WS.
Using yarn B, which is still attached at base of thumb, and 4.5mm (UK7/US7) needles, with RS facing, pick up and k 2sts from thumb cast-on and k to end of row. (41sts)
Next row: P.
Work 10 rows without shaping (8 rows B, 2 rows A). Change to 3.75mm (UK9/US5) needles, and using A, starting with a k row, work 10 rows st st. Cast off using 4.5mm (UK7/US7) needles, leaving a long tail of yarn for sewing up.
Darn in all ends and join row ends and thumb seams using mattress stitch (see p.227).

RIGHT ARMWARMER
Work as given for Left Armwarmer to **.
Thumb Gusset
Row 1: (Working in yarn A) k29, [M1, k4] twice, M1, k to end. (43sts)
Row 2 and all foll alt rows: P.
Row 3: K38, M1, k to end. (44sts)
Row 5: K29, M1, k6, M1, k4, M1, k to end. (47sts)
Row 7: K29, M1, k8, M1, k to end. (49sts)

Row 9: K29, M1, k10, M1, k to end. (51sts)
Row 13: Using yarn B, k41 and turn, leaving rem sts unworked. Leave yarn B hanging, join in yarn A, cast on 2sts and p12. Complete as given for Left Armwarmer from Thumb.

WORKING THE STRIPES

TWIST THE UNWORKED colour with the yarn you are working with at the end of even-numbered rows. The unworked colour is "stitched" in up the side of the stripe – no multiple ends to darn in.

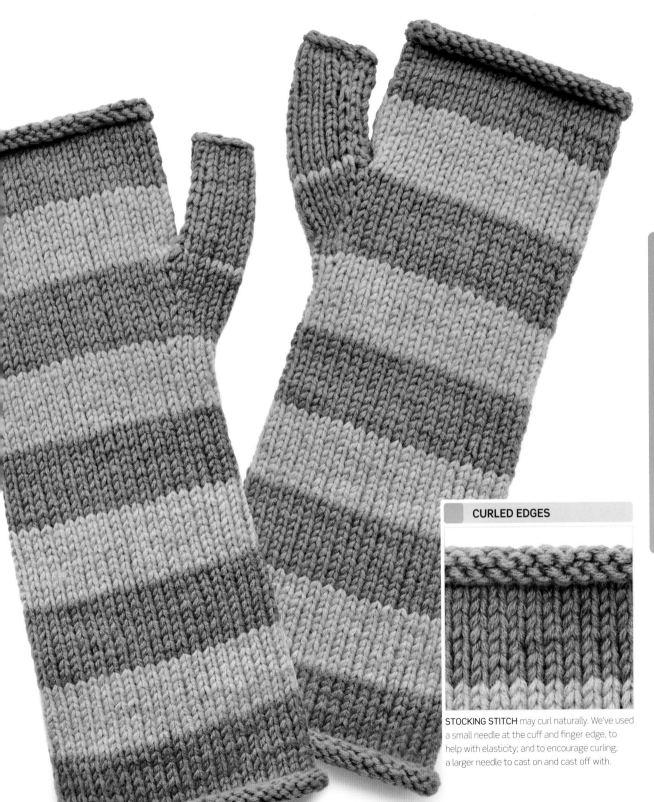

CURLED EDGES

STOCKING STITCH may curl naturally. We've used a small needle at the cuff and finger edge, to help with elasticity; and to encourage curling, a larger needle to cast on and cast off with.

FINGERLESS GLOVES

What better way to treat and accessorize your deserving, hard-working hands than with these useful fingerless gloves. Each finger is insulated near the knuckle with a taut, tightly ribbed knitted fabric, keeping the fingers warm but leaving the fingertips free. A stretchy, double-twisted ribbed cuff hugs the wrists and keeps the gloves in place. When sewing up the fingers and wrist seams, a discreet mattress stitch (see p.227) gives a professional finish.

DIFFICULTY LEVEL
Moderate

SIZE
To fit an adult female

YARN
Rowan Cashsoft 4-ply 50g

A   B

A: 442 Forest x 1 **B**: 458 Almond x 1

NEEDLES
A: 1 pair of 2.75mm (UK12/US2) needles
B: 1 pair of 3.25mm (UK10/US3) needles

——————————————————— A

——————————————————— B

TENSION
28sts and 36 rows to 10cm (4in) in st st on 3.25mm (UK10/US3) needles

PATTERN
LEFT HAND
Using 2.75mm (UK12/US2) needles and double cast-on method (see p.91), cast on 45sts in yarn A.
Row 1 (RS): K1, *p1, k1 tbl, rep from * to end.
Row 2: *P1 tbl, k1, rep from * to last st, p1.
These 2 rows set twisted rib.
Rep last 2 rows until work measures 9cm (3½in), ending with a RS row.
Next row (WS): Rib 7, M1, [rib 8, M1] four times, patt to end. Break off A. (50sts)
Change to 3.25mm (UK10/US3) needles and working in yarn B, starting with a k row, work in st st for 8 rows, ending with a WS row.**

Thumb Gusset
Row 1 (RS): K22, M1, k3, M1, k to end. (52sts)
Starting with a p row, work 3 rows st st.
Row 5: K22, M1, k5, M1, k to end. (54sts)
Row 6 and all foll alt rows: P.
Row 7: K22, M1, k7, M1, k to end. (56sts)
Row 9: K22, M1, k9, M1, k to end. (58sts)
Row 11: K22, M1, k11, M1, k to end. (60sts)
Row 13: K22, M1, k13, M1, k to end. (62sts)
Row 15: K22, M1, k15, M1, k to end. (64sts)
Row 16: P.
Row 17: K40. Turn. Break off yarn B and join in A.
Row 18: P17. Turn.
Working on these 17sts only, work 8 rows as given for twisted rib. Cast off.
Using yarn B, rejoin yarn at base of thumb and k to end.
Starting with a WS row (p), work 15 rows st st without shaping.
First Finger
Next row: K30. Turn. Break off yarn B, join in A.
Next row (WS): P13. Turn. Cast on 2sts. (15sts for finger)
Working on these 15sts only, work 8 rows as given for twisted rib. Cast off in rib leaving a 15cm (6in) tail of yarn.
Second Finger
With RS facing and using yarn A, pick up and k 2sts from base of first finger, k6. Turn.
Next row (WS): P14. Turn and cast on 2sts. (16sts for second finger)
Working on these 16sts only, work 8 rows as given for twisted rib. Cast off in rib leaving a 15cm (6in) tail of yarn.
Third Finger
With RS facing and using yarn A, pick up and k 2sts from base of first finger, k5. Turn.
Next row (WS): P14. Turn and cast on 2sts. (16sts for third finger)
Working on these 16sts only, work 8 rows as given for twisted rib. Cast off in rib leaving a 15cm (6in) tail of yarn.

Fourth Finger
With RS facing and using yarn A, pick up and k 2sts from base of first finger, k5. Turn.
Next row: P12. Turn and cast on 2sts. (14sts for fourth finger)
Working on these 14sts only, work 6 rows as given for twisted rib. Cast off in rib leaving a long tail of yarn.
Use all long tails of yarn to sew up corresponding finger using mattress stitch (see p.227), being especially careful to run as fine a seam as possible. Continue fourth finger seam to cuff. Contrasting coloured yarn should not show if mattress stitch is being worked correctly. Block according to ballband instructions, but do not block rib areas.

RIGHT HAND
Work as given for left hand to **.
Thumb
Row 1 (RS): K25, M1, k3, M1, k to end. (52sts)
Starting with a p row, work 3 rows st st.
Row 5: K25, M1, k5, M1, k to end. (54sts)
Row 6 and all foll alt rows: P.
Row 7: K25, M1, k7, M1, k to end. (56sts)
Row 9: K25, M1, k9, M1, k to end. (58sts)
Row 11: K25, M1, k11, M1, k to end. (60sts)
Row 13: K25, M1, k13, M1, k to end. (62sts)
Row 15: K25, M1, k15, M1, k to end. (64sts)
Row 16: P.
Row 17: K43. Turn.
Row 18: P17. Turn. Break off yarn B and join in A.
Complete as given for left glove.

FULLY-FASHIONED SHAPING

BY INCREASING WITH the subtle M1 stitch (see pp.131–133), the shaping forms a vertical line around the base of the thumb. This is generally the preferred outcome when hand-knitting gloves.

DOUBLE-TWISTED RIB

TWISTING THE STITCHES on every row of a ribbed edge adds grip and helps prevent ribbing losing its shape over time. The reinforced edge of the double cast-on provides sturdiness too.

MOSAIC ARMWARMERS

This geometric Fair Isle pattern is easy to work, as you only ever use two colours together at a time. The pattern is very attractive and can create quite interesting effects when you increase or lower the amount of contrast between colours in order to achieve a stark or subtle effect. Here we've chosen to use a selection of double-knit (DK) yarns of varying fibre mixes to provide texture changes between stitches as well as different colours.

DIFFICULTY LEVEL
Moderate

SIZE
To fit an adult female

YARN
A and B: Rowan Baby Alpaca DK 50g
C: Rowan Pure Wool DK **D:** Rowan Cashsoft DK

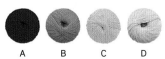

| A | B | C | D |

A: 216 Skipper x1 **B:** 223 Electric x1
C: 044 Frost x 1 **D:** 501 Sweet x 1

NEEDLES
A: 4 x 3.25mm (UK10/US3) double-pointed needles
B: 4 x 4mm (UK8/US6) double-pointed needles

A

B

TENSION
24sts and 26 rows to 10cm (4in) over patt, slightly stretched, on 4mm (UK8/US6) needles

PATTERN

LEFT ARMWARMER
Using yarn A and 3.25mm (UK10/US3) needles, cast on 44sts and divide evenly between four needles.
Cuff round: K1, *p2, k2, to last 3 sts, p2, k1. Rep last round nine times more (10 rounds rib worked in total).
Next round: Rib 4, M1, [rib 10, M1] four times, rib to end of round. (49sts)
Next round: K, at same time changing to 4mm (UK8/US6) dpns.
Working every row using the Fair Isle method and

repeating 7sts of chart seven times for each round, work until armwarmer measures 18cm (7in) from cast-on edge, ending with chart row 11.**

Thumb Opening
Next round: Work as given for chart for 9sts, cast off 6sts, patt to end of round.
Next round: Work as given for chart for 9sts, cast on 6sts, patt to end of round.
Work a further 12 rows in patt as given for 7st chart repeat, ending with chart row 1.
Dec round: Using yarn A, k3, k2tog, [k7, k2tog] four times, k to end of round, at same time changing dpns to 3.25mm (UK10/US3).
Work in rib as given for cuff round for 7 rounds. Cast off in rib.

Thumb
Using yarn A and 3.25mm (UK10/US3) dpns, pick up and knit 6sts from cast-off edge, pick up loop between sts and M1, 6sts from cast-on edge of thumb opening. Pick up another loop between sts to M1. (14sts)
Thumb round: *K1, p1, rep from * to end. Rep last round five times. Cast off in rib. Darn in all ends and press lightly under a damp cloth.

RIGHT ARMWARMER
Work as given for Left Armwarmer to **.
Thumb Opening
Next round: Work as given for chart to last 15sts, cast off 6sts, patt to end of round.
Next round: Work as given for chart for 34sts, cast on 6sts, patt to end of round.
Complete as given for Left Armwarmer.

CHART

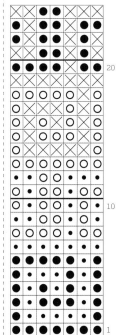

KEY

● A   • B

○ C   ⊠ D

THUMB TUBE

BY USING DOUBLE-POINTED needles to work the thumb, you eliminate seams. Also, ribbed stitches begin a round on k1 and end on p1: no uneven seams break the consistency of the pattern.

FAIR ISLE KNITTING

WHEN WORKING THREE or more stitches between colour changes on a row, catch the unworked yarn to the back of the work. It prevents it snagging in wear.

MEN'S MITTENS

These chunky mittens are quick to make and use simple-fashioned shapings. They are knitted in a thick merino and mohair mixture, which is soft and warm. Start with a rib to make an elasticated cuff and follow with a simple Stocking stitch, dividing the stitches and knitting a separate strip when you reach the thumb. When you reach the fingertip area, the special cast-off takes care of some of the sewing up, just leaving the side seams to do.

DIFFICULTY LEVEL
Easy

SIZE
To fit an adult male

YARN
Rowan Cocoon 100g

825 Clay x 2

NEEDLE
A: 1 pair of 5mm (UK6/US8) needles
B: 1 pair of 6.5mm (UK3/US10½) needles

A

B

TENSION
14sts and 16 rows to 10cm (4in) over st st on 6.5mm (UK3/US10½) needles.

SPECIAL ABBREVIATIONS
s1 k1 psso Slip 1, knit 1, pass slipped stitches over.

p2tog tbl Purl 2 together through back loop.

PATTERN
RIGHT MITTEN
Using 5mm (UK6/US8) needles, cast on 45sts using double cast-on method (see p.91).
Row 1 (RS): K1, *p1, k1, rep from * to end.
Row 2: P1, *k1, p1, rep from * to end.
Rep last 2 rows seven times more (16 rows worked in total).
Change to 6.5mm (UK3/US10½) needles and work in st st for 4 rows.**
Shape Thumb
Row 1 (RS): K22, M1, k4, M1, k to end. (47sts)
Work 3 rows without shaping.

Row 5: K22, M1, k6, M1, k to end. (49sts)
Row 6: P.
Row 7: K22, M1, k8, M1, k to end. (51sts)
Row 8: P.
Row 9: K22, M1, k10, M1, k to end. (53sts)
Row 10: P.
Row 11: K34sts and turn, leaving rem 19sts on left needle on a holder.
Row 12: P12sts and turn, leaving rem 22sts on left needle on a holder. (12sts)
Working only on these 12sts, work 8 rows in st st ending with a WS row.
Next row: *K1, k2tog, rep from * to end. (8sts)
Next row: P.
Next row: *K2tog, rep from * to end. (4sts)
Break off yarn leaving a long tail and thread through rem sts.
Transfer the 19sts from left holder to needle, rejoin yarn and k to end.
Next row: P across 19sts, then p the 22sts from rem holder. (41sts)
Work 14 rows st st without shaping.
Shape Top
Row 1: K2, s1 k1 psso, k14, k2tog, k2, s1 k1 psso, k14, k2tog, k1. (37sts)
Rows 2 and 4: P.
Row 3: K2, s1 k1 psso, k12, k2tog, k2, s1 k1 psso, k12, k2tog, k1. (33sts)
Row 5: K2, s1 k1 psso, k10, k2tog, k2, s1 k1 psso, k10, k2tog, k1. (29sts)
Row 6: P1, p2tog, p8, p2tog tbl, p2, p2tog tbl, p8, p2tog, p2. (25sts)
Row 7: K2, s1 k1 psso, k6, k2tog, k2, s1 k1 psso, k6, k2tog, k1. (21sts)
Next row: P9, p2tog, and with WS facing, cast off using three-needle cast-off method, leaving a long tail. Use long ends to sew up thumb and hand seam using mattress stitch (see p.227).

LEFT MITTEN
Work as given for right mitten to **.
Shape Thumb
Row 1 (RS): K19, M1, k4, M1, k to end. (47sts)
Work 3 rows without shaping.
Row 5: K19, M1, k6, M1, k to end. (49sts)
Row 6: P.
Row 7: K19, M1, k8, M1, k to end. (51sts)
Row 8: P.
Row 9: K19, M1, k10, M1, k to end. (53sts)
Row 10: P.
Row 11: K31sts and turn, leaving rem 22sts on left needle on a holder.
Row 12: P12sts and turn, leaving rem 19sts on left needle on a holder. (12sts)
Complete as for right mitt.

THUMB GUSSET

THE M1 INCREASE (see p.131) is a professional and smart finish. When done correctly, it should not leave any gaps or uneven areas of knitting.

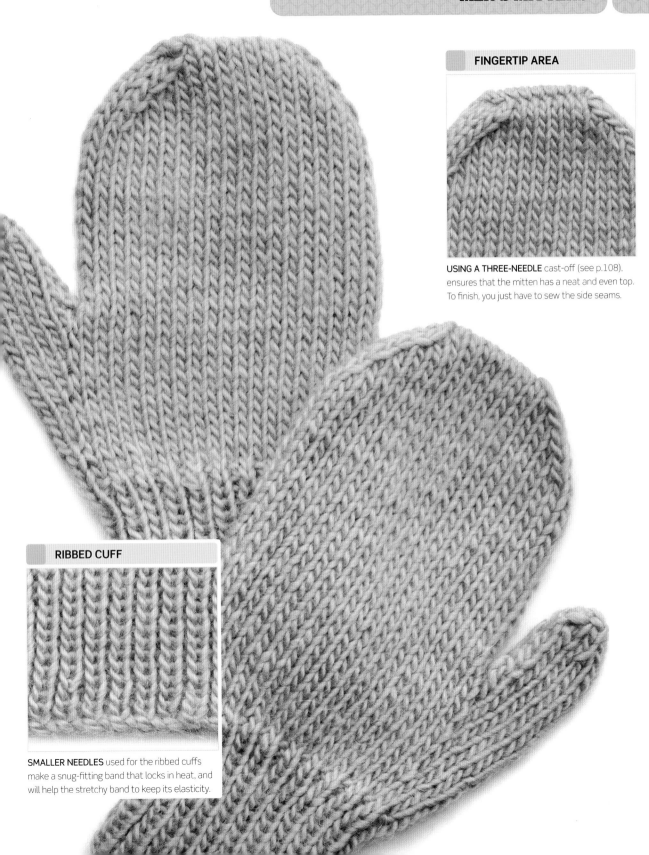

FINGERTIP AREA

USING A THREE-NEEDLE cast-off (see p.108), ensures that the mitten has a neat and even top. To finish, you just have to sew the side seams.

RIBBED CUFF

SMALLER NEEDLES used for the ribbed cuffs make a snug-fitting band that locks in heat, and will help the stretchy band to keep its elasticity.

CABLED ARMWARMERS

Practical and stylish, these cabled armwarmers will keep your arm and hands warm but allow your fingers to remain free. The cable is easy to follow, with a simple, buttonhole-style thumb opening, which is worked in the same way as a buttonhole (see p.213).

DIFFICULTY LEVEL
Moderate

SIZE
To fit an adult female

YARN
Rowan Silky Tweed 50g

752 Ember x 2

NEEDLES
A: 4 x 4.5mm (UK7/US7) double-pointed needles
B: Cable needle

TENSION
20sts and 28 rows to 10cm (4in) over 2 x 2 rib using 4.5mm (UK7/US7) needles

SPECIAL ABBREVIATIONS
C6F (cable 6 front)
RS: S3 to cable needle, hold in front, k3, k3 from cable needle.
C6B (cable 6 back)
RS: S3 to cable needle, hold in back, k3, k3 from cable needle.

PATTERN
LEFT ARMWARMER
Using cable cast-on method (see p.89), cast on 40sts on to one needle. Divide these sts between three dpns: 13sts on needles 1 and 3, and 14sts on needle 2.

Working in circular rounds, work 10 rounds of 1 x 1 rib as foll:

*K1, p1 rep from * to end of round.

Increase round: Rib 14, M1p, [rib 4, M1p] three times, rib to end of round. (44sts)

You should now have 13sts on needles 1 and 3, and 18sts on needle 2.

Set Cable Panel
Rib 13, work next 18 sts from chart, rib 13.

Rep last row until work measures 22cm (9in).**

Shape Thumb
Round 1: Rib 3, cast off 6sts, patt to end of round. (38sts)

Round 2: Rib 3, cast on 4sts using single cast-on method (see p.87), work in patt to end of round. (42sts)

Round 3: K1, p1, k2, p1, k2, work in patt to end of round.

Rep round 3 until work measures 3cm (1¼in) from thumb opening, ending at least 2 rounds after the last cable row.

Dec round: Patt 3, k2tog tbl, patt 8, k2tog tbl, k2, k2tog, p2, k2tog tbl, k2, k2tog patt to end of round. (37sts)

Change to 2 x 2 rib as folls:

Next round: K1, [p2, k2] to last 3 sts, p2, k1.

Rep last round four more times.

Cast off in rib.
Darn in ends.

RIGHT ARMWARMER
Work as given for Left Armwarmer to **.

Shape Thumb
Round 1: Work in patt as set to last 9sts. Cast off 6sts, rib to end of round. (38sts)

Round 2: Work in patt as set to last 3sts, cast on 4sts, patt to end. (42sts)

Round 3: Patt to last 7sts, k2, p1, k2, p1, k1.

Rep round 3 until work measures 3cm (1¼in) from thumb opening, ending at least 2 rounds after the last cable row.

Dec round: Patt 15, k2tog tbl, k2, k2tog, p2, k2tog tbl, k2, k2tog, p2, k1, p1, k1, p1, k2tog tbl, k1, p1, k1.

Next round: K1, [p2, k2] to last 3sts, p2, k1.

Rep last round four times.
Cast off in rib.
Darn in ends.
Handwash each armwarmer, reshape and dry flat.

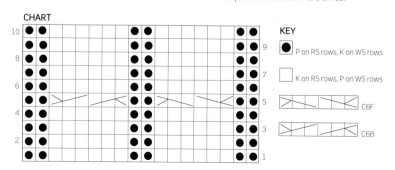

CHART

KEY

● P on RS rows, K on WS rows

□ K on RS rows, P on WS rows

⧖ C6F

⧖ C6B

RIBBED EDGE

FOR AN ELASTICATED fit, we chose 2 x 2 ribbing (a k2, p2 repeat) for the finger ends of the gloves. The stretchy edge prevents the gloves from losing their shape in wear.

CABLES

IN A CABLE, the twisted stitches result in a narrower width of knitted fabric. To counter this, you usually increase shortly before a cable. An M1 increase (see p.130) is a subtle way of doing it.

MEN'S GLOVES

To make these gloves, you will be working M1 increases (see p.131), dividing stitches, and working on part of a row at a time to form long strips of fabric for the fingers. The organic wool used still contains some lanolin, making it durable and slightly waterproof.

DIFFICULTY LEVEL
Moderate

SIZE
To fit an adult male

YARN
Rowan British Sheep Breeds DK Undyed 50g

783 Bluefaced Leicester Marl x 2

NEEDLES
A: 1 pair of 3.25mm (UK10/US3) needles
B: 1 pair of 3.75mm (UK9/US5) needles

———————————————————— A

———————————————————— B

TENSION
24sts and 30 rows to 10cm (4in) over stocking stitch using 3.75mm (UK9/US5) needles

PATTERN
LEFT HAND
Using 3.25mm (UK10/US3) needles and double cast-on method (see p.91), cast on 45sts.
Row 1 (RS): K1, *p1, k1 tbl, rep from * to end.
Row 2: *P1 tbl, k1, rep from * to end.
These two rows set twisted rib.
Rep last 2 rows until work measures 6.5cm (2½in), ending with a RS row.
Next row (WS): Rib 7, M1, [rib 8, M1] four times, patt to end. (50sts)
Change to 3.75mm (UK9/US5) needles and work in st st for 6 rows, ending on a WS row.
Thumb
Row 1 (RS): K22, M1, k3, M1, k to end. (52sts)
Starting with a p row, work 3 rows st st.
Row 5: K22, M1, k5, M1, k to end. (54sts)
Row 6 and all foll alt rows: P.
Row 7: K22, M1, k7, M1, k to end. (56sts)
Row 9: K22, M1, k9, M1, k to end. (58sts)

Row 11: K22, M1, k11, M1, k to end. (60sts)
Row 13: K22, M1, k13, M1, k to end. (62sts)
Row 15: K22, M1, k15, M1, k to end. (64sts)
Row 16: P.
Row 17: K39. Turn.
Row 18: P17. Turn.
Working on these 17sts only, work 19 rows st st ending with a RS row.
**Next row: P1, [p2tog] eight times. (9sts)
Leaving a long tail, break yarn and thread through rem sts.
Rejoin yarn at base of thumb and k to end.
Starting with a p row, work 13 rows st st without shaping.
First Finger
Next row: K30. Turn.
Next row: P13. Turn, cast on 2sts. (15sts for finger)
Working on these 15sts only, work 24 rows st st.
Next row: K1, [k2tog] seven times. (8sts)
Leaving a long tail, break yarn and thread through rem sts.
Second Finger
With RS facing, pick up and knit 2sts from base of first finger, k6. Turn.
Next row: P14. Turn and cast on 2sts. (16sts for second finger)
Working on these 16sts only, work 24 rows st st.
Next row: [K2tog] eight times.
Leaving a long tail, break yarn and thread through rem sts.
Third Finger
With RS facing, pick up and knit 2sts from base of first finger, k6. Turn.
Next row: P14. Turn and cast on 2sts. (16sts for third finger)
Working on these 16sts only, work 22 rows st st.
Next row: [K2tog] eight times.
Leaving a long tail, break yarn and thread through rem sts.
Fourth Finger
With RS facing, pick up and knit 2sts from base of first finger, k5. Turn.
Next row: P12. Turn and cast on 2sts. (14sts for fourth finger)

Working on these 14sts only, work 15 rows st st.
Next row (WS): [P2tog] seven times.
Leaving a long tail, break yarn and thread through rem sts.
Use all long tails of yarn to sew up corresponding finger using mattress stitch, being especially careful to run as fine a seam as possible. Continue fourth finger seam to cuff. Block according to instructions on yarn, but do not block rib.

RIGHT HAND
Work as for left-hand glove up to Thumb.
Thumb
Row 1 (RS): K25, M1, k3, M1, k to end. (52sts)
Starting with a p row, work 3 rows st st.
Row 5: K25, M1, k5, M1, k to end. (54sts)
Row 6 and all foll alt rows: P.
Row 7: K25, M1, k7, M1, k to end. (56sts)
Row 9: K25, M1, k9, M1, k to end. (58sts)
Row 11: K25, M1, k11, M1, k to end. (60sts)
Row 13: K25, M1, k13, M1, k to end. (62sts)
Row 15: K25, M1, k15, M1, k to end. (64sts)
Row 16: P.
Row 17: K39. Turn.
Row 18: P17. Turn.
Working on these 17sts only, work 19 rows st st ending with a RS row.
Work from ** to end of instructions for the left-hand glove.

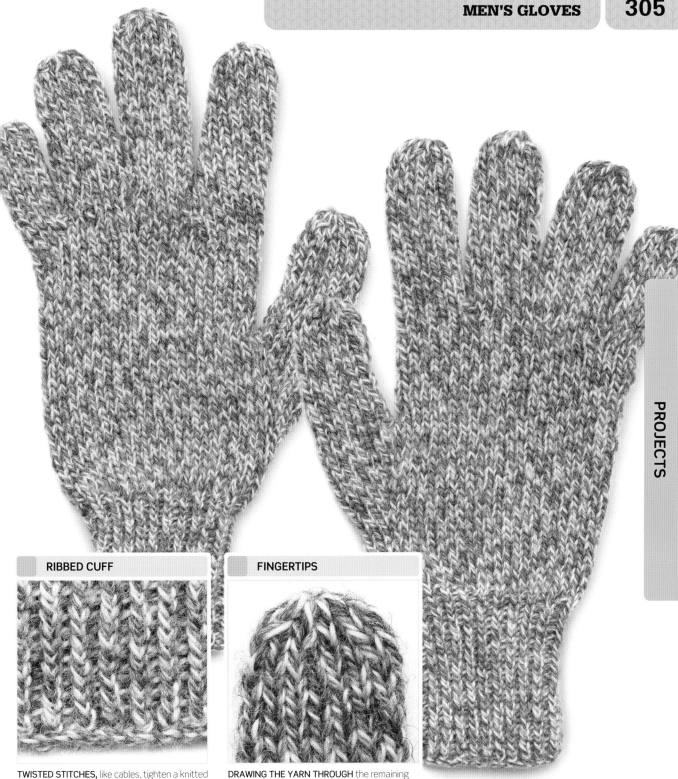

RIBBED CUFF

TWISTED STITCHES, like cables, tighten a knitted fabric and make a more elasticated wrist. Blocking ribbing can loosen it and is not advised.

FINGERTIPS

DRAWING THE YARN THROUGH the remaining stitches to finish encourages the area of work to curve, which is perfect for creating fingertips.

ANKLE SOCKS

These thick, cosy socks are quick to knit and made from a machine-washable wool blend. They have a reinforced heel, which is worked as a short flap, and then on the following rounds you pick up stitches along the edge of the flap to turn the heel.

DIFFICULTY LEVEL
Moderate

SIZE
To fit an adult female, shoe size UK 5–8

YARN
Gedifra Riana Colour 50g

5845 Red x 2

NEEDLES
4 x 4.5mm (UK7/US7) double-pointed needles

TENSION
19sts and 25 rows to 10cm (4in) over st st

PATTERN
(Make 2)
CUFF
Using the double cast-on method (see p.91), cast on 40sts.
Divide sts between three needles and arrange as foll:
Needle 1: 10 heel sts.
Needle 2: 20 instep sts.
Needle 3: 10 heel sts.
Next round: [K1 tbl, p1] to end of round.
Last row sets twisted rib. Work in this patt as set for a further 9 rows.

LEG
Work in stocking stitch (k every round) until work measures 13cm (5½in).

DIVIDE FOR HEEL
K10, turn.
S1 purlwise, p19 on to same dpn. Divide remaining 20sts between two dpn.
With RS facing, work back and forth as follows:

Row 1: *S1 purlwise, k1. Repeat from * to end.
Row 2: S1 purlwise, p to end.
Repeat these 2 rows three more times (8 rows worked in total).

TURN HEEL
Row 1 (RS): K 11, s1 k1 psso, k1. Turn.
Row 2 (WS): S1, p4, p2tog, p1. Turn.
Row 3: S1, k5, s1 k1 psso, k1. Turn.
Row 4: S1, p6, p2tog, p1. Turn.
Row 5: S1, k7, s1 k1 psso, k1. Turn.
Row 6: S1, p8, p2tog, p1. Turn.
Row 7: S1, k9, s1 k1 psso, k1. Turn.
Row 9: S1, p10, p2tog. Turn.
12sts remain. K6.

HEEL GUSSET
Rearrange sts on needles 2 and 3 so they now sit on the same needle. One needle is now spare. Use this spare needle to knit across the remaining 6 heel sts.
Continuing with the same needle, pick up 6sts along the side of the heel, pick up a loop of yarn to M1 from between instep and heel sts (needle 1 has 13sts in total).
On next needle, k across 20 instep sts (needle 2). With free needle, pick up and knit from row below the first heel st to M1.
With same needle, pick up 6sts along side of the heel and work across remaining heel sts (needle 3 has 13sts in total).
Shape Gusset
Round 1: (Dec round.)
Needle 1: K to 3sts from end. K2tog, k1.
Needle 2: (Instep.) Work even.
Needle 3: K1, s1 k1 psso, work to end.
Round 2: K.
Repeat rounds 1 and 2 twice more. (40sts)

FOOT
Continue working in rounds until foot measures 20cm (8in) from base of heel.

SHAPE TOE
Round 1: Work to last 3sts on needle 1, k2tog, k1.

Needle 2, k1, ssk, work to last 3sts, k2tog, k1.
Needle 3, k1, ssk, complete round.
Round 2: Work even.
Repeat rounds 1 and 2 until 28sts remain in total.
Work round 1 only until 12sts remain (6 instep sts, 6 sole sts).

FINISHING
K across sts on needle 1. Turn sock inside out through the middle of the needles. Slip sts from needle 3 to opposite end of needle 1.
Holding two needles together, and with WS facing, cast off using three-needle cast-off (see p.108). Darn in ends. Work second sock.

SLIPPED STITCH HEEL

BY SLIPPING STITCHES at the heel, you line the inside of the sock with strands of yarn, making the area stronger, which is important when a soft fibre is used.

DOUBLE CAST-ON

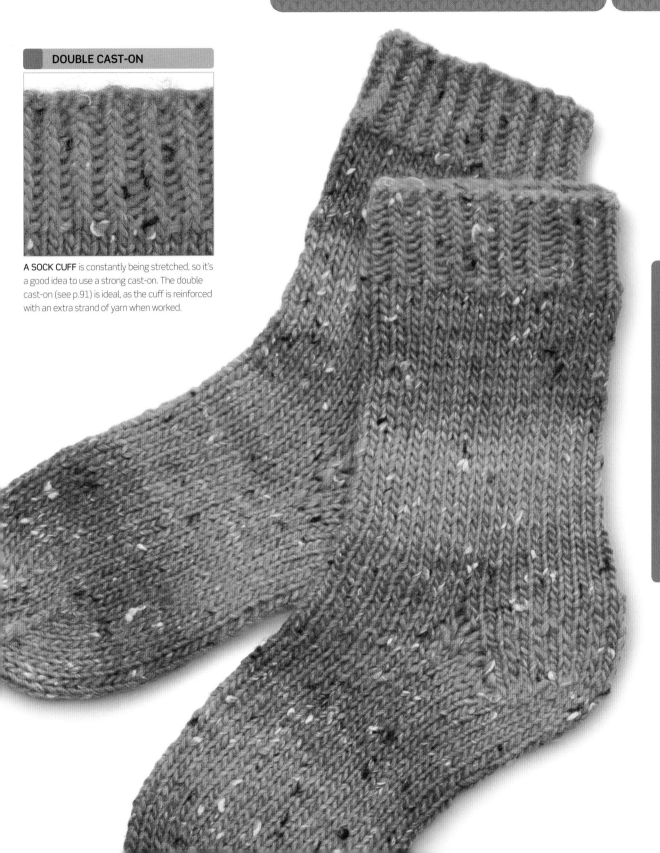

A SOCK CUFF is constantly being stretched, so it's a good idea to use a strong cast-on. The double cast-on (see p.91) is ideal, as the cuff is reinforced with an extra strand of yarn when worked.

CABLED SOCKS

These socks are finished with a strong inner seam that protects against wear and tear at the toe. The subtle cable is not difficult to work, but you will be using cable needles alongside double-pointed needles, which can feel awkward.

DIFFICULTY LEVEL
Difficult

SIZE
To fit an adult male, shoe size UK 9-12

YARN
Rowan Felted Tweed DK 50g

152 Watery x 2

NEEDLES
A: 4 x 3mm (UK11/US n/a) double-pointed needles
B: Cable needle

TENSION
30sts and 36 rows to 10cm (4in) over patt, when slightly stretched

SPECIAL ABBREVIATIONS
C2L Slip one stitch on to cable needle and leave at front of work, k1, then k1 from cable needle.
C2R Slip one stitch on to cable needle and leave at back of work, k1, then k1 from cable needle.
T3F Slip 2 stitches on to cable needle and leave at front of work, k1, then k2 from cable needle.

PATTERN
Using only two dpn, cast on 68sts using double cast-on method (see p.91). Rearrange sts over three needles so that there are 22, 22, and 24 sts.

CUFF EDGING
Round 1: K1, *p2, k2, to last 3 sts, p2, k1.
Rep last round seventeen times more (18 rounds worked in total).
Set-up round: *C2R, C2L, rep from * to end.
Next round: *P1, k2, p1, rep from * to end.
Increase round: *P1, k1, M1, k1, p1, rep from * to end. (85sts)

LEG
Commence Patt
Patt round 1: *P1, k3, p1, rep from * to end.
Patt round 2: *P1, T3F, p1, rep from * to end.
Patt rounds 3 and 4: As round 1
Repeat patt rounds 1–4 until work measures 16cm (6¼in), ending with round 3.

DIVIDE FOR HEEL
Row 1: [P1, k2tog, k1, p1] four times. Turn.
Row 2: S1p, p16, [p2tog, p3] three times, p2tog, p2. Turn. (77sts)
These 32sts set heel. Divide remaining 45sts between two dpn and work heel flap as follows:
Row 1 (RS): S1, k31. Turn.
Row 2: S1, p31. Turn.
Rep last 2 rows thirteen times, ending with a WS row (28 rows worked in total).

TURN HEEL
Set-up row: S1, k19, s1 k1 psso, k1. Turn.
Row 1: S1k, p9, p2tog, p1. Turn.
Row 2: S1k, k10, s1 k1 psso, k1. Turn.
Row 3: S1k, p11, p2tog, p1. Turn.
Row 4: S1k, k12, s1 k1 psso, k1. Turn.
Cont shaping in this way, taking one stitch more into heel shaping on every row until row "s1k p17, p2tog, p1, turn" has been worked.
Next row: S1k, k18, s1 k1 psso. Turn.
Next row: S1k, p18, p2tog. Turn (20 live sts remain).
Knit across these 20sts, pick up and knit 16sts down left-hand side of heel flap, work in patt across 45 instep sts, pick up and knit 16sts up right-hand side of heel flap, k10. This point marks end of round. (97sts)
Rearrange sts so that 26sts lie on needles 1 and 3 and 45 instep sts sit separately on needle 2.
Next round: K10, k16 tbl, work in patt across 45 instep sts, k16 tbl, k10.
Instep-shaping round: K to last 3sts on needle 1, k2tog, k1, work in patt across 45 instep sts, k1, s1 k1 psso, k to end.
Next round: K.
Rep last 2 rounds until 77sts remain (16sts on needles 1 and 3, 45sts on needle 2).

Cont in patt with st st on sole, and instep in patt until work measures 20cm (8in) from start of heel shaping.

SHAPE TOE
Dec round: K16, [p1, k2tog, k1, p1] nine times, k to end. (68sts)
Rearrange sts so that there are17sts on needles 1 and 3, and 34sts on needle 2.
Next round: K.
Toe-shaping round: K to last 3sts on needle 1, k2tog, k1. On needle 2, k1, s1 k1 psso, k to last 3sts on needle, k2tog, k1. On needle 3, k1, s1 k1 psso, k to end. (64sts)
Knit 3 rounds without shaping.
Decreasing as set by toe-shaping round, dec on next and foll third round, then on 2 foll alt rounds and every foll round until 20sts remain.
Next round: K across 5 rem sts on needle 1, turn work inside out through the centre of dpn. Slide 5sts from needle 3 to needle 1 (10sts on each needle). Cast off using three-needle cast-off.
Darn in ends. Work second sock.
To wash the socks, hand-wash in warm water, reshape and dry flat.

TEXTURE

WITH CHANNELS OF PURL stitches between each cable, the pattern resembles a rib and adds stretch to help the sock spring back into shape.

RIBBED CUFF

THE FUNCTION OF A RIBBED CUFF or collar is usually as an elasticated edging, but it can also "frame" a garment and prevent curled edges in single-sided stitches.

TOE

THE THREE-NEEDLE CAST-OFF (see p.108) creates a durable seam at the toe, with a smooth and professional finish on the right side of the work.

PROJECTS

QUEEN OF HEARTS SOCKS

Knitted from cuff to toe of the sock, this lace pattern is worked in reverse, with the hearts appearing upside down as you knit. The pattern uses basic yarn-over and decreasing techniques, with more advanced short-row shaping to turn the "corner" at the heel.

DIFFICULTY LEVEL

Moderate

SIZE

To fit an adult female, shoe size UK 5–8

YARN

Rowan Cashsoft 4-Ply 50g

455 Fiesta x 1

NEEDLES

4 x 3mm (UK11/US n/a) double-pointed needles

TENSION

30sts and 37 rows to 10cm (4in) over st st using 3mm (UK11) double-pointed needles

PATTERN

(Make 2)

Cast on 60sts using double cast-on method (see p.91), and join to form a round.

CUFF

Cuff round: *K1, p1, rep from * to end of round. Rep cuff round eighteen more times (19 rounds worked in total).

Increase for sock: [Rib 15, M1] four times. (64sts) Knit 2 rounds.

PLACE CHART

For every following round, work as given for 32sts of chart twice. Remember that working in the round, you will only ever in this instance read the chart from right to left. Continue working in chart until work measures 18cm (7in), or desired length to heel shaping, ending after chart row 12 or 26.

DIVIDE FOR HEEL

Next row: K16, turn. S1, p31 on to same needle. These set 32 heel sts. Rearrange sts so that 32sts

sit on one needle for heel, and remaining 32sts are divided across two needles, unworked.

HEEL

Next row: S1, k31.
Next row: S1, p31.
Rep last 2 rows eleven times more (22 rows worked in total for heel flap).

TURN HEEL

Next row: S1, k21, s1 k1 psso, k1, turn.
Next row: S1, p13, p2tog, p1, turn.
Next row: S1, k14, s1 k1 psso, k1, turn.
Next row: S1, p15, p2og, p1, turn.
Cont working short-row shaping in this way, bringing an extra stitch into heel shaping, finishing with the following rows:
Next row: S1, k20, s1 k1 psso, turn.
Next row: S1, p21, p2tog, turn. 22 live sts remain.

REJOIN ROUND

Next round: S1, k21, pick up and k 15sts along side of heel, work next 32sts as given for chart, pick up and k15 from other side of heel flap, k11. This point marks end of round. Rearrange sts so

that 26sts are on needles 1 and 3, 32 patt instep sts on needle 2.
Next round: K.
Next round: K to last 3sts on needle 1, k2tog, k1. Work as given for chart across 32 instep sts. On needle 3, k1, s1 k1 psso, and k to end.
Rep last round until 64sts remain.
Cont working in st st for underside of heel and in chart patt on instep until work measures 17cm (6¾in) from start of heel shaping, ending with an all-knit row.

SHAPE TOE

Toe-shaping round: K to last 3sts on needle 1, k2tog, k1. Work as given for chart across 32 instep sts. On needle 3, k1, s1 k1 psso, and k to end. Work 2 rounds without shaping.
Decreasing as set by toe-shaping round, dec on next round, foll alt round, and then every foll round until 16sts remain in total. Turn sock inside out through middle of dpns, p4, and then cast off using the three-needle cast-off method (see p.108). Darn in ends and block if desired. Work second sock.

CHART

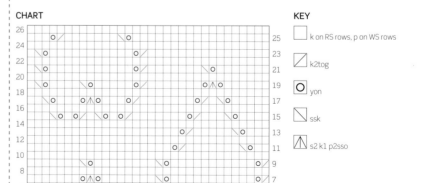

KEY

☐ k on RS rows, p on WS rows

◿ k2tog

◯ yon

◻ ssk

△ s2 k1 p2sso

RIBBED CUFF

A MID-CALF CUFF needs good elasticity to grip the shin. This ribbing starts off a bit smaller than the rest of the sock, at 60sts. Collars, cuffs, and ribbed edgings usually have fewer stitches than the rest of the garment.

WORK FROM CUFF TO TOE

WHEN WORKING A PATTERN in a sock, you start with the cuff and work downwards. As a result, any chart you apply to a sock has to be inverted so the pattern doesn't end up the wrong way up.

HEEL SHAPING

A LOOSE TENSION may cause gaps in the heel flap stitches. To twist the stitches and stop gaps, knit across these stitches through the back of the loop for the first round after picking them up.

TUTTI-FRUTTI BAG

This fun project is made up of square pieces of knitted fabric, so it is incredibly easy to make as you only need to know the basic knit and purl stitches and how to join in colours. The aran-weight yarn is knitted with reasonably large needles, so the bag will not take long to knit. We've included two options for strap size, so you can make a bag for a child if you wish.

DIFFICULTY LEVEL
Easy

SIZE
22 x 18cm (8½ x 7in)

YARN
Rowan Summer Tweed 50g

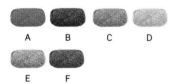

A: 528 Brilliant x 2 B: 529 Denim x 2
C: 500 Powder x 1 D: 538 Butterball x 1
E: 552 Bamboo x 1 F: 546 Loganberry x 1
Oddments of two different coloured yarns for marking (we've used red and black)

NEEDLES
A: 1 pair of 4.5mm (UK7/US7) needles
B: 1 pair of 5mm (UK6/US8) needles
C: 1 pair of 80cm (32in) long, 4.5mm (US7/UK7) circular needles

TENSION
16sts and 23 rows to 10cm (4in) over st st using 5mm (UK6/US8) needles

PATTERN
STRIPE PATT
6 rows yarn F, 4 rows A, 4 rows C, 6 rows B, 4 rows A, 6 rows F, 4 rows A, 6 rows D, 6 rows E, 4 rows yarn A. 50 rows in total.

BAG (MAIN BODY)
Using 4.5mm (UK7/US7) needles and yarn A, cast on 34sts. Starting with a k row, work 4 rows g st, ending with a WS row.

Set Border and Stripe Patt
Change to 5mm (UK6/US8) needles. Working as given for stripe patt, set border as foll:
Row 1 (RS): K.
Row 2: K3, p to last 3sts, k3.
Last 2 rows set border. Rep last 2 rows throughout. At same time, place black markers at each end of rows 56 and 65, and red markers at each end of rows 121 and 130. Cont in patt until work measures 80cm (32in) from cast-on edge, ending with a RS row.
Change to 4.5mm (UK7/US7) needles; join in yarn A. Starting with a k row, work 3 rows g st. Cast off. Darn in all ends and block as given on ballband instructions.

STRAP
Using 4.5mm (US7/UK7) circular needles and yarn B, cast on 200sts for a child's bag, or 300sts for an adult's bag, placing black markers at 44th and 156th sts [or 256th st for adult's bag] st. Starting with a k row (RS), work 4 rows g st. Break off B, join in C and work a further 4 rows g st. Cast off, placing black markers at 44th and 156th sts [256th st for adult's bag]. Darn in ends.

MAKING UP
Lay main piece of bag flat with WS facing, align row ends of strap with bag row ends between red markers. Sew in place using backstitch (see p.229). Fold main bag piece around strap so that black markers on both pieces meet. Pin in place along bag row ends and strap cast-on/cast-off edges. Sew these side seams using backstitch (see p.229). Darn in ends.

GARTER STITCH EDGE

GARTER STITCH (see p.116) makes a double-sided edge that won't curl. Stitches at each end of a row are worked in knit; the rest are stocking stitch, so knit on the right side, purl on the wrong side.

FITTING THE STRAP

MARKERS SHOW YOU exactly where the base end of the strap will sit, and how far up the bag you need to sew it. There is no need to worry that the strap will be wrongly positioned.

STRAP

CHOOSE ANY TWO COLOURS for the stripy strap. The pattern could be adjusted with regard to the number of rows for each stripe. Garter stitch makes a thick, strong fabric, ideal for bag straps.

CHANGING STRIPE COLOURS

IF USING MANY COLOURS, it may be best to cut off each colour when you finish a stripe. Knit in ends as you go, twisting them in at the back of the work every other stitch.

GLIMMER CLUTCH

This sophisticated evening bag is made from a simple pattern. It is embellished with knitted-in beads (see pp.236–240 for knitting with beads). Strand beads on the yarn, place the beads at points allocated on the chart, and push the unworked beads down the yarn as you work.

LEVEL
Moderate

SIZE
18 x 13cm (7 x 5⅛in)

YARN
Rowan Cotton Glace 50g

727 Black x 1

NEEDLE
1 pair of 3.5mm (UKn/a/US4) needles

NOTIONS
18cm (7in) zip
450 x 3mm (⅛in) glass knitting beads
23 x 33cm (8½ x 13in) strong lining fabric
Matching ribbon, 3mm (⅛in) wide (optional)
Beads for wrist strap (optional)

TENSION
22sts and 32 rows over st st

PATTERN
BAG PIECES (Make 2)
Cast on 42sts using knit-on cast-on method (see p.88). Work 2 rows st st, ending with a WS row.

PLACE CHART
Row 1: K1, [work next 8sts as given for row 1 of chart] five times, k1.
Row 2: P1, [work next 8sts as given for row 1 of chart] five times, k1.
These two rows set position of chart. Cont working from chart until piece measures 11.5cm (4¾in) repeating the 12 row patt and ending on a patt row 12.
Beginning with a k row, work 2 rows st st.
Cast off.

MAKING UP
With WS facing each other, sew row ends and cast-on edges together using backstitch (see p.229). Turn work inside out and press lightly under a damp cloth. Sew assembled bag pieces to zip. Make the lining. Fold the fabric in half along the long edge, RS together. Trim to size: it should be slightly larger than the side of the bag, and have a 1cm (½in) seam allowance on each side edge and the top edge. Stitch the side seams and turn RS out. With the bag WS out, insert the lining. Catch the corners of the fabric to the corners of the inside of the bag to prevent the lining floating about. Fold the top edges over, and oversew to the bag.
To make wrist strap, thread 40cm (16in) strands of ribbon through the zip pull, and knot together. Thread beads on ends of ribbon and trim so that they are each of equal length. Knot the end of each beaded strand.

BEAD CHART

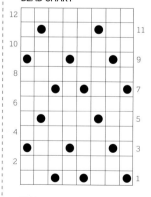

KEY

K on RS rows, p on WS rows

● Place bead

LINING THE BAG

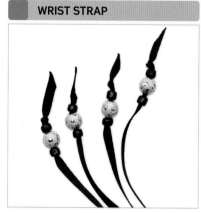

INSERT A LINING to prevent the bag's contents from warping the knitted fabric. We've used a mercerized cotton, which is very strong; it needs to be slightly larger than the area of the inside of the bag, with a seam allowance of 10mm (½in).

WRIST STRAP

THIS EASY WRIST STRAP is made from ribbon trimmed with beads, which are secured with a knot. We have used some of the remaining knitting beads plus a larger sparkly bead.

GLASS KNITTING BEADS

GLASS BEADS are very reflective, even black ones. Knitting beads are washable and able to withstand wear; they have a large eye and so will slide smoothly along yarn during knitting.

GIFT BAG

This delicate, pretty pouch makes a great "wrapping" for a gift, and could also double as an evening bag. Shiny yarns, such as the one used here, highlight texture and patterns, drawing attention to all your hard work. The rows of eyelets are pulled into a zigzag shape by increases and decreases which "warp" the shape of the rows as they are knitted. For more on increasing and decreasing techniques, see pp.130–151.

DIFFICULTY LEVEL
Moderate

SIZE
18cm (7in) tall

YARN
Gedifra Amara 50g

3705 Lilac x 1

NEEDLES
1 pair of 4.5mm (UK7/US7) needles

NOTIONS
60cm (24in) matching ribbon, 7mm–2cm (3/8–3/4in) wide
Decorative beads (optional)

TENSION
19sts and 24 rows to 10cm (4in) over st st using 4.5mm (UK7/US7) needles

SPECIAL ABBREVIATIONS
p2sso/p3sso Pass 2/pass 3 slipped stitches over. Please note that all slipped stitches are worked knitwise throughout.

PATTERN
BAG (All one piece)
Cast on 57sts using 4.5mm (UK7/US7) needles. Work 3 rows g st (knit every row), ending with a WS row.
Row 1 (RS): *K2tog, yo, rep from * to last st, k1.
Row 2: P.
Commence Patt
Row 1: K1, [M1, k5, s2 k1 p2sso, k5, M1, k1] four times.
Row 2 and all foll alt rows: P.
Last 2 rows set chevron patt. Work 4 more rows in patt.
Work Ribbon Eyelets
Row 1: K1, [yo, k5, s2 k1 p2sso, k5, yo, k1] four times.
Row 2 and all foll alt rows: P.
Row 3: K1, M1, k5, *yo, s2 k1 p2sso, yo, k5, M1, k1, M1, k5, rep from * to last 9sts, yo, s2 k1 p2sso, yo, k5, M1, k1. (65sts)
Row 5: K1, [yo, k6, s2 k1 p2sso, k6, yo, k1] four times.
Cont working in chevron patt until work measures 15cm (6in) from cast-on edge at protruding chevron points, ending with a WS row.
Next row (RS): *K2tog, yo, rep from * to last st, k1. Cont working in chevron patt until work measures 20cm (8in) from cast-on edge at protruding chevron points, ending with a WS row.
Shape Base
Row 1 (RS): K1, [M1, k5, s3, k2tog, p3sso, k5, M1, k1] four times. (57sts)
Row 2 and all foll alt rows: P.
Row 3: K1, [M1, k5, s2 k1 p2sso, k5, M1, k1] four times.
Row 5: K1, [M1, k4, s3, k2tog, p3sso, k4, M1, k1] four times. (49sts)
Row 7: K1, [M1, k3, s3, k2tog, p3sso, k3, M1, k1] four times. (41sts)
Row 9: K1, [M1, k2, s3, k2tog, p3sso, k2, M1, k1] four times. (33sts)
Row 11: S1 k1 psso, k1, *s2 k1 p2sso, k1, rep from * to last 2sts, k2tog. (17sts)
Row 13: *S1 k1 psso, rep from * to last 3sts, s2 k1 p2sso. (8sts)
Break off yarn leaving a long tail, draw it through rem sts and pull tight. Block lightly if desired, and join row ends, with RS facing, using mattress stitch (see p.227). Thread ribbon through ribbon eyelets and add decorative beads if desired.

EMBELLISHMENTS

PRETTY RIBBONS AND BEADS that match the yarn are a lovely way to add a decorative finish to a project. Try chiffon or lurex ribbon; crystal or clear beads complement any colour of yarn.

BASE OF THE BAG

A CHEVRON PATTERN forms distinct columns where the increases and decreases lie. By following the column lines for decreases at the base, we create this star-like, professional finish.

EYELETS FOR RIBBON

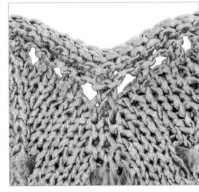

THE EYELET ROW is pulled into a V-shape by the constantly worked increases and decreases. By adding and removing stitches at strategic points, it makes the stitches travel in opposite directions.

PROJECTS

BABY'S CARDIGAN

This soft, luxurious cardigan is perfect for a newborn. You only need to know stocking stitch for the body, and garter stitch for the stylized yoke and sleeves. Boys' and girls' buttonholes appear on different sides, so follow the relevant instructions below.

DIFFICULTY LEVEL
Easy

SIZE
To fit a newborn baby

YARN
Rowan Pure Cashmere DK 25g

829 Violetta x 3

NEEDLES
1 pair of 3.25mm (UK10/US3) needles

NOTIONS
1 button

TENSION
27sts and 37 rows to 10cm (4in) over st st using 3.25mm (UK10/US3) needles

PATTERN
Using cable cast-on method (see p.89), cast on 62sts.
Row 1 (WS): K.
Rows 2 and 3: As row 1.
Row 4 (RS): K.
Row 5: P.
Last 2 rows set st st. Continue working in st st until work measures 17cm (6¾in) from cast-on edge, ending with a WS row.

SHAPE ARMS
Next 2 rows: Cast on 36sts knit to end. (134sts)
Cont in g st as set for a further 32 rows.

SHAPE RIGHT FRONT
Next row: K57 and turn, leaving rem 77sts on a holder.

SHAPE NECK
Row 1 (WS): K1, s1 k1 psso, k to end. (56sts)
Row 2 (RS): K to last 3sts, k2tog, k1. (55sts)
Row 3: As row 1. (54sts)
Knit 11 rows ending with a RS row.
Inc row (WS): K1, M1, k to end. (55sts)
Knit 3 rows without shaping.
Cont increasing at neck edge as set by inc row on next and foll 3 alt rows, then at neck edge of foll 2 rows. (61sts)
Next row: Cast on and k 7sts, k to end. (68sts)
For a Girl Only:
Place buttonhole: K to last 5sts, cast off 3sts, k1.
Next row: K2, cast on 3sts, k to end.
For a Boy Only:
Knit 2 rows.
For Boy and Girl:
Shape underarm (RS): Cast off 36sts, k to end.
Row 1 (WS): K5, p to end.
Row 2 (RS): Knit to end.
Last 2 rows set st st with g st border.
Rep last 2 rows until work measures 16cm (6¼in) from underarm, ending with a RS row.
Knit 3 rows, cast off.

LEFT FRONT
With RS facing, rejoin yarn to rem sts.
Cast off next 20 sts, k to end. (57sts)
Row 1 (WS): K to last 3sts, k2tog, k1. (56sts)
Row 2 (RS): K1, s1, k1, psso, k to end. (55sts)
Row 3(WS): As row 1. (54sts)
Knit 12 rows without shaping, ending with a WS row.
Inc row (RS): K1, M1, k to end. (55sts)
Knit 2 rows without shaping.
Cont increasing at neck edge as set by inc row on next and foll 3 alt rows, then at neck edge of foll 2 rows. (61sts)
Next row (WS): K.
Next row (RS): Cast on and k 7sts, k to end. (68sts)
For a Girl Only:
Knit 2 rows

For a Boy Only:
Place buttonhole: K to last 5sts, cast off 3sts, k1.
Next row: K2, cast on 3sts, k to end.
For Boy and Girl:
Shape underarm (WS): Cast off 36sts, k to end.
Row 1 (RS): Knit to end.
Row 2 (WS): P to last 5 sts, k5.
Rep last 2 rows until work measure 16cm (6 1/4in) from underarm ending with a RS row.
Knit 3 rows. Cast off. Join side and underarm seams using mattress stitch (see p.227).
Steam gently and attach button.

GARTER STITCH

GARTER STITCH (see p.116) makes a thick fabric. It is used here on the arms to help keep the baby warm, and also to provide a variation in texture.

STOCKING STITCH

STOCKING STITCH (see p.116) uses only basic knits and purls, and works well in this yarn as it produces a professional and taut fabric that looks store-bought.

BUTTONS

A PROFESSIONAL FINISH can be achieved with the right trimmings and embellishments. This understated shell button has flashes of many colours and will blend with anything.

BABY'S FIRST HAT

This hat is designed to match the Baby's cardigan on p.318. It is sized to fit a newborn baby, but can be made bigger by using a thicker yarn with the appropriate needles. For example, try a different double-knit yarn with 4mm (UK8/US6) needles to make a hat for a baby aged 3–6 months. A tiny hat like this is very quick to knit. We have chosen cashmere for its warmth and buttery softness, but another very soft easy-care yarn would make an ideal substitute.

DIFFICULTY LEVEL
Easy

SIZE
To fit a newborn baby

YARN
Rowan Pure Cashmere DK 25g

Violetta 829 x 1

NEEDLES
1 pair of 3.25mm (UK10/US3) needles

TENSION
25sts and 34 rows to 10cm (4in) over st st.

SPECIAL ABBREVIATIONS
rib Work in rib, knitting all presented knit stitches and purling all presented purl stitches.
rib2tog Working in rib, k2tog.

PATTERN
Cast on 83sts using cable cast-on method (see p.89).
Row 1 (RS): *K1, p1, rep from * to last st, k1.
Row 2: *P1, k1, rep from * to last st, p1.
Rep last 2 rows once more.
Row 5: [Rib 13, rib2tog] five times, rib to end. (78sts)
Next row: P.
Next row: K.
These 2 rows form st st.
Work in st st for a further 17 rows.

SHAPE CROWN
Row 1 (RS): [K6, k2tog] nine times, k to end. (69sts)
Row 2 and every foll alt row: P.
Row 3: K.
Row 5: [K5, k2tog] nine times, k to end. (60sts)
Row 7: [K4, k2tog] nine times, k to end. (51sts)
Row 9: [K3, k2tog] ten times, k to end. (41sts)
Row 11: [K2, k2tog] ten times, k to end. (31sts)
Row 13: [K1, k2tog] ten times, k to end. (21sts)
Row 15: [K2tog] ten times, k1. (11sts)
Break off yarn leaving a long tail and draw this through rem sts twice. Use this end to join row ends using mattress stitch. Steam lightly.

TOP OF CROWN

BY TIGHTLY PULLING the yarn through the stitches twice at the top of the hat, you will prevent gaps from forming in the future. Loosely gathered stitches may slide apart over time as a result of wear and tear.

TIGHTLY KNITTED FABRIC

A TIGHTLY KNITTED FABRIC is created by using smaller needles than those specified on the yarn label. The tight fabric prevents heat escaping.

SEAM

IN BABIES' GARMENTS, it is important not to add extra bulk with chunky seams. Use mattress stitch (see p.227) for a tidy hidden seam.

SOFT RIBBING

THIS DAINTY CAP sits against the baby's head, holding its shape with soft ribbing that is just snug enough to retain warmth. By using the same needles throughout for the hat, the ribbing does not end up too tight.

BABY'S BLANKET

This blanket is smooth and will not shed fibres with wear, making it ideal for a baby or small child. The fresh, lightweight, glossy yarn is made from a mixture of viscose and linen, and will feel smooth against sensitive skin. This is an ideal project for improving your knitting and purling skills; as an added bonus, you don't have to follow any complex charts to create the attractive diamond pattern. A double-sided moss stitch is used to border the blanket and prevent the edges from curling.

DIFFICULTY LEVEL
Easy

SIZE
62 x 87cm (24½ x 34¼in)

YARN
Rowan Lenpur Linen 50g

571 Blanch x 7

NEEDLES
1 pair of 4mm (UK8/US6) needles

TENSION
22sts and 30 rows to 10cm (4in) over patt

PATTERN
BOTTOM EDGING
Cast on 137 sts.
Moss St Row: [K1, p1] to last st, k1.
This row forms moss st.
Rep this row 5 more times.

COMMENCE PATT
Row 1: [K1, p1] twice, k4, *p1, k7, rep from * to last 9sts, p1, k4, [p1, k1] twice.
Rows 2 and 8: [K1, p1] twice, p3, *k1, p1, k1, p5, rep from * to last 10sts, k1, p1, k1, p3, [p1, k1] twice.
Rows 3 and 7: [K1, p1] twice, k2, *p1, k3, rep from * to last 7sts, p1, k2, [p1, k1] twice.
Rows 4 and 6: [K1, p1] twice, p1, *k1, p5, k1, p1, rep from * to last 4sts, [p1, k1] twice.
Row 5: [K1, p1] twice, *p1, k7 rep from * to last 5sts, p1, [p1, k1] twice.
Rep rows 1-8 until work measures 84cm (33in) from cast-on edge, ending with row 8.

TOP EDGING
Moss St Row: [K1, p1] to last st, k1.
This row forms moss st.
Rep this row 5 more times.
Cast off in patt.
Darn in ends on WS and block according to ballband instructions.

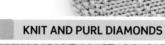
KNIT AND PURL DIAMONDS

THIS SUBTLE KNIT AND PURL TEXTURE adds interest and is easier to see in a neutral, pale, or muted shade. Very dark colours may disguise a great deal of carefully created detail.

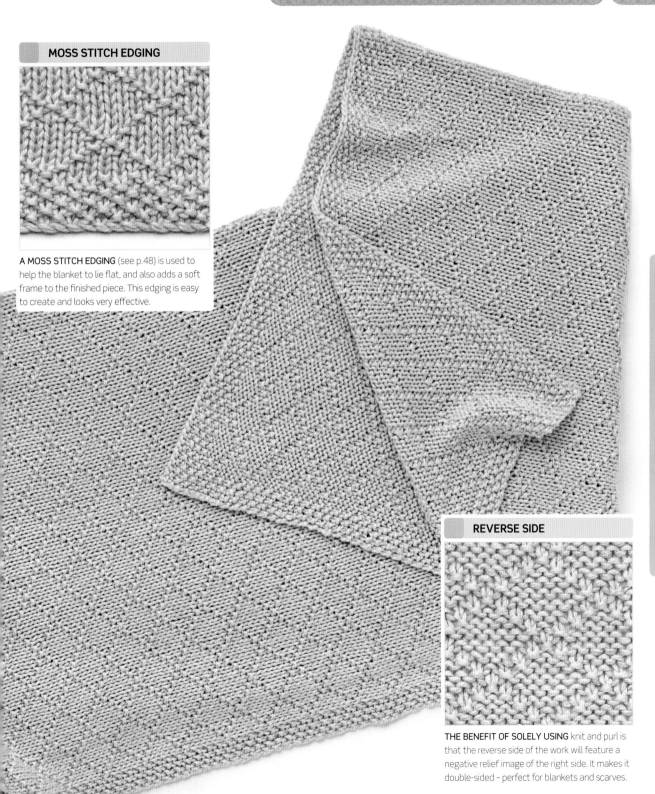

MOSS STITCH EDGING

A MOSS STITCH EDGING (see p.48) is used to help the blanket to lie flat, and also adds a soft frame to the finished piece. This edging is easy to create and looks very effective.

REVERSE SIDE

THE BENEFIT OF SOLELY USING knit and purl is that the reverse side of the work will feature a negative relief image of the right side. It makes it double-sided – perfect for blankets and scarves.

BABY'S BOOTIES

As with the heel of a sock, these booties need to curve to fit a very irregular shape – a baby's foot. To achieve a good fit, we use increases and decreases to push the curvature of the work in the right direction. We've chosen a DK yarn and used smaller than recommended needles to achieve a taut, firm fabric suitable for these tiny shoes.

DIFFICULTY LEVEL
Moderate

SIZE
To fit a baby aged 0–6 months

YARN
Rowan Lenpur Linen 50g

571 Blanch x 1

NEEDLES
A: 1 pair of 2.75mm (UK12/US2) needles
B: 1 pair of 3mm (UK11/US n/a) needles

⎯⎯⎯⎯⎯⎯⎯⎯⎯⎯ A

⎯⎯⎯⎯⎯⎯⎯⎯⎯⎯ B

NOTIONS
70cm (27½in) matching ribbon, 5–7mm (¼–⅜in) wide

TENSION
25sts and 46 rows to 10cm (4in) over g st using 3mm (UK11) needles

PATTERN
BOOTIES (Make 2)
Using 3mm (UK11) needles, cast on 37sts.
Row 1 (WS): K.
Row 2: Inc in next st, k15, inc in next st, k3, inc in next st, k15, inc in last st. (41sts)
Row 3 and all foll alt rows: K.
Row 4: Inc in next st, k17, inc in next st, k3, inc in next st, k17, inc in last st. (45sts)
Row 6: Inc in next st, k19, inc in next st, k3, inc in next st, k19, inc in last st. (49sts)
K 16 rows, ending with a WS row.

Shape for Toe
Row 1 (RS): K17, s1 k1 psso, k11, k2tog, k17. (47sts)

Row 2: K17, s1 k1 psso, k9, k2tog, k17. (45sts)
Row 3: K17, s1 k1 psso, k7, k2tog, k17. (43sts)
Row 4: K17, s1 k1 psso, k5, k2tog, k17. (41sts)
Row 5: K17, s1 k1 psso, k3, k2tog, k17. (39sts)
Row 7: K17, s1 k1 psso, k1, k2tog, k17. (37sts).
Row 8: K17, s1 k2tog psso, k17. (35sts)
Shape for Ankle
Change to 2.75mm (UK12/US2) needles and work as foll:
Next row (RS): K1, *p1, k1, rep from * to end.
Next row: P1, *k1, p1, rep from * to end.
Rep last 2 rows twice more.
Eyelet row: K1, *yo, k2tog, rep from * to end.
Next row: P1, *k1, p1, rep from * to end.
Work Edging
Next row: (Casting off) *k2, pass first st over second so that one st remains on right-hand needle as if casting off, place this one st back on left-hand needle, rep from * until one st remains.

Fasten off, leaving a long tail of yarn.
Join row ends with mattress stitch (see p.227), using long tail of yarn from cast-off edge. Fold over ribbed edging and catch to main bootie with a long running stitch (see p.247). Thread ribbon through eyelets and tie in a bow.

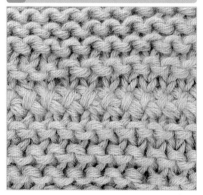

OVERSEWN SEAMS

THESE GARTER STITCH booties have an oversewn seam (see p.229). This will sit completely flat and not form an uncomfortable, bulky seam on the right or wrong side of the work.

TOE SHAPING

INCREASES AND DECREASES, at regular points in the rows, shape the toe. They are hidden behind the ridges of the garter stitch, giving the bootie a completely smooth appearance.

ANKLE CUFF

THE CUFF is knitted as a long piece, then folded and stitched to create a casing for the ribbon. The cast-off adds a wavy edge to the design.

BUNNY TOY

This irregularly shaped rabbit is a great way to play with knitted fabric, using it in a three-dimensional way, and the project will hone your skill at increasing and decreasing. We've used simple embroidery to create the facial features, and mattress stitch for an almost seamless back. A simple pom-pom, neatly trimmed, makes a perfect fluffy tail.

DIFFICULTY LEVEL
Moderate

SIZE
12cm (5in) tall

YARN

Blue colourway

Rowan Wool Cotton 50g

A   B

A: 968 Cypress x 1 **B:** 941 Clear x 1

Pink colourway

Rowan Wool Cotton 50g

A   B

A: 943 Flower x 1 **B:** 951 Tender x 1

NEEDLES
1 pair of 3mm (UK11/US n/a) needles

NOTIONS
Polyester toy stuffing
Dried chickpeas for stuffing
Darning needle
2 plastic eyes or buttons
Short length of yarn in contrasting colour for embroidery
Stitch marker

TENSION
30sts and 37 rows to 10cm (4in) over st st on 3mm (UK11) needles

PATTERN

BODY
Cast on 16sts in yarn A, placing marker at centre of cast-on edge.
Row 1: Inc into every st to end. (32sts)
Row 2 and all foll alt rows: P.
Row 3: [K1, inc in next st] to end. (48sts)
Row 5: [K2, inc in next st] three times, k to last 7sts, [inc in next st, k2] twice, inc in last st. (54sts)
Row 7: K.
Row 9: [K3, inc in next st] three times, [k2, inc in next st] to last 12sts, [inc in next st, k3] to end. (70sts)
Row 11: K.
Row 13: [K4, inc in next st] three times, k to last 16sts, [inc in next st, k4] twice, inc in last st. (76sts)
Work 13 rows without shaping.

Shape Back
Row 1: [K3, k2tog] six times, k to last 27sts, [k2tog, k3] five times, k2tog. (64sts)
Work 3 rows without shaping.
Row 5: [K2, k2tog] six times, k to last 22sts, [k2tog, k2] five times, k2tog. (52sts)
Next and all foll alt rows: P.
Row 7: [K1, k2tog] four times, k to last 11sts, [k2tog, k1] three times, k2tog. (44sts)
Row 9: K12, k2tog, k2, k2tog, k8, k2tog, k2, k2tog, k to end. (40sts)
Row 11: K1, k2tog, k to last 3sts, k2tog, k1. (38sts)
Row 13: K10, k2tog, k2, k2tog, k6, k2tog, k2, k2tog, k to end. (34sts)
Row 15: K1, k2tog, k to last 3sts, k2tog, k1. (32sts)
Work 7 rows without shaping.

Shape Head
Row 1: *K2, k2tog, rep from * to end. (24sts)
Row 2 and all foll alt rows: P.
Row 3: [K1, k2tog] to end. (16sts)
Row 5: [K2tog] to end. (8sts)
Using a darning needle, draw yarn through rem sts twice. Join row ends to form back seam, using mattress stitch (see p.227) and leaving bottom open. Stuff firmly with toy stuffing, inserting a

layer of chickpeas at the base of the bunny. Line up back seam with marker at bunny's front and squash flat. Oversew (see p.229) this seam together. Make a 3cm (1¼in) pom-pom (see p.252) from yarn B. Using picture as a guide, affix to the back of the bunny.

Spots (Make 3)
Using yarn B, cast on 3sts.
Row 1: K.
Row 2: Inc in first st, p1, inc in last st. (5sts)
Row 3: K.
Row 4: P.
Row 5: K.
Row 6: P2tog, p1, p2tog. (3sts)
Row 7: K.
Cast off, leaving a long tail of yarn.
Arrange spots randomly on bunny and, using long tail of yarn and running stitch (see p.247), sew in place.

FEET (Make 2)
Using yarn A, cast on 6sts.
Row 1: K.
Row 2: P.
Rep last 2 rows five times more. Cast off. With RS facing, oversew cast-on and cast-off edge together. This seam forms the back of the foot. Using picture as a guide, pin in place and oversew to underside of body.

EARS (Make 2)
Using yarn A, cast on 6sts and work 10 rows st st.
Next row (RS): K1, s1 k1 psso, k2tog, k1. (4sts)
Next row: P.
Change to yarn B.
Next row: K2, M1, k2. (5sts)
Beginning with a p row, work 9 rows st st.
Cast off.
Fold ear piece in half to match cast-on to cast-off edge. Join row ends and stitch in position; catch the left ear down with a single stitch to affix to bunny's head.
Sew on eyes. Using yarn in a contrasting colour, embroider nose in satin stitch (see p.246).

WEIGHTING THE TOY

FILL THE BUNNY with chickpeas at its bottom end to help the toy sit upright. An entire filling of chickpeas would make him heavy and lumpy, but combining them with a light stuffing works well.

POM-POM

A POM-POM is quick to make (see p.252). When tying yarn around the centre of it, leave two long ends: use to sew it in place. Run the yarn into the bunny and cut so it disappears into the body.

FACIAL FEATURES

THE BUNNY'S FACE can wear any expression: use the embroidery stitches shown on pp.245-248 to create it. For the eyes, buttons make a charming alternative to plastic eyes.

CABLED HOTTIE

This sparkly hot water bottle cover is easily worked by holding two strands of yarn together and treating them as if they were the same yarn – no twisting is required.

LEVEL

Moderate

SIZE

To fit an average hot water bottle, approx. 33 x 20cm (13 x 8in)

YARN

Rowan Felted Tweed Aran 50g
Rowan Shimmer 50g

A   B

A: 728 Dusty x 3
B: 092 Silver x 1

NEEDLE

A: 1 pair of 5mm (UK6/US8) needles
B: 1 pair of 5.5mm (UK5/US9) needles

A

B

NOTIONS

30cm (12in) length silver lamé ribbon 7-10mm (³⁄₈-¹⁄₂in) wide

TENSION

18sts x 20 rows to 10cm (4in) over patt on 5.5mm (UK5/US9) needles

SPECIAL ABBREVIATIONS

CR2L Place one stitch on cable needle and leave at front of work, p1, then k1 from cable needle.
CR2R Place one stitch on cable needle and leave at back of work, k1, then p1 from cable needle.
C8F Slip 4 stitches on to cable needle and leave at front of work, k4, then k4 from cable needle.
C8B Slip 4 stitches on to cable needle and leave at back of work, k4, then k4 from cable needle.

PATTERN
MAIN BODY

Using 5mm (UK6/US8) needles and one strand each of yarns A and B held together, cast on 34sts.

Row 1 (RS): K2, *p2, k2, rep from * to end.
Row 2: P2, *k2, p2, rep from * to end.
These 2 rows set rib. Rep these 2 rows twice more, then row 1 again (7 rows worked in total).
Next row (WS): P2tog, k2, p2, k1, M1p, k3 [(p2, M1) twice, p2, k2] twice, k1, M1p, k1, p2, k2, p2tog. (38sts)
Change to 5.5mm (UK5/US9) needles and cont in patt as foll:
Row 1 (RS): K1, p2, k2, p1, CR2L, p2, k8, p2, k8, p2, CR2R, p1, k2, p2, k1.
Row 2: P1, k2, p2, k2, p1, k2, p8, k2, p8, k2, p1, k2, p2, k2, p1.
Row 3: K1, p2, k2, p2, CR2L, p1, k8, p2, k8, p1, CR2R, p2, k2, p2, k1.
Row 4: P1, k2, p2, k3, p1, k1, p8, k2, p8, k1, p1, k3, p2, k2, p1.
Row 5: K1, p2, k2, p3, k1, p1, C8F, p2, C8B, p1, k1, p3, k2, p2, k1.
Row 6: P1, k2, p2, k3, p1, k1, p8, k2, p8, k1, p1, k3, p2, k2, p1.
Row 7: K1, p2, k2, p2, CR2R, p1, k8, p2, k8, p1, CR2L, p2, k2, p2, k1.
Row 8: P1, k2, p2, k2, p1, k2, p8, k2, p8, k2, p1, k2, p2, k2, p1.
Row 9: K1, p2, k2, p1, CR2R, p2, k8, p2, k8, p2, CR2L, p1, k2, p2, k1.
Row 10: P1, k2, p2, k1, p1, k3, p8, k2, p8, k3, p1, k1, p2, k2, p1.
Row 11: K1, p2, k2, p1, k1, p3, k8, p2, k8, p3, k1, p1, k2, p2, k1.
Row 12: P1, k2, p2, k1, p1, k3, p8, k2, p8, k3, p1, k1, p2, k2, p1 **.
Rows 1-12 set patt. Rep rows 1-12 until work measures 20cm (8in) from cast-on edge, ending with a WS row.
Shape Base
Row 1: K1, p2tog, patt to last 3sts, p2tog tbl, k1. (36sts)
Row 2: K all k sts and p all p sts as they present themselves.
Row 3: K1, k2tog, patt to last 3sts, s1 k1 psso, k1. (34sts)
Row 4: As row 2; place markers at each end of row.
Row 5: K1, M1p, patt to last 2sts, M1p, k1. (36sts)
Row 6: P1, k1, p2, patt to last 4sts, p2, k1, p1.
Row 7: K1, M1p, patt to last 2sts, M1p, k1. (38sts)

Cont working in patt until work measures 27cm (10³⁄₄in) from markers.
Shape Top
Row 1: K1, p2tog, patt to last 3sts, p2tog tbl, k1. (36sts)
Row 2: K all k sts and p all p sts as they present themselves.
Row 3: K1, k2tog, patt to last 3sts, s1 k1 psso, k1. (34sts)
Row 4 (WS): Cast off 8sts, [p2, p2tog] twice, k2, [p2, p2tog] twice, patt to end. (22sts)
Row 5: Cast off 8sts, k to end.
Row 6: P.
Row 7: K1, [yo, s1 k1 psso] six times, k1.
Row 8: P.
Work in st st until top measures 6cm (2¹⁄₂in) from ribbon eyelet row. Cast off.

BACK FLAP

Work as given for main body to **.
Rep rows 1-12 until work measures 18cm (7in) from cast-on edge, ending with a WS row.
Shape Top
Row 1: K1, p2tog, patt to last 3sts, p2tog tbl, k1. (36sts)
Row 2: K all k sts and p all p sts as they present themselves.
Row 3: K1, k2tog, patt to last 3sts, s1 k1 psso, k1. (34sts)
Row 4 (WS): Cast off 8sts, [p2, p2tog] twice, p2, k2, [p2, p2tog] twice, patt to end. (22sts)
Row 5: Cast off 8sts, k to end.
Row 6: P.
Row 7: K1, [yo, s1 k1 psso] six times, k1.
Row 8: P.
Work in st st until top measures 6cm (2¹⁄₂in) from ribbon eyelet row. Cast off.

MAKING UP

Handwash both pieces, reshape and dry flat. Fold main body at markers, and lay back flap so that cast-off edges meet, and it lies over main body piece at back. Using mattress stitch (see p.227), join main body row ends in this position, then sew back flap over the top. Darn in ends. Thread a strand of ribbon through top eyelets and tie in a bow.

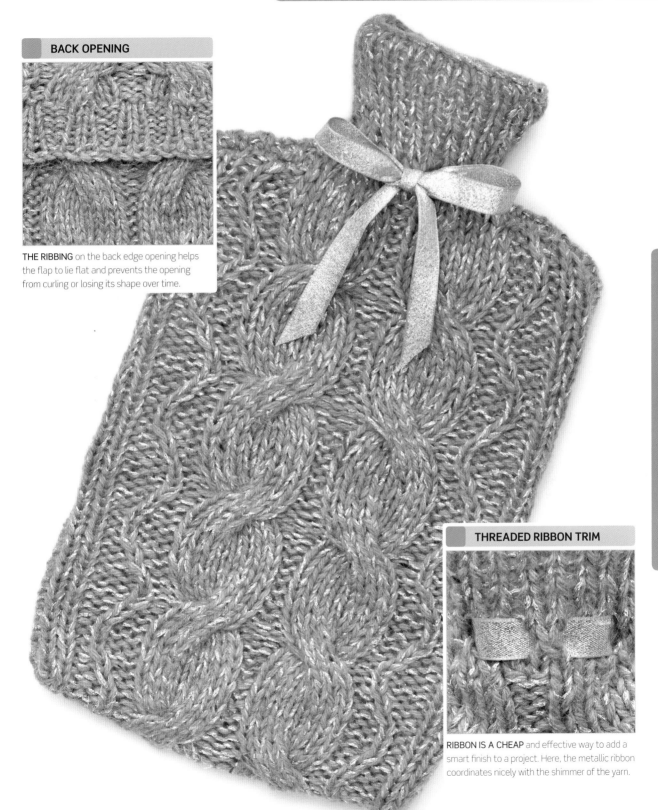

BACK OPENING

THE RIBBING on the back edge opening helps the flap to lie flat and prevents the opening from curling or losing its shape over time.

THREADED RIBBON TRIM

RIBBON IS A CHEAP and effective way to add a smart finish to a project. Here, the metallic ribbon coordinates nicely with the shimmer of the yarn.

FAIR ISLE HOTTIE

This hot water bottle cover is a great project for practising Fair Isle techniques (see p.167). It is embellished with running stitch (see p.247), and a satin ribbon to draw in the neck.

DIFFICULTY LEVEL
Moderate

SIZE
To fit an average hot water bottle, 33 x 20cm (13 x 8in)

YARN
Rowan Silk Twist 50g

A   B

A: 668 Ruby x 3 B: 660 Parchment x 1

NEEDLES
A: 1 pair of 5mm (UK6/US8) needles
B: 1 pair of 4.5mm (UK7/US7) needles

A

B

NOTIONS
3 x 15mm (⅝in) press studs
30cm (12in) cream satin ribbon, 10mm (½in) wide
1 skein Anchor Stranded Embroidery Cotton in shade 972

TENSION
17sts and 23 rows to 10cm (4in) over st st using 5mm (UK6/US8)needles

PATTERN
FRONT
Using 5mm (UK6/US8) needles, cast on 32sts.
Row 1 (RS): K.
Row 2: P.
Row 3: K1, M1, k to last st, M1, k1. (34sts)
Row 4: P.
Rep rows 3 and 4 once, then row 3 again. (38sts)
*Next row (WS): K.
Place Chart
Next row: Join in yarn B and using Fair Isle method, [work as given for row 1 of chart] twice.
Cont working from chart as set for a further 6 rows, ending with a RS row. Break off yarn B.

Row 1 (WS): P.
Row 2: K.
Row 3: K.
Beginning with a k row, work 11 rows st st ending with a RS row.*
Rep from * to * once more.
Next row (WS): K.**
Place Chart
Next row: Join in yarn B and using Fair Isle method, [work as given for row 1 of chart] twice.
Cont working from chart as set for a further 6 rows, ending with a RS row. Break off yarn B.
Row 1 (WS): P.
Row 2: K.
Row 3: K.
Decrease for Top
Row 1: K1, s1 k1 psso, k to last 3sts, k2tog, k1. (36sts)
Row 2 and every foll alt row: P.
Rows 3 and 5: As row 1. (32sts)
Row 7: Cast off 11sts, k to end. (21sts)
Row 8: Cast off 11sts purlwise, p to end. (10sts)
Eyelet row (RS): K1, [yo, s1 k1 psso, k1] three times.
Beginning with a p row, work 14 rows in st st, ending with a RS row.
Change to 4.5mm (UK7/US7) needles and starting with a k row, work 4 further rows in g st.
Cast off in k on WS.

BACK
Lower Back
Work as given for front to **.
Change to 4.5mm (UK7/US7) needles. With RS facing, and starting with a k row, work 4 rows g st.
Cast off in k on WS.
Upper Back
Using 4.5mm (UK7/US7) needles, cast on 38sts.
Starting with a k row, work 6 rows in g st, ending with

a WS row.
Change to 5mm (UK6/US8) needles and beginning with a k row, work 11 rows st st ending with a RS row.
Next row (WS): K.
Place Chart
Next row: Join in yarn B and using Fair Isle method, [work as given for row 1 of chart] twice.
Cont working from chart as set for a further 6 rows, ending with a RS row. Break off yarn B.
Row 1 (WS): P.
Row 2: K.
Row 3: K.
Decrease for Top
Row 1: K1, s1 k1 psso, k to last 3sts, k2tog, k1. (36sts)
Row 2 and every foll alt row: P.
Rows 3 and 5: As row 1. (32sts)
Row 7: Cast off 11sts, k to end. (21sts)
Row 8: Cast off 11sts purlwise, p to end. (10sts)
Eyelet row (RS): K1, [yo, s1 k1 psso, k1] three times.
Beginning with a p row, work 14 rows in st st, ending with a RS row.
Change to 4.5mm (UK7/US7) needles and starting with a k row, work 4 further rows in g st.
Cast off in k on WS.
Making Up
Block all pieces according to ballband instructions. With WS facing, lay back pieces with lower back flapped over upper back. Sandwich the sides with front, RS facing. Join side and bottom seams using backstitch (see p.229). Darn in all ends, turn RS out and block again lightly. Holding yarn B double, embroider a loose running stitch (see p.247) along outer edge of Fair Isle stripes and top opening edge. Sew press studs, evenly spaced, along inner back opening edges with embroidery cotton. Thread ribbon through top eyelets, and tie a bow.

CHART

KEY

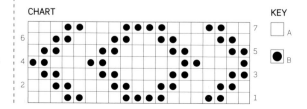

BACK OPENING EDGE

TAKE CARE WITH THE FINISHING and sewing up of the knitted pieces to give a professional finish. Align the flap edges before sewing so that they will lie perfectly parallel when finished, as shown.

PROJECTS

FLAP FASTENING

PRESS STUDS ARE AN EASY way to hold the flap closed. Sew them on with embroidery thread, which is stronger than a soft-fibred yarn. A matching colour makes for a quality finish.

RHUBARB TEA COSY

Knitted accessories for the home can make great gift ideas. This easy tea cosy is knitted in two pieces and sewn together afterwards. Use your teapot as a guide to where to leave gaps for the spout and handle, and embellish with pom-poms made from leftover yarn. As you get more creative, you can even coordinate this project with other matching items. Use a machine-washable yarn with a high wool content to ensure your tea is insulated and kept warm.

DIFFICULTY LEVEL
Easy

SIZE
To fit a small teapot, approx. 35cm (14in) in diameter

YARN
Rowan Belle Organic DK 50g

A   B   C

A: 015 Slate **B**: 012 Tomato **C**: 016 Cilantro

NEEDLES
A: 1 pair of 3.25mm (UK10/US3) needles
B: 1 pair of 3.75mm (UK9/US5) needles

——————————————————— A

——————————————————— B

NOTIONS
Pom-pom maker or cardboard

TENSION
23sts and 32 rows to 10cm (4in) over st st using 3.75mm (UK9/US5) needles

PATTERN
SIDE OF TEA COSY (Make 2)
Using yarn A and 3.25mm (UK10/US3) needles, cast on 42sts using cable cast-on method (see p.89).
Row 1 (RS): *K1, p1, rep from * to end.
This row forms rib.
Work a further 9 rows in rib. Join in yarn B.
Change to 3.75mm (UK9/US5) needles and work in yarn B as foll:
Row 1 (RS): K.
Row 2: P.

Row 3: K3, [M1, k6] six times, M1, k3. (49sts)
Row 4: As row 1.
Cont in st st, commencing stripe patt as foll:
Work 2 rows in yarn A, 4 rows in C, 2 rows in A, 4 rows in B; and then 2 rows in A and 4 rows in C, 2 rows in A and 2 rows in B, ending with a WS row.
Cont working in yarn B; shape top as foll:
Row 1 (RS): *K5, k2tog, rep from * to end. (42sts)
Row 2 and all foll alt rows: P. Break off yarn B.
Work 2 rows without shaping in yarn A. Break off yarn A.
Row 5: Using yarn C, *k4, k2tog, rep from * to end. (35sts)
Row 7: *K3, k2tog, rep from * to end. (28sts)
Row 9: *K2, k2tog, rep from * to end. (21sts)
Row 11: *K1, k2tog, rep from * to end. (14sts)
Row 13: [K2tog] seven times. (7sts)
Cast off purlwise.
Block both pieces lightly with a warm iron under a damp cloth. With WS facing, and leaving openings for handle and spout, join row ends using backstitch (see p.229). Darn in all ends.
Make one pom-pom in each of yarns A, B, and C. Sew to top of tea cosy.

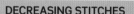

WORKING THE STRIPES

THESE STRIPES have an even number of rows, so the yarn can travel up the side of the work rather than being cut off. For stripes of more than 2 rows, twist yarns at row ends to catch them in.

DECREASING STITCHES

DECREASES AT THE TOP of any item made to fit a half-spherical area are more attractive when evenly spaced around it. As more and more rows are worked, sections create attractive ridges.

POM-POMS

POM-POMS are an easy way to jazz up knitted accessories. For how to make one, see p.252. The more wool you manage to pull through the middle of it, the tighter and firmer it will be.

EGG COSIES

Kids will love these cute cosies. They are quick and easy to make and use very little yarn. Choosing a pure wool yarn, like that used here, over a synthetic blend will keep your eggs warmer for longer. Working in short, two-row stripes, it is best to carry your yarns up the side of the work when they are not being used. The head is shaped using simple knit two togethers (k2tog), shown on p.139.

DIFFICULTY LEVEL
Easy

SIZE
To fit a large egg

YARN
Rowan Pure Wool 4-Ply 50g

A   B   C

A: 411 Navy x 1 **B:** 436 Kiss x 1
C: 451 Porcelaine x 1

NEEDLES
1 pair of 3.25mm (UK10/US3) needles

NOTIONS
Sew-on eyes for a toy (or buttons)

TENSION
28sts and 36 rows to 10cm (4in) over st st using 3.25mm (UK10/US3) needles

PATTERN
Using yarn A and cable cast-on method (see p.89), cast on 37sts.
Row 1 (RS): *K1, p1, rep from * to last st, k1.
Row 2: P1, *k1, p1, rep from * to end.
Rep last 2 rows once more (4 rows worked in total). Join in yarn B.
Using yarn B and working in st st, work 2 rows in B, 2 rows in A, and 2 rows in B again (6 rows worked).
Next row (RS): Using yarn A, k.
Next row (WS): Using yarn B, k.
Break off yarns A and B, and join in yarn C.
Working in yarn C, and starting with a k row, work 2 rows st st, ending with a WS row.

SHAPE TOP
Row 1 (RS): *K4, k2tog, rep from * to last st, k1. (31sts)
Row 2 and all foll alt rows: P.
Row 3: *K3, k2tog, rep from * to last st, k1. (25sts)
Row 5: *K2, k2tog, rep from * to last st, k1. (19sts)
Row 7: *K1, k2tog, rep from * to last st, k1. (13sts)
Row 8 (WS): P1, [p2tog] six times. (7sts)
Break yarn, leaving a long tail, and draw through rem sts. Join row ends with RS facing, using mattress stitch (see p.227). Using the photograph as a guide, and with seam centred at back of work, stitch on eyes or buttons.
Work another cosy using the same pattern, but swapping yarn A for yarn B, to achieve the alternative colourway stripe.

EYES

IT IS BEST to use sew-on eyes rather than stick-on ones, to ensure that they stay permanently attached. Although a stick-on version may last a while, the eyes are likely to fall off eventually.

SEAM

MATTRESS STITCH (see p.227) runs a smooth seam, ideal for lining up stripes, as you stitch from the right side of your work.

JOINING IN A NEW COLOUR

THESE FUNKY STRIPES are very easy to knit: you carry the yarn up the side of the work instead of constantly cutting it off and re-joining it.

KNITTING THE RIDGE

THIS NIFTY RIDGE provides a clear border between the egg's jumper and his head. It is made by working 2 rows of garter stitch (knit every row) on a stocking stitch background.

LAVENDER BAG

It is important to protect knitted items from moths – after all your hard work, the last thing you want is to discover that they have been nibbling holes. Lavender repels moths and has traditionally been placed in small bags which are kept in wardrobes and drawers. Pot-pourri with a few drops of citronella or grapefruit oil makes an alternative filling.

DIFFICULTY LEVEL
Easy

SIZE
17cm (6¾in) across (approx.)

YARN
Rowan Belle Organic DK 50g

008 Peony x 1

NEEDLES
1 pair of 3.25mm (UK10/US3) needles

NOTIONS
Fresh dried lavender
Polyester toy stuffing

TENSION
24sts and 34 rows to 10cm (4in) over st st using 3.25mm (UK10/US3) needles

PATTERN
MAIN BOW
Cast on 12sts.
Starting with a k row, work 8 rows in st st ending with a WS row.

SHAPE LEFT BOW
Row 1 (RS): *[Inc in next st, k2] 3 times, inc in next st k1, inc in last st. (17 sts)
Work 3 rows without shaping.
Row 3: Inc in first st, k to last st, inc in last st. (19sts)
Work 3 rows without shaping.
Inc as set by row 3 at both ends of next and two foll 4th rows. (25sts)
Starting with a WS row, work 15 rows without shaping, placing markers at each end of 7th row in a contrasting coloured yarn.

Next row: S1 k1 psso, k to last 2sts, k2tog. (23sts)
Dec as set by prev row, dec at each end of four foll 4th rows. (15sts)
Work 3 rows without shaping.
Next row: S1 k1 psso, *k2, k2tog, rep from * to last 3sts, k1, k2tog. (12sts).**
Work 15 rows without shaping, ending with a WS row.

RIGHT BOW
Rep as given for ** to **, remembering to place markers where indicated.
Work 8 rows without shaping. Cast off on WS.
With RS facing, join cast-on and cast-off edges using mattress stitch (see p.227), and turn work inside out. Fold bow flat at markers and join row ends using backstitch (see p.229), leaving a small 3–4cm (1¼–1½in) gap open to turn work right side out for stuffing. Fill first with lavender, then toy stuffing, for padding and shape. Close open edge with mattress stitch.

BOW MIDDLE
Cast on 14sts.
Row 1 (RS): P2, k10, p2.
Row 2: K2, p10, k2.
Rep last 2 rows nineteen times (40 rows worked in total). Cast off, leaving a long tail of yarn.
With RS facing and WS against main bow piece, wrap bow middle around centre of main bow piece, so that cast-on and cast-off edges meet. Oversew (see p.229) these together and place a few stitches through the bow middle to catch to the main bow. Stitch another piece of yarn (or ribbon) just underneath the back top edge of the bow middle's seam at the back, and make a loop of yarn by securing the other end to underside of the bow middle seam, for hanging.

BOW MIDDLE

THE BOW MIDDLE curls at the sides in order to create a slight 3D effect when attached to the main bow. This produces a nice neat edge without the need for blocking or extra sewing.

MATTRESS STITCH SEAM

MATTRESS STITCH (see p.227) is the best option for any project that needs a smooth edge on the outside. This is particularly useful in the bow middle piece, for giving the illusion that it has no seam at all.

STUFFING

A BAG STUFFED entirely with lavender would be too heavy to hold its shape when hung up, so mix it with polyester stuffing to fill out the shape and prevent the bow from sagging.

TABLE RUNNER

Yarns in 100 per cent cotton are great for homewares as they wash well. The simple, understated lace pattern in the centre of the runner is lovely to work: the leaves "grow" from the needles and form as each row is worked. Simple eyelets, as shown on pp.158–159, connect the column of lace to the easy stocking-stitch side panels. A decorative metallic lace trimming highlights the lace motif. The runner matches the Coasters on pp.340–341.

DIFFICULTY LEVEL
Moderate

SIZE
34 x 130cm (13½ x 51in) (excluding trimming)

YARN
Rowan Siena 4-Ply 50g

667 Shadow x 4

NEEDLES
1 pair of 3mm (UK11/US n/a) needles

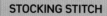

NOTIONS
3.5m (3⅞yd) metallic trimming (optional)

TENSION
28sts and 38 rows to 10cm (4in) over st st using 3mm (UK11/US2) needles

PATTERN
Cast on 93sts using knit-on cast-on method (see p.88).

Row 1 (RS): K35, yo, k3, k2tog, p1, s1k, k1, psso, k3, yo, k1, yo, k3, k2tog, p1, s1k, k1, psso, k3, yo, k to end.

Row 2: K1, p39, k1, p11, k1, p to last st, k1.

Row 3: K35, yo, k1, yo, k2, k2tog, p1, s1k, k1, psso, k1, k2tog, p1, s1k, k1, psso, k1, k2tog, p1, s1k, k1, psso, k2, yo, k1, yo, k to end. (91sts)

Row 4: K1, p40, k1, [p3, k1] twice, k1, p to last st, k1.

Row 5: K35, yo, k3, yo, k1, k2tog, p1, s1k, k1, psso, k1, p1, k1, k2tog, p1, s1k, k1, psso, k1, yo, k3, yo, k to end.

Row 6: K1, p41, k1, p2, k1, p2, k1, p to last st, k1.

Row 7: K35, yo, k5, yo, k2tog, p1, s1k, k1, psso, p1, k2tog, p1, s1k, k1, psso, yo, k5, yo, k to end.

Row 8: K1, p42, k1, [p1, k1] twice, p to last st, k1.

Row 9: K35, yo, k7, yo, s1k, k2tog, psso, p1, k3tog, yo, k7, yo, k to end.

Row 10: K1, p44, k1, p to last st, k1.

Row 11: K35, yo, k9, yo, s1k, k2tog, psso, yo, k9, yo, k to end. (93sts)

Row 12: P.

These 12 rows set lace patt. Cont repeating rows 1–12 until work measures 130cm (52in), ending with patt row 12.

Cast off.

Pin out and block using a hot iron over a damp cloth. Affix trimming using a short running stitch (see p.247), leaving some slack on corners to prevent pulling.

LACE PATTERN

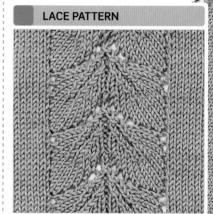

THIS REPEATING PATTERN runs in a column, using eyelets to separate it from the stocking stitch. Cables, too, are often separated from the main knitting with columns of purl to create a border.

STOCKING STITCH

STOCKING STITCH may seem dull next to the lace panel, but it will lie nice and flat on a table. A mercerized cotton yarn such as this one is shiny and highlights the structure of the fabric.

ATTACHING THE TRIMMING

USE A SHARP NEEDLE with a large eye, such as a chenille needle. Some lace trims include eyelets: just sew through these. Leave some slack around the corners so that the trim lies flat.

COASTERS

These coasters appear to be worked in the same way as a medallion – knitted on double-pointed needles from the centre outwards. However, the coasters are worked flat from the outer edge inwards and seamed, which is easier to do and yet creates the same geometric result. You decrease at quarter points across each row to work to a tight centre.

DIFFICULTY LEVEL
Easy

SIZE
10cm (4in) square excluding trimming

YARN
Rowan Siena 4-Ply 50g

667 Shadow x 1 (Makes 2 coasters)

NEEDLES
1 pair of 3mm (UK11/US n/a) needles

NOTIONS
45cm (18in) metallic trimming, 2cm (¾in wide) (optional)

TENSION
28sts and 38 rows to 10cm (4in) over st st on 3mm (UK11/US2) needles

PATTERN
Cast on 119sts using knit-on cast-on method (see p.88).

Row 1 (RS): K1, s1 k1 psso, [k26, s2 k1 p2sso] three times, k26, k2tog, k1. (111sts)

Row 2 and all foll alt rows: P.

Row 3: K1, s1 k1 psso, [k24, s2 k1 p2sso] three times, k24, k2tog, k1. (103sts)

Row 5: K1, s1 k1 psso, [k22, s2 k1 p2sso] three times, k22, k2tog, k1. (95sts)

Row 7: K1, s1 k1 psso, [k20, s2 k1 p2sso] three times, k20, k2tog, k1. (87sts)

Row 9: K1, s1 k1 psso, [k18, s2 k1 p2sso] three times, k18, k2tog, k1. (79sts)

Row 11: K1, s1 k1 psso, [k16, s2 k1 p2sso] three times, k16, k2tog, k1. (71sts)

Row 13: K1, s1 k1 psso, [k14, s2 k1 p2sso] three times, k14, k2tog, k1. (63sts)

Row 15: K1, s1 k1 psso, [k12, s2 k1 p2sso] three times, k12, k2tog, k1. (55sts)

Row 17: K1, s1 k1 psso, [k10, s2 k1 p2sso] three times, k10, k2tog, k1. (47sts)

Row 19: K1, s1 k1 psso, [k8, s2 k1 p2sso] three times, k8, k2tog, k1. (39sts)

Row 21: K1, s1 k1 psso, [k6, s2 k1 p2sso] three times, k6, k2tog, k1. (31sts)

Row 23: K1, s1 k1 psso, [k4, s2 k1 p2sso] three times, k4, k2tog, k1. (23sts)

Row 25: K1, s1 k1 psso, [k2, s2 k1 p2sso] three times, k2, k2tog, k1. (15sts)

Row 27: K1, s1 k1 psso, [s2 k1 p2sso] three times, k2tog, k1. (7sts)

Draw a long tail of yarn through rem sts and join row ends using mattress stitch (see p.227).
Pin out and block lightly, using a hot iron over a damp cloth, until work no longer curls. Affix trimming around edges using a short running stitch (see p.247), leaving some slack on the corners so that coaster lies flat.

STOCKING STICH

INCREASING OR DECREASING will alter the way that stocking stitch appears. Where columns of stitches would usually run parallel, rows will instead sit in different directions.

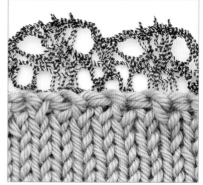

KNIT-ON CAST-ON

THIS KNIT-ON CAST-ON (see p.88) blends neatly into any lacy stitch, but also lends itself to appliqué as it sits flat when sewn with a fine seam close to the cast-on.

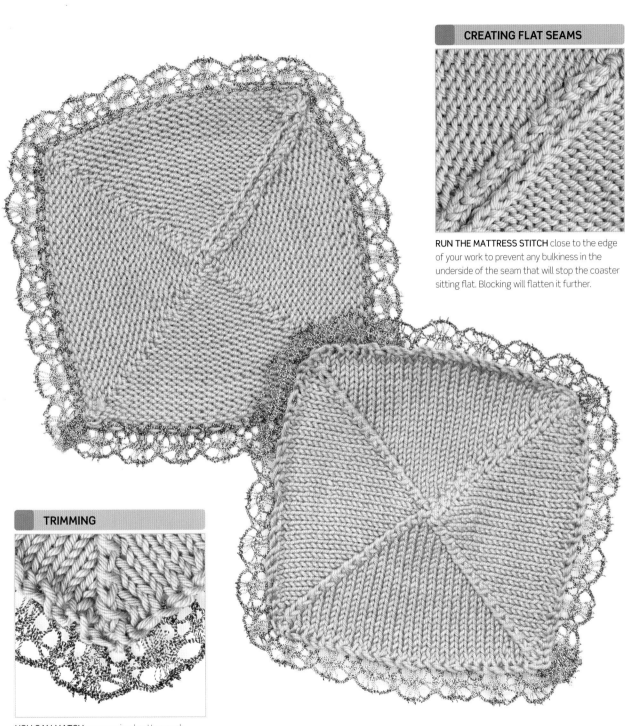

CREATING FLAT SEAMS

RUN THE MATTRESS STITCH close to the edge of your work to prevent any bulkiness in the underside of the seam that will stop the coaster sitting flat. Blocking will flatten it further.

TRIMMING

YOU CAN MATCH a mercerized cotton such as this yarn with a metallic trim to good effect; however, the coasters look just as nice with no trim at all.

STRAWBERRY CUSHION

This cushion has a cover that consists of two squares sewn together and is a good project for practising cables. Springy pure wool yarns such as the one used here work well to highlight and define stitches – details that might get lost with a yarn such as a mohair blend.

DIFFICULTY LEVEL
Moderate

SIZE
40 x 40cm (16 x 16in) approx.

YARN
Rowan Pure Wool Aran 100g

A

689 Burlesque x 3

NEEDLES
A: 1 pair of 5mm (UK6/US8) needles
B: Cable needle

A

B

NOTIONS
35cm or 40cm (14in or 16in) zip

TENSION
18sts and 21 rows to 10cm (4in) over patt using 5mm (UK6/US8) needles

SPECIAL ABBREVIATIONS
C8F

RS: S4 to cable needle, hold in front, k4, k4 from cable needle.

C8B

RS: S4 to cable needle, hold in back, k4, k4 from cable needle.

PATTERN
CUSHION SIDE (Make 2)
Cast on 66sts using cable cast-on method (see p.89).
Row 1 (RS): K11, [inc in next st, k4, inc in next st, k15] twice, inc in next st, k4, inc in next st, k to end. (72sts)
Row 2 (WS): K9 [p12, k9] to end.

COMMENCE PATT
Work all RS (odd) rows from R to L and all WS (even) rows from L to R.
Row 1 (RS): K9, [work next 21sts as given for chart] three times.
Row 2 (WS): [Work next 21sts as given for chart] three times, k9.
Cont working last 2 rows in patt as set, repeating 12 rows of chart until work measures 40cm (16in), ending with a RS row.
Dec row: K9, (p3, p2tog, p2, p2tog, p3, k9) three times. (66sts)
Cast off.

CHART

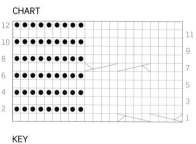

KEY

 C8F

☐ K on RS rows, p on WS rows

● K on WS rows

 C8B

BACKSTITCHED SEAM

BACKSTITCH CREATES a firm, straight seam, which is ideal for furnishings. However, it is harder to line up cables or other patterned stitches because the wrong side of the work is facing you.

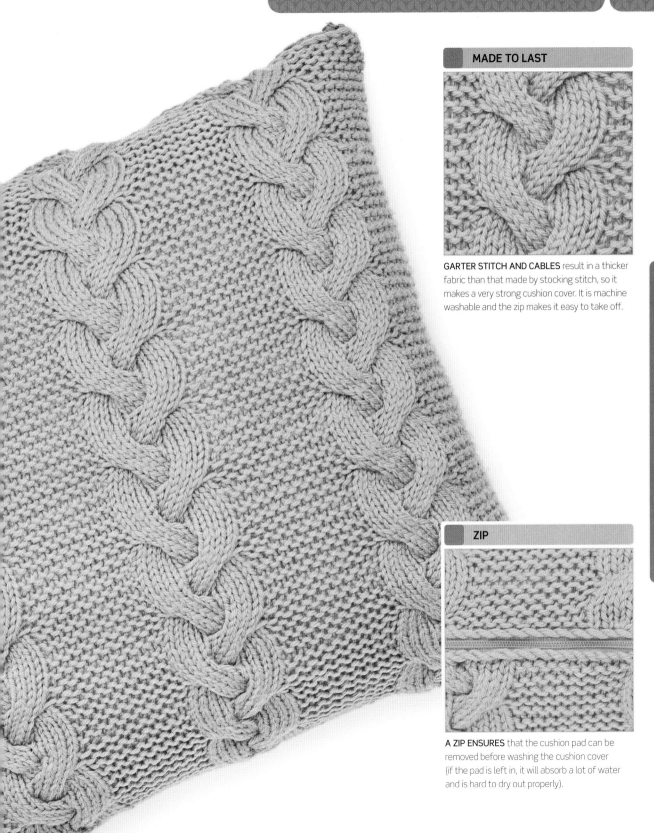

MADE TO LAST

GARTER STITCH AND CABLES result in a thicker fabric than that made by stocking stitch, so it makes a very strong cushion cover. It is machine washable and the zip makes it easy to take off.

ZIP

A ZIP ENSURES that the cushion pad can be removed before washing the cushion cover (if the pad is left in, it will absorb a lot of water and is hard to dry out properly).

LEMON AND LIME CUSHION

Liven up your sofa with this zingy, cuddly cushion. In a super-chunky bold yarn, it is an ideal first project as it requires no shaping. All you need to know is how to do Garter stitch (see p.116) and how to join in a new colour. The seams are oversewn, rather than having a bulky seam on the reverse side of the work. It is advisable to insert a zip in one seam to make the cushion cover easier to remove for washing (see p.235).

DIFFICULTY LEVEL
Easy

SIZE
50 x 50cm (20 x 20in)

YARN
Gedifra Highland Alpaca 100g

A   B   C

A: 2967 Lime Green x 3
B: 2969 Forest Green x 2
C: 2908 Yellow x 2

NEEDLES
1 pair of 12mm (UK n/a/US17) needles

NOTIONS
50cm (20in) zip (optional)
50 x 50cm (20 x 20in) cushion pad or polyester stuffing

TENSION
8sts and 12 rows to 10cm (4in) over g st

PATTERN
Cushion cover is constructed of four strips, worked bottom to top, as follows:

STRIP 1 (Make 2)
Using yarn A, and 12mm (US17) needles, cast on 21sts. Work 30 rows in g st (k every row).
Change to yarn B, and work 30 rows. Cast off.

STRIP 2 (Make 2)
Using yarn C, and 12mm (US17) needles, cast on

21sts. Work 30 rows in g st.
Change to yarn A, and work 30 rows. Cast off.

MAKING UP
Lay strips alongside each other, in order, using the photograph as a guide, to form the two sides. Sew up each side, with RS facing, using mattress stitch (see p.227). Oversew sides (see p.229), with WS facing, to make whole cushion (enclosing polyester stuffing, or leaving one side open to insert a zip if using a cushion pad). Darn in all ends. Make four 10cm (4in) tassels (see below right and p.253) of three strands each and affix to each corner of the cushion.

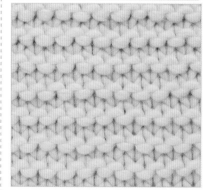

GARTER STITCH

GARTER STITCH is plain knitting on every row. It forms ridges on both sides of the work, making a thick, double-sided knitted fabric. It is the simplest way to add texture to a project.

COLOUR JOINS

WHEN JOINING in new colours in garter stitch, or working in stripes, colours will be cleanly divided in a straight line on the right side of your work. You can easily identify the right and wrong sides because the join looks different at the back.

TASSELS

WHEN THE STRANDS OF YARN for the tassels are pulled through your work, they inevitably lose their alignment, making the ends of the tassel uneven, so it is best to trim them to length afterwards.

LEMON AND LIME BLANKET

Blankets knitted on large needles with an appropriately proportioned yarn result in a luxuriously thick and warm fabric. To maximize a blanket's insulating properties, choose a yarn made of animal fibres such as pure wool or the wool and alpaca blend we've used here.

DIFFICULTY LEVEL
Easy

SIZE
100 x 125cm (40 x 49in)

YARN
Gedifra Highland Alpaca 100g

A   B   C   D

A: 2967 Lime Green x 4 **B:** 2969 Forest Green x 5
C: 2908 Yellow x 6 **D:** 2907 Green x 2

NEEDLES
1 pair of 12mm (UK n/a/US17) needles

TENSION
8sts and 12 rows to 10cm (4in) over g st

CHART

A	C	D	B
B	A	B	C
C	B	C	A
A	C	D	B
C	B	C	A

Strip 1   Strip 2   Strip 3   Strip 4

PATTERN
Blanket is constructed of four strips, worked bottom to top, as follows (see chart also):

STRIP 1
Using yarn C and 12mm (US17) needles, cast on 21sts and k 30 rows.
Change to yarn A and work 30 rows.
Change to yarn C and work 30 rows.
Change to yarn B and work 30 rows.
Change to yarn A and work 30 rows.
Strip should measure 125cm (49in). Cast off.

STRIP 2
Using yarn B and 12mm (US17) needles, cast on 21sts and k 30 rows.
Change to yarn C and work 30 rows.
Change to yarn B and work 30 rows.
Change to yarn A and work 30 rows.
Change to yarn C and work 30 rows.
Strip should measure 125cm (49in). Cast off.

STRIP 3
Using yarn C and 12mm (US17) needles, cast on 21sts and k 30 rows.
Change to yarn D and work 30 rows.
Change to yarn C and work 30 rows.
Change to yarn B and work 30 rows.
Change to yarn D and work 30 rows.
Strip should measure 125cm (49in). Cast off.

STRIP 4
Using yarn A and 12mm (US17) needles, cast on 21sts and k 30 rows.
Change to yarn B and work 30 rows.
Change to yarn A and work 30 rows.
Change to yarn C and work 30 rows.
Change to yarn B and work 30 rows.
Strip should measure 125cm (49in).
Cast off.

MAKING UP
Lay the strips alongside each other and match cast-on and cast-off edges. Sew up, with WS facing, using overcast stitch (see p.229). Block and darn in all ends. Affix one tassel to each corner of the blanket (15cm/6in long and made of three strands of yarn).

OVERSEW STRIPS TOGETHER

IT IS BEST to oversew (see p.229) garter stitch strips as this blends with the ridged texture of the knitted fabric. It also doesn't form a reverse-side seam, which in a blanket is more attractive.

GARTER STITCH

GARTER STITCH (see p.116) is easy and is identical on both sides, which prevents the knitted fabric from curling, so little blocking is required. Perfect for hand-knitted blankets.

CAMPFIRE BLANKET

This cosy blanket uses Stocking stitch and the intarsia technique to create large patches of colour inlaid into background shades. There are four designs in the blanket, but you could use just one, or a mixture of two or three. The charts for these motifs are on p.391.

DIFFICULTY LEVEL
Moderate

SIZE
127 x 107cm (50 x 42in) approx.

YARN
Rowan Silky Tweed 50g

A   B   C   D   E

A: 754 Tabby x 4
B: 759 Mardi Gras x 6
C: 756 Bechamel x 3
D: 753 Inky x 1
E: 752 Ember x 1

NEEDLES
A: 1 pair of 5mm (UK6/US8) needles
B: 1 pair of 4.5mm (UK7/US7) circular needles

A

B

NOTIONS
Yarn bobbins

TENSION
19sts and 25 rows to 10cm (4in) over st st using 5mm (UK6/US8) needles

PATTERN
Use the intarsia method and yarn bobbins (see p.172).

BORDERED SQUARE (Make 10)
Using yarn B and 5mm (UK6/US8) needles, cast on 48sts. Work as given for bordered square chart (see p.391) for 68 rows, then cast off.

HEART SQUARE (Make 5)
Using yarn A and 5mm (UK6/US8) needles, cast on 48sts. Work as given for heart square chart (see p.391) for 68 rows, then cast off.

MOON SQUARE (Make 2)
Using yarn D and 5mm (UK6/US8) needles, cast on 48sts. Work as given for moon square chart (see p.391) for 68 rows, then cast off.

STAR SQUARE (Make 3)
Using yarn A and 5mm (UK6/US8) needles, cast on 48sts. Work as given for star square chart (see p.391) for 68 rows, then cast off.

Block all squares according to ballband instructions and arrange squares in to a 4 x 5 pattern of your choice. Oversew all squares together, or use mattress stitch if desired.

BOTTOM AND TOP BORDERS
Using yarn B and 4.5mm (UK7/US7) circular needles, and with RS facing, pick up and k 192sts across bottom edge of blanket (cast-on edge of squares). Work 10 rows garter stitch, cast off. Repeat for top edge of blanket

SIDE BORDERS
Using yarn B and 4.5mm (UK7/US7) circular needles, pick up and k 5sts from right bottom border edge, 210sts along blanket squares, and 5sts from top border edge. Work 10 rows in garter stitch and cast off. Repeat for left border. Darn in ends. Steam entire blanket lightly under a damp cloth.

PICKING UP STITCHES

PICKING UP STITCHES around your blanket for the final border can look very professional. Remember to evenly space your stitches along the edge you will be picking up along, to prevent wavy or puckered areas along your trim.

INTARSIA

THE INTARSIA COLOURWORK method is a nifty way to work two or more strands of yarn and "stitch" them together with a twist at each colour change point on a row.

MATTRESS STITCH SEAMS

MATTRESS STITCH (see p.227) is a great way to make sewn-up seams appear as if the seam were knitted together in the first place. It only forms a small seam on the wrong side of the work.

FELTED TOTE BAG

This quick and easy tote bag is a good design to start off with if you're interested in knitting bags. In a felting project, the colour changes present in a variegated yarn make the knitting of large stretches of plain stocking stitch more enjoyable. Refer to the felting section (see pp.264–266) before starting, and remember to felt a sample swatch before attempting the final project.

DIFFICULTY LEVEL
Easy

SIZE
32 x 38cm (12¾ x 15in) (approx.)

YARN
Rowan Colourscape Chunky 100g

447 Jungle x 2

NEEDLES
1 pair of 7mm (UK2/US n/a) needles

NOTIONS
20 (approx.) rhinestone studs

TENSION
(Before felting) 14sts and 28 rows to 10cm (4in) over st st

PATTERN
Cast on 50sts.
Starting with a k row, and working in st st, inc at both ends of 5th row. Work 9 rows without shaping. (52sts)
Row 16 (RS): Inc in first st, k15, cast off 20sts, k15, inc in last st. (54sts)
Row 17: K17, cast on 20sts, k to end.
Cont working in st st, inc on 8th and every foll 10th row, until there are 66sts.
Work 19 rows without shaping.
Dec at each end of next and every foll 10th row until 54sts remain.
Work 8 rows without shaping.
Next row (WS): P17, cast off 20sts, p to end.
Next row: S1 k1 psso, k15, cast on 20sts, k to last 2sts, k2tog. (52sts)
Cont working in st st, dec on foll 10th row. Work 5 more rows without shaping. Cast off.

Fold work with wrong sides facing you so that cast-on and cast-off edges meet. Join row ends using a long backstitch (see p.229), and felt in the washing machine at 60°C. Stuff the felted bag with clean plastic bags to hold it in its pear shape and leave to dry. Add rhinestone studs on the bag, using the photograph as a guide.

BAG HANDLE

THESE LARGE SLITS are worked as a buttonhole, casting off on the first row and the following row, then casting on over the top of these stitches.

SEAM

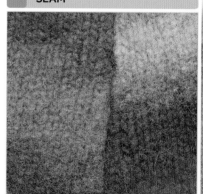

WHEN A KNITTED FABRIC is going to be felted, seams need only be sewn loosely. The high-temperature wash for felting will cause the fabric to "glue" itself together, strengthening the seam.

FELTED FABRIC

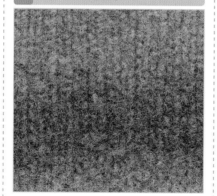

ANIMAL FIBRES such as wool and alpaca will release hair during the felting process, creating a lovely fuzzy fabric. Excess "fuzz" can be pulled off by hand shortly after felting has finished.

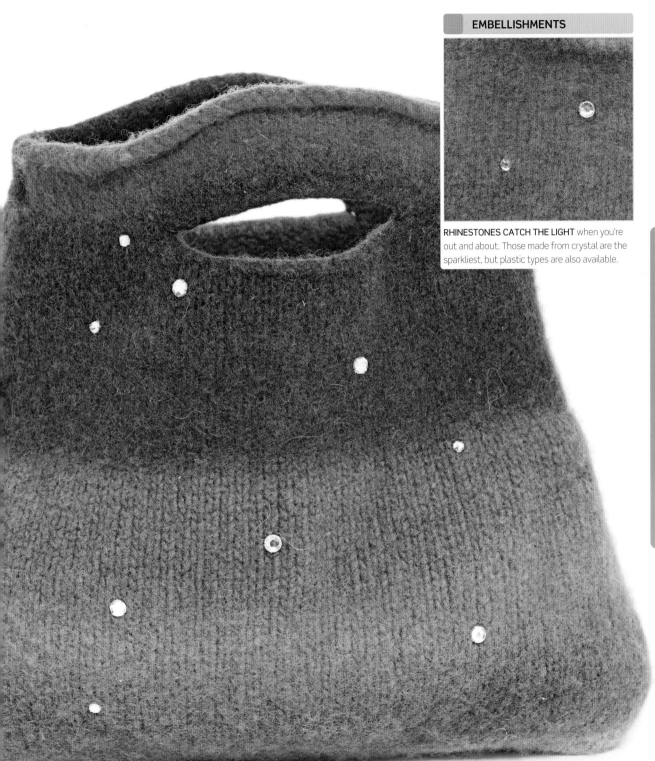

RHINESTONES CATCH THE LIGHT when you're out and about. Those made from crystal are the sparkliest, but plastic types are also available.

MAGMA FELTED CUSHION

The intarsia method of colourwork (see p.172) is employed here to create a gentle and mesmerizing flow of shapes. The blobs of colour are eased into shape by the felting process (see pp.264–266); remember to felt a test swatch before starting on the final cushion.

LEVEL
Difficult

SIZE
(After Felting) 30cm (12in) square (approx.)

YARN
Rowan Kid Classic 50g

A   B

A: 847 Cherry Red x 2
B: 852 Victoria x 2

NEEDLE
1 pair of 5mm (UK6/US8) needles

NOTIONS
Yarn bobbins
1 blunt-ended darning needle
1 sharp-ended darning needle
Mercerized cotton thread
Large safety pins
30cm (12in) zip (optional)
30 x 30cm (12 x 12in) cushion pad

TENSION
(Before felting) 19sts and 25 rows to 10cm (4in)
over st st using 5mm (UK6/US8) needles

PATTERN
CUSHION PIECES (Make 2)
Cast on 88sts. Using the intarsia method and yarn bobbins, complete rows 1–120 as given for chart. Cast off.

MAKING UP
Darn in all ends. Pin pieces together with right sides facing, matching cast-on and cast-off edges. Join row ends and cast-off edges using blunt needle and a long backstitch. Turn right side out. Tack

cast-on edges together using mercerized cotton. **Felt in the washing machine** at 60°C. Remove tacking, reshape, stuff with plastic bags and safety-pin the cast-on edges together to hold the cover in shape while it dries. Leave to dry.

Insert zip (see p.235). The felt will be very thick, so you need to use the sharp needle. Put the cushion pad inside the cushion cover. Alternatively, insert cushion pad and close bottom edge using mattress stitch.

CHART   KEY ● A   □ B

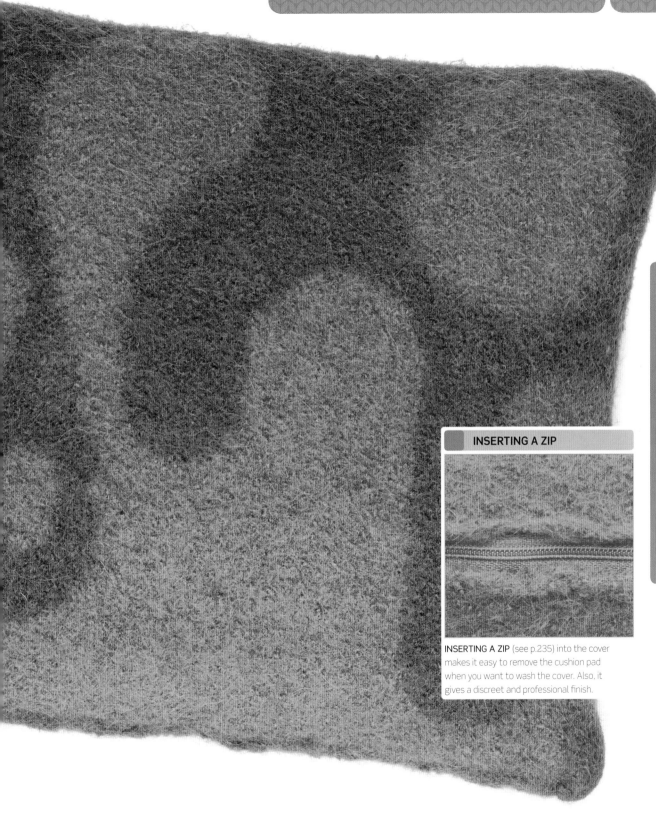

INSERTING A ZIP

INSERTING A ZIP (see p.235) into the cover makes it easy to remove the cushion pad when you want to wash the cover. Also, it gives a discreet and professional finish.

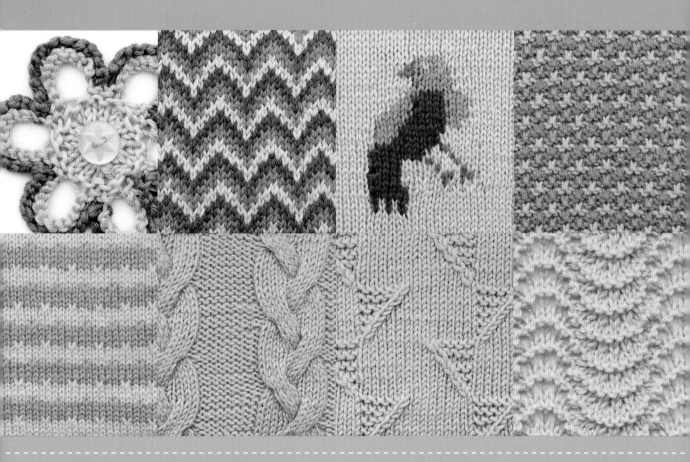

STITCH PATTERNS

KNIT AND PURL STITCH PATTERNS

MOSS STITCH (RICE STITCH)

INSTRUCTIONS

For an even number of sts:
Row 1: *K1, p1, rep from *.
Row 2: *P1, k1, rep from *.
Rep rows 1 and 2 to form patt.

For an odd number of sts:
Row 1: *K1, p1, rep from * to
last st, k1.
Rep row 1 to form patt.

SINGLE RIB

INSTRUCTIONS

For an even number of sts:
Row 1: *K1, p1, rep from * to end.
Rep row 1 to form patt.

For an odd number of sts:
Row 1: *K1, p1, rep from * to last
st, k1.
Row 2: *P1, k1, rep from * to last
st, p1.
Rep rows 1 and 2 to form patt.

DOUBLE RIB

INSTRUCTIONS

Cast on a multiple of 4sts.
Row 1: *K2, p2, rep from *.
Rep row 1 to form patt.

BASKETWEAVE STITCH

INSTRUCTIONS

Cast on a multiple of 8sts.
Rows 1–5: *K4, p4, rep from *.
Rows 6–10: *P4, k4, rep from *.
Rep rows 1–10 to form patt.

TEXTURED CHECK STITCH

INSTRUCTIONS

Cast on a multiple of 4sts plus
3 extra sts.
Row 1: K3, *p1, k3, rep from *.
Row 2: K1, *p1, k3, rep from * to last
2sts, p1, k1.
Rows 3–6: [Rep rows 1 and 2] twice.
Row 7: K1, *p1, k3, rep from * to last
2sts, p1, k1.
Row 8: K3, *p1, k3, rep from *.
Rows 9–12: [Rep rows 7 and 8] twice.
Rep rows 1–12 to form patt.

STRIPED CHECK STITCH

INSTRUCTIONS

Cast on a multiple of 6sts plus
3 extra sts.
**Row 1 and all odd-numbered rows
(RS):** K.
Row 2: K.
Rows 4 and 6: P3, *k3, p3, rep from *.
Rows 8 and 10: K.
Rows 12 and 14: K3, *p3, k3, rep
from *.
Row 16: K.
Rep rows 1–16 to form patt.

LITTLE CHECK STITCH

INSTRUCTIONS

Cast on a multiple of 10sts plus
5 extra sts.
Row 1: *K5, p5, rep from * to last
5sts, k5.
Row 2: P.
Repeat last 2 rows twice more, then
row 1 again.
Row 8: K5, *p5, k5, rep from * to end.
Row 9: K.
Repeat last 2 rows twice more, then
row 8 again.

DIAMOND STITCH

INSTRUCTIONS

Cast on a multiple of 9sts.
Row 1 (RS): K2, *p5, k4, rep from *
to last 7sts, p5, k2.
Row 2: P1, *k7, p2, rep from *
to last 8sts, k7, p1.
Row 3: P.
Row 4: Rep row 2.
Row 5: Rep row 1.
Row 6: P3, *k3, p6, rep from *
to last 6sts, k3, p3.
Row 7: K4, *p1, k8, rep from *
to last 5sts, p1, k4.
Row 8: Rep row 6.
Rep rows 1–8 to form patt.

ENGLISH RIB

INSTRUCTIONS

Cast on an odd number of sts.
Row 1: S1, *p1, k1, rep from * to end.
Row 2: S1, *k1b, p1, rep from * to end.
Rep rows 1 and 2 to form patt.

FISHERMAN'S RIB

INSTRUCTIONS

Cast on an odd number of sts
and knit 1 row.
Row 1 (RS): S1, *k1b, p1, rep
from * to end.
Row 2: S1, *p1, k1b, rep from * to
last 2sts, p1, k1.
Rep rows 1 and 2 to form patt.

DOUBLE MOSS STITCH

INSTRUCTIONS

Cast on an odd number of sts.
Row 1 (RS): *K1, p1, rep from * to last
st, k1.
Row 2: *P1, k1, rep from * to last st,
p1.
Row 3: As row 2.
Row 4: As row 1.
Rep rows 1–4 to form patt.

HALF MOSS STITCH

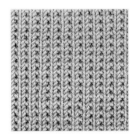

INSTRUCTIONS

Cast on an odd number of sts.
Row 1 (RS): *P1, k1, rep from *
to last st, k1.
Row 2: K.
Rep rows 1 and 2 to form
patt.

TRAVELLING RIB

INSTRUCTIONS

Cast on a multiple of 4sts.
Row 1 (RS): *K2, p2, rep from * to end.
Row 2: As row 1.
Row 3: *K1, p2, k1, rep from * to end.
Row 4: *P1, k2, p1, rep from * to end.
Row 5: *P2, k2, rep from * to end.
Row 6: As row 5.
Row 7: As row 4.
Row 8: As row 3.
Rep rows 1–8 to form patt.

BROKEN RIB

INSTRUCTIONS

Cast on a multiple of 4sts plus
2 extra sts.
Row 1 (RS): *K3, p1, rep from * to last
2sts, k2.
Row 2: P1, *k3, p1, rep from * to last
st, k1.
Rep rows 1 and 2 to form patt.

BROKEN MOSS STITCH

INSTRUCTIONS

Cast on an odd number of sts.
Row 1 (RS): K.
Row 2: *P1, k1, rep from * to last st, k1.
Rep rows 1 and 2 to form patt.

GARTER RIB

INSTRUCTIONS

Cast on a multiple of 8sts plus
4 extra sts.
Row 1 (RS): K4, *p4, k4, rep from *
to end.
Row 2: P.
Rep rows 1 and 2 to form patt.

MOSS STITCH COLUMNS

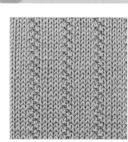

INSTRUCTIONS

Cast on a multiple of 6sts plus 4
extra sts.
Row 1 (RS): K4, *k1, p1, k4, rep from
* to end.
Row 2: *P5, k1, rep from * to last
4sts, p4.
Rep rows 1 and 2 to form patt.

HONEYCOMB STITCH

INSTRUCTIONS

Cast on a multiple of 6sts plus 2
extra sts.
Row 1 (RS): K.
Row 2: K2, *p4, k2, rep from * to end.
Row 3: As row 1.
Row 4: P2, *p1, k2, p3, rep from *
to end.
Rep rows 1–4 to form patt.

INCREASING AND DECREASING

BASIC CHEVRON

INSTRUCTIONS

Cast on a multiple of 12sts.
Row 1 (RS): *K2tog, k3, [inc in next st] twice, k3, s1 k1 psso, rep from * to end.
Row 2: P.
Rep rows 1 and 2 to form patt.

GARTER CHEVRON

INSTRUCTIONS

Cast on a multiple of 11sts.
Row 1 (WS): K.
Rows 2, 3, 4, and 5: As row 1.
Row 6: *K2tog, k2, [inc in next st] twice, k3, s1 k1 psso, rep from * to end.
Row 7: P.
Rep last 2 rows twice more, then row 6 again.
Rep rows 1–12 to form patt.

FEATHER AND FAN STITCH

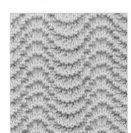

INSTRUCTIONS

Cast on a multiple of 18sts plus 2 extra sts.
Row 1 (RS): K.
Row 2: P.
Row 3: K1, *[k2tog] three times, [yo, k1] six times, [k2tog] three times, rep from * to last st, k1.
Row 4: K.
Rep rows 1–4 to form patt.

DIAGONAL RIB

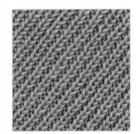

INSTRUCTIONS

Cast on a multiple of 2sts.
Row 1 (WS): *K1, p1, rep from * to end.
Row 2: S1 p1 psso, *k1, p1, rep from * to last 2sts, k1, [p1, k1] into next st.
Row 3: *P1, k1, rep from * to last 2sts, p2.
Row 4: S1 k1 psso, *p1, k1, rep from * to last 2sts, p1 [k1 p1] into next st.
Rep rows 1–4 to form patt.

BLACKBERRY STITCH

INSTRUCTIONS

Cast on a multiple of 4sts plus 2 extra sts.
Row 1 (RS): P.
Row 2: K1, *[k1, p1, k1] into next st, p3tog, rep from * to last st, k1.
Row 3: P.
Row 4: K1, *p3tog, [k1, p1, k1] into next st, rep from * to last st, k1.
Rep rows 1–4 to form patt.

PUFF STITCH

INSTRUCTIONS

Cast on a multiple of 4sts plus one extra st.
Row 1 (RS): K.
Row 2: P.
Row 3: K1, *p3tog without removing these sts from needle, yrn, re-insert RH needle into 3 previously worked sts and p3tog, this time removing them from LH needle, k1, rep from * to end.
Row 4: P.
Rep rows 1–4 to form patt.

BOBBLE STITCH

INSTRUCTIONS

Cast on an odd number of sts.
Row 1 (RS): K.
Row 2: K1, *work [p1, k1] twice into next st, pass 2nd, 3rd, and 4th sts over the first st on RH needle, k1, rep from * to end.

Row 3: As row 1.
Row 4: K2, *work [p1, k1] twice into next st, pass 2nd, 3rd, and 4th sts over the first st on RH needle, k1, rep from * to last st, k1.
Rep rows 1–4 to form patt.

INCREASING AND DECREASING: FLOWER PATTERNS

TWELVE-PETAL FLOWER

INSTRUCTIONS

Worked in yarn A (petals) and yarn B (flower centre).
Using knit-on cast-on method (see p.88) and yarn A, cast on 12sts, leaving a yarn tail at least 25cm (10in) long.
Row 1 (RS): Cast off 10sts knitwise and slip st on RH needle back on to LH needle. (2sts)
Note: Do not turn work when working petals, but keep RS always facing.
Row 2 (RS): Cast on 12sts on LH needle using knit-on cast-on method, then cast off 10sts knitwise and slip st on RH needle back on LH needle. (4sts)
Rows 3–12: [Rep row 2] ten times more to make a total of 12 petals (24sts – 2sts at base of each petal).
Cut off yarn A.
Using yarn B and working across all 24sts, cont in usual rows for flower

centre as foll:
Row 13 (RS): [K2tog] twelve times. (12sts)
Row 14 (WS): K.
Row 15 (RS): K.
Slip all sts back on LH needle. Then cut off yarn, leaving a yarn tail at least 25cm (10in) long. Thread yarn tail through a blunt-ended yarn needle. With RS facing, thread yarn through rem sts, slipping them off knitting needle as you proceed. Pull yarn tightly to gather sts firmly. With WS facing and still using threaded yarn needle, oversew row ends of flower centre together, working from centre to beginning of petal yarn. Knot ends of matching yarn together, close to work on WS, then knot all yarn ends together close to WS. To form stem, plait together yarn ends, holding two ends of A together and using B strands singly for three strands of plait. Knot end of stem and trim yarn ends.
Do not press.

SPINNING-PETAL FLOWER

INSTRUCTIONS

Worked in yarn A (petals) and yarn B (flower centre).
Using knit-on cast-on method (see p.88) and yarn A, cast on 10sts, leaving a yarn tail at least 25cm (10in) long.
Row 1 (RS): K8 and turn, leaving rem sts unworked.
Row 2 (WS): K to end.
Rows 3 and 4: Rep rows 1 and 2.
Row 5 (RS): Cast off 8sts loosely knitwise, slip st on RH needle back on to LH needle. (2sts)
Note: Do not turn work after last row of each petal (cast-off row), but keep RS facing for next row.
Row 6 (RS): Cast on 10sts on LH needle using knit-on cast-on method, k8

and turn.
Rows 7, 8, 9, and 10: Rep rows 2–5 of first petal. (4sts)
[Rep rows 6–10] five times more to make a total of 7 petals (14sts – 2sts at base of each petal).
Cut off yarn A.
Using yarn B and working across all 14sts, cont in usual rows for flower centre as foll:
K 3 rows.
P 1 row.
K 1 row, so ending with a RS row.
Finish as for Twelve-Petal Flower from ** to **.
Do not press.
Decorate centre with small button if desired.

ANEMONE

INSTRUCTIONS

Note: Slip all slip sts purlwise with yarn at WS of work.

Worked in yarn A (petals) and yarns B and C (flower centre).

Using double cast-on method (see p.91) and yarn A, cast on 41sts, leaving a yarn tail at least 25cm (10in) long.

Row 1 (RS): *S1, k7, rep from * to last st, p1.

Row 2: *S1, k to end.

Row 3: Rep row 1.

Row 4: *S1, p7, *s1, take yarn to back of work between two needles then around knitting over cast-on edge, over top of knitting between two needles and around cast-on edge again, so ending at front of work, pull yarn to gather knitting tightly, p7, rep from * to last st, k1.

Cut off yarn A and change to B.

Row 5: *K2tog, rep from * to last 3sts, s1 k2tog psso. (20sts)

Row 6: K.

Cut off yarn B and change to C.

Row 7: [K2tog] ten times. (10sts)

Finish as for Twelve-Petal Flower from ** to **, but also using yarn A to sew short petal seam (leaving part of seam unworked to create indent between petals as between other petals) and making plait with two strands each of A, B, and C.

Do not press.

PUFFBALL FLOWER

INSTRUCTIONS

Cast on 7sts.

Row 1 (RS): *K1, yo, rep from * to last st, k1. (13sts)

Row 2 and all foll alt rows: P.

Row 3: *K2, yo, rep from * to last st, k1. (19sts)

Row 5: *K3, yo, rep from * to last st, k1. (25sts)

Row 7: *K4, yo, rep from * to last st, k1. (31sts)

Row 9: *K5, yo, rep from * to last st, k1. (37sts)

Row 11: *K6, yo, rep from * to last st, k1. (43sts)

Row 13: *K7, yo, rep from * to last st, k1. (49sts)

Row 15: K.

Row 17: *K6, k2tog, rep from * to last st, k1. (43sts)

Row 19: *K5, k2tog, rep from * to last st, k1. (37sts)

Row 21: *K4, k2tog, rep from * to last st, k1. (31sts)

Row 23: *K3, k2tog, rep from * to last st, k1. (25sts)

Row 25: *K2, k2tog, rep from * to last st, k1. (19sts)

Row 27: *K1, k2tog, rep from * to last st, k1. (13sts)

Row 29: *K2tog, rep from * to last st, k1. (7sts)

Cut yarn, leaving a long tail, and draw through remaining 7sts. Using the tail of yarn, continue to join row ends using mattress stitch with RS facing, draw through cast-on edge, and pull tight. Align cast-on edge centre with cast-off edge, and squash flower flat so that these two edges meet. Join with a few stitches through the centre, and embellish with beads or buttons at centre if desired.

LARGE LEAF

INSTRUCTIONS

Note: Although the stem is worked on two double-pointed needles, you can change to ordinary needles after row 1. Using any cast-on method, cast on 3sts on a double-pointed needle and k 1 row (this is RS). Cord row (RS): With RS still facing, slide sts to opposite end of needle, then take yarn across WS of work, pull yarn tightly and k to end. Rep cord row until stem is desired length.

Row 1 (RS): With RS of work still facing, slide sts to opposite end of needle, then take yarn across WS of work, pull yarn tightly and work k1, [yfwd, k1] twice. (5sts)

Cont in rows, turning work in usual way.

Row 2 (WS): K2, p1, k2.

Row 3: K2, yfwd, k1, yfwd, k2. (7sts)

Row 4 (WS): Cast on one st on LH needle (using knit-on cast-on method), cast off one st (knitwise), k to centre st, p centre st, k to end. (7sts)

Row 5: Cast on one st on LH needle, cast off one st, k to centre st, yfwd, k centre st, yfwd, k to end. (9sts)

Rows 6–9: [Rep rows 4 and 5] twice. (13sts)

Row 10: Rep row 4. (13sts)

Row 11: Cast on one st on LH needle, cast off one st, k to end. (13sts)

Row 12: Rep row 4. (13sts)

Row 13: Cast on one st on LH needle, cast off one st, k to 2sts before centre st, k2tog, k centre st, ssk, k to end. (11sts)

Rows 14–19: [Rep rows 4 and 13] three times. (5sts)

Row 20: K2, p1, k2.

Row 21: K2tog, k1, ssk. (3sts)

Row 22: K1, p1, k1.

Row 23: S1 k2tog psso and fasten off. Darn in yarn ends. Do not press.

FLOWER WITH SMALL CENTRE

INSTRUCTIONS

Worked in yarn A (outer petal), yarn B (inner petal), and yarn C (flower centre).
Using double cast-on method (see p.91) and yarn A, cast on 90sts, leaving a yarn tail at least 25cm (10in) long.

Row 1 (WS): K6, s1 k2tog psso, *k12, s1 k2tog psso, rep from * to last 6sts, k6.
Cut off yarn A and change to B.
Row 2 (RS): *K1, cast off next 11sts knitwise, rep from *. (12sts)
Cut off yarn B and change to C.
Row 3: P.
Row 4: *K2tog, k1, rep from *. (8sts)
Finish as for Twelve-Petal Flower from ** to **, but also using yarn A to sew beginning and end of cast-on sts together and making plait with two strands each of A, B, and C. Do not press.

FLOWER WITH LARGE CENTRE

INSTRUCTIONS

Worked in yarn A (outer petal), yarn B (inner petal), and yarn C (flower centre). Using double cast-on method (see p.91) and yarn A, cast on 72sts, leaving a yarn tail at least 25cm (10in) long. Cut off yarn A and change to B.

Row 1 (RS): K.
Row 2: *Kfb, cast off next 10sts knitwise, rep from *. (18sts)
Cut off yarn B and change to C.
Row 3: K.
Row 4: *K4, k2tog, rep from *. (15sts)
Row 5: K.
Row 6: P.
Row 7: *K1, k2tog, rep from * to end. (10sts)
Finish as for Twelve-Petal Flower from ** to **, but also using yarn A to sew beginning and end of cast-on sts together and making plait with two strands each of A, B, and C. Do not press. Decorate centre with small button if desired.

CABLE AND TWIST STITCH PATTERNS

KEY

☐ K on RS rows, P on WS rows	T2L
● P on RS rows, K on WS rows	T2R
	MB = make bobble	k2tog	s1 k2tog psso	CR4L
C4B		○ yfwd	ssk	s2 K1 p2sso	CR4R
C4F	C6B		C8B	CR2R
	C6F		C8F	CR2L

FOUR-STITCH CABLE PATTERN

INSTRUCTIONS

Special abbreviations

C4F: Slip next 2sts on to cable needle and hold at front of work, k2 from LH needle, then k2 from cable needle.
C4B: Slip next 2sts on to cable needle and hold at back of work, k2 from LH needle, then k2 from cable needle.

Cast on a multiple of 14sts plus 3 extra sts.
Row 1 (RS): P3, *k4, p3, rep from *.
Row 2: K3, *p4, k3, rep from *.
Row 3: P3, *k4, p3, C4F, p3, rep from *.
Row 4: Rep row 2.
Row 5: P3, *C4B, p3, k4, p3, rep from *.
Rep rows 2–5 to form patt.

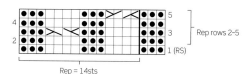

Rep rows 2–5

Rep = 14sts

CHAIN CABLE STITCH

INSTRUCTIONS

Special abbreviations

C4F: Slip next 2sts on to cable needle and hold at front of work, k2 from LH needle, then k2 from cable needle.

C4B: Slip next 2sts on to cable needle and hold at back of work, k2 from LH needle, then k2 from cable needle.

Cast on a multiple of 22sts plus 3 extra sts.

Row 1 (RS): P3, *k8, p3, rep from *.

Row 2 and all even-numbered (WS) rows: K3, *p8, k3, rep from *.

Row 3: P3, *k8, p3, C4B, C4F, p3, rep from *.

Row 5: P3, *C4B, C4F, p3, k8, p3, rep from *.

Row 7: P3, *k8, p3, C4F, C4B, p3, rep from *.

Row 9: P3, *C4F, C4B, p3, k8, p3, rep from *.

Rep rows 2–9 to form patt.

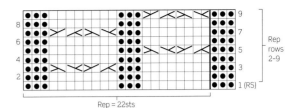

Rep = 22sts

SIX-STITCH CABLE PATTERN

INSTRUCTIONS

Special abbreviations

C6F: Slip next 3sts on to cable needle and hold at front of work, k3 from LH needle, then k3 from cable needle.

C6B: Slip next 3sts on to cable needle and hold at back of work, k3 from LH needle, then k3 from cable needle.

Cast on a multiple of 18sts plus 3 extra sts.

Row 1 (RS): P3, *k6, p3, rep from *.

Row 2 and all even-numbered (WS) rows: K3, *p6, k3, rep from *.

Row 3: P3, *k6, p3, C6F, p3, rep from *.

Row 5: Rep row 1.

Row 7: P3, *C6B, p3, k6, p3, rep from *.

Row 9: Rep row 1.

Rep rows 2–9 to form patt.

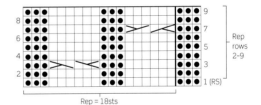

Rep = 18sts

HORSESHOE CABLE

INSTRUCTIONS

Special abbreviations

C4F: Slip next 2sts on to cable needle and hold at front of work, k2 from LH needle, then k2 from cable needle.

C4B: Slip next 2sts on to cable needle and hold at back of work, k2 from LH needle, then k2 from cable needle.

Cast on a multiple of 22sts plus 3 extra sts.

Row 1 (RS): P3, *k8, p3, rep from *.

Row 2 and all even-numbered (WS) rows: K3, *p8, k3, rep from *.

Row 3: P3, *k8, p3, C4B, C4F, p3, rep from *.

Row 5: Rep row 1.

Row 7: P3, *C4B, C4F, p3, k8, p3, rep from *.

Row 9: Rep row 1.

Rep rows 2–9 to form patt.

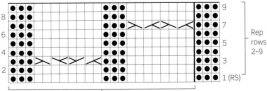

Rep = 22sts

PLAIT CABLE

INSTRUCTIONS

Special abbreviations

C8F: Place 4sts on cable needle and leave at front of work, k4, then k4 from cable needle.

C8B: Place 4sts on cable needle and leave at back of work, k4, then k4 from cable needle.

Cast on a multiple of 20sts.

Row 1: *P4, k12, p4, rep from * to end.

Row 2 and all foll alt rows: *K4, p12, k4, rep from * to end.

Row 3: *P4, C8F, k4, p4, rep from * to end.

Rows 5 and 7: As row 1.

Row 9: *P4, k4, C8B, rep from * to end.

Row 11: As row 1.

Row 12: As row 2.

Rep rows 1–12 to form patt.

DIAMOND CABLE

INSTRUCTIONS

Special abbreviations

CR4L: Place 2sts on cable needle and leave at front of work, p2, then k2 from cable needle.

CR4R: Place 2sts on cable needle and leave at back of work, k2, then p2 from cable needle.

C4F: Place 2sts on cable needle and leave at front of work, k2, then k2 from cable needle.

Cast on a multiple of 20sts.

Row 1: *P8, C4F, p8, rep from * to end.

Row 2: *K8, p4, k8, rep from * to end.

Row 3: *P6, CR4R, CR4L, p6, rep from * to end.

Row 4: *K6, p2, k4, p2, k6, rep from * to end.

Row 5: *P4, CR4R, p4, CR4L, p4, rep from * to end.

Row 6: *K4, p2, k8, p2, k4, rep from * to end.

Row 7: *P2, CR4R, p8, CR4L, p2, rep from * to end.

Row 8: *K2, p2, k12, p2, k2, rep from * to end.

Row 9: *P2, CR4L, p8, CR4R, p2, rep from * to end.

Row 10: As row 6.

Row 11: *P4, CR4L, p4, CR4R, p4, rep from * to end.

Row 12: As row 4.

Row 13: *P6, CR4L, CR4R, p6, rep from * to end.

Row 14: As row 2.

Rep rows 1–14 to form patt.

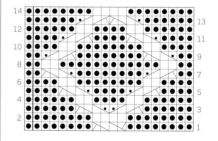

SMOCKING

INSTRUCTIONS

Special abbreviation

smock 5sts: Slip next 5sts on to cable needle and leave at front of work, bring yarn to the front of work, and wrap anti-clockwise around these stitches twice so that yarn now sits at back of work. Work (K1, p3, k1) from cable needle.

Cast on a multiple of 8sts, plus 7 extra sts.

Row 1 (RS): P1, k1, *p3, k1, rep from * to last st, p1.

Row 2: K1, p1, *k3, p1, rep from * to last st, k1.

Row 3: P1, smock 5sts, *p3, smock 5sts, rep from * to last st, p1.

Row 4: As row 2.

Row 5: As row 1.

Rep last 2 rows once more, and row 2 again.

Row 9: P1, k1, p3, *smock 5sts, p3, rep from * to last 2sts, k1, p1.

Rows 10 and 12: As row 2.

Row 11: As row 1.

Rep rows 1–12 to form pattern.

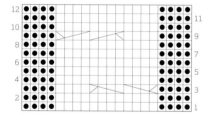

GARTER ZIGZAG TWIST

INSTRUCTIONS

Special abbreviations

T2R (twist 2 right): Skip first st on LH needle and k 2nd st through front of loop (do not drop st off LH needle), then k first st on LH needle and drop both sts off LH needle at same time.

T2L (twist 2 left): Skip first st on LH needle and k 2nd st by taking RH needle behind first st to do so (do not drop st off LH needle), then k first st on LH needle and drop both sts off LH needle at same time.

Row 1 (RS): K.
Row 2: *K5, p1, rep from * to last st, k1.
Row 3: K1, *T2L, k4, rep from *.
Row 4: *K4, p1, k1, rep from * to last st, k1.
Row 5: K1 *k1, T2L, k3, rep from *.
Row 6: *K3, p1, k2, rep from * to last st, k1.
Row 7: K1, *k2, T2L, k2, rep from *.
Row 8: *K2, p1, k3, rep from * to last st, k1.
Row 9: K1, *k3, T2L, k1, rep from *.
Row 10: *K1, p1, k4, rep from * to last st, k1.

Row 11: K1, *k3, T2R, k1 rep from *.
Row 12: Rep row 8.
Row 13: K1, *k2, T2R, k2, rep from *.
Row 14: Rep row 6.
Row 15: K1, *k1, T2R, k3, rep from *.
Row 16: Rep row 4.
Row 17: K1, *T2R, k4, rep from *.
Row 18: Rep row 2.
Rep rows 3–18 to form patt.

Rep rows 3-18

Rep = 6sts

GARTER STITCH CABLE

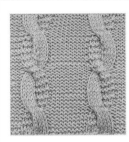

INSTRUCTIONS

Special abbreviation

C8F: Place 4sts on cable needle and leave at front of work, k4, then k4 from cable needle.

Cast on a multiple of 18sts.
Row 1 (RS): *P5, k8, p5, rep from * to end.
Row 2: *K9, p4, k5, rep from * to end.
Rep last 2 rows twice more.
Row 7: *P5, *C8F, p5, rep from * to end.
Row 8: *K5, p4, k9, rep from * to end.
Row 9: As row 1.
Rep last 2 rows four times more, then row 8 again.
Row 19: As row 7.
Row 20: As row 2.
Row 21: As row 1.
Row 22: As row 2.
Row 23: As row 1.
Row 24: As row 2.
Rep rows 1–24 form pattern.

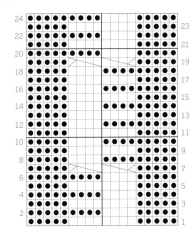

BOBBLE CABLE

INSTRUCTIONS

Special abbreviations

C8B: Place 4sts on cable needle and leave at back, k4, then k4 from cable needle.

MB: Make bobble as follows. [(K1, yo) twice, k1, turn, p5, turn, slip 4sts on to RH needle, k1, then pass 4 slipped stitches over (one by one), all into next st. Cast on a multiple of 8sts, plus 4 extra sts.

Row 1: K.
Row 2 and all foll alt rows: P.
Row 3: K.
Row 5: K2, *C8B, rep from * to last 2sts, k2.
Row 7: K2, *MB, k7, rep from * to last 2sts, k2.
Row 9: K.
Row 11: K6, *C8B, rep from * to last 6sts, k6.
Row 13: K6, *MB, k7, rep from * to last 13sts, k13.
Row 14: As row 2.
Rep rows 3-14 to form patt.

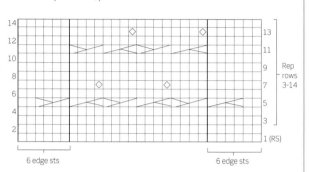

Rep rows 3-14

6 edge sts   6 edge sts

WOVEN CABLE

INSTRUCTIONS

Special abbreviations

C6F: Place 3sts on cable needle and leave at front of work, k3, then k3 from cable needle.

C6B: Place 3sts on cable needle and leave at back of work, k3, then k3 from cable needle.

Cast on a multiple of 6sts (a minimum of 12sts).

Row 1 (RS): K.
Row 2 and all foll alt rows: P.
Row 3: K3, *C6B, rep from * to last 3sts, k3.
Row 5: K.
Row 7: * C6F, rep from * to end.
Row 8: As row 2.
Rep rows 1-8 to form patt.

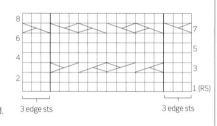

3 edge sts   3 edge sts

CABLE CHECK

INSTRUCTIONS

Special abbreviation

C4F: Place 2sts on cable needle and leave at front of work, k2, then k2 from cable needle.

Cast on a multiple of 8sts plus 4 extra sts.

Row 1 (RS): *P4, k4, rep from * to last 4sts, p4.
Row 2: K4, *p4, k4, rep from *.
Row 3: As row 1.
Row 4: As row 2.
Row 5: *P4, C4F, rep from * to last 4sts, p4.
Rows 6 and 7: As row 2.
Row 8: As row 1.
Row 9: As row 2.
Row 10: As row 1.
Row 11: *C4F, p4, rep from * to last 4sts, C4F.
Row 12: As row 1.
Rep rows 1-12 to form patt.

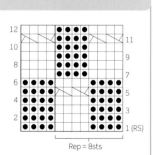

Rep = 8sts

CABLE-EFFECT STITCH

INSTRUCTIONS

Cast on a multiple of 5sts plus 2 extra sts.

Note: The stitch count varies from row to row.

Row 1 (RS): P2, *yarn to back of work between 2 needles, s1 purlwise, k2, pass slipped st over last 2 k sts and off RH needle, p2, rep from *.

Row 2: K2, *p1, yrn, p1, k2, rep from *.

Row 3: P2, *k3, p2, rep from *.

Row 4: K2, *p3, k2, rep from *.

Rep rows 1–4 to form patt.

WAVY CABLE

INSTRUCTIONS

Special abbreviations

CR2R: Skip first st on LH needle and k 2nd st through front of loop (do not drop st off LH needle), then p first st on LH needle and drop both sts off this needle at same time.

CR2L: Skip first st on LH needle and p 2nd st by taking RH needle behind first st to do so (so do not drop st off LH needle), then k first st on LH needle and drop both sts off together.

Cast on a multiple of 3sts (a minimum of 9sts).

Row 1 (RS): *P1, CR2R, rep from * to end.

Row 2: * K1, p1, k1, rep from * to end.

Row 3: *CR2R, p1, rep from * to end.

Row 4: *K2, p1, rep from * to end.

Row 5: *K1, p2, rep from * to end.

Row 6: As row 4.

Row 7: *CR2L, p1, rep from * to end.

Row 8: As row 2.

Row 9: *P1, CR2L, rep from * to end.

Row 10: *P1, k2, rep from * to end.

Row 11: *P2, k1, rep from * to end.

Row 12: As row 10.

Rep rows 1–12 to form patt.

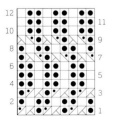

FAN CABLE

INSTRUCTIONS

Read all odd (WS) rows from L to R.

Read all even (RS) rows from R to L.

Special abbreviations

CR2R: Skip first st on LH needle and k 2nd st through front of loop (do not drop st off LH needle), then p first st on LH needle and drop both sts off this needle at same time.

CR2L: Skip first st on LH needle and p 2nd st by taking RH needle behind first st to do so (so do not drop st off LH needle), then k first st on LH needle and drop both sts off together.

Cast on a multiple of 14sts plus 2 extra sts.

Row 1 and all foll alt rows (WS): P.

Row 2: *K6, CR2R, k6, rep from * to last 2sts, k2.

Row 4: *K5, CR2R, p1, k6, rep from * to last 2sts, k2.

Row 6: *K4, CR2R, p2, k6, rep from * to last 2sts, k2.

Row 8: *K3, CR2R, p3, k6, rep from * to last 2sts, k2.

Row 10: *K2, CR2R, p4, k6, rep from * to last 2sts, k2.

Row 12: * K8, CR2L, k4, rep from * to last 2sts, k2.

Row 14: *K8, p1, CR2L, k3, rep from * to last 2sts, k2.

Row 16: *K8, p2, CR2L, K2, rep from * to last 2sts, k2.

Row 18: *K8, p3, CR2L, k1, rep from * to last 2sts, k2.

Row 20: *K8, p4, CR2L, rep from * to last 2sts, k2.

Rep rows 1–20 to form patt.

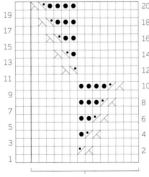

Rep = 14sts

LACE STITCH PATTERNS

KEY

☐	K on RS rows, P on WS rows
⬤	P on RS rows, K on WS rows

O	yfwd
╱	k2tog
╲	ssk

⋀	s1 k2tog psso
⋀	s2 k1 p2sso

EYELET MESH STITCH

INSTRUCTIONS

Cast on a multiple of 3sts.
Row 1 (RS): K2, *k2tog, yfwd, k1, rep from * to last st, k1.
Row 2: P.
Row 3: K2, *yfwd, k1, k2tog, rep from * to last st, k1.
Row 4: P.
Rep rows 1–4 to form patt.

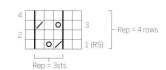

Rep = 4 rows
Rep = 3sts

LEAF EYELET PATTERN

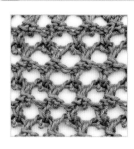

INSTRUCTIONS

Cast on a multiple of 8sts plus 7 extra sts.
Row 1 (RS): K.
Row 2 and all even-numbered (WS) rows: P.
Row 3: K2, *yfwd, s1 k2tog psso, yfwd, k5, rep from * to last 5 sts, yfwd, s1 k2tog psso, yfwd, k2.
Row 5: K2, *k1, yfwd, ssk, k5, rep from * to last 5sts, k1, yfwd, ssk, k2.
Row 7: K.
Row 9: K2, *k4, yfwd, s1 k2tog psso, yfwd, k1, rep from * to last 5sts, k5.
Row 11: K2, *k5, yfwd, ssk, k1, rep from * to last 5sts, k5.
Row 12: P.
Rep rows 1–12 to form patt.

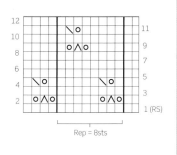

Rep = 8sts

GRAND EYELET MESH STITCH

INSTRUCTIONS

Note: This fabric looks the same on both sides. When blocking, stretch vertically to open eyelets.
Cast on a multiple of 3sts plus 4 extra sts.
Row 1: K2, *s1 k2tog psso, yfwd twice, rep from * to last 2sts, k2.
Row 2: K2, *[p1, k1] into double yfwd, p1, rep from * to last 2sts, k2.
Row 3: K.
Rep rows 1–3 to form patt.

VERTICAL MESH STITCH

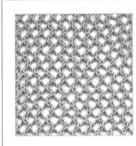

INSTRUCTIONS

Cast on an odd number of sts.
Row 1: K1, *yfwd, k2tog, rep from *.
Row 2: P.
Row 3: *Ssk, yfwd, rep from * to last st, k1.
Row 4: P.
Rep rows 1–4 to form patt.

MINI-LEAF STITCH

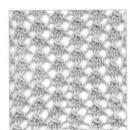

INSTRUCTIONS

Cast on a multiple of 6sts plus 2 extra sts.
Row 1 (RS): K1, *k3, yfwd, s1 k2tog psso, yfwd, rep from * to last st, k1.
Row 2: P.
Row 3: K1, *yfwd, s1 k2tog psso, yfwd, k3, rep from * to last st, k1.
Row 4: P.
Rep rows 1–4 to form patt.

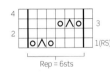

Rep = 6sts

ARROWHEAD LACE

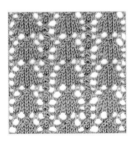

INSTRUCTIONS

Cast on a multiple of 8sts plus 5 extra sts.
Row 1 (RS): K1, yfwd, s1 k2tog psso, yfwd, *k5, yfwd, s1 k2tog psso, yfwd, rep from * to last st, k1.
Row 2 and all even-numbered (WS) rows: P.
Row 3: Rep row 1.
Row 5: K4, *yfwd, ssk, k1, k2tog, yfwd, k3, rep from * to last st, k1.
Row 7: K1, yfwd, s1 k2tog psso, yfwd, *k1, yfwd, s1 k2tog psso, yfwd, to last st, k1.
Row 8: P.
Rep rows 1–8 to form patt.

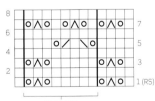

Rep = 8sts

ZIGZAG MESH STITCH

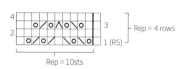

Rep = 4 rows

Rep = 10sts

INSTRUCTIONS

Cast on a multiple of 10sts plus one extra st.
Row 1 (RS): K1, *[yfwd, ssk] twice, k1, [k2tog, yfwd] twice, k1, rep from *.
Row 2: P.
Row 3: K1, *k1, yfwd, ssk, yfwd, s1 k2tog psso, yfwd, k2tog, yfwd, k2, rep from * to end.
Row 4: P.
Rep rows 1–4 to form patt.

STAR EYELET STITCH

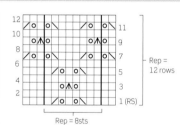

Rep = 12 rows

Rep = 8sts

INSTRUCTIONS

Special abbreviation
s2 k1 p2sso: Slip 2sts, knit 1st, pass 2 slipped sts over.

Cast on a multiple of 8sts plus 5 extra sts.
Row 1 (RS): K4, *ssk, yfwd, k1, yfwd, k2tog, k3, rep from * to last st, k1.
Row 2 and all even-numbered (WS) rows: P.
Row 3: K5, *yfwd, s2 k1 p2sso, yfwd, k5, rep from *.
Row 5: Rep row 1.
Row 7: Ssk, yfwd, k1, yfwd, k2tog, *k3, ssk, yfwd, k1, yfwd, k2tog, rep from *.
Row 9: K1, *yfwd, s2 k1 p2sso, yfwd, k5, rep from *, ending last rep k1 (instead of k5).
Row 11: Rep row 7.
Row 12: P.
Rep rows 1–12 to form patt.

BIG LEAF LACE

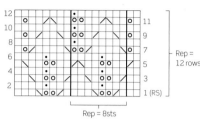

Rep = 12 rows

Rep = 8sts

INSTRUCTIONS

Cast on a multiple of 8sts plus 2 extra sts.
Row 1 (RS): K2, *k1, k2tog, yfwd twice, ssk, k3, rep from * to end.
Row 2 and all even-numbered (WS) rows: P, working [k1, p1] into every double yfwd and p1 into single yfwd at beg and end of row.
Row 3: K2, *k2tog, k1, yfwd twice, k1, ssk, k2, rep from *.
Row 5: K1, *k2tog, k2, yfwd twice, k2, ssk, rep from * to last st, k1.
Row 7: K1, yfwd, *ssk, k4, k2tog, yfwd twice, rep from * to last 9sts, ssk, k4, k2tog, yfwd, k1.
Row 9: K1, yfwd, *k1, ssk, k2, k2tog, k1, yfwd twice, rep from * to last 9sts, k1, ssk, k2, k2tog, k1, yfwd, k1.
Row 11: K1, yfwd, *k2, ssk, k2tog, k2, yfwd twice, rep from * to last 9sts, k2, ssk, k2tog, k2, yfwd, k1.
Row 12: Rep row 2.
Rep rows 1–12 to form patt.

DOMINO EYELET PATTERN

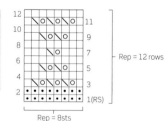

Rep = 12 rows

Rep = 8sts

INSTRUCTIONS

Cast on a multiple of 8sts.
Row 1 (RS): P.
Row 2: K.
Row 3: *K1, [yfwd, ssk] three times, k1, rep from *.
Row 4 and all foll even-numbered (WS) rows: P.
Row 5: *K2, [yfwd, ssk] twice, k2, rep from *.
Row 7: *K3, yfwd, ssk, k3, rep from *.
Row 9: Rep row 5.
Row 11: Rep row 3.
Row 12: P.
Rep rows 1–12 to form patt.

LEAVES LACE

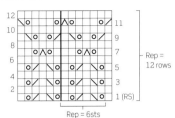

Rep = 12 rows

Rep = 6sts

INSTRUCTIONS

Cast on a multiple of 6sts plus one extra st.

Row 1 (RS): K1, *yfwd, ssk, k1, k2tog, yfwd, k1, rep from *.

Row 2: P.

Rows 3–6: [Rep rows 1 and 2] twice.

Row 7: K2, *yfwd, s1 k2tog psso, yfwd, k3, rep from *, ending last rep k2 (instead of k3).

Row 8 and all foll even-numbered (WS) rows: P.

Row 9: K1, *k2tog, yfwd, k1, yfwd, ssk, k1, rep from *.

Row 11: K2tog, *yfwd, k3, yfwd, s1 k2tog psso, rep from * to last 5sts, yfwd, k3, yfwd, ssk.

Row 12: P.

Rep rows 1–12 to form patt.

DIAMOND LACE STITCH

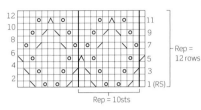

Rep = 12 rows

Rep = 10sts

INSTRUCTIONS

Cast on a multiple of 10sts plus one extra st.

Row 1 (RS): K1, *k1, k2tog, [k1, yfwd] twice, k1, ssk, k2, rep from *.

Row 2 and all even-numbered (WS) rows: P.

Row 3: K1, *k2tog, k1, yfwd, k3, yfwd, k1, ssk, k1, rep from *.

Row 5: K2tog, *k1, yfwd, k5, yfwd, k1, s1 k2tog psso, rep from *, ending last rep ssk (instead of s1 k2tog psso).

Row 7: K1, *yfwd, k1, ssk, k3, k2tog, k1, yfwd, k1, rep from *.

Row 9: K1, *k1, yfwd, k1, ssk, k1, k2tog, k1, yfwd, k2, rep from *.

Row 11: K1, *k2, yfwd, k1, s1 k2tog psso, k1, yfwd, k3, rep from *.

Row 12: P.

Rep rows 1–12 to form patt.

VICTORY LACE

INSTRUCTIONS

Cast on a multiple of 8sts plus 6 extra sts.

Row 1: K5, *s1 k1 psso, yo, k6, rep from * to last st, k1.

Row 2 and all foll alt rows: P.

Row 3: K4, *s1 k1 psso, yo, k1, yo, k2tog, k3, rep from * to last st, k1.

Row 5: K3, *s1 k1 psso, yo, k3, yo, k2tog, k1, rep from * to last st, k1.

Row 7: K.

Row 8: P.

Rep rows 1–8 to form patt.

OPENWORK DIAMONDS

INSTRUCTIONS

Cast on a multiple of 12sts plus 7 extra sts.

Row 1 (RS): *K2, k2tog, yo, k8, rep from * to last 7sts, k2, k2tog, yo, k3.

Row 2 and all foll alt rows: P.

Row 3: *K1, k2tog, yo, k2tog, yo, k7, rep from * to last 7sts, k1, k2tog, yo, k2tog, yo, k2.

Row 5: As row 1.

Row 7: K.

Row 9: *K8, k2tog, yo, k2, rep from * to last 7sts, k7.

Row 11: *K7, k2tog, yo, k2tog, yo, k1, rep from * to last 7sts, k7.

Row 13: As row 9.

Row 15: K.

Row 16: P.

Rep these 16 rows to form patt.

FAGGOTING

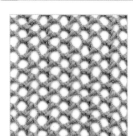

INSTRUCTIONS

Cast on an even number of sts.
Row 1 (RS): K1, *yrn, p2tog, rep from * to last st, k1.
Row 2: As row 1.
Rep rows 1 and 2 to form patt.

LACE OPENWORK

INSTRUCTIONS

Cast on any number of sts.
Row 1 (WS): P.
Row 2: K.
Row 3: P.
Row 4: *Insert RH needle into next st as if to knit, wrap yarn around RH needle three times and bring all 3 loops through this st, rep from * to end.
Row 5: *Purl next st in first of the 3 loops only, allowing remaining 2 loops in this st to fall off LH needle and extend to full length, rep from * to end.
Rep rows 2–5 to form patt.

LADDER LACE

INSTRUCTIONS

Cast on a multiple of 6sts plus 3 extra sts.
Row 1 (RS): K3, *yo, s1k, k2tog, psso, yo, k3, rep from * to end.
Row 2: P.
Rep rows 1 and 2 to form patt.

EYELET LINES

INSTRUCTIONS

Cast on a multiple of 2sts.
Row 1 (RS): K.
Row 2 and all foll alt rows: P.
Row 3: As row 1.
Row 5: K1, *k2tog, yo, rep from * to last st, k1.
Row 6: P.
Rep rows 1–6 to form patt.

NAUTICAL MOTIF

INSTRUCTIONS

Cast on a minimum of 17sts.
Row 1 (RS): K7, k2tog, yo, k to end.
Row 2: P6, p2tog tbl, yrn, p1, yrn, p2tog, p to end.
Row 3: K5, [k2tog, yo] twice, k1, yo, s1, k1, psso, k to end.
Row 4: P4, p2tog tbl, yrn, p5, yrn, p2tog, p to end.
Row 5: K3, k2tog, yo, k2, k2tog, yo, k3, yo, s1, k1, psso, k to end.
Row 6: P.
Row 7: [K2tog, yo] twice, k3, k2tog, yo, k4, [yo, s1,k1, psso] twice.

Row 8: P.
Row 9: K7, k2tog, yo, k to end.
Rep last two rows twice more, then row 8 again.
Row 15: K5 [k2tog, yo] twice, k1, yo, s1, k1, psso, k to end.
Row 16: P
Row 17: As row 9.
Row 18: P
Row 19: As Row 9.
These 19 rows set the motif.

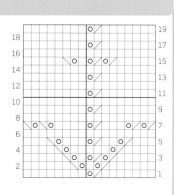

HORSESHOE LACE

INSTRUCTIONS

Cast on a multiple of 10sts plus one extra st.

Row 1 (RS): K1, *yo, k3, s1 k2tog psso, k3, yo, k1, rep from * to end.

Row 2 and all foll alt rows: P.

Row 3: K2, *yo, k2, s1 k2tog psso, k2, yo, k3, rep from * to last 9sts, yo, k2, s1 k2tog psso, k2, yo, k2.

Row 5: K3, *yo, k1, s1 k2tog psso, k1, yo, k5, rep from * to last 8sts, yo, k1, s1 k2tog psso, k1, yo, k3.

Row 7: K4, *yo, s1 k2tog psso, yo, k7, rep from * to last 7sts, yo, s1 k2tog psso, yo, k4.

Row 8: P.

Rep rows 1–8 to form patt.

DIAGONAL LACE RIBS

INSTRUCTIONS

Cast on a multiple of 7sts plus one extra st.

Row 1 (RS): P1, *yo, s1 k1 psso, k4, p1, rep from * to end.

Row 2 and all foll alt rows: K1, *p6, k1, rep from * to end.

Row 3: P1, * k1, yo, s1 k1 psso, k3, p1, rep from * to end.

Row 5: P1, *k2, yo, s1 k1 psso, k2, p1, rep from * to end.

Row 7: P1, *k3, yo, s1 k1 psso, k1, p1, rep from * to end.

Row 9: P1, *k4, yo, s1 k1 psso, p1, rep from * to end.

Row 10: As row 2.

Rep rows 1–10 to form patt.

DROPPED STITCH PATTERN

INSTRUCTIONS

Cast on a multiple of 4sts plus 2 extra sts.

Row 1 (RS): K.

Row 2 and all foll alt rows: P.

Row 3: K1, *k2, yo, k2, rep from * to last st, k1.

Row 5: K.

Row 7: K1, *yo, k2, drop next st off LH needle and allow to ladder down to yo worked on row 3, k2, rep from * to last st, k1.

Row 9: K.

Row 11: K1, *drop next st off LH needle and allow to ladder down to yo worked on row 7, k2, yo, rep from * to last st, k1.

Row 12: P.

Rep rows 5–12 to form patt.

Cast off on WS.

INTERWOVEN EYELETS

INSTRUCTIONS

Cast on a multiple of 2sts plus one extra st.

Row 1 (RS): K1, *s1 k1 psso, yo, rep from * to last st.

Row 2: K1, p1, *yrn, p2tog, rep from * to last st, k1.

Rep rows 1 and 2 to form patt.

COLOURWORK PATTERNS

SIMPLE BORDERS

INSTRUCTIONS

Use the Fair Isle technique to work these border patterns. Change background and motif colours as desired for each band of pattern.

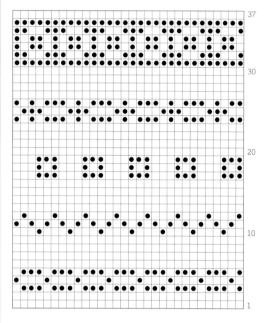

REPEATING CIRCLES

INSTRUCTIONS

Use the Fair Isle technique to work this repeating pattern. Choose four colours: two motif colours and two background colours.

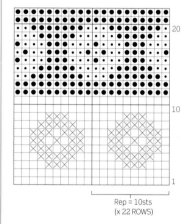

Rep = 10sts
(x 22 ROWS)

HEART MOTIF

INSTRUCTIONS

Use the intarsia technique to work this heart. Choose four colours: three motif colours and one background colour.

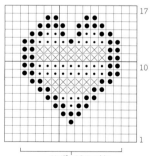

Motif = 13sts wide
(x 14 rows tall)

FAIR ISLE BLOSSOMS

INSTRUCTIONS

Use the Fair Isle technique to work this repeating pattern. Choose two colours: one motif colour and one background colour.

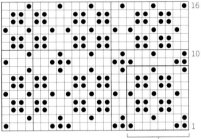

Rep = 8sts wide
(x 8 rows tall)

ZIGZAGS

INSTRUCTIONS

Use the three-stranded Fair Isle technique to work this repeating pattern. Choose three colours: a light, medium, and dark shade work best.

Rep = 8sts

BIRD MOTIF

INSTRUCTIONS

Use the intarsia technique to work this bird. Choose five colours: four motif colours and one background colour. Work a single motif on the knitting or arrange motifs across the knitting at random intervals or in regular repeating positions.

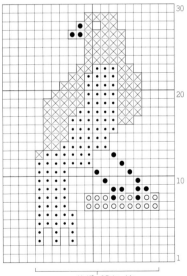

Motif = 15sts wide
(x 27 rows tall)

STITCH PATTERNS

INTARSIA FLOWERS

INSTRUCTIONS

Use the intarsia technique to work the flowers in this repeating pattern and the Fair Isle technique to work only the background colour. Choose four colours, two motif colours for each flower and one background colour.

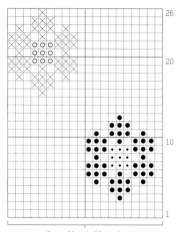

Rep = 20sts (x 26 rows)

NUMBERS AND LETTERS

INSTRUCTIONS

Use the intarsia technique to work these motifs and the Fair Isle technique to work only the background colour. Choose eight colours: seven motif colours and one background colour.

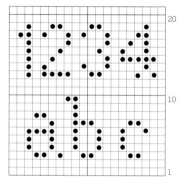

FLOWER MOTIF

INSTRUCTIONS

Use the intarsia technique to work the flower motif in this pattern and the Fair Isle technique to work only the background colour. Choose two colours, one motif colour and one background colour.

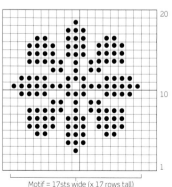

Motif = 17sts wide (x 17 rows tall)

PUSSY CAT MOTIF

INSTRUCTIONS

Use the intarsia technique to work this cat motif. Choose two colours: one motif colour and one background colour.

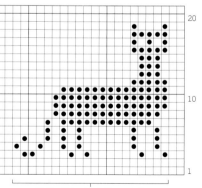

Motif = 20sts wide (x 17 rows tall)

TULIP MOTIF

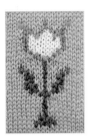

INSTRUCTIONS

Use the intarsia technique to work the tulip motif and the background around the tulip head in this pattern. When working the stem, use the Fair Isle technique to work only the background colour. Choose four colours: three motif colours and one background colour.

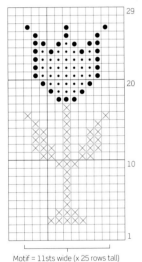

Motif = 11sts wide (x 25 rows tall)

HEARTS

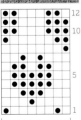

INSTRUCTIONS

Use the Fair Isle technique to work this repeating pattern. Choose two colours: one colour for the motif and another colour for the background.

Rep = 8sts

LITTLE LADY MOTIF

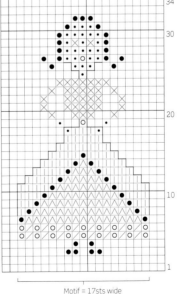

INSTRUCTIONS

Use the intarsia technique to work this motif. Choose eight colours: seven motif colours and one background colour. Work a single motif on the knitting or arrange motifs across the knitting at random intervals or in regular repeating positions.

Motif = 17sts wide
(x 30 rows tall)

DUCK MOTIF

INSTRUCTIONS

Use the intarsia technique to work this duck motif. Choose four colours: three motif colours and one background colour.

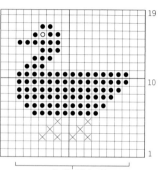

19

10

1

Motif = 15sts wide
(x 15 rows tall)

ARGYLE

INSTRUCTIONS

Use the intarsia and Fair Isle methods to work this pattern. Choose three colours: one for the motif, one for the background, and one for the stripe.

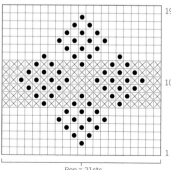

19

10

1

Rep = 21sts

SKULL AND CROSSBONES MOTIF

INSTRUCTIONS

Use the intarsia method to work this motif. Choose two colours: one colour for the motif and the other for the background.

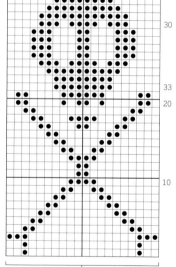

30

33
20

10

Motif = 20sts wide

CLIMBING VINE

INSTRUCTIONS

Use the intarsia method to work this motif. Choose three colours: two for the motif and one for the background.

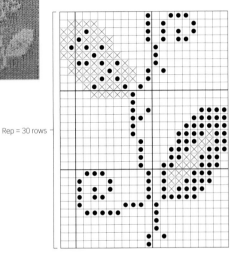

Rep = 30 rows

SNOWFLAKE MOTIF

INSTRUCTIONS

Use the intarsia method to work this motif. Choose two colours: one colour for the motif and another for the background.

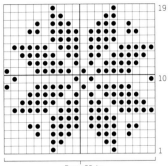

19

10

1

Rep = 20sts

FAUX COLOURWORK PATTERNS

PEEPING PURL STITCH

INSTRUCTIONS

Note: All sts to be slipped purlwise.
Using yarn A, cast on an odd number of sts.
Row 1 (RS): Using yarn A, k.
Row 2: Using yarn A, p.
Rows 3 and 4: As rows 1 and 2.
Row 5: Using yarn B, k1, *s1 wyib, k1, rep from * to end.
Row 6: Using yarn B, k1, *s1 wyif, k1, rep from * to end.
Row 7: As row 1.
Row 8: As row 2.
Rep last 2 rows once more.
Row 11: Using yarn B, s1 wyib, *k1, s1 wyib, rep from * to end.
Row 12: Using yarn B, s1 wyif, *k1, s1 wyif, rep from * to end.
Rep rows 2–9 to form patt.

BROKEN STRIPES

INSTRUCTIONS

Note: All sts to be slipped purlwise.
Using yarn A, cast on a multiple of 4sts plus 2 extra sts.
Row 1 (RS): Using yarn A, k.
Row 2: Using yarn A, p.
Rows 3 and 4: As rows 1 and 2.
Row 5: Using yarn B, k2, *s1, k3, rep from * to end.
Row 6: Using yarn B, p.
Row 7: Using yarn B, k.
Row 8: Using yarn B, p.
Row 9: Using yarn A, k4, *s1, k3, rep from * to last 2sts, s1, k1.
Rep rows 2–9 to form patt.

ARROWHEAD STITCH

INSTRUCTIONS

Special abbreviations

C3L: Place one st on cable needle and hold at front of work, k2, then k1 from cable needle.
C3R: Place 2sts on cable needle and hold at back of work, k1, then k2 from cable needle.

Note: All sts to be slipped purlwise.
Using yarn A, cast on a multiple of 7sts plus one extra st.
Row 1 (RS): Using yarn A, k.
Row 2: Using yarn A, p.
Rows 3: Using yarn B, *k1, s1, k4, s1, rep from * to last st, k1.
Row 4: Using yarn B, p1, *s1, p4, s1, p1, rep from * to last st, p1.
Row 5: As row 3.
Row 6: As row 4.
Row 7: Using yarn B, *k1, C3L, C3R, rep from * to last st, k1.
Row 8: Using yarn B, p.
Row 9: Using yarn A, *k1, s1, k4, s1, rep from * to last st, k1.
Row 10: Using yarn A, p1, *s1, p4, s1, p1, rep from * to last st, p1.
Row 11: As row 9.
Row 12: As row 10.
Row 13: Using yarn A, *k1, C3L, C3R, rep from * to last st, k1.
Row 14: Using yarn A, p.
Rep rows 3–14 to form patt.

GARTER SLIP STITCH

INSTRUCTIONS

Note: All sts to be slipped purlwise.
Using yarn C, cast on a multiple of 4sts plus 3 extra sts.
Row 1 (RS): Using yarn A, k1, *s1, k3, rep from * to last 2sts, s1, k1.
Row 2: Using yarn A, k1, *s1 wyif, k3, rep from * to last 2sts, s1 wyif, k1.
Row 3: Using yarn B, k3, *s1, k3, rep from * to end.
Row 4: Using yarn B, k3, *s1 wyif, k3, rep from * to end.
Row 5: Using yarn C, k1, *s1, k3, rep from * to last 2sts, s1, k1.
Row 6: Using yarn C, k1, *s1 wyif, k3, rep from * to last 2sts, s1 wyif, k1.
Row 7: Using yarn A, k3, *s1, k3, rep from * to end.
Row 8: Using yarn A, k3, *s1 wyif, k3, rep from * to end.
Row 9: Using yarn B, k1, *s1, k3, rep from * to last 2sts, s1, k1.
Row 10: Using yarn B, k1, *s1 wyif, k3, rep from * to last 2sts, s1 wyif, k1.
Row 11: Using yarn C, k3, *s1, k3, rep from * to end.
Row 12: Using yarn C, k3, *s1 wyif, k3, rep from * to end.
Rep rows 1–12 to form patt.

WEAVERS STITCH

INSTRUCTIONS

Note: All sts to be slipped purlwise.
Using yarn A, cast on an even number of sts.
Row 1 (RS): Using yarn A, *k1, s1 wyif, rep from * to end.
Row 2: Using yarn A, *p1, s1 wyib, rep from * to end.
Row 3: Using yarn B, *k1, s1 wyif, rep from * to end.
Row 4: Using yarn B, *p1, s1 wyib, rep from * to end.
Rep rows 1–4 to form patt.

VERTICAL STRIPES

INSTRUCTIONS

Note: All sts to be slipped purlwise. Tension will be tighter as a result of slipped stitch columns, so it is advisable to cast on an extra third to requirements.
Using yarn A, cast on a multiple of 4sts (minimum 12sts).
Row 1 (RS): Using yarn A, k.
Row 2: Using yarn A, p.
Row 3: Using yarn B, k3, s2, *k2, s2, rep from * to last 3sts, k3.
Row 4: Using yarn B, p3, s2, *p2, s2, rep from * to last 3sts, p3.
Row 5: Using yarn A, k1, s2, *k2, s2, rep from * to last st, k1.
Row 6: Using yarn A, p1, s2, *p2, s2, rep from * to last st, p1.
Rep rows 3–6 to form patt.

HONEYCOMB STITCH

INSTRUCTIONS

Note: All sts to be slipped purlwise.

Using yarn A, cast on a multiple of 4sts plus one extra st.

Row 1 (RS): Using yarn A, k.

Row 2: Using yarn A, p.

Rows 3: Using yarn B, *s1, k3, rep from * to last st, k1.

Row 4: Using yarn B, p1, *p3, s1, rep from * to last st, k1.

Row 5: As row 3.

Row 6: As row 4.

Row 7: Using yarn A, k.

Row 8: Using yarn A, p.

Row 9: Using yarn C, *k2, s1, k1, rep from * to last st, k1.

Row 10: Using yarn C, p1, *p1, s1, p2, rep from * to last st, k1.

Row 11: As row 9.

Row 12: As row 10.

Row 13: Using yarn A, k.

Row 14: Using yarn A, p.

Rep rows 3-14 to form patt.

EDGING PATTERNS

PETAL EDGING

INSTRUCTIONS

Cast on 6sts.

Row 1 (RS): K.

Row 2: Yfwd, k2, k2tog, yfwd, k2. (7sts)

Row 3: K.

Row 4: Yfwd, k to last 4sts, k2tog, yfwd, k2. (8sts)

Rows 5–10: (Rep rows 3 and 4) three times. (11sts)

Row 11: K.

Row 12: Cast off 5sts loosely knitwise, k1, k2tog, yfwd, k2. (6sts)

Rep rows 1-12 until edging is desired length, ending with a row 12.

Cast off knitwise.

PEAKS EDGING

INSTRUCTIONS

Cast on 6sts.

Row 1 and all odd-numbered (RS) rows: K.

Row 2: Yfwd, k2, k2tog, yfwd, k2. (7sts)

Row 4: Yfwd, k3, k2tog, yfwd, k2. (8sts)

Row 6: Yfwd, k4, k2tog, yfwd, k2. (9sts)

Row 8: Yfwd, k5, k2tog, yfwd, k2. (10sts)

Row 10: Yfwd, k6, k2tog, yfwd, k2. (11sts)

Row 12: Yfwd, s1 k2tog psso, k4, k2tog, yfwd, k2. (10sts)

Row 14: Yfwd, s1 k2tog psso, k3, k2tog, yfwd, k2. (9sts)

Row 16: Yfwd, s1 k2tog psso, k2, k2tog, yfwd, k2. (8sts)

Row 18: Yfwd, s1 k2tog psso, k1, k2tog, yfwd, k2. (7sts)

Row 20: Yfwd, s1 k2tog psso, k2tog, yfwd, k2. (6sts)

Rep rows 1-20 until edging is desired length, ending with a row 20.

Cast off knitwise.

PICOT RUFFLE EDGING

INSTRUCTIONS

Note: This edging is worked widthways.

Cast on an odd number of sts.

Row 1 (RS): K.

Row 2: K.

Row 3: *K2tog, yfwd, rep from * to last st, k1.

Rows 4, 5 and 6: K.

Row 7: K1, *[k1, p1, k1] into next st, [k1, p1] into next st, rep from *. (This row increases the number of stitches on the needle by about two and a half times.)

Row 8: P.

Row 9: K.

Rows 10, 11, 12, and 13: [Rep rows 8 and 9] twice.

Row 14 (WS): P.

Rows 15 and 16: K.

Work picots along cast-off as follows:

Picot cast-off: *Cast on 2sts on LH needle using knit-on cast-on method, cast off 5sts knitwise, transfer st on RH needle back to LH needle, rep from *, ending last cast-off as required by sts remaining.

CHRISTENING EDGING

INSTRUCTIONS

Cast on 7sts.

Row 1 (RS): K2, yfwd, k2tog, yfwd twice, k2tog, k1. (8sts)

Row 2: K3, p1, k2, yfwd, k2tog.

Row 3: K2, yfwd, k2tog, k1, yfwd twice, k2tog, k1. (9sts)

Row 4: K3, p1, k3, yfwd, k2tog.

Row 5: K2, yfwd, k2tog, k2, yfwd twice, k2tog, k1. (10sts)

Row 6: K3, p1, k4, yfwd, k2tog.

Row 7: K2, yfwd, k2tog, k6.

Row 8: Cast off 3sts knitwise, k4, yfwd, k2tog. (7sts)

Rep rows 1–8 until edging is desired length, ending with a row 8.

Cast off knitwise.

PICOT EDGING

INSTRUCTIONS

Cast on a multiple of 2sts plus one extra st.

Work in st st to the point of turning, finishing with a WS row (minimum 6 rows st st worked).

Picot row (RS): *K2tog, yo, rep from * to last st, k1.

Starting with a p row, work 5 rows st st and cast off. Fold work along picot row and catch to back of work using the overcast technique (see p.229).

ARCHWAY EDGING

INSTRUCTIONS

All stitches are cast on using the single cast-on method
(see p.87).
Cast on a multiple of 6sts plus 2 extra sts.
Row 1 (RS): K.
Row 2: *K1, cast off 3sts, rep from * to end.
Row 3: K1, *cast on one st, k2, rep from * to last st, cast on
one st, k1.
Rows 4, 5, and 6: K.

FRINGE EDGING

INSTRUCTIONS

Note: When making this edging, hold 2 strands of yarn together
throughout and knit tightly. You can alter length of fringe by adding
to or subtracting from number of knit stitches at end of row 1 and
adjusting purl stitches at beg of row 2 by same number.
Cast on 12sts.
Row 1 (RS): K2, yfwd, k2tog, k8.
Row 2: P7, k2, yfwd, k2tog, k1.
Rep rows 1 and 2 until edging is desired length, ending with a row 2.
Cast off (RS): Cast off first 5sts knitwise, cut yarn and draw through
loop on RH needle to fasten off, then drop rem 6sts off LH needle
and unravel them to form fringe.
Smooth out unravelled strands, and, if necessary, lightly steam to
straighten the strands. Then cut through loops at end of fringe.
Knot strands together in groups of four strands, positioning knots
close to edge of knitting. Trim fringe ends slightly if necessary to
make them even.

GODMOTHER'S EDGING

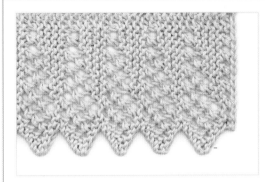

INSTRUCTIONS

Note: Slip first st of even-numbered rows purlwise, then take yarn to
back of work between two needles ready to k next st.
Cast on 15sts.
Row 1 (RS): K.
Row 2: S1, k2, [yfwd, k2tog] five times, yfwd, k2. (16sts)
Row 3 and all odd-numbered (RS) rows: K.
Row 4: S1, k5, [yfwd, k2tog] four times, yfwd, k2. (17sts)
Row 6: S1, k8, [yfwd, k2tog] three times, yfwd, k2. (18sts)
Row 8: S1, k11, [yfwd, k2tog] twice, yfwd, k2. (19sts)
Row 10: S1, k18.
Rows 11: Cast off 4sts knitwise, k to end. (15sts)
Rep rows 2–11 until edging is desired length, ending with a row 11.
Cast off knitwise.

BEADED EDGING

INSTRUCTIONS

Pre-thread the beads and push them down the yarn until you are instructed to use them.
Cast on 6sts.
Rows 1 and 2 (RS): K.
Row 3: Push 10 beads up the working yarn and press against first presenting stitch on LH needle, k1 tbl, k to end as normal, leaving bead loop in place.
Rows 4, 5, and 6: K.
Rep rows 1–6 to form patt.

CABLED EDGING

INSTRUCTIONS

Special abbreviation
C8B: Place 2sts on cable needle and leave at back of work, k2, then k2 from cable needle.

Cast on 12sts.
Row 1 (RS): K.
Row 2: K2, p8, k2.
Rep last 2 rows twice more.
Row 7: K2, C8B, k2.
Row 8: K2, p8, k2.
Row 9: K.
Rep last 2 rows twice more, then row 8 again.
Rep rows 1–14 to set patt.

OPEN WEAVE EDGING

INSTRUCTIONS

Cast on a multiple of 6sts plus one extra st.
Row 1 (RS): K.
Row 2: P.
Row 3: *[K1, p1, k1, p1, k1] into next st, k5tog, rep from * to end.
Row 4: P.
Rep rows 1–4 to form patt.

MEDALLIONS

SIMPLE CIRCLE

INSTRUCTIONS

Cast on 8sts on one needle. Then distribute 2sts on each of four double-pointed needles and knit with a 5th double-pointed needle as foll:

Round 1: [K1 tbl] twice on each of four needles.
Round 2: [Kfb in each st] on each of four needles. (16sts)
Rounds 3, 4, and 5: K.
Round 6: [Kfb in each st] on each of four needles. (32sts)
Rounds 7, 8, 9, 10, and 11: K.
Round 12: Rep round 6. 64sts.
Rounds 13, 14, 15, 16, 17, 18, and 19: K.
Round 20: [Kfb into every 2nd st] on each of four needles. (96sts)

Rounds 21, 22, 23, 24, and 25: K.
Round 26: [Kfb into every 3rd st] on each of four needles. (128sts)
Rounds 27, 28, 29, 30, and 31: K.
Round 32: [Kfb into every 4th st] on each of four needles. (160sts)
Cont in this way, increasing 32 stitches in every 6th round and working the next increase round with kfb into every 5th stitch, the following into every 6th stitch, and so on, until the circle is the desired size.
Cast off knitwise.

SQUARE WITH SWIRL INCREASES

INSTRUCTIONS

Cast on 8sts on one needle. Then distribute 2sts on each of four double-pointed needles, and knit with a 5th double-pointed needle as foll:

Row 1: [K1 tbl] twice on each of four needles.
Row 2: [K, working yfwd before first st] on each of four needles. (12sts)
Rep round 2 (increasing 4sts in every round) until square is desired size.
Cast off knitwise.

SIMPLE SQUARE

INSTRUCTIONS

Cast on 8sts on one needle. Then distribute 2sts on each of four double-pointed needles and knit with a 5th double-pointed needle as foll:

Round 1: [K1 tbl] twice on each of four needles.
Round 2: [Kfb in each st] on each of four needles. (16sts)
Round 3: K.
Round 4: [K, working kfb in first and last st] on each of four needles. (24sts)
Rep rounds 3 and 4 (increasing 8sts in every alt round) until square is desired size.
Cast off knitwise.

HEXAGON

INSTRUCTIONS

Cast on 12sts on one needle. Then distribute 4sts on each of three double-pointed needles and knit with a 4th double-pointed needle as foll:

Round 1: [K1 tbl] four times on each of three needles.

Round 2: [Yfwd, k2, yfwd, k2] on each of three needles. (18sts)

Round 3: K.

Round 4: [Yfwd, k3, yfwd, k3] on each of three needles. (24sts)

Round 5: K.

Round 6: [Yfwd, k half of rem sts on needle, yfwd, k to end of needle] on each of three needles. (30sts)

Rep rounds 5 and 6 (increasing 6sts in every alt round) until hexagon is desired size.

Cast off knitwise.

SIMPLE OCTAGON

INSTRUCTIONS

Cast on 8sts on one needle. Then distribute 2sts on each of four double-pointed needles and knit with a 5th double-pointed needle as foll:

Round 1: [K1 tbl] twice on each of four needles.

Round 2: [Kfb in each st] on each of four needles. (16sts)

Round 3 and all odd-numbered rounds: K.

Round 4: [K1, kfb, k1, kfb] on each of four needles. (24sts)

Round 6: [K2, kfb, k2, kfb] on each of four needles. (32sts)

Round 8: [K3, kfb, k3, kfb] on each of four needles. (40sts)

Round 10: [K4, kfb, k4, kfb] on each of four needles. (48sts)

Round 12: [K5, kfb, k5, kfb] on each of four needles. (56sts)

Cont in this way (increasing 8sts in every alt round) until octagon is desired size.

Cast off knitwise.

MITRED SQUARE

INSTRUCTIONS

Cast on 55sts.

Row 1 (RS): K26, s2k, k1, p2sso, k to end. (53sts)

Row 2 and all foll alt rows: K.

Row 3: K25, s2k, k1, p2sso, k to end. (51sts)

Row 5: K24, s2k, k1, p2sso, k to end. (49sts)

Continue working RS row decrease at centre of row as set, knitting one stitch fewer before decreasing on each row (i.e. row 6: k23, row 5: k22) until 3sts remain, ending with a WS row.

Next row: S2 k1 p2sso (one st). Draw yarn through remaining stitch to fasten off.

SQUARE WITH OPENWORK

INSTRUCTIONS

Cast on 8sts on one needle. Then distribute 2sts on each of four double-pointed needles and knit with a 5th double-pointed needle as foll:

Round 1: [K1 tbl] twice on each of four needles.

Round 2: [Yfwd, k1, yfwd, k1] on each of four needles. (16sts)

Round 3: K.

Round 4: [Yfwd, k3, yfwd, k1] on each of four needles. (24sts)

Round 5: k.

Round 6: [Yfwd, k to last st, yfwd, k1] on each of four needles. (32sts)

Rep rounds 5 and 6 (increasing 8sts in every alt round) until square is desired size.

Cast off knitwise.

BEADING STITCH PATTERNS

SUBTLE SPARKLES

INSTRUCTIONS

Special abbreviation

pb: Place bead.

Cast on a multiple of 6sts plus 2 extra sts.

Row 1 (RS): K.

Row 2: P.

Row 3: K1, *pb, k5, rep from * to last st, k1.

Row 4: P.

Row 5: K.

Row 6: P.

Row 7: K1, *k3, pb, k2, rep from * to last st, k1.

Row 8: P.

Rep rows 1–8 to form patt.

DIAGONAL BEADING

INSTRUCTIONS

Special abbreviation

pb: Place bead.

Cast on a multiple of 5sts plus 2 extra sts.

Row 1: K1, *k2, pb, k2, rep from * to last st, k1.

Row 2 and all foll alt rows: P.

Row 3: K1, *k1, pb, k3, rep from * to last st, k1.

Row 5: K1, *pb, k4, rep from * to last st, k1.

Row 7: K1, *k4, pb, rep from * to last st, k1.

Row 9: K1, *k3, pb, k1, rep from * to last st, k1.

Row 10: P.

Rep rows 1–10 to form patt.

BEADED STOCKING STITCH

INSTRUCTIONS

Special abbreviation

pb: Place bead.

Cast on an odd number of sts.

Row 1: K1, *pb, k1, rep from * to end.

Row 2: P.

Row 3: K1, *k1, pb, rep from * to last st, k1.

Row 4: P.

Rep rows 1–4 to form patt.

BEADED CHEVRON

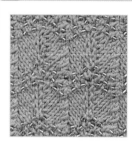

INSTRUCTIONS

Special abbreviation
pb: Place bead.

Cast on a multiple of 10sts plus one extra st.
Starting with a k row, work 2 rows st st.
Row 1 (RS): K1, *pb, k1, rep from * to end.
Row 2 and all foll alt rows (WS): *P1, M1p, p3, s1, p2tog, psso, p3, M1, rep from * to last st, p1.

Rows 3 and 5: As row 1.
Rows 7, 9, and 11: K.
Row 12: As row 2.
Rep rows 1–12 to form patt.

BEADED CHEQUERBOARD

INSTRUCTIONS

Special abbreviation
pb: Place bead.

Cast on a multiple of 10sts plus 7 extra sts.
Row 1 (RS): K1, *[pb, k1] three times, k4, rep from * to last 6sts, [pb, k1] three times.
Row 2 and all foll alt rows: P.

Rows 3: K2, *[pb, k1] twice, k6, rep from * to last 5sts, [pb, k1] twice, k1.
Row 5: As row 1.
Row 7: K6, *[pb, k1] three times, k4, rep from * to last 5sts, k to end.
Row 9: K7, *[pb, k1] twice, k6, rep from * to end.
Row 11: As row 7.
Rep rows 1–12 to form patt.

DIAMANTÉ STITCH

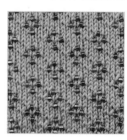

INSTRUCTIONS

Special abbreviation
pb: Place bead.

Cast on a multiple of 8sts plus 2 extra sts.
Row 1 (RS): K1, *k1, pb, k3, pb, k2, rep from * to last st, k1.
Row 3: K1, *k4, pb, k1, pb, k1, rep from * to last st, k1.
Row 5: K1, *k1, pb, k3, pb, k2, rep from * to last st, k1.
Row 7: K1, *pb, k1, pb, k5, rep from * to last st, k1.
Row 8: P.
Rep rows 1– 8 to form patt.

BEADED GARTER STITCH

INSTRUCTIONS

Special abbreviation
pb: Place bead.

Cast on an odd number of sts.
Row 1 (RS): K.
Row 2 and all foll alt rows: K.
Rows 3: K1, *pb, k1, rep from * to end.
Rows 5 and 6: K.
Rep rows 1–6 to form patt.

PEEKABOO BEADS

INSTRUCTIONS

Special abbreviation
pb: Place bead.

Cast on a multiple of 10sts plus
5 extra sts.
Row 1 (RS): K.
Row 2: P1, *k3, p7, rep from * to last
4sts, k3, p1.
Row 3: K2, *pb, k9, rep from * to last
2sts, k2.
Row 4: P.
Row 5: K.
Row 6: P6, *k3, p7, rep from * to last
9sts, k3, p to end.
Row 7: K7, *pb, k9, rep from * to last
8sts, pb, k7.
Row 8: P.
Rep rows 1–8 to form patt.

BEADED STRIPES

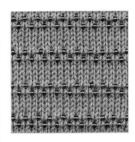

INSTRUCTIONS

Special abbreviation
pb: Place bead.

Cast on an odd number of sts.
Row 1 (RS): K.
Row 2 and all foll alt rows: P.
Row 3: * K1, pb, rep from * to last st,
k1.
Row 5: K2, *pb, k1, rep from * to last
st, k1.
Row 7: K.
Row 8: P.
Rep rows 1–8 to form patt.

VERTICAL SEQUIN STRIPES

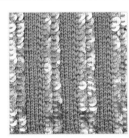

INSTRUCTIONS

Special abbreviation
pb: Place bead – sequin.

Cast on a multiple of 8sts plus one
extra st.
Row 1: K1, *k2, pb, k1, pb, k3, rep from
* to end.
Row 2: P.
Rep rows 1 and 2 to form patt.

ALL-OVER SEQUINS

INSTRUCTIONS

Special abbreviation
pb: Place bead – sequin.

Cast on an odd number of sts.
Row 1: K1, *pb, k1, rep from * to end.
Row 2: P.
Row 3: *K1, pb, rep from * to last st,
k1.
Row 4: P.
Rep rows 1–4 to form patt.

TOY PATTERN: KNITTED MONKEY
(SEE PAGES 256–261)

BODY AND HEAD
The body and head are worked in one piece, starting at the lower end of the body.
Using a stripe colour (B, C, D, or E), cast on 20sts, leaving a long loose end for back seam.
Row 1 (RS): [Kfb, k1] 10 times. 30sts.
Row 2: P.
Row 3: K1, [M1, K3] 9 times, M1, k2. 40sts.
Row 4: P.
Row 5: K2, [M1, K4] 9 times, M1, k2. 50sts.
Cont in st st in random stripes for 13 rows more, ending with RS facing for next row.
Cont in st st in random stripes (of B, C, D, and E) throughout as foll:
Next row (RS): K6, [k2tog, k10] 3 times, k2tog, k6. 46sts.
P 1 row.
Next row: K1, [k2tog, k4] 7 times, k2tog, k1. 38sts.
P 1 row.
Next row: K3, [k2tog, k8] 3 times, k2tog, k3. 34sts.
P 1 row.
Next row: K4, [k2tog, k3] 6 times. 28sts.
Work 9 rows without shaping, ending with RS facing for next row.
Shape shoulders
Next row (RS): K6, k2tog, k12, k2tog, k6. 26sts.
P 1 row.
Next row: K5, s1 k2tog psso, k10, s1 k2tog psso, k5. 22sts.
P 1 row.
Next row: K4, s1 k2tog psso, k8, s1 k2tog psso, k4. 18sts.
P 1 row.
Head
Next row (RS): K2, [kfb, k1] 8 times. 26sts.
P 1 row.
Next row: K2, [M1, K3] 8 times. 34sts.
P 1 row.
Next row: K4, [M1, k5] 6 times. 40sts.
Work 17 rows without shaping, ending with RS facing for next row.
Next row: K2 [k2tog, k3] 7 times, k2tog, k1. 32sts.
P1 row.
Next row: K1, [k2tog, k2] 7 times, k2tog, k1. 24sts.
P 1 row.
Next row: [K2tog, k1] 8 times. 16sts.
P 1 row.
Next row: [K2tog] 8 times. 8sts.
Next row: [P2tog] 4 times. 4sts.
Cut off yarn, leaving a long loose end. Thread end onto a blunt-ended yarn needle and pass needle through 4 remaining sts as they are dropped from needle. Pull yarn to gather stitches and secure with a few stitches.

LEGS (make 2)
Each leg is started at the foot end.
Using A (foot and hand colour), cast on 6sts using the single cast-on method (see p.87) and leaving a long loose end.
Row 1 (RS): [Kfb] 5 times, k1. 11sts.
Row 2: P.
Row 3: K1, [M1, k1] 10 times. 21sts.
Beg with a P row, work 9 rows in st st, ending with RS facing for next row.
Row 13 (RS): K2, [k2tog, k3] 3 times, k2tog, k2. 17sts.
Row 14: P.
Cut off A.

Cont in st st in random stripes (of B, C, D, and E) throughout as follows:
Work 10 rows without shaping, ending with RS facing for next row.
Next row (RS): K4, k2tog, k6, k2tog, k3. 15sts.
Work 15 rows without shaping.
Next row (RS): K3, [k2tog, k2] twice, k2tog, k2. 12sts.**
Work 11 rows without shaping.
Cast off knitwise.

ARMS (make 2)
Each arm is started at the foot end.
Work as for leg to **.
Work 7 row without shaping.
Cast off 2sts at beg of next 4 rows.
Cast off rem 4sts, leaving a long loose end for sewing arm to body.

MUZZLE
Using a stripe colour (B, C, D, or E), cast on 6sts, using single cast-on method (see p.87) and leaving a long loose end.
Row 1 (RS): [Kfb] 5 times, K1. 11sts.
Row 2: P.
Row 3: K1, [M1, K1] 10 times. 21sts.
Row 4: P.
Cut off first stripe colour and change to a second stripe colour for remainder of muzzle.
Row 5: K1, [M1, K2] 10 times. 31sts.
Beg with a p row, work 5 rows in st st.
Cast off knitwise, leaving a long loose end for sewing muzzle to body.

EARS (make 2)
Using F (ear and tail colour), cast on 3 sts.
Row 1 (WS): [Kfb] twice, k1. 5sts.
Note: Work the remaining increases as yarnovers, ensuring that each yarnover is crossed when it is knit in the following row to close the hole by knitting it through the back of the loop.
Row 2 (RS): [K1, yfwd] 4 times, k1. 9sts.
Row 3: K to end, knitting each yfwd through back loop.
Row 4: [K2, yfwd] 4 times, k1. 13sts.
Row 5: Rep row 3.
Row 6: K.
K 2 rows.
Cast off loosely knitwise, leaving a long loose end for gathering ear into cupped shape and sewing to head.

TAIL
Using F (ear and tail colour), cast on 3sts, leaving a long loose end for sewing tail to body.
Work in garter stitch (k every row) until tail is a little longer than leg (or desired length).
Next row s1 k2tog psso, then fasten off.
Tail will swirl naturally – do not press out this swirl.

FINISHING
Finish as explained on pages 260–261.

CAMPFIRE BLANKET CHARTS (SEE PAGES 348-349)

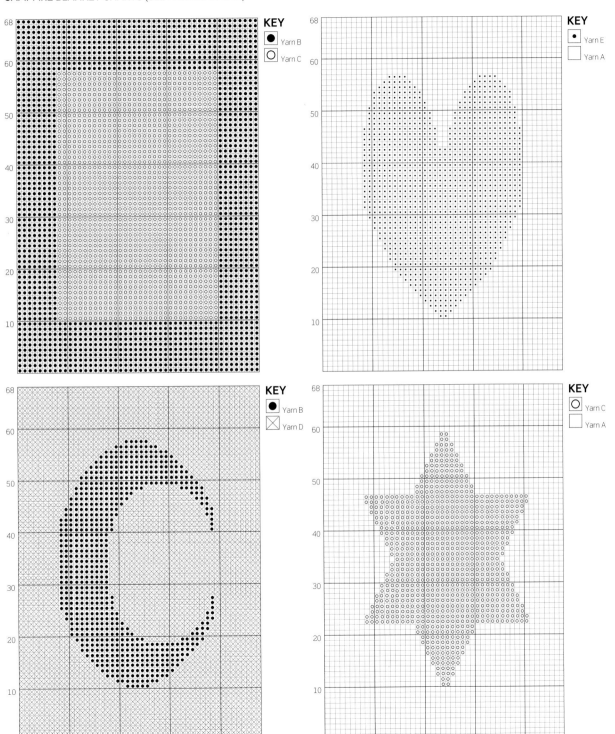

KEY
- ● Yarn B
- ○ Yarn C

KEY
- ● Yarn E
- ☐ Yarn A

KEY
- ● Yarn B
- ⊠ Yarn D

KEY
- ○ Yarn C
- ☐ Yarn A

GLOSSARY

aran yarn
Also called medium, 12-ply, worsted, or Afghan (yarn symbol 4). A medium yarn suitable for jumpers, cabled menswear, blankets, hats, scarves, and mittens.

backstitch
A sewing stitch used for firm, straight seams, which is worked from the wrong side.

ballband
The wrapper around a ball of yarn, which usually details fibre content, weight, length, needle size, tension, and cleaning instructions.

ball-winder
A device for winding hanks of yarn into balls; also to wind two or more strands together to make a double-stranded yarn. Often used in conjunction with a swift.

bias knitting
Diagonally shaped pieces of knitting, which slope to the left or the right.

blocking
The finishing process for a piece of knitting, in which it is set in shape using water or steam.

blocking wire
Wire for insertion around the edge of a piece of very fine lace work, which is left in to keep it in shape.

bulky or chunky yarn
Also called 14-ply, craft, or rug (yarn symbol 5). A chunky yarn suitable for rugs, jackets, blankets, hats, legwarmers, and winter accessories.

cable
A design made by crossing one or more stitches over other stitches in a row; it frequently resembles a rope or cable. Twist stitches belong to the same family.

cable cast-on
A method of casting on that produces a firm, cord-like edge, which holds a neat and defined edge.

cable needle
A needle with a kink or U-shape, used when working cables.

carrying up the side
A method for keeping the edges of a two-coloured, even-row stripe pattern tidy. The yarns are twisted around each other and carried up the side of the piece.

casting off/binding off
Completing a piece of knitting by finishing off the loops of the stitches so that they cannot unravel.

casting on
Forming an initial number of stitches on a needle at the start of a piece of knitting. There are various methods, depending on the effect you want to achieve.

circular knitting
Working on circular needles or double-pointed needles to produce a seamless item such as a hat. There is no need to turn the work and no wrong-side row. Sometimes called tubular knitting.

circular needles
A pair of short needles connected by a flexible tube, usually used for circular knitting and very wide projects that do not fit on conventional straight needles.

colourwork
Any method of incorporating colour into your knitting. This includes stripes, Fair Isle, intarsia, and slipped stitch patterns.

Continental-style knitting
A way of holding the yarn as you knit, lacing it around your left hand and using these fingers to position the yarn to make a stitch.

darning in ends
The process of completing a piece of knitting by weaving yarn ends (such as from the cast-on and cast-off edges) into the knitting to disguise them.

decreases/decreasing
Techniques that subtract stitches. Used to shape knitting, and to form textures in combination with other stitches.

double cast-on
See **two-strand cast-on** and **long-tail cast-on**.

double-knit yarn (DK)
A medium-weight yarn. Also called DK, 5–6-ply, or light worsted (yarn symbol 3). A light yarn suitable for jumpers, lightweight scarves, blankets, and toys.

double-pointed needles
Knitting needles with a tip at each end; a set of four or five is used for the circular knitting of small items, such as mittens and socks.

double-sided or double knitting
See **tubular knitting**.

English-style knitting
A way of holding the yarn as you knit, lacing it around your right hand and using the right forefinger to wrap the yarn around the needle.

Fair Isle Patterns
Various multicoloured, stranded, geometric patterns originating from Fair Isle and latterly the Shetland Islands.

Fair Isle knitting
A method in which yarn colours not being worked are carried across the back of the work until required. This unworked yarn can also be woven in.

faux colourwork
Adding yarn in another colour without having to knit with two different yarns in each row. It involves manipulating stitches from previous rows.

fibres
Yarn is made up of fibres, such as the hair from an animal, man-made (synthetic) fibres, or fibres derived from a plant. The fibres are processed and spun into a yarn.

fine yarn
Also called 4-ply, sport, or baby (yarn symbol 2). A fine yarn suitable for lightweight jumpers, babywear, socks, and accessories.

fisherman's rib
A pattern of knit and purl stitches, in which alternating stitches are double knitted, making a thick, warm, textured fabric.

fully fashioned shaping
An attractive method for increasing or decreasing when working stocking stitch, in which a line of stitches is preserved to follow the edge of the piece.

garter stitch
Working in knit stitches on every row, whichever side of the knitting is facing you. It produces a thick fabric, which is identical on both sides and will not curl at the edges.

hank
A twisted ring of yarn, which needs to be wound into one or more balls before it can be used.

I-cord
A narrow tube of knitting, created on a knitting dolly or cord-maker, or knitted on double-pointed needles. Used as cords, straps, ties, or as a trimming.

increases/increasing
Creating stitches during knitting. Can be combined with other stitches in order to form shapes and textures.

intarsia
A method for working with different coloured yarns to create blocks of colour. A separate length of yarn is used for each colour of the motif and twisted where the colour changes to prevent a hole; yarns are not stranded across the reverse of the work. Uses less yarn than Fair Isle knitting.

knit-on cast-on
This cast-on uses two needles to combine a cast-on with the knitting of the first row. If worked through the front of the loops, it produces a soft edge; if through the back of the loops, the edge is firmer.

knit stitch
One of the two basic stitches used to form knitting.

knitting beads
Beads with a central hole in various sizes for specific thicknesses of yarn. Most are washable and colourfast.

knitting needle gauge
A tool for identifying needle size by pushing it through holes.

knitting through back of loop
Stitches that twist the stitch in the row below so that the legs of the stitch cross at the base.

knitwise
Working with knit stitches facing you, inserting the right-hand needle into a stitch as if to knit it. See also **purlwise**.

lace cast-on method
A cast-on that produces a looser, more open effect than other cast-ons, and is particularly suitable for lacy designs.

lace yarn
Also called 2-ply or fingering (yarn symbol 0). A very fine yarn for knitting lace.

lanolin
An oily substance contained in a sheep's wool.

live stitches
Stitches that are currently being worked.

long-tail cast-on method
See also **two-strand cast-on**. This method is also known as a double cast-on. It produces a sturdy, reinforced edge and so is good for ribbing.

mattress stitch
A seaming stitch, which is almost invisible, used to sew pieces of knitting together with the right side facing. It only forms a small seam on the wrong side of the work.

medallion
A circular, hexagonal, octagonal, or square flat shape made of knitting, which is knitted from the centre outwards.

mercerized cotton
Cotton thread, fabric, or yarn that has been treated in order to strengthen it and add a sheen. The yarn is a good choice for items that need to be strong and hold a shape, such as a bag.

organic wool
Wool produced from sheep that graze on land that is not treated with herbicides, pesticides, or artificial fertilizers. The wool is not given any manmade chemical treatments.

oversewing/overcasting
Stitch used to seam two pieces of knitting by placing them right sides together and then sewing through the edge stitches. Also called whip stitch.

pilling
When the surface of a knitted item rubs up into tiny balls, due to wear and friction.

plied yarn
A yarn made from more than one strand of spun fibre, so 4-ply is four strands plied together. Most knitting yarns are plied, as plying prevents the yarn twisting and resulting fabric slanting diagonally.

pom-pom
A small fluffy ball made of yarn, used as a trimming or decoration.

purl stitch
One of the two basic stitches used in knitting.

purlwise
Working with stitches facing you, inserting the right-hand needle into a stitch as if to purl it. See also **knitwise**.

put-up
A specific quantity of yarn packaged for sale, such as a ball, hank, or skein.

ribbing/rib/rib stitch
Knitting with great elasticity, used where fabric needs to hold tightly to the body, but is capable of expanding. Single ribbing or 1 x 1 rib is knit 1, purl 1; 2 x 2 rib is knit 2, purl 2; 3 x 3 rib is knit 3, purl 3 etc.

short-row shaping
Used for shaping shoulders, curving hems, making darts, and turning sock heels. Rows are added in only one part of the fabric by knitting part of a row instead of knitting it to the end. It uses one of three turning methods to close holes.

single rib/ribbing
See **ribbing**.

single-strand cast-on
A group of methods for casting on using one strand of yarn. Tends to produce a soft edge, but this can be made firmer by twisting the stitches.

skein
Yarn sold wound into a long oblong shape, which is ready to knit.

slip knot
A knot that you form when you place the first loop on the needle as you start casting on stitches.

slip stitch
Sliding a stitch from the left-hand needle to the right-hand needle without working it. The usual method is to slip stitches purlwise; less frequently, stitches are slipped knitwise. Slipped stitches at the beginning of each row – slipped selvedge – can help to create a very neat edge.

sock blocker
A flat plastic or wooden shape that is inserted into a finished sock and used to mould it to shape in conjunction with moisture.

stock stoppers
Plastic caps used to stop stitches falling off double-pointed needles.

stocking stitch
A stitch formed by knitting all stitches when the right side of the work is facing you, and purling all stitches when the wrong side of the work is facing you.

stranded beading method
A process for streamlining the knitting-in of beads by threading them on yarn before you begin, using a needle and thread looped through the yarn. Beads are later arranged in the knitting when brought to the front of the work and wrapped around a slipped stitch.

super bulky or super chunky yarn
Also called 16-ply (and upwards), bulky, or roving (yarn symbol 6). A chunky yarn suitable for heavy blankets, rugs, and thick scarves.

superfine yarn
Also called 3-ply, fingering, or baby (yarn symbol 1). A very fine yarn suitable for fine-knit socks, shawls, and babywear.

swift
A wooden frame used with a ball-winder to transform a hank of yarn into convenient balls.

tape yarn
A wide, flat, or tubular yarn, flattened when wound into a ball. Can be knitted to produce a nubbly or smooth result.

tension square
A square knitted to the required number of stitches and rows to match the stated tension of a project, usually 10cm (4in) square. A knitter must achieve the tension stated in a pattern, or else the knitted item will not end up the correct size.

three-needle cast-off/bind-off
A method of casting off which binds two sets of stitches together, whilst casting off simultaneously. This creates a firm, neat seam, with a smooth finish on the right side of the work. It is a good way of finishing the toe of a sock or the fingertip area of a mitten.

tubular cast-on/cast-off
Also known as an invisible cast-on/off. Produces a good edge for a single rib; best to use needles that are at least two sizes smaller than the main fabric in order to prevent the ribbing stretching out of shape.

tubular knitting
Also known as double knitting or double-sided knitting. It is worked on straight needles by slipping every other stitch and produces a double-sided fabric. See also **circular knitting**.

Tunisian knitting
A style of knitting where the finished fabric resembles crocheted work.

twist
Two stitches twisted together to form a narrow cable, which slants to the right or left. A cable needle is not used.

two-strand cast-on
A group of methods for casting on using two strands of yarn. Tends to produce a strong, elastic edge.

yarn
Fibres that have been spun into a long strand in order for you to knit with them. Yarns may be made of natural fibres, man-made fibres, a blend of the two, or even non-standard materials.

yarn bobbins
Small plastic shapes for holding yarn when doing intarsia work, where there are many yarns in different colours.

yarn over (yo)
An instruction to increase by adding stitches and creating holes at the same time. Yarnovers (yos) are used for decorative purposes, such as producing lacy knitting. There are various types: yfwd (US yo), yarn over between knit stitches; yrn (US yo), yarn over between purl stitches; yfrn and yon (US yo), yarn over between knit and purl stitches; and yfwd (US yo), yarn over at the beginning of a row.

INDEX